ASSESSMENT RESOURCES

Addison-Wesley
Chemistry

TestWorks™ Testbank File

Prentice
Hall

Needham, Massachusetts
Upper Saddle River, New Jersey
Glenview, Illinois

ASSESSMENT RESOURCES

Addison-Wesley Chemistry

Cover photographs: Clockwise from top left: Test tube with zinc in acid, Richard Megma, Fundamental Photographs, Molecular structure of "Bucky ball," Ken Edward, Photo Researchers; Bunsen burner flame and flask containing precipate of lead (II) iodide, Richard Megma, Fundamental Photographs; Scanning tunneling microscope image, Fran Heyl Associates.

ISBN 0-201-35671-6

2 3 4 5 6 7 8 9 10   05 04 03 02 01

Contents

About the Assessment Resources v
About the Prentice Hall Dial-A-Test® Service vii

Test Questions and Answer Keys   **Chapter page**

Chapter 1   Introduction to Chemistry
             Answer Key 1-4

Chapter 2   Matter and Change
             Answer Key 2-9

Chapter 3   Scientific Measurement
             Answer Key 3-10

Chapter 4   Problem Solving in Chemistry
             Answer Key 4-9

Chapter 5   Atomic Structure and the Periodic Table
             Answer Key 5-12

Chapter 6   Chemical Names and Formulas
             Answer Key 6-13

Chapter 7   Chemical Quantities
             Answer Key 7-14

Chapter 8   Chemical Reactions
             Answer Key 8-12

Chapter 9   Stoichiometry
             Answer Key 9-10

Chapter 10   States of Matter
             Answer Key 10-9

Chapter 11   Thermochemistry
             Answer Key 11-14

Chapter 12   The Behavior of Gases
             Answer Key 12-10

Chapter 13   Electrons in Atoms
             Answer Key 13-13

Chapter 14   Chemical Periodicity
             Answer Key 14-7

Chapter 15   Ionic Bonding and Ionic Compounds
             Answer Key 15-10

Chapter 16   Covalent Bonding
             Answer Key 16-12

Chapter 17   Water and Aqueous Systems
             Answer Key 17-12

Contents continued

Chapter 18   Solutions
              Answer Key 18-12

Chapter 19   Reaction Rates and Equilibrium
              Answer Key 19-13

Chapter 20   Acids and Bases
              Answer Key 20-13

Chapter 21   Neutralization
              Answer Key 21-10

Chapter 22   Oxidation-Reduction Reactions
              Answer Key 22-10

Chapter 23   Electrochemistry
              Answer Key 23-11

Chapter 24   The Chemistry of Metals and Nonmetals
              Answer Key 24-16

Chapter 25   Hydrocarbon Compounds
              Answer Key 25-15

Chapter 26   Functional Groups and Organic Reactions
              Answer Key 26-13

Chapter 27   The Chemistry of Life
              Answer Key 27-6

Chapter 28   Nuclear Chemistry
              Answer Key 28-12

About the Assessment Resources

The *Assessment Resources Test Works™ Test Generator* for *Addison-Wesley Chemistry* gives you unparalleled flexibility in creating tests. You can design tests to reflect your particular teaching emphasis. You can use TestWorks to create tests for different classes or to create alternate forms of the same test. You can also create tests for one chapter or for any combination of chapters, as well as for midterm and final exams

The TestWorks Testbank File is a printed version of all the questions available on the TestWorks CD-ROM. The Testbank File is organized by chapter, question type, and section. It is a convenient reference source that allows you to review all of the questions from which you may choose when creating tests or quizzes for *Addison-Wesley Chemistry.*

For information on using the TestWorks Test Generator software, consult the TestWorks User's Guide on the CD-ROM.

QUESTION ORGANIZATION

Test questions in TestWorks are organized by chapter for each of the 28 chapters of *Addison-Wesley Chemistry.* Within each chapter the questions are organized by question type and section. The questions are in a variety of formats, including matching, multiple choice, essay, and problems. Some multiple choice questions are bimodal, meaning that they may be used as either a multiple choice or short answer question. In total, TestWorks contains over 2100 questions.

AVAILABLE IN WINDOWS AND MACINTOSH FORMATS

A CD-ROM has been included inside the front cover of this book. On the CD-ROM, the TestWorks Test Generator is provided in both Macintosh and Windows formats. The User's Guide is also provided in a file on the CD that allows you to print out all of the guide, or just the pages that you need.

FLEXIBLE TEST-MAKING

The TestWorks software allows you to edit existing questions, create your own test questions, scramble the question sequence to create multiple versions of the same test, and create custom answer keys. For information on using the TestWorks Test Generator software, consult the TestWorks User's Guide.

NEED HELP?

Stuck at any point? Simply call our toll-free HELP hotline (1-800-234-5TEC) for continuous and reliable support.

NO COMPUTER? USE DIAL-A-TEST®

If you don't have access to a computer, one way to create worksheets or tests is to photocopy and paste exercises from this print version of TestWorks Test Generator. A far less tedious way is to use Prentice Hall's free Dial-A-Test® service. With Dial-A-Test, you tell Prentice Hall which items you want on a test and let us create the test for you. For details, see page vi.

About the Dial-A-Test® Service

If you do not have access to a computer or would like the convenience of designing your own tests without typing a word, you may want to take advantage of our free Dial-A-Test® Service. Available to all users of *Addison-Wesley Chemistry,* Dial-A-Test® is simple to use.

Dial-A-Test® OFFERS YOU THE ABILITY TO:

* Customize tests for different ability levels.

* Focus your testing on mastery of specific content, skills, or critical thinking.

* Scramble your questions for each class you teach.

HERE'S HOW IT WORKS

1. **Choose the questions you want** from the ready-made Chapter Tests.

2. **Enter the numbers of the questions** in the order you want on a Dial-A-Test® Order Form (see page vii). Be sure to include the book abbreviation and chapter number on the form. For example, in the case of test question 17, taken from the Chapter 1 test, mark the order form with the designation **AWC 01–17.**

3. **Use a separate Dial-A-Test® order form** for each original test you request. You may use one form, however, to order multiple versions of the same original test.

4. **If you would like another version** of your original test with the questions scrambled, or put in another sequence, simply check the blank labeled *Scramble Questions* on the order form. If you would like more than one scrambled version of your original test, note this on your order form or inform the Dial-A-Test® operator. Please note that Prentice Hall reserves the right to limit the number of tests and versions you can request at any one time, especially during the busier times of the year when midterms and finals are given.

5. **Choose the method** by which you would like to order your original test and/or multiple versions of your original test. To order by telephone, call toll free 1-800-468-8378 between 9:00 A.M. and 4:30 P.M. Eastern Standard Time and read the test question numbers to our Dial-A-Test® operator. Use the ISBN 0-201-3567-6 for *Addison-Wesley Chemistry.* To order by mail, send your completed Dial-A-Test® order form to the address listed below. Now you may also FAX your order to 1-614-771-7365.

6. **You may order** up to 100 questions per test by telephone on our toll-free 800 number or up to 200 questions per test by mail.

7. **Please allow a minimum of two weeks** for shipping, especially if you are ordering by mail. Although we process your order within 48 hours of your call or the receipt of your form by mail, mailing may take up to two weeks. Thus we ask you to plan accordingly and expect to receive your original test, any alternate test versions that you requested, and complete answer keys within a reasonable amount of time.

8. **Tests are available all year.** You can order tests before the school year begins, during vacation, or as you need them.

9. **For additional order forms,** or to ask questions regarding this service, please write to the following address:

Dial-A-Test®
Prentice Hall School Division
4350 Equity Drive
Columbus, OH 43228

DIAL-A-TEST®
PRENTICE HALL SCHOOL DIVISION
CUSTOMIZED TESTING SERVICE
TOLL-FREE NUMBER 800-468-8378 (H-O-T-T-E-S-T)

You may call the PH Dial-A-Test® toll-free number during our business hours (9:00 A.M.–4:30 P.M. EST).
Now you may also FAX your order to 1-614-771-7365 any time.

DIAL-A-TEST®
PRENTICE HALL SCHOOL DIVISION
4350 EQUITY DRIVE
COLUMBUS, OH 43228

FOR PH USE	DATE REC. DATE SENT
___ PHONE ___ MAIL ___ FAX	_____ _____

EXACT TEXT TITLE/VOL. *Addison-Wesley Chemistry* _____ © **DATE** 2002
CODE 0-201-35671-6 _____

CUSTOMER INFORMATION
NAME _____
SCHOOL _____
ADDRESS _____
CITY _____STATE ____ ZIP _____
PHONE _____ EXT. _____

DATE BY WHICH TEST IS NEEDED _____

TEST USAGE (CHECK ONE)
__ SAMPLE __ QUIZ __ CHAPTER TEST
__ UNIT TEST __ SEMESTER TEST __ FINAL EXAM

VERSIONS (SEE page vi INSTR. #4)
(CHECK ONE)
____ 1. ORIGINAL ____ 2. SCRAMBLE QUESTIONS

TEST IDENTIFICATION (This information will appear at the top of your test.)
_____
_____
_____
_____
(You may use up to 4 lines with a maximum of 38 characters per line.)

EXAMPLE: Mr Holzman
Chemistry 101, Period 5
Test
(Spaces count as characters.)

1 ___	26 ___	51 ___	76 ___	101 ___	126 ___	151 ___	176 ___
2 ___	27 ___	52 ___	77 ___	102 ___	127 ___	152 ___	177 ___
3 ___	28 ___	53 ___	78 ___	103 ___	128 ___	153 ___	178 ___
4 ___	29 ___	54 ___	79 ___	104 ___	129 ___	154 ___	179 ___
5 ___	30 ___	55 ___	80 ___	105 ___	130 ___	155 ___	180 ___
6 ___	31 ___	56 ___	81 ___	106 ___	131 ___	156 ___	181 ___
7 ___	32 ___	57 ___	82 ___	107 ___	132 ___	157 ___	182 ___
8 ___	33 ___	58 ___	83 ___	108 ___	133 ___	158 ___	183 ___
9 ___	34 ___	59 ___	84 ___	109 ___	134 ___	159 ___	184 ___
10 ___	35 ___	60 ___	85 ___	110 ___	135 ___	160 ___	185 ___
11 ___	36 ___	61 ___	86 ___	111 ___	136 ___	161 ___	186 ___
12 ___	37 ___	62 ___	87 ___	112 ___	137 ___	162 ___	187 ___
13 ___	38 ___	63 ___	88 ___	113 ___	138 ___	163 ___	188 ___
14 ___	39 ___	64 ___	89 ___	114 ___	139 ___	164 ___	189 ___
15 ___	40 ___	65 ___	90 ___	115 ___	140 ___	165 ___	190 ___
16 ___	41 ___	66 ___	91 ___	116 ___	141 ___	166 ___	191 ___
17 ___	42 ___	67 ___	92 ___	117 ___	142 ___	167 ___	192 ___
18 ___	43 ___	68 ___	93 ___	118 ___	143 ___	168 ___	193 ___
19 ___	44 ___	69 ___	94 ___	119 ___	144 ___	169 ___	194 ___
20 ___	45 ___	70 ___	95 ___	120 ___	145 ___	170 ___	195 ___
21 ___	46 ___	71 ___	96 ___	121 ___	146 ___	171 ___	196 ___
22 ___	47 ___	72 ___	97 ___	122 ___	147 ___	172 ___	197 ___
23 ___	48 ___	73 ___	98 ___	123 ___	148 ___	173 ___	198 ___
24 ___	49 ___	74 ___	99 ___	124 ___	149 ___	174 ___	199 ___
25 ___	50 ___	75 ___	100 ___	125 ___	150 ___	175 ___	200 ___

Chapter 1 Introduction to Chemistry

Matching Questions

Chapter 1: Matching I

1) organic chemistry

2) inorganic chemistry

3) biochemistry

4) analytical chemistry

5) physical chemistry

A) concerned with the theories and experiments that describe chemical behavior

B) the study of all substances containing carbon

C) the study of the chemistry of living organisms

D) the study of the composition of substances

E) the study of substances that do not contain carbon

Multiple Choice and Bimodal Questions

1) The study of the composition and structure of matter is the domain of which field of science?

   A) physics   B) biology   C) chemistry   D) geology

2) Which of the following changes would be most appropriately considered in a study of chemistry, rather than any other science?

   A) a rock sinking in the water

   B) a rock melting as the result of being heated

   C) a rock breaking upon impact

   D) a rock rolling down a hill

   E) a rock warming in the sun

3) Chemistry is chiefly concerned with the study of which of the following types of changes in substances?

   A) changes in composition

   B) changes in shape

   C) changes in volume

   D) changes in amount

   E) changes in location

4) Which of the five major divisions of chemistry requires the most extensive mathematical background?

   A) analytical chemistry

   B) biochemistry

   C) inorganic chemistry

   D) organic chemistry

   E) physical chemistry

5) Which of the following is a significant contributor to the greenhouse effect?

   A) decaying radioactive waste   B) ozone layer depletion

   C) carbon dioxide gas   D) pheromones

6) Previous periods in history were known as the stone age, the iron age, and the bronze age. The modern world is primarily the age of _____ .

   A) recycling   B) plastics   C) aluminum   D) solar power

7) What fuel source provides most of the world's energy?

   A) fossil fuels   B) the sun   C) nuclear fusion   D) nuclear fission

8) What is the first step of the scientific method?

   A) reaching a conclusion

   B) conducting an experiment

   C) formulating a hypothesis

   D) making an observation

   E) stating a theory

9) The difference between a scientific theory and a scientific law is that _____ .

   A) a law only summarizes observations; a theory attempts to explain observations

   B) a theory only summarizes observations; a law attempts to explain observations

   C) There is no difference.

10) A hypothesis is _____ .

   A) an observation recorded from an experiment

   B) a descriptive model for observations

   C) a concise statement that summarizes the results of a wide variety of experiments

   D) a thoroughly tested model

11) An important characteristic of an accepted scientific theory is that _____ .

   A) it can be disproved at any time.   B) it can be proven true.

   C) it cannot be modified.   D) it is agreed upon by all scientists.

12) Which of the following statements is false?

    A) The photos, art, and captions in your text book contain valuable information.

    B) Chemistry is always best learned by studying it by yourself..

    C) Taking notes often results in a greater understanding of the material.

    D) Working the Practice Problems in the text book will help you understand the material.

Essay Questions

1) Name the five major divisions of chemistry and give examples of the types of subjects studied within each division.

2) Describe some of the ways the world's future energy needs might be met.

3) Explain why plastics are valuable in the construction of a modern automobile.

4) Explain the relationships among observation, hypothesis, experiment, theory, and law, with respect to the scientific method.

5) What is the difference between a scientific law and a theory?

6) Illustrate the process of testing and refining a hypothesis with an example from your own life or a situation known to you.

7) Set up a controlled experiment to determine how the water content of food influence how well it heats in a microwave oven. Outline the steps you would follow.

8) Discuss how a scientist's use of the word theory is different from the way the word is used in everyday speech.

Chapter 1 Introduction to Chemistry

Matching Questions

    1) Answer: B

    2) Answer: E

    3) Answer: C

    4) Answer: D

    5) Answer: A

Essay Questions

    1) Answer: Inorganic Chemistry: geology, manufacturing; Organic Chemistry: biology, medicine, agriculture; Analytical Chemistry: geology, manufacturing; Physical Chemistry: geology, physics, manufacturing; Biochemistry: biology, agriculture, medicine.

    2) Answer: Answers will vary, but might include conservation, solar power, nuclear fission, nuclear fusion, or a breakthrough in extracting oil from tar sands and oil shales.

    3) Answer: The high strength–to–weight ratio of structural plastics allows them to replace heavier steel parts. The resulting weight reduction allows the vehicle to be more fuel efficient.

    4) Answer: A hypothesis is formulated on the basis of observations. Experiments are then planned and conducted to test the validity of the hypothesis. The results of the experiments may confirm the hypothesis or they may cause the hypothesis to be refined so as to better explain the results. Additional experiments must be done to test the validity of the refined hypothesis. Once the hypothesis has been refined and confirmed by the results of many experiments it can be stated as a theory. A theory is a thoroughly tested model that explains why experiments give certain results. A scientific law is a concise statement that summarizes a broad variety of observations and the results of many experiments. A scientific law describes a natural phenomenon, but does not attempt to explain it.

    5) Answer: A scientific law is different from a theory in that the law only describes a natural phenomenon; it does not attempt to explain the phenomenon. A theory is an attempt at explanation.

    6) Answer: The student's example should include the following steps: A hypothesis should be formulated on the basis of observations; experiments should be undertaken to test the hypothesis; the hypothesis may need to be refined on the basis of the results of the experiments. Additional experiments would need to be done to test the refined hypothesis.

7) Answer: Accept all answers supported by logical reasoning. Students may suggest testing several samples of the same kind of food with different water content. The samples of food with different water content could be microwaved for the same period of time and their temperature measured. To produce samples of food with different water content, the food samples could be dried initially for various periods of time in a conventional oven. One control would be a sample of food that had not been dried.

8) Answer: Scientists use the word theory to mean a thoroughly tested explanation of why experiments give certain results. In everyday speech the word theory often refers to a simple guess or idea about why something happens.

Chapter 2 Matter and Change

Matching Questions

Chapter 2: Matching I

1) mixture

2) product

3) phase

4) reactant

5) heterogeneous mixture

6) vapor

A) a new substance formed in a chemical reaction

B) part of a system having uniform composition and properties

C) gas that is normally a liquid or solid at room temperature

D) not uniform in composition

E) a physical blend of two or more substances

F) starting substance in a chemical reaction

Chapter 2: Matching II

7) distillation

8) mass

9) chemical reaction

10) compound

11) element

12) homogeneous mixture

A) a process in which a liquid is boiled to produce a vapor that is condensed again into a liquid

B) of completely uniform composition

C) amount of matter in a substance

D) substance that cannot be changed into a simpler substance under normal laboratory conditions

E) composed of two or more substances chemically bound together

F) process in which substances are changed into different substances

Multiple Choice and Bimodal Questions

1) Matter is defined as anything that _____ .
   A) has a fixed volume and weight   B) has a definite volume
   C) can be weighed on a balance   D) has mass and takes up space

2) A vapor is which state of matter?
   A) solid   B) liquid   C) gas   D) plasma

3) A substance that forms a vapor is generally in what physical state at room temperature?
   A) solid
   B) liquid
   C) gas
   D) plasma
   E) liquid or solid

4) Which state of matter has a definite volume and takes the shape of its container?
   A) solid   B) liquid   C) gas   D) both B. and C.

5) Which state of matter takes both the shape and volume of its container?
   A) solid   B) liquid   C) gas   D) both B. and C.

6) Which state of matter is characterized by having an indefinite shape, but a definite volume?
   A) gas   B) liquid   C) solid   D) plasma

7) Which state of matter is characterized by having a definite shape and a definite volume?
   A) gas   B) liquid   C) solid   D) plasma

8) Which state of matter is characterized by low density and high compressibility?
   A) gas   B) liquid   C) solid

9) Which of the following is NOT an example of matter?

    A) air

    B) heat

    C) smoke

    D) water

    E) water vapor

10) Which of the following materials is a pure substance?

    A) air   B) tea   C) brass   D) diamond   E) gasoline

11) All of the following are physical properties of matter EXCEPT _____.

    A) mass

    B) hardness

    C) melting point

    D) color

    E) explosiveness

12) Which of the following CANNOT be classified as a substance?

    A) table salt   B) air   C) nitrogen   D) gold

13) A golf ball has more mass than a tennis ball because it _____.

    A) takes up more space   B) contains more matter

    C) contains different kinds of matter   D) has a definite composition

14) Physical properties of a substance include _____.

    A) color and odor   B) melting and boiling points

    C) density and hardness   D) all of the above

15) Which of the following states of matter is characterized by having definite shape?

    A) solid   B) liquid   C) gas   D) plasma

16) Which of the following is NOT a physical property of water?

    A) It has a boiling point of 100°C.   B) It is a colorless liquid.

    C) It is composed of hydrogen and oxygen.   D) Sugar dissolves in it.

17) All of the following are physical properties of a substance in the liquid state EXCEPT _____.

    A) indefinite volume   B) definite mass

    C) virtual incompressibility   D) indefinite shape

18) All of the following changes to a metal are physical changes EXCEPT _____.

    A) bending   B) melting   C) rusting   D) cutting   E) polishing

19) Which of the following is NOT a physical change?

    A) the cutting of cheese   B) the melting of cheese   C) the spoiling of cheese

20) Which of the following is a physical change?

    A) corrosion   B) explosion   C) evaporation   D) food spoilage

21) Which of the following does NOT involve a physical change?

    A) mixing   B) melting   C) grinding   D) tarnishing

22) Which of the following is NOT a pure substance?

    A) mercury   B) apple juice   C) liquid oxygen   D) liquid helium

23) Separating a solid from a liquid by evaporating the liquid is called _____.

    A) emulsification.   B) condensation.   C) theorizing.   D) distillation.

24) Which of the following is a heterogeneous mixture?

    A) air   B) brine   C) steel   D) soil

25) Which of the following is a homogeneous mixture?

    A) brine

    B) beef stew

    C) sand and water

    D) soil

    E) raisin bread

26) Which of the following CANNOT be considered a single phase?

    A) a pure solid

    B) a pure liquid

    C) a pure gas

    D) a homogeneous mixture

    E) a heterogeneous mixture

27) Which of the following is a true statement about homogeneous mixtures?

    A) They are known as solutions.

    B) They consist of two or more phases.

    C) They have compositions that never vary.

    D) They can consist only of liquids.

28) Which of the following is a homogeneous mixture?

    A) oil in water   B) soot in water   C) alcohol in water

29) Approximately how many elements exist in nature?

    A) 30   B) 100   C) 1000   D) 10 000   E) 1 000 000

30) Which of the following household items is NOT a pure compound?
  A) baking soda
  B) distilled water
  C) sugar
  D) salt
  E) salad dressing

31) Which of the following is a true statement about compounds?
  A) They can be physically separated into their constituent elements.
  B) They have variable compositions.
  C) They are pure substances.
  D) They have properties similar to those of their constituent elements.

32) A homogeneous substance that can be separated into two or more pure substances only by a chemical change is a(n) _____.
  A) phase   B) element   C) mixture   D) compound   E) solution

33) One difference between a mixture and a compound is that _____.
  A) a compound is made up of more than one phase.
  B) a compound can only be separated into its components by chemical means.
  C) a mixture can only be separated into its components by chemical means.
  D) a mixture must be uniform in composition.

34) What is the chemical symbol for sodium?
  A) Ag   B) Fe   C) Hg   D) Na   E) Sn

35) What is the name of the element having the chemical symbol K?
  A) antimony   B) copper   C) iron   D) lead   E) potassium

36) What is the chemical symbol for copper?
  A) Ag   B) Cu   C) Hg   D) Na   E) Sn

37) What is the chemical symbol for lead?
  A) Ag   B) Fe   C) Na   D) Pb   E) Sn

38) What is the name of the element having the chemical symbol Hg?
  A) antimony   B) copper   C) iron   D) lead   E) mercury

39) What is the chemical symbol for gold?
  A) Ag   B) Au   C) Hg   D) Na   E) Sn

40) What is the name of the element having the chemical symbol Ag?
  A) antimony   B) copper   C) iron   D) lead   E) silver

41) What is the name of the element having the chemical symbol Ca?

   A) cadmium   B) calcium   C) carbon   D) chromium   E) chlorine

42) What is the name of the element having the chemical symbol N?

   A) nickel

   B) niobium

   C) neptunium

   D) nitrogen

   E) neon

43) The chemical formula of a compound indicates the _____.

   A) identity of the elements in the compound only

   B) relative proportions of the elements in the compound

   C) three-dimensional structure of the compound

   D) type and arrangement of the bonds in the compound

44) A copper-colored wire changes to a darker color after it is heated and then cooled. What type of change has likely taken place to cause this color change?

   A) a physical change

   B) a chemical change

   C) neither a physical nor a chemical change

45) Consider the chemical reaction in which carbon reacts with oxygen to produce carbon dioxide. What mass of carbon dioxide would be produced if 24 grams of carbon reacted completely with 64 grams of oxygen?

   A) 40 g   B) 48 g   C) 130 g   D) 88 g   E) 64 g

46) What happens to the individual atoms in a chemical reaction?

   A) They are rearranged.

   B) Some are destroyed.

   C) Some are created.

   D) Some are destroyed and some are created.

47) How will the mass of a rusted iron nail compare with the mass of the same nail before it rusted?

   A) The rusted nail will have the greater mass.

   B) The unrusted nail will have the greater mass.

   C) The two masses will be the same.

48) What must occur for a process to be a chemical reaction?

   A) The process must involve a change in chemical properties.

   B) The process must involve a change in physical properties.

   C) The process must involve a change in mass.

   D) The process must involve a change in volume.

49) In the chemical reaction in which carbon, hydrogen, and oxygen absorb heat and combine to form carbon dioxide and water, which of the following is considered to be a reactant?

A) oxygen   B) carbon dioxide   C) water   D) heat

50) Which of the following processes does NOT involve a change in chemical properties?

A) rusting   B) fermenting   C) boiling   D) burning

51) A chemical change occurs when a piece of wood _____.

A) is split   B) is painted   C) decays   D) is cut

52) Which of the following is a chemical property of water as it exists at 4°C?

A) its color

B) its physical state

C) its specific gravity

D) the fact that it may decompose into hydrogen and oxygen

53) Which of the following is a chemical property of butter?

A) its greasy feel   B) the fact that it becomes rancid

C) its yellow color   D) the fact that it melts at 110°C

54) Which of the following is a chemical property of butter?

A) its greasy feel   B) the fact that it becomes rancid

C) its yellow color   D) the fact that it melts at 110°C

55) When paper becomes yellow–brown in color upon exposure to sunlight, what type of change is likely taking place?

A) a physical change

B) a chemical change

C) neither a physical nor a chemical change

56) Which of the following is a chemical property of an antacid tablet?

A) lack of color   B) tart taste

C) white color   D) ability to neutralize acid

57) Which of the following is true for all chemical reactions?

A) The total mass of the reactants increases.

B) The total mass of the products is greater than the total mass of the reactants.

C) Water is given off.

D) The total mass of the reactants equals the total mass of the products.

Essay Questions

1) Identify five examples of matter and five examples of nonmatter.

2) Explain what is meant by a substance. Give an example.

3) Is there any difference between the chemical properties of water that has been boiled and then condensed and the chemical properties of water that has been frozen and then thawed?

4) What is the difference between a solution and a mixture? Give an example of each.

5) Give five examples of heterogeneous mixtures and five examples of homogeneous mixtures.

6) Give an example of a mixture of two substances for each of the six different two-state mixture systems.

7) Give an example of a mixture of two or more substances in a two-state system and describe how you would separate the substances.

8) Select an element you are familiar with, and a compound you know contains that element. What can you infer about the properties of the compound based on the properties of the element?

9) Explain the difference between an element and a compound.

10) What does the chemical formula of a compound indicate? Use an example to illustrate your points.

11) Describe some of the physical and chemical changes involved in cooking.

12) Explain the difference between chemical properties and physical properties. Give an example of each.

13) Discuss the difference between physical changes and chemical changes. Use an example to illustrate the difference.

14) State the law of conservation of mass. Apply the law to the answering of this question: What would be the total mass of the products of a reaction in which 10 grams of water (H_2O) decomposes into the elements hydrogen (H_2) and oxygen (O_2)?

Chapter 2 Matter and Change

Matching Questions

    1) Answer: E

    2) Answer: A

    3) Answer: B

    4) Answer: F

    5) Answer: D

    6) Answer: C

    7) Answer: A

    8) Answer: C

    9) Answer: F

    10) Answer: E

    11) Answer: D

    12) Answer: B

Multiple Choice and Bimodal Questions

    1) Answer: D

    2) Answer: C

    3) Answer: E

    4) Answer: B

    5) Answer: C

    6) Answer: B

    7) Answer: C

    8) Answer: A

    9) Answer: B

    10) Answer: D

    11) Answer: E

    12) Answer: B

    13) Answer: B

    14) Answer: D

    15) Answer: A

    16) Answer: C

    17) Answer: A

    18) Answer: C

    19) Answer: C

    20) Answer: C

    21) Answer: D

    22) Answer: B

    23) Answer: D

    24) Answer: D

    25) Answer: A

    26) Answer: E

    27) Answer: A

28) Answer: C

29) Answer: B

30) Answer: E

31) Answer: C

32) Answer: D

33) Answer: B

34) Answer: D

35) Answer: E

36) Answer: B

37) Answer: D

38) Answer: E

39) Answer: B

40) Answer: E

41) Answer: B

42) Answer: D

43) Answer: B

44) Answer: B

45) Answer: D

46) Answer: A

47) Answer: A

48) Answer: A

49) Answer: A

50) Answer: C

51) Answer: C

52) Answer: D

53) Answer: B

54) Answer: B

55) Answer: B

56) Answer: D

57) Answer: D

Essay Questions

1) Answer: The examples should follow this rule: Matter has mass and volume; nonmatter has no mass or volume. Examples of matter are: air, water, metal, rock, solutions. Examples of nonmatter are: energy, vacuum, force, magnetic or electric or gravitational fields.

2) Answer: A substance is a particular kind of matter that has a uniform and definite composition. A diamond is a substance.

3) Answer: No. Changes in the physical properties of a substance do not affect the chemical properties of the substance.

4) Answer: A solution is a type of mixture, namely a mixture that has a uniform composition. A mixture can have a nonuniform composition, but a solution cannot. All solutions are mixtures, but not all mixtures are solutions. Salt water (brine) is a solution; sand in water is a mixture.

5) Answer: The examples should follow this rule: A homogeneous mixture is uniform in composition, whereas a heterogeneous mixture is not. An example of a homogeneous mixture is air; an example of a heterogeneous mixture is soup.

6) Answer: Gas–Gas: air; Liquid–Gas: a spray; Gas–Liquid: a foam; Liquid–Liquid: a salad dressing; Solid–Liquid: a medicinal suspension; Solid–Solid: conglomerate rock

7) Answer: One example would be a solution of salt in water. The salt and water can be separated by distillation. Another example would be a mixture of iron and sulfur, which can be separated by placing the mixture in a magnetic field.

8) Answer: You can infer very little, because generally the chemical and physical properties of compounds are quite different from the properties of their component elements. One inference you could draw is that the mass of the compound must be greater than that of the element. Mass is a physical property that is unchanged in the chemical reaction creating the compound.

9) Answer: An element cannot be broken down into simpler components in chemical reactions. Compounds are substances that can be broken down into simpler substances in chemical reactions.

10) Answer: The chemical formula shows the elements that are in the compound and gives the proportions in which the atoms of these elements are found in the compound. The formula for sodium chloride (NaCl), for instance, indicates that the elements in the compound are sodium (Na) and chlorine (Cl), and that the two atoms are present in a proportion of 1:1 in the compound.

11) Answer: Physical changes in cooking include the melting of solids and the boiling of liquids. Examples of physical changes would be the melting of fats and the boiling of water. Chemical changes involve the production of new substances. Examples of chemical changes would be the carmelization of sugar during candy-making and the release of carbon dioxide during the baking of bread.

12) Answer: The ability of a substance to undergo particular chemical reactions and to form new substances constitutes its set of chemical properties. Chemical properties can only be observed when a substance undergoes a change in composition. Physical properties can be observed without altering the composition of a substance. The fact that iron will rust is a chemical property of iron. The fact that iron is a solid at room temperature is a physical property of iron.

13) Answer: Physical changes do not alter the composition of a substance, but chemical changes do. When water is boiled the resulting gas is still made up of water molecules just like those in the liquid. However, when water molecules are broken down into elemental hydrogen and oxygen in a chemical reaction, the water molecules no longer exist. The latter is a chemical change; the former a physical change.

14) Answer: The law of conservation of mass states that in any physical or chemical reaction, mass is neither created nor destroyed. According to this law, the total mass the products in the reaction referred to here would be 10 grams, namely the same mass as that of the reactants.

Chapter 3 Scientific Measurement

Matching Questions

Chapter 3: Matching I

1) accuracy

2) precision

3) qualitative

4) significant figure

5) quantitative

A) closeness to true value

B) known or estimated in a measurement

C) descriptive and nonnumeric

D) definite and usually numeric

E) narrowness of range of measurements

Chapter 3: Matching II

6) absolute zero

7) Kelvin temperature scale

8) Celsius temperature scale

9) weight

10) mass

A) the non–SI scale for temperature

B) the force of gravity on an object

C) the quantity of matter an object contains

D) the lowest point on the Kelvin scale

E) the SI scale for temperature

Multiple Choice and Bimodal Questions

1) The diameter of a carbon atom is 0.000 000 000 154 m. What is this number expressed in scientific notation?

A) 1.54×10^{12} m   B) 1.54×10^{-12} m   C) 1.54×10^{10} m   D) 1.54×10^{-10} m

2) What is 5928 km expressed in scientific notation?

A) 5.928×10^{0} B) 5.928×10^{3} C) 5.928×10^{2} D) 5.928×10^{-3}

3) What is the result of multiplying $(2.5 \times 10^{10}) \times (3.5 \times 10^{-7})$?

A) 8.75×10^{-3} B) 8.75×10^{17} C) 8.75×10^{3} D) 8.75×10^{-17}

4) What is the result of adding $(2.5 \times 10^{3}) + (3.5 \times 10^{2})$?

A) 2.85×10^{3} B) 6.0×10^{3} C) 2.85×10^{2} D) 6.0×10^{5}

5) Which of the following is the best example of a quantitative measurement?

A) 2.01   B) 2.011   C) 2.011 1   D) 2.011 11   E) 2.01 grams

6) Which of the following is NOT a quantitative measurement?

A) 5 liters

B) 17 millimeters

C) 10 meters

D) 200 milliliters

E) very small

7) When a test instrument is calibrated, does its accuracy, precision, or reliability improve?

A) precision   B) accuracy   C) reliability

8) The closeness of a measurement to its true value is a measure of its _____.

A) precision   B) accuracy   C) reproducibility   D) usefulness

9) In the measurement 0.503 L, which digit is the estimated digit?

A) 5

B) the 0 immediately to the left of the 3

C) 3

D) the 0 to the left of the decimal point

E) There is no estimated digit in this measurement.

10) How many significant figures are there in the measurement 0.003 4 kg?

A) two

B) three

C) four

D) five

E) This cannot be determined.

11) How many significant figures are there in the measurement 40 500 mg?

A) two

B) three

C) four

D) five

E) This cannot be determined.

12) How many significant figures are there in the measurement 811.40 grams?

A) two   B) three   C) four   D) five

13) What is the measurement 111.009 mm rounded off to four significant digits?

A) 111 mm   B) 111.0 mm   C) 111.01 mm   D) 110 mm   E) 100 mm

14) What is the measurement 1042 L rounded off to two significant digits?

A) 1.0×10^3 L

B) 1040 L

C) 1050 L

D) 1.1×10^3 L

E) none of the above

15) Express the sum of 1111 km and 222 km using the correct number of significant digits.

A) 1300 km   B) 1330 km   C) 1330. km   D) 1333 km   E) 1333.0 km

16) Express the sum of 7.68 m and 5.0 m using the correct number of significant digits.

A) 12.68

B) 12.7

C) 13

D) 10 m

E) none of the above

17) Express the product of 2.2 mm and 5.00 mm using the correct number of significant digits.

A) 10 mm^2

B) 11 mm^2

C) 11.0 mm^2

D) 11.00 mm^2

E) none of the above

18) Express the product of 4.0×10^{-2} m and 8.1×10^2 m using the correct number of significant digits.

A) 3×10^1 B) 3.0×10^1 C) 3.2×10^1 D) 3.24×10^1 E) 3.3×10^1

19) Which of the following measurements (of different masses) is the most accurate?

A) 3.1000 g

B) 3.100 00 g

C) 3.122 00 g

D) 3.122 22 g

E) 3.000 000 g

20) Which group of measurements is the most precise? (Each group of measurements is for a different object.)

A) 2 g, 3 g, 4 g

B) 2.0 g, 3.0 g, 4.0 g

C) 2 g, 2.5 g, 3 g

D) 2.0 g, 3.0 g, 4.0 g, 5.0 g

E) 1 g, 3 g, 5 g

21) Three different people weigh a standard mass of ?   ch person obtains a reading of 7.32 g for the ma   at the balance that was used is _____.

A) accurate

C) accurate and precise   nor precise

22) Which of the following measu   significant figures?

A) 0.007 m   B) 70   C) 7.30 x 10^{-7} km   D) 0.070 mm

23) Which of the following meas   contains two significant figures?

A) 0.004 00 L   B)   C) 0.000 44 L   D) 0.004 40 L

24) When multiplying and div   easured quantities, the number of significant figures in the result should be equal   umber of significant figures in _____ .

A) all of the measuremen

B) the least and most pre   easurements.

C) the most precise mea   ent.

D) the least precise mea   ent.

25) What quantity is repres   by the metric system prefix deci–?

A) 1000   B)   C) 0.1   D) 0.01   E) 0.001

26) What is the metric sys   prefix for the quantity 0.000 001?

                    i–   C) kilo–   D) micro–   E) milli–

                    75 meters expressed in centimeters?

                    75 cm   C) 7.5 cm   D) 70.5 cm   E) 705.0 cm

                    96 millimeters expressed in meters?

A) 7.896 m

B) 78.96 m

C) 789.6 m

D) 789 600 m

E) 7 896 000 m

29) A nanosecond is equivalent to how many seconds?

A) 10^{-6} s   B) 10^9 s   C) 10^{-9} s

30) What is the quantity 78 liters expressed in cubic meters?
   A) 0.000 078 m^3
   B) 0.078 m^3
   C) 0.78 m^3
   D) 78 000 m^3
   E) 78 000 000 m^3

31) What is the volume of a salt crystal measuring 2.44 x 10^{-2} ... 1.4 x 10^{-3} m by 8.4 x 10^{-3} m?
   A) 2.9 x 10^{-7} m^3 B) 2.9 x 10^{-6} m^3 C) 2.9 x 1... ^{3} D) 2.9 x 10^{-4} m^3

32) What is the quantity 987 milligrams expressed in grams?
   A) 0.000 987 g
   B) 0.987 g
   C) 9.87 g
   D) 98 700 g
   E) 987 000 g

33) The chief advantage of the metric system over other systems o... asurement is that it
   _____.
   A) has more units   B) is in multip... f 10
   C) is in French   D) is derived f... nature itself

34) Which of the following units is NOT an official SI unit?
   A) kilogram   B) candela   C) ampere   D) mo...   E) liter

35) Which of the following units is NOT a derived SI unit?
   A) millimeter of mercury
   B) grams per cubic centimeter
   C) newtons per cubic meter
   D) cubic meter
   E) moles per gram

36) Which of the following equalities is NOT correct?
   A) 100 cg = 1 g   B) 1000 mm = 1 m   C) 1 cm^3 = 1 mL   D) 10 kg = 1 g

37) Which of the following mass units is the largest?
   A) 1 cg   B) 1 dg   C) 1 mg   D) 1 ng

38) For which of the following quantities are the units derived?
   A) mass   B) volume   C) length   D) width

39) Which of the following volumes is the smallest?
   A) one microliter   B) one liter   C) one milliliter

40) A cubic meter is about the same as the volume occupied by _____ .

   A) a kilogram of water   B) a cup of milk

   C) a washing machine   D) a basketball arena

41) The weight of an object _____ .

   A) is the same as its mass

   B) depends on its location

   C) is not affected by gravity

42) What is the SI unit of mass?

   A) liter   B) joule   C) pascal   D) candela   E) kilogram

43) If a liter of water is heated from 20°C to 50°C, what happens to its volume?

   A) The volume decreases.

   B) The volume increases.

   C) The volume does not change.

   D) The volume first increases, then decreases.

   E) The volume first decreases, then increases.

44) What is the density of an object having a mass of 8.0 g and a volume of 25 cm^3?

   A) 0.32 g/cm^3

   B) 2.0 g/cm^3

   C) 3.1 g/cm^3

   D) 200 g/cm^3

   E) none of the above

45) If the temperature of a piece of steel decreases, what happens to its density?

   A) The density decreases.

   B) The density increases.

   C) The density does not change.

   D) The density first increases, then decreases.

   E) The density first decreases, then increases.

46) As the density of a substance increases, the volume of a given mass of that substance _____ .

   A) increases   B) is not affected   C) decreases

47) What is the volume of 80.0 g of ether if the density of ether is 0.70 g/mL?

   A) 5.6×10^1 B) 1.1×10^2 C) 8.8×10^{-3} D) 8.0×10^1

48) What is the volume of 344 g of ice, if the density of the ice is 0.92 g/mL?

   A) 0.002 67 mL   B) 37.4 mL   C) 316 mL   D) 370 mL

49) What is the volume of 45.6 g of silver if the density of silver is 10.5 g/mL?

A) 0.23 mL

B) 4.34 mL

C) 479 mL

D) none of the above

50) If the density of a particular liquid is 0.98 g/cm^3 at 4°C, how does the specific gravity of this liquid compare to that of water?

A) It is greater than that of water.

B) It is less than that of water.

C) It is equal to that of water.

D) No determination can be made from the information.

51) If the density of a substance is 4.8 g/cm^3 at a particular temperature and the density of water at the same temperature is 0.96 g/cm^3, what is the specific gravity of the substance at that temperature?

A) 5.0

B) 0.2

C) 5.65

D) No determination can be made from the information given.

52) The derived unit for density is _____.

A) m/cm^3 B) kg/m^2 C) kg/m^3 D) g/cm^3

53) The density is found by dividing _____.

A) mass by volume

B) volume by mass

C) mass by area

D) area by mass

E) mass by length

54) The specific gravity of a liquid _____.

A) is a number without a unit

B) can be determined with a hydrometer

C) is the ratio of the density of the liquid to the density of water

D) all of the above

55) What is the temperature –34°C expressed in kelvins?

A) 139 K   B) 207 K   C) 239 K   D) 307 K   E) 339 K

56) What is the temperature of absolute zero measured in °C?

A) –373°C   B) –273°C   C) –173°C   D) –73°C   E) 0°C

57) Which temperature scale has no negative temperatures?

A) Celsius   B) Fahrenheit   C) Joule   D) Kelvin

58) What is the boiling point in kelvins of water at 1 atmosphere of pressure?

   A) 0 K   B) 100 K   C) 273 K   D) 373 K   E) 473 K

59) If the temperature changes by 100 K, by how much does it change in °C?

   A) 0°C   B) 37°C   C) 100°C   D) 273°C   E) 373°C

60) Chlorine boils at 239 K. What is the boiling point of chlorine expressed in degrees Celsius?

   A) 93°C   B) 34°C   C) –61°C   D) –34°C

Problems

1) The following length measurements were taken by students using several different measuring devices. Find the average of the measurements. Make sure that your answer has the correct number of significant figures.
   10.02 cm, 10.5 cm, 9.75 cm, 10.9 cm, 10.2 cm

2) Round off the measurement 417.10 g to three significant figures.

3) Round off the measurement 0.003 095 5 m to three significant figures.

4) What is the sum of 2.7 g and 2.47 g expressed in the correct number of significant digits?

5) What is the sum of 6.210 L and 3 L expressed in the correct number of significant digits?

6) What is the product of the number 1000 and the measurement 0.003 57 m expressed in the correct number of significant digits?

7) The mass of the electron is 9.109 39 x 10^{-31} kg. Express the mass of the electron to 1, 2, 3, and 4 significant figures.

8) Perform the following operation: 3.43 cm x 5.2 cm. Make sure that your answer has the correct number of significant figures.

9) Express 0.06 liters in cubic meters, using the correct abbreviations.

10) Express 0.05 grams in kilograms, using the correct abbreviations.

) What is the density of an object having a mass of 4.0 g and a volume of 39.0 cubic centimeters?

) What is the volume of an object with a density of 8.03 g/cm^3 and a mass of 6.00 x 10^{2}g?

) A cube of a gold-colored metal with a volume of 59 cm^3 has a mass of 980 g. The density of the gold is 19.3 g/cm^3. Is the metal pure gold? Show calculations to justify your answer.

14) If the density of a particular substance is 7.2 g/cm^3 at a particular temperature and the density of water at the same temperature is 1.0 g/cm^3, what is the specific gravity of the substance at that temperature?

15) The density of osmium, which is the densest metal, is 22.57 g/cm^3. What is the mass of a block of osmium that measures 1.00 cm x 4.00 cm x 2.50 cm?

16) If the specific gravity of a substance is 3.6 at 20°C, and the density of water is 0.95 g/cm^3 at 20°C, what is the density of the substance at 20°C?

17) What is the temperature 198 K expressed in degrees Celsius?

Essay Questions

1) Explain the difference between a qualitative and a quantitative measurement. Provide examples to illustrate this difference.

2) Explain the difference between precision and accuracy. Suppose you made three different mass measurements of a sugar sample you knew to have a mass of 1 g. How would you know whether or not the measurements were accurate? How would you know whether or not they were precise? Could the three measurements be precise, but not accurate? Explain.

3) Describe the rules that are used to determine the number of significant figures in the results of addition, subtraction, multiplication, and division.

4) Why is the metric system the preferred system of measurement for science?

5) Explain the difference between mass and weight. Provide an example to illustrate the distinction.

6) Why is the density of a metal greater than the density of water?

7) Why do the densities of most substances decrease with temperature?

8) Explain what is wrong with the statement, "Gold is heavier than bone".

9) Explain the difference between specific gravity and density.

10) Describe how a hydrometer works to measure specific gravity.

11) You are given a jar containing a mixture of three different solid substances. The particles of each substance are larger than 0.5 cm in diameter. All you know about the substances is that each is a pure metal. Describe a method for determining the identities of the metals that make up the mixture. Assume that each metal is a different color, so you can tell one from the others.

12) Explain the difference between the Celsius and Kelvin temperature scales.

Chapter 3 Scientific Measurement
Matching Questions
1) Answer: A
2) Answer: E
3) Answer: C
4) Answer: B
5) Answer: D
6) Answer: D
7) Answer: E
8) Answer: A
9) Answer: B
10) Answer: C

Multiple Choice and Bimodal Questions
1) Answer: D
2) Answer: B
3) Answer: C
4) Answer: A
5) Answer: E
6) Answer: E
7) Answer: B
8) Answer: B
9) Answer: C
10) Answer: A
11) Answer: B
12) Answer: D
13) Answer: B
14) Answer: A
15) Answer: D
16) Answer: B
17) Answer: B
18) Answer: C
19) Answer: E
20) Answer: C
21) Answer: B
22) Answer: C
23) Answer: C
24) Answer: D
25) Answer: C
26) Answer: D
27) Answer: B
28) Answer: A
29) Answer: C
30) Answer: B

31) Answer: A

32) Answer: B

33) Answer: B

34) Answer: E

35) Answer: A

36) Answer: D

37) Answer: B

38) Answer: B

39) Answer: A

40) Answer: C

41) Answer: B

42) Answer: E

43) Answer: B

44) Answer: A

45) Answer: B

46) Answer: C

47) Answer: B

48) Answer: D

49) Answer: B

50) Answer: B

51) Answer: A

52) Answer: D

53) Answer: A

54) Answer: D

55) Answer: C

56) Answer: B

57) Answer: D

58) Answer: D

59) Answer: C

60) Answer: D

Problems

1) Answer: Average = 10.3 cm

2) Answer: 417 g

3) Answer: 0.003 10 m

4) Answer: 5.2 g

5) Answer: 9 L

6) Answer: 3.57 m

7) Answer: one: 9×10^{-31} kg; two: 9.1×10^{-31} kg; three: 9.11×10^{-31} kg; four: 9.109×10^{-31} kg

8) Answer: 3.43 cm x 5.2 cm = 18 cm^2

9) Answer: 0.06 L x 1 m^3/1000 L = 0.000 06 m^3

10) Answer: 0.05 g x 1 kg/1000 g = 0.000 05 kg

11) Answer: Density = $\dfrac{\text{mass}}{\text{volume}}$ = $\dfrac{4.0 \text{ g}}{39.0 \text{ cm}^3}$ = 0.10 g/cm^3

12) Answer: Volume $= \dfrac{\text{mass}}{\text{density}} = \dfrac{600 \text{ g}}{8.03 \text{ g}/\text{cm}^3} = 74.7 \text{ cm}^3$

13) Answer: No.

$$\text{Density} = \dfrac{\text{mass}}{\text{volume}} = \dfrac{980 \text{ g}}{59 \text{ cm}^3} = 17 \text{ g}/\text{cm}^3$$

14) Answer: Specific gravity $=$ density of substance / density of water

$$= \dfrac{7.2 \text{ g}/\text{cm}^3}{1.0 \text{ g}/\text{cm}^3} = 7.2$$

15) Answer: Mass $=$ density x volume

$= 22.57 \text{ g}/\text{cm}^3 \times 1.00 \text{ cm} \times 4.00 \text{ cm} \times 2.50 \text{ cm} = 226 \text{ g}$

16) Answer: Density of substance

$=$ density of water x specific gravity of substance

$= 0.95 \text{ g}/\text{cm}^3 \times 3.6 = 3.4 \text{ g}/\text{cm}^3$

17) Answer: $^{\circ}\text{C} = \text{K} - 273 = 198 - 273 = -75^{\circ}\text{C}$

Essay Questions

1) Answer: A qualitative measurement is a measurement that gives descriptive, nonnumeric results; a quantitative measurement is a measurement that gives definite, usually numeric results. "The rock is heavy" would be a qualitative measurement. "The rock weighs 110 grams" would be a quantitative measurement.

2) Answer: Precision is the reproducibility, under the same conditions, of a measurement; accuracy is the closeness of a measurement to the true value of what is being measured. The three measurements would be precise if they were very close to each other in value; they would be accurate if they were close to the actual 1–g value for the mass of the sample. If the measurements are very close to each other, they are precise, regardless of how close they are to the real value. Therefore, the measurements could be precise, but not accurate.

3) Answer: The answer of an addition or subtraction can have no more digits to the right of the decimal point than are contained in the measurement with the least number of digits to the right of the decimal point. The answer of a multiplication or division can have no more significant figures than the measurement having the least number of significant figures. For these two operations, the position of the decimal point has nothing to do with the number of significant figures.

4) Answer: The primary reason for this is that the metric system is based on units that are multiples of ten, thus simplifying conversions between units. In addition, all necessary units can be derived from the seven basic units of the metric system.

5) Answer: Mass is a measure of the quantity of matter in an object. The mass of an object does not vary with location. Weight, on the other hand, is a measure of the strength of the pull of a gravitational force (usually the earth's) on an object. The weight of the object changes with the object's distance from the center of the gravitational field it is in. The mass of a person, for instance, will be exactly the same whether the person is on the earth or on the moon. The weight of that person, however, will be much less on the moon than on the earth because the gravitational pull of the moon is much less than that of the earth.

6) Answer: The student should infer from the text that this is true either because the metal's atoms are heavier than the water molecules or because the metal atoms are more closely packed than the water molecules, or both.

7) Answer: The student should infer that this is because a substance's atoms or molecules tend to move farther apart with an increase in temperature. Consequently, the volume of the substance increases. There is no change in the mass of the substance, however, and therefore the density (mass/volume) decreases.

8) Answer: When comparing masses of two substances, the volumes of both must be known. Only when volumes are equal can it be said that one substance is heavier than another. This relationship between mass and volume is called density. As the density of a substance decreases, the volume of a given mass of that substance increases.

9) Answer: Density has units and is absolute, depending only on temperature. Specific gravity has no units and is a comparison of the density of a substance to the density of a reference substance, usually at the same temperature. The density of aluminum at 25°C is 2.76 g/cm^3. The specific gravity of aluminum at 25°C, using the reference standard of water at 4°C, is simply 2.70.

10) Answer: A typical hydrometer is a long, slender glass float that is weighted at the lower end, and provided with a scale so graduated that the depth to which the instrument sinks in a liquid indicates the specific gravity of that liquid by direct reading on the scale. The weight of the hydrometer is constant and the hydrometer will sink to the depth at which it is buoyed up by the weight of the displaced liquid. The less dense the sample liquid is, the deeper the hydrometer will sink.

11) Answer: If each substance is a pure metal, they should be identifiable by determining their densities. Separate the solids by color into three separate batches of pure metals. Determine the mass of each metal using a balance. Determine the volume of each metal as follows. Immerse each metal in a measured volume of a suitable liquid. Measure the volume of the liquid plus the metal, for example, using a graduated cylinder. Calculate the difference between the volume of the liquid plus the metal and the liquid by itself. To calculate the density, divide the mass of each metal by the volume. Compare the density and color of each metal to the density and color listed in reference books.

12) Answer: Both scales use the freezing point and boiling point of water as reference temperature values. The Celsius scale designates the freezing point of water as 0°C and the boiling point as 100°C. The region between these two points is divided into equal intervals known as degrees. The Kelvin scale designates 0 K as the temperature at which the volume of an ideal gas would be zero. It is called the absolute zero because it is the lowest temperature that is theoretically attainable. Absolute zero corresponds to –273°C on the Celsius scale. The Kelvin scale uses degree intervals that are the same size as the intervals on the Celsius scale. The difference between the scales lies in how the zero point is chosen. On the Celsius scale, the zero point is the freezing point of water. On the Kelvin scale, it is the point at which the volume of an ideal gas would theoretically be zero. The scales are related by the following formulas:

K = 0°C + 273 or 0°C = K - 273.

Chapter 4 Problem Solving in Chemistry
Matching Questions
Chapter 4: Matching I

1) conversion factor

2) dimension

3) dimensional analysis

4) unit

5) variable

6) constant

A) a scale of measurement

B) value established as fact

C) ratio of equivalent measurements

D) unknown or changing value

E) technique of obtaining correct unit for answer

F) unit of measurement

Multiple Choice and Bimodal Questions

1) The best way to become a better problem solver is by _____.
   A) doing problems
   B) watching your teacher work out problems on the board
   C) practicing one and only one approach to problem solving
   D) There is no way to improve. Problem solvers are born, not made.

2) Which of the following is at the "heart" of problem solving?
   A) identifying the unknown
   B) identifying what is known or given
   C) planning a solution
   D) doing the calculations
   E) finishing up

3) What is the volume of 60.0 g of ether if the density of ether is 0.70 g/mL?
   A) 42 mL   B) 8.6 x 10^1 mL   C) 0.012 mL   D) 60.0 mL

4) How are the numerator and denominator in a conversion factor related?
   A) They are equal.
   B) One is greater than or less than the other.
   C) They each have the same units.
   D) Both equal the value 1.

5) How many significant figures are there in the conversion factor 100 cm/1 m?

   A) one

   B) two

   C) three

   D) four

   E) an unlimited number

6) If the correct conversion factor is $\dfrac{100 \text{ cm}}{1 \text{ m}}$ and the known measurement is 25 m, what is the answer given by dimensional analysis?

   A) 0.25 m   B) 0.25 cm   C) 2500 m   D) 2500 cm

7) If the correct conversion factor is $\dfrac{1 \text{ L}}{1000 \text{ mL}}$ and the known measurement is 33 mL, what is the answer given by dimensional analysis?

   A) 0.033 mL   B) 0.033 L   C) 33 000 mL   D) 33 000 L

8) What is the volume 1×10^4 L expressed in cubic centimeters?

   A) 1×10^1 cm^3 B) 1×10^2 cm^3 C) 1×10^6 cm^3 D) 1×10^7 cm^3

9) How many centimeters are there in 3 kilometers?

   A) 3×10^{-5} cm   B) 3×10^{-3} cm   C) 3×10^3 cm   D) 3×10^5 cm

10) How many miles does light travel in 1 microsecond in a vacuum? (The speed of light in a vacuum is 186 000 miles/second.)

   A) 0.000 186 miles   B) 0.186 miles   C) 1.86 miles   D) 186 miles

11) On a typical day you inhale about 1×10^4 liters of air. What conversion factor would you use to express the volume in cubic centimeters?

   A) $\dfrac{1.0 \times 10^3 \text{ cm}^3}{1 \text{ L}}$ B) $\dfrac{1 \text{ L}}{1.0 \times 10^3 \text{ cm}^3}$ C) $\dfrac{1.0 \times 10^2 \text{ cm}^2}{1 \text{ L}}$ D) $\dfrac{1 \text{ L}}{1.0 \times 10^2 \text{ cm}^3}$

12) What is the result of converting 31 kg to nanograms?

   A) 0.000 000 031 ng

   B) 0.000 031 ng

   C) 0.031 ng

   D) 31 000 000 ng

   E) 31 000 000 000 ng

13) What is the result of converting 197 μm to kilometers?

   A) 0.000 000 197 km

   B) 0.000 197 km

   C) 0.197 km

   D) 197 000 km

   E) 197 000 000 km

14) What is the result of converting 0.256 μL to kiloliters?

    A) 0.000 000 000 000 256 kL

    B) 0.000 000 000 256 kL

    C) 0.000 000 256 kL

    D) 0.000 256 kL

    E) 0.002 56 kL

15) What is the result of converting 0.04 kmol to centimoles?

    A) 40 000 cmol

    B) 4000 cmol

    C) 40 cmol

    D) 4 cmol

    E) 0.4 cmol

16) What is the result of converting 794 dg to centigrams?

    A) 79 400 cg   B) 7940 cg   C) 79.4 cg   D) 7.94 cg   E) 0.794 cg

17) What is the result of converting 631 mm to m?

    A) 0.063 1 m   B) 631 m   C) 63.1 m   D) 6.31 m   E) 0.631 m

18) Word problems normally deal with relationships between which quantities?

    A) numbers   B) measurements   C) vectors

19) Which of the following ratios represents a correct conversion factor?

    A) $\dfrac{100\ L}{1000\ L}$ B) $\dfrac{100\ L}{1000\ g}$ C) $\dfrac{100\ L}{1000\ dL}$ D) $\dfrac{100\ L}{1000\ mL}$ E) $\dfrac{100\ L}{1000\ cL}$

20) Which of the following units can be converted into grams?

    A) liters   B) joules   C) kelvins   D) pounds   E) meters

21) Which of the following ratios represents a correct conversion factor?

    A) $\dfrac{10\ cN}{1\ J}$ B) $\dfrac{0.01\ L}{1\ cm}$ C) $\dfrac{10\ g}{1000\ mL}$ D) $\dfrac{0.01\ g}{1\ cg}$ E) $\dfrac{1000\ cal}{1\ kN}$

22) Which of the following ratios is a correct conversion factor for changing kilometers to meters?

    A) $\dfrac{0.001\ km}{1\ m}$ B) $\dfrac{1000\ km}{1\ m}$ C) $\dfrac{1000\ m}{1\ km}$ D) $\dfrac{0.01\ m}{1\ km}$

23) Which of the following ratios is a correct conversion factor for changing grams to micrograms?

    A) $\dfrac{1\ 000\ 000\ \mu g}{1\ g}$ B) $\dfrac{1000\ \mu g}{1\ g}$ C) $\dfrac{1000\ g}{1\ \mu g}$ D) $\dfrac{1\ 000\ 000\ g}{1\ \mu g}$

24) What is the ratio of the conversion factor 1 mg/0.001 g?

  A) greater than 1

  B) equal to 1

  C) less than 1

  D) A ratio cannot be determined from the information given.

25) A conversion factor _____.

  A) is equal to 1

  B) is a ratio of equivalent measurements

  C) does not change the value of a measurement

  D) all of the above

26) Which of the following steps of problem solving is aided by the process of dimensional analysis?

  A) identifying the unknown

  B) identifying what is known

  C) planning a solution based on the units

27) Dimensional analysis involves which of the following processes?

  A) solving a formula

  B) estimating the magnitude of the answer

  C) splitting a problem into steps

  D) multiplying a known measurement by a conversion factor

28) Which of the following conversion factors can be used to change kilograms to grams?

  A) $\dfrac{1\ kg}{1000\ g}$ B) $\dfrac{1000\ g}{1\ kg}$ C) $\dfrac{1\ kg}{0.001\ g}$ D) $\dfrac{0.001\ g}{1\ kg}$

29) Which of the following conversion factors can be used to change liters to centiliters?

  A) $\dfrac{1\ L}{100\ cL}$ B) $\dfrac{100\ cL}{1\ L}$ C) $\dfrac{1\ L}{0.01\ cL}$ D) $\dfrac{0.01\ cL}{1\ L}$

30) Which of the following conversion can be used to change centimeters to kilometers?

  A) $(\dfrac{100\ cm}{1\ m}) \times (\dfrac{1\ km}{1000\ m})$ B) $(\dfrac{100\ cm}{1\ m}) \times (\dfrac{1000\ m}{1\ km})$

  C) $(\dfrac{1\ m}{100\ cm}) \times (\dfrac{1\ km}{1000\ m})$ D) $(\dfrac{1\ m}{100\ cm}) \times (\dfrac{1000\ m}{1\ km})$

31) Which of the following conversion can be used to change kilomoles to nanomoles?

  A) $(\dfrac{1\ kmol}{1000\ mol}) \times (\dfrac{10^9\ nmol}{1\ mol})$ B) $(\dfrac{1000\ mol}{1\ kmol}) \times (\dfrac{10^9\ nmol}{1\ mol})$

  C) $(\dfrac{1\ kmol}{1000\ mol}) \times (\dfrac{1\ mol}{10^9\ nmol})$ D) $(\dfrac{1000\ mol}{1\ kmol}) \times (\dfrac{1\ mol}{10^9\ nmol})$

32) The density of aluminum is 2.70 g/cm^3. What is the mass of a cube of aluminum 1.0 cm on each edge?

    A) 2.70 g   B) 5.4 g   C) 27.0 g   D) 81 g

33) What is the result of converting 48 m to centimeters?

    A) 0.000 48 cm   B) 0.48 cm   C) 4800 cm   D) 4 800 000 cm

34) What is the result of converting 63 mL to liters?

    A) 0.063 L   B) 0.63 L   C) 630 L   D) 63 000 L

35) Five kilometers is equal to how many centimeters?

    A) 5.0×10^{-3} cm   B) 5.0×10^{5} cm   C) 5.0×10^{-5} cm   D) 1.0×10^{3} cm

36) If 20 gits equal 1 erb, and 1 futz equals 2 hews, and 10 erbs equal 1 futz, how many gits equal 5 hews?

    A) 50 gits   B) 100 gits   C) 500 gits   D) 1000 gits

37) Express the density 5.6 g/cm^3 in kg/m^3.

    A) 5 600 000 kg/m^3

    B) 5600 kg/m^3

    C) 560 kg/m^3

    D) 0.0056 kg/m^3

    E) 0.000 005 6 kg^3/m

38) How would the rate 60 m/s be expressed in km/hr?

    A) 21 600 km/hr

    B) 216 km/hr

    C) 2.16 km/hr

    D) 0.216 km/hr

    E) 0.002 16 km/hr

39) How would the ratio 18 g/mol be expressed in kilograms per kilomole?

    A) 0.018 kg/kmol   B) 18 kg/kmol

    C) 18 000 kg/kmol   D) 18 000 000 kg/kmol

40) Which of the following approaches is often useful when trying to plan a solution to a complex problem?

    A) eliminating unnecessary facts

    B) rounding off the numbers

    C) using fewer significant figures

    D) simplifying the equation

    E) splitting the problem into easier steps

41) The number of seconds in an 8–hour work day can be calculated as _____.

A) $60 \text{ s} \times \dfrac{1 \text{ min}}{60 \text{ s}} \times \dfrac{1 \text{ h}}{60 \text{ min}} =$

B) $8 \text{ h} \times \dfrac{60 \text{ min}}{1 \text{ h}} \times \dfrac{60 \text{ s}}{1 \text{ min}} =$

C) $1 \text{ s} \times \dfrac{1 \text{ min}}{60 \text{ s}} \times \dfrac{8 \text{ h}}{60 \text{ min}} =$

D) $8 \text{ h} \times \dfrac{60 \text{ min}}{8 \text{ h}} \times \dfrac{60 \text{ s}}{60 \text{ min}} =$

42) The diameter of a sodium atom is 3.7 nanometers. What conversion factor(s) would you use to express this measurement in centimeters?

A) $\dfrac{1 \text{ m}}{10^9 \text{ nm}}$

B) $\dfrac{10^9 \text{ nm}}{1 \text{ m}}$

C) $\dfrac{1 \text{ m}}{10^9 \text{ nm}} \times \dfrac{100 \text{ cm}}{1 \text{ m}}$

D) $\dfrac{10^9 \text{ nm}}{1 \text{ m}} \times \dfrac{1 \text{ m}}{100 \text{ cm}}$

43) A blacksmith has to put new shoes on a stable of 20 horses. Each shoe requires 3 nails. How can he or she calculate the number of nails that must be brought to the stable?

A) number of nails $\times \dfrac{4 \text{ shoes}}{3 \text{ nails}} \times \dfrac{1 \text{ horse}}{4 \text{ shoes}} =$

B) number of horses $\times \dfrac{4 \text{ shoes}}{1 \text{ horse}} \times \dfrac{3 \text{ nails}}{1 \text{ shoe}} =$

C) number of shoes $\times \dfrac{1 \text{ horse}}{4 \text{ shoes}} \times \dfrac{3 \text{ nails}}{1 \text{ horse}} =$

D) number of nails $\times \dfrac{1 \text{ shoe}}{\text{nails}} \times \dfrac{3 \text{ nails}}{1 \text{ shoe}} =$

Problems

1) What is the mass of a bone that has a volume of 80.0 cm^3 and a density of 1.9 g/cm^3?

2) What is the volume of a liquid that has a density of 0.90 g/cm^3 and a mass of 60.0 g?

3) What is the volume of 500.0 g of ice if the density of ice is 0.92 g/mL?

4) List four different conversion factors for kilometers and meters.

5) List four different conversion factors for micrograms and grams.

6) Give a conversion factor that may be used to convert kiloliters to nanoliters.

7) Give a conversion factor that may be used to convert micrograms to kilograms.

8) If the known is expressed in units of kilometers and the unknown is to be expressed in units of centimeters, what is the appropriate conversion factor?

9) If the known is expressed in units of micromoles and the unknown is to be expressed in units of kilomoles, what is the appropriate conversion factor?

10) Convert 0.300 mol to kilomoles.

11) Convert 549 kg to grams.

12) Convert 0.0349 mm to meters.

13) Convert 673 m to kilometers.

14) Convert 0.945 dL to liters.

15) Convert 0.968 kL to liters.

16) Convert 13 µg to kilograms.

17) Convert 121 g to milligrams.

18) Convert 7600 micrograms to centigrams.

19) Convert 332 mmol to kilomoles.

20) Convert 0.769 kg to decigrams.

21) In 1976, an airplane was flown at a speed of 2193 miles per hour. What was the speed of the plane in meters per second? (1 km = 0.621 mi)

22) The density of water is 1.0 g/mL. What is the density of water in pounds/gallon? (1 quart = 9.46 x 10^{-1} L; 1 g = 2.20 x 10^{-3} lb.)

23) Express the density 4.2 g/cm^3 in kg/m^3.

24) Express the rate 21 m/s in km/hr.

25) Express the ratio 99.5 g/mol in kg/kmol.

26) Light travels at a speed of 186 000 miles/second in a vacuum. How many kilometers will it travel in two hours? (1 km = 0.621 mile)

27) An automobile can travel 21.0 miles on 1 gallon of gasoline. How many kilometers per liter is this? (1.61 km = 1 mi; 1 L = 1.06 quart; 1 gallon = 4 quarts)

28) Gold has sold for $500/ounce. Considering that there are 16 ounces (or 454 grams) in a pound, how many milligrams of gold could you buy for one cent?

Essay Questions

1) Describe each step in the 3–step problem solving process.

2) How does a conversion factor differ from a measurement? Give an example of each.

3) Explain why the value of a conversion factor is always equal to 1 even though both the units and the numbers in the conversion factor are different from each other. Use an example to illustrate your explanation.

4) Explain what is meant by dimensional analysis. Use an example in your explanation.

5) In the dimensional analysis method, what must be checked particularly carefully in every problem?

Chapter 4 Problem Solving in Chemistry

Matching Questions

    1) Answer: C

    2) Answer: F

    3) Answer: E

    4) Answer: A

    5) Answer: D

    6) Answer: B

Multiple Choice and Bimodal Questions

    1) Answer: A

    2) Answer: C

    3) Answer: B

    4) Answer: A

    5) Answer: E

    6) Answer: D

    7) Answer: B

    8) Answer: D

    9) Answer: D

    10) Answer: B

    11) Answer: A

    12) Answer: E

    13) Answer: A

    14) Answer: B

    15) Answer: B

    16) Answer: B

    17) Answer: E

    18) Answer: B

    19) Answer: C

    20) Answer: D

    21) Answer: D

    22) Answer: C

    23) Answer: A

    24) Answer: B

    25) Answer: D

    26) Answer: C

    27) Answer: D

    28) Answer: B

    29) Answer: B

    30) Answer: C

    31) Answer: B

    32) Answer: A

    33) Answer: C

    34) Answer: A

35) Answer: B

36) Answer: C

37) Answer: B

38) Answer: B

39) Answer: B

40) Answer: E

41) Answer: B

42) Answer: C

43) Answer: B

Problems

1) Answer: Mass = density x volume = 1.9 g/cm^3 x 80.0 cm^3 = 150 g

2) Answer: Volume = $\dfrac{mass}{density}$ = $\dfrac{60.0 \text{ g}}{0.90 \text{ g/cm}^3}$ = 67 cm^3

3) Answer: Volume = $\dfrac{mass}{density}$ = $\dfrac{500.0 \text{ g}}{0.92 \text{ g/mL}}$ = 540 mL

4) Answer: 1 km/1000 m, 1000 m/1 km, 1 m/0.001 km, 0.001 km/1 m

5) Answer: 1 000 000 μg/1 g, 1 g/1 000 000 μg, 1 μg/0.000 001 g, 0.000 001 g/1 μg

6) Answer: 1000 L/1 kL x 1 000 000 000 nL/1 L = 1 x 10^{12} nL/1 kL

7) Answer: 1 g/1 000 000 μg x 1 kg/1000 g = 1 kg/10^9 μg

8) Answer: 1 kilometer = 1000 meters; 1 meter = 100 centimeters; 1 kilometer = 100 000 cm
   conversion factor = 100 000 cm/1 km

9) Answer: 1 kilomole = 1000 moles; 1 mol = 1 000 000 μmol; 1 kmol = 10^9 μmol
   conversion factor = 10^9 μmol/kmol

10) Answer: 0.300 mol x 1 kmol/1000 mol = 0.000300 kmol

11) Answer: 549 kg x 1000 g/1 kg = 549 000 g

12) Answer: 0.0349 mm x 1 m/1000 mm = 0.0000349 m

13) Answer: 673 m x 1 km/1000 m = 0.673 km

14) Answer: 0.945 dL x 1 L/10 dL = 0.0945 L

15) Answer: 0.968 kL x 1000 L/1 kL = 968 L

16) Answer: 0.000 000 013 kilograms

17) Answer: 121 g x 1000 mg/1 g = 121 000 mg

18) Answer: 7600 μg x 1 g/10^6 μg x 100 cg/1 g = 0.76 cg

19) Answer: 332 mmol x 1 mol/1000 mmol x 1 kmol/1000 mol = 0.000332 kmol

20) Answer: 0.769 kg x 1000 g/kg x 10 dg/g = 7690 dg

21) Answer: 2193 mi/h x 1 h/60 min x 1 min/60 s x 1 km/0.621 mi x 1000 m/1 km
    = 9.81 x 10^2 m/s

22) Answer: $\dfrac{1.0 \text{ g H}_2\text{O}}{1 \text{ mL}}$ x $\dfrac{2.20 \times 10^{-3} \text{ lb}}{1 \text{ g}}$ x $\dfrac{4 \text{ qt}}{1 \text{ gal}}$ x $\dfrac{9.46 \times 10^{-1} \text{ L}}{1 \text{ qt}}$ x $\dfrac{1000 \text{ mL}}{1 \text{ L}}$
    = 8.3 lb/gal

23) Answer: 4.2 g/cm^3 x 1 kg/1000 g x 1 000 000 cm^3/1 m^3 = 4200 kg/m^3

24) Answer: 21 m/1 s x 1 km/1000 m x 60 s/1 min x 60 min/1 h = 76 km/h

25) Answer: 99.5 g/1 mol x 1 kg/1000 g x 1000 mol/1 kmol = 99.5 kg/kmol

26) Answer: Distance = speed x time

$$= 2 \text{ h} \times 60 \text{ min}/1 \text{ h} \times 60 \text{ s}/1 \text{ min} \times 1.86 \times 10^5 \text{ mi}/\text{s} \times 1 \text{ km}/0.621 \text{ mi}$$

$$= 2.16 \times 10^9 \text{ km}$$

27) Answer: $21.0 \text{ mi}/1 \text{ gal} \times 1.6 \text{ km}/1 \text{ mi} \times 1 \text{ gal}/4 \text{ qt} \times 1.06 \text{ qt}/1 \text{ L}$

$$= 8.90 \text{ km}/\text{L}$$

28) Answer: $1 \text{ oz}/500 \text{ dollars} \times 1 \text{ dollar}/100 \text{ cents} \times 1 \text{ lb}/16 \text{ oz} \times 454 \text{ g}/1 \text{ lb} \times 1000 \text{ mg}/1 \text{ g}$

$$= 0.57 \text{ mg}/\text{cent}$$

Essay Questions

1) Answer: (1) ANALYZE: Determine what is known and unknown, and plan a strategy for solving the problem. (2) CALCULATE: Perform required calculations. (3) EVALUATE: Check the answer to make sure it is reasonable.

2) Answer: A measurement is a physical quantity expressed with numbers and units. A conversion factor is a ratio of defined units of measurement. This ratio always has the value of 1. A conversion factor has no units; it is dimensionless. An example of a measurement is 1000 m. An example of a conversion factor is 1000 m/1 km.

3) Answer: The essence of a conversion factor is that it shows the exact same quantity written in two different ways (e.g. the conversion factor 1000 m/1 km shows the same quantity in kilometers and in meters, i.e. the distance represented by 1000 m is exactly the same distance as is represented by 1 km, by definition). The result of dividing one quantity by the exact same quantity is 1. Therefore, since 1000 m is equal to 1 km by definition, the conversion factor 1000 m/1 km must be equal simply to 1.

4) Answer: In the dimensional analysis approach to problem solving, the units of the unknown are identified. Then the relationship between the knowns is established and an appropriate conversion factor or series of conversion factors is selected. The conversion factor or series of factors is appropriate if, when it is applied to the knowns, the units cancel so as to yield the units of the unknown. If the units do not cancel in this way, it can be inferred that something has gone wrong during the problem solving process.

For instance, suppose the problem is to determine an airplane's speed in km/h when you know that the plane travels 2000 m every 10 seconds. The units of the unknown are km/h. The knowns are 2000 m and 10 seconds, and they are related by the fact that the plane travels 2000 m in each 10 seconds, i.e. the plane's speed is 2000 m/10 s. According to dimensional analysis, it is necessary to go from the units of the known (m/s) to the units of the unknown (km/h). The appropriate conversion factors to do this are 1 km/1000 m and 60 s/h.

Units of knowns x conversion factor x conversion factor = units of unknown

m/s x km/m x s/h = km/h

By applying these conversion factors to the related knowns the answer is obtained in the correct units.

5) Answer: Each conversion factor must be checked to verify that the numerator and denominator are equal to one another. In addition, the units of the knowns and of the conversion factor(s) must be checked to make sure that they cancel to give the units of the unknown.

Chapter 5 Atomic Structure and the Periodic Table

Matching Questions

Chapter 5: Matching I

1) proton

2) nucleus

3) atom

4) electron

5) neutron

A) the smallest particle of an element that retains the properties of that element

B) a negatively charged subatomic particle

C) a positively charged subatomic particle

D) the central part of an atom, containing protons and neutrons

E) a subatomic particle with no charge

Chapter 5: Matching II

6) mass number

7) atomic mass unit

8) atomic number

9) atomic mass

10) isotope

A) the number of protons in the nucleus of an element

B) the total number of protons and neutrons in the nucleus of an atom

C) the weighted average of the masses of the isotopes of an element

D) atoms with the same number of protons, but different numbers of neutrons in the nucleus of an atom.

E) one–twelfth the mass of a carbon atom having six protons and six neutrons

Mutliple Choice and Bimodal Questions

1) What is the smallest particle of an element that retains the properties of that element?

A) an atom

B) an electron

C) a proton

D) a neutron

E) a molecule

2) Who was the first person to suggest the idea of atoms, in the fourth century B. C.?

A) Atomos

B) Dalton

C) Democritus

D) Galileo

E) Thomson

3) The comparison of the number of atoms in a copper coin the size of a penny with the number of people on earth is made to illustrate which of the following?

A) that atoms are indivisible

B) that atoms are very small

C) that atoms are very large

D) in a copper penny, there is one atom for every person on earth

E) there are fewer atoms in a copper penny than there are people on earth

4) Dalton's atomic theory included which idea?

A) All atoms of all elements are the same size.

B) Atoms of different elements always combine in one–to–one ratios.

C) Atoms of the same element are always identical.

D) Individual atoms can be seen with a microscope.

E) When an atom of an element changes into another element, a chemical reaction takes place.

5) Which of the following is NOT a part of Dalton's atomic theory?

A) All elements are composed of atoms.

B) Atoms are always in motion.

C) Atoms of the same element are alike in mass and size.

D) Atoms that combine do so in simple whole–number ratios.

6) What particles form the nucleus of an atom?

A) protons and neutrons

B) protons and electrons

C) electrons only

D) neutrons and electrons

E) None of the above

7) Which of the following was originally a tenet of Dalton's atomic theory, but had to be revised about a century ago?

   A) Atoms are tiny indivisible particles.

   B) Atoms of the same element are identical.

   C) Compounds are molecules made by uniting atoms.

   D) Atoms of different elements can combine with one another in simple whole number ratios.

   E) In a chemical reaction, atoms of one element are not changed into atoms of another element.

8) Which statement is true about the discovery of electrons?

   A) Electrons were discovered by experimental chemists.

   B) Electrons were discovered after the TV tube was invented.

   C) Electrons were discovered in a vacuum tube.

   D) Electrons were discovered when anode rays were identified in an anode ray tube.

   E) Electrons were discovered when an electric current was passed through gases at low pressures.

9) Why did J. J. Thomson reason that electrons must be a part of the atoms of all elements?

   A) Cathode rays are negatively–charged particles.

   B) Cathode rays can be deflected by magnets.

   C) An electron is 2000 times lighter than a hydrogen atom.

   D) Cathode rays are always made of electrons, regardless of the gas used.

   E) Cathode rays were always accompanied by anode rays.

10) Which hypothesis led to the discovery of the proton?

   A) When a neutral hydrogen atom loses an electron, a positively–charged particle should remain.

   B) A proton should be 1840 times heavier than an electron.

   C) Cathode rays should be attracted to a positively–charged plate.

   D) The nucleus of an atom should contain neutrons.

   E) A neutral atom should have dozens of subatomic particles.

11) Which of the following is correct concerning subatomic particles?

   A) The electron was discovered by Goldstein in 1886.

   B) The neutron was discovered by Chadwick in 1932.

   C) The proton was discovered by Thomson in 1880.

   D) Cathode rays were found to be made of protons.

   E) Canal rays were found to be made of protons, electrons, and neutrons.

12) Select the correct statement about subatomic particles.

   A) Electrons are negatively charged and are the heaviest subatomic particle.

   B) Protons are positively charged and the lightest subatomic particle.

   C) Neutrons have no charge and are the lightest subatomic particle.

   D) The mass of a neutron nearly equals the mass of a proton.

   E) Electrons, protons, and neutrons all have the same mass.

13) Dalton theorized that atoms are indivisible and that all atoms of an element are identical. We now know that _____.

   A) Dalton's theories are correct

   B) Atoms of an element can have different numbers of protons

   C) Atoms are divisible

   D) All atoms of an element are not identical but they must all have the same mass

14) As a consequence of the discovery of the nucleus by Rutherford, which model of the atoms is believed to be true?

   A) A model in which the protons, electrons, and neutrons are evenly distributed throughout the volume of the atom

   B) A model in which the nucleus is made of protons, electrons, and neutrons

   C) A model in which the nucleus is made of neutrons only

   D) A model in which the nucleus is made of electrons and protons.

   E) A model in which the region outside the nucleus is largely empty space in which the electrons are situated

15) The nucleus of an atom is _____.

   A) positively charged and has a high density

   B) positively charged and has a low density

   C) negatively charged and has a high density

   D) negatively charged and has a low density

16) Which of these statements is FALSE?

   A) Protons have a positive charge.

   B) Electrons are negatively charged and have a mass of 1 amu.

   C) The nucleus of an atom is positively charged.

   D) The neutron is found in the nucleus of an atom.

17) All atoms are _____.

   A) positively charged, with the number of protons exceeding the number of electrons

   B) negatively charged, with the number of electrons exceeding the number of protons

   C) neutral, with the number of protons equaling the number of electrons

   D) neutral, with the number of protons equaling the number of electrons, which is equal to the number of neutrons

   E) neutral, with the number of protons equaling the number of neutrons, which is equal to half the number of electrons

18) In which of the following sets are the symbol of the element, the number of protons, and the number of electrons given correctly?

  A) In, 49 protons, 49 electrons

  B) Zn, 30 protons, 60 electrons

  C) Cs, 55 protons, 132.9 electrons

  D) F, 19 protons, 19 electrons

  E) He, 4 protons, 4 electrons

19) The atomic number of an element is the total number of which particles in the nucleus?

  A) neutrons

  B) protons

  C) electrons

  D) protons and electrons

  E) protons and electrons and neutrons

20) An element has an atomic number of 80. How many protons and electrons are in a neutral atom of the element?

  A) 80 protons, 80 electrons

  B) 40 protons, 40 electrons

  C) 160 protons, 80 electrons

  D) 80 protons, 0 electrons

  E) 0 protons, 80 electrons

21) The mass number of an element is equal to _____.

  A) the total number of electrons in the nucleus

  B) the total number of protons and neutrons in the nucleus

  C) less than twice the atomic number

  D) a constant number for the lighter elements

22) How are the number of neutrons in the nucleus of an atom calculated?

  A) add the number of electrons and protons together

  B) subtract the number of electrons from the number of protons

  C) subtract the number of protons from the mass number

  D) add the mass number to the number of electrons

23) The sum of the protons and neutrons in an atom equals the _____.

  A) atomic number   B) nucleus number

  C) atomic mass   D) mass number

24) Using the periodic table, determine the number of neutrons in ^{16}O.

  A) ^{16}O B) 8   C) 124   D) 26   E) 61

25) How many protons, electrons, and neutrons does an atom with an atomic number 50 and a mass number 120 contain?

A) 50 protons, 50 electrons, and 70 neutrons

B) 70 electrons, 50 protons, and 50 neutrons

C) 120 neutrons, 50 protons, and 70 electrons

D) 70 neutrons, 70 protons, and 50 electrons

26) How do the isotopes hydrogen–1 and hydrogen–2 differ?

A) Hydrogen–2 has one more electron than hydrogen–1.

B) Hydrogen–2 has one neutron; hydrogen–1 has none.

C) Hydrogen–2 has two protons; hydrogen–1 has one.

D) Hydrogen–1 has no protons; hydrogen–2 has one.

27) What does the number 84 in the name krypton–84 represent?

A) the atomic number   B) the mass number

C) the sum of the protons and electrons   D) None of these

28) What unit is used to measure average relative atomic mass?

A) amus   B) grams   C) angstroms   D) nanograms

29) Different elements have different numbers of _____.

A) subatomic particles   B) protons

C) electrons   D) all of the above

30) All atoms of the same element have the same _____.

A) number of neutrons   B) number of protons

C) mass numbers   D) mass

31) Why do chemists use relative comparisons of masses of atoms?

A) The actual mass of an electron is very large compared to the actual mass of a proton.

B) The actual masses of protons and neutrons are very small.

C) The number of subatomic particles in atoms of different elements varies.

D) The actual masses of protons, electrons, and neutrons are not known.

32) Which of the following equals one atomic mass unit?

A) the mass of one electron

B) the mass of one helium atom

C) the mass of one carbon atom

D) one–twelfth the mass of one carbon atom

E) one gram

33) Isotopes of the same element have different _____.

    A) numbers of neutrons

    B) numbers of protons

    C) numbers of electrons

    D) atomic numbers

    E) symbols

34) Isotopes of the same element have different _____.

    A) positions on the periodic table

    B) chemical behavior

    C) atomic numbers

    D) mass numbers

    E) symbols

35) In which of the following is the number of neutrons correctly represented?

    A) $^{19}_{9}F$ has 0 neutrons.

    B) $^{75}_{33}As$ has 108 neutrons.

    C) $^{24}_{12}Mg$ has 24 neutrons.

    D) $^{197}_{79}Au$ has 79 neutrons.

    E) $^{238}_{92}U$ has 146 neutrons.

36) Which of the following sets of symbols represents isotopes of the same element?

    A) $^{91}_{42}J$ $^{92}_{42}J$ $^{93}_{40}J$

    B) $^{50}_{19}L$ $^{50}_{20}L$ $^{50}_{21}L$

    C) $^{80}_{38}M$ $^{81}_{38}M$ $^{83}_{38}M$

    D) $^{132}_{55}Q$ $^{133}_{55}Q$ $^{133}_{54}Q$

    E) $^{58}_{59}Z$ $^{60}_{30}Z$ $^{62}_{31}Z$

37) Which of these statements is NOT true?

    A) Atoms of the same element can have different masses.

    B) Atoms of isotopes of an element have different numbers of protons.

    C) The nucleus of an atom has a positive charge.

    D) Atoms are mostly empty space.

38) If E is the symbol for an element, which two of the following symbols represent isotopes of the same element?

1. $_{10}^{20}E$ 3. $_{9}^{21}E$

2. $_{11}^{20}E$ 4. $_{10}^{21}E$

   A) 1 and 2   B) 3 and 4   C) 1 and 4   D) 2 and 3

39) The atomic mass of an element is equal to _____.

   A) the total number of subatomic particles in its nucleus

   B) the average of the number of protons, neutrons and electrons in its nucleus

   C) the total mass of the isotopes of the element

   D) the average of the mass number and the atomic number for the element

   E) the weighted average of the masses of the isotopes of the element

40) Consider an element Z that has two naturally occurring isotopes with the following percent abundances: the isotope with a mass number of 20 is 25% abundant; the isotope with a mass number of 22 is 75% abundant. What is the average atomic mass for element Z?

   A) 2.0 g   B) 20.5 g   C) 21.0 g   D) 21.5 g   E) 42.0 g

41) The atomic mass of an element _____.

   A) depends upon the number of isotopes of that element

   B) depends upon the mass of each isotope of that element

   C) depends upon the relative abundance of each isotope of the element

   D) all of the above

42) What are the Group A elements known as?

   A) representative elements

   B) transition elements

   C) inner transition elements

   D) periodic elements

   E) metallic elements

43) Of the elements Fe, Hg, U, Te, and Y, which is a representative element?

   A) Fe   B) Hg   C) U   D) Te   E) Y

44) Of the elements Pt, Sc, V, Li, and Kr, which is a nonmetal?

   A) Pt   B) Sc   C) V   D) Li   E) Kr

45) What is each vertical column of elements in the periodic table called?

   A) row   B) list   C) group or family   D) transition

46) Approximately how many elements exist?
   A) one dozen
   B) one hundred
   C) one million
   D) 6.02×10^{24}
   E) an infinite number

47) What criterion is used to arrange the elements in rows and columns on the periodic table?
   A) similarity in size
   B) similarity in properties
   C) similarity in symbol
   D) similarity in date of discovery
   E) similarity in melting point

48) Which of the following categories includes the majority of the elements?
   A) gases   B) liquids   C) metals   D) nonmetals   E) metalloids

49) A mystery element Q is a nonlustrous solid and a poor conductor of electricity. To what category of elements does it belong?
   A) metals
   B) nonmetals
   C) transition metals
   D) semimetals
   E) metalloids

50) Who first arranged the elements according to nuclear charge?
   A) Louis Pasteur
   B) Henry Moseley
   C) Antoine Lavoisier
   D) John Dalton
   E) Dmitri Mendeleev

51) Who first arranged the elements according to atomic mass and noticed a periodic recurrence of their physical and chemical properties?
   A) Louis Pasteur
   B) Henry Moseley
   C) Antoine Lavoisier
   D) John Dalton
   E) Dmitri Mendeleev

52) The modern periodic table is arranged in order of increasing atomic _____.
   A) mass   B) charge   C) number   D) radius

53) The periodic law states that there is a periodic repetition of the physical and chemical properties of elements _____.

A) when they are arranged in order of increasing atomic mass

B) if only metals are considered

C) when they are arranged in order of increasing atomic radii

D) when they are arranged in order of increasing atomic number

54) Which of the following elements is in the same period as phosphorus?

A) carbon   B) magnesium   C) nitrogen   D) oxygen

55) Which subatomic particle plays the greatest part in determining the physical and chemical properties of an element?

A) electron   B) neutron   C) proton   D) muon   E) quark

Problems

1) Complete this table:

Atomic number	Mass number	Number of protons	Number of neutrons	Number of electrons
8	_____	_____	8	_____
_____	14	_____	7	_____
_____	_____	_____	21	20
11	23	_____	_____	_____
_____	56	26	_____	_____

2) List the number of protons, neutrons, and electrons in each of the following atoms.

	Protons	Neutrons	Electrons
$^{13}_{6}C$	_____	_____	_____
$^{15}_{7}N$	_____	_____	_____
$^{20}_{10}Ne$	_____	_____	_____
$^{11}_{5}B$	_____	_____	_____
$^{9}_{4}Be$	_____	_____	_____

3) There are four naturally occurring isotopes of the element chromium. The relative abundance of each is:

$^{50}Cr = 4.31\%$, $^{52}Cr = 83.76\%$, $^{53}Cr = 9.55\%$, $^{54}Cr = 2.38\%$.

Calculate the average atomic mass of chromium.

Essay Questions

1) Explain how the atoms of one element differ from those of another element.

2) In what way are two isotopes of the same element different? Explain why isotopes of the same element have the same chemical behavior.

3) Explain how Moseley's periodic arrangement of the elements differed from Mendeleev's.

Chapter 5 Atomic Structure and the Periodic Table
Matching Questions
    1) Answer: C

    2) Answer: D

    3) Answer: A

    4) Answer: B

    5) Answer: E

    6) Answer: B

    7) Answer: E

    8) Answer: A

    9) Answer: C

    10) Answer: D

Mutliple Choice and Bimodal Questions
    1) Answer: A

    2) Answer: C

    3) Answer: B

    4) Answer: C

    5) Answer: B

    6) Answer: A

    7) Answer: A

    8) Answer: E

    9) Answer: D

    10) Answer: A

    11) Answer: B

    12) Answer: D

    13) Answer: C

    14) Answer: E

    15) Answer: A

    16) Answer: B

    17) Answer: C

    18) Answer: A

    19) Answer: B

    20) Answer: A

    21) Answer: B

    22) Answer: C

    23) Answer: D

    24) Answer: B

    25) Answer: A

    26) Answer: B

    27) Answer: B

    28) Answer: A

    29) Answer: D

30) Answer: B

31) Answer: B

32) Answer: D

33) Answer: A

34) Answer: D

35) Answer: E

36) Answer: C

37) Answer: B

38) Answer: C

39) Answer: E

40) Answer: D

41) Answer: D

42) Answer: A

43) Answer: D

44) Answer: E

45) Answer: C

46) Answer: B

47) Answer: B

48) Answer: C

49) Answer: B

50) Answer: B

51) Answer: E

52) Answer: C

53) Answer: D

54) Answer: B

55) Answer: A

Problems

1) Answer: Atomic number: 8, 7, 20, 11, 26
Mass number: 16, 14, 41, 23, 56
Number of protons: 8, 7, 20, 11, 26
Number of neutrons: 8, 7, 21, 12, 30
Number of electrons: 8, 7, 20, 11, 26

2) Answer: Protons: 6, 7, 10, 5, 4
Neutrons: 7, 8, 10, 6, 5
Electrons: 6, 7, 10, 5, 4

3) Answer: 50 amu x 0.0431 = 2.16 amu
52 amu x 0.8376 = 43.56 amu
53 amu x 0.0955 = 5.06 amu
<u>54 amu x 0.0238 = 1.29 amu</u>
= 52.07 amu
= 52 amu

Essay Questions

1) Answer: Differences among the atoms of different elements result from different numbers of protons in the nuclei of atoms. All atoms of the same element have the same number of protons. Since atoms are neutral, the number of electrons in an atom equals the number of protons. The atoms of an element may have different numbers of neutrons in their nuclei and still be atoms of the same element.

2) Answer: Isotopes of the same element have different numbers of neutrons, and therefore, different mass numbers and different atomic masses. Isotopes of the same element have the same number of protons and electrons and it is the electrons, not the neutrons, that are primarily responsible for an element's chemical behavior.

3) Answer: Mendeleev arranged the elements into groups having similar properties, and in order of increasing atomic mass. Moseley arranged the elements in order of atomic charge (atomic number). The order developed by Moseley is slightly different from that proposed by Mendeleev because the order by atomic mass is not always the same as the order by atomic number.

Chapter 6 Chemical Names and Formulas

Matching Questions

Chapter 6: Matching I

1) formula unit

2) molecular formula

3) chemical formula

4) law of definite proportions

5) law of multiple proportions

A) when two elements form more than one compound, the masses of one element that combine with the same mass of the other element are in the ratio of small, whole numbers

B) shows the kinds and numbers of atoms in the smallest proportions representative of a unit of the substance

C) in any chemical compound the elements are always proportions combined in the same proportion by mass

D) shows the lowest whole number ratio of ions in an ionic compound

E) shows the number and kinds of atoms present in a molecule

Chapter 6: Matching II

6) cation

7) ternary compound

8) molecule

9) polyatomic ion

10) binary compound

11) ionic compound

12) anion

A) tightly bound group of atoms that behaves as a unit and carries a net charge

B) smallest unit of a substance having properties of the substance

C) any atom or group of atoms having a negative charge

D) compound composed of two different elements

E) compound composed of three different elements

F) a compound composed of cations and anions

G) atom or group of atoms having a positive charge

Multiple Choice and Bimodal Questions

1) What type of ions have names ending in –ide?

    A) only cations

    B) only anions

    C) only metal ions

    D) only gaseous ions

    E) only metalloid ions

2) What is the electrical charge of a cation?

    A) a positive charge   B) no charge

    C) a negative charge   D) None of the above

3) In which of the following is the symbol for the ion and the number of electrons it contains given correctly?

    A) H^+ has 1 electron.

    B) Br^- has 34 electrons.

    C) Al^{3+} has 16 electrons.

    D) Ca^{2+} has 18 electrons.

    E) S^{2-} has 2 electrons.

4) In which of the following sets is the number of electrons in each species the same?

    A) Mg^{2+}, O^{2-}, Ne^{2+}

    B) Na^+, K^+, Rb^+

    C) F^-, Cl^-, Br^-

    D) Al^{3+}, Cl^-, Ar

    E) Sr^{2+}, Kr, Br^-

5) Which of the following statements is correct concerning ions?

    A) Cations form when an atom gains electrons.

    B) Cations form when an atom loses electrons.

    C) Anions form when an atom gains protons.

    D) Anions form when an atom loses protons.

    E) Cations are negatively charged particles and anions are positively charged particles.

6) Ions form when atoms gain or lose _____.

    A) protons

    B) neutrons

    C) electrons

    D) atomic number

    E) mass number

7) Which of the following is a pure compound?

    A) salt water

    B) fresh air

    C) aluminum

    D) calcium iodide

    E) neon

8) In any chemical compound, the elements are always combined in the same proportion by _____.

    A) charge

    B) mass

    C) volume

    D) density

    E) number of protons

9) The law of definite proportions applies to _____.

    A) all compounds

    B) gases only

    C) solids only

    D) molecular compounds only

    E) ionic compounds only

10) Which of the following statements is true concerning molecular compounds?

    A) They are composed of only one element.

    B) They are composed of ions.

    C) They are crystalline solids at room temperature.

    D) They have low melting points.

    E) They are formed from a metallic element and a nonmetallic element.

11) Which of the following statements is true concerning the composition of ionic compounds?

    A) They are composed of anions and cations.

    B) They are composed of anions only.

    C) They are composed of cations only.

    D) They are formed from two or more nonmetallic elements.

    E) They are formed from two or more metallic elements.

12) What is the lowest whole–number ratio of ions in an ionic compound called?

A) a molecule   B) an atom   C) an ion   D) a formula unit

13) Which of the following formulas represents an ionic compound?

A) CS_2 B) BaI_2 C) N_2O_4 D) PCl_3 E) Kr

14) Which of the following formulas represents a molecular compound?

A) ZnO B) Xe C) SO_2 D) BeF_2 E) Mg_3N_2

15) Molecular compounds are usually _____.

A) composed of two or more transition elements

B) composed of positive and negative ions

C) composed of two or more nonmetallic elements

D) exceptions to the law of definite proportions

E) solids at room temperature

16) Which element when combined with fluorine would most likely form an ionic compound?

A) lithium   B) carbon   C) phosphorus   D) chlorine

17) Compounds that are composed of ions _____.

A) are molecular compounds

B) have relatively high melting and boiling points

C) are for the most part composed of two or more metallic elements

D) fit all of the above descriptions

18) Select the correct statement concerning the formula C_2H_6O.

A) It is a molecular formula.

B) It is a formula unit.

C) It gives information about molecular structure.

D) It is the formula of an ionic compound.

E) It represents a molecule made of 1 carbon atom, 2 hydrogen atoms, and 6 oxygen atoms.

19) Select the correct statement about the formula K_2O.

A) It represents a molecule of potassium oxide.

B) It represents a substance composed of potassium atoms and oxygen atoms.

C) It represents a substance containing 1 potassium atom and 2 oxygen atoms.

D) It represents an electrically neutral compound.

E) It represents a molecular compound.

20) Ionic compounds are composed of _____.

A) positive and negative ions

B) semimetallic elements

C) molecules

D) elements that are gases at room temperature

E) elements that are found in the same column of the periodic table

21) A molecular formula _____.

A) gives information about molecular structure

B) can be written for ionic compounds

C) shows the number and kinds of atoms in a molecule of a compound

D) shows the number of atoms of each kind by a superscript written after the symbol

22) Which of the following pairs of substances best illustrates the law of multiple proportions?

A) H_2 and O_2

B) P_2O_5 and PH_3

C) $CaCl_2$ and $CaBr_2$

D) NO and NO_2

E) $^{235}_{92}U$ and $^{238}_{92}U$

23) What is the usual charge on an ion from Group 7A?

A) –1 B) 0 C) +1 D) +2 E) +7

24) In which of the following sets are the charges given correctly for all the ions?

A) Na^+, Mg^+, Al^+

B) K^+, Sr^{2+}, O^{2-}

C) Rb^-, Ba^{2-}, P^{3+}

D) N^-, O^{2-}, F^{3-}

E) H^{2+}, Li^+, Ne^-

25) In which of the following are the symbol and name for the ion given correctly?

A) Fe^{2+}:ferrous ion; Fe^{3+}:ferric ion

B) Sn^{2+}:stannic ion; Sn^{4+}:stannous ion

C) Co^{2+}:cobalt(II) ion; Co^{3+}:cobaltous ion

D) Pb^{2+}:lead ion; Pb^{4+}:lead(4) ion

E) I^-:iodine ion; Cl^-:chlorine ion

26) In which of the following groups of ions are the charges all shown correctly?

   A) Li^-, O^{2-}, S^{2+}

   B) Ca^{2+}, Al^{3+}, Br^-

   C) K^{2-}, F^-, Mg^{2+}

   D) Na^+, I^-, Rb^-

   E) Be^{2+}, Cl^{2-}, Sr^{2+}

27) When Group 2A elements form ions, they _____.

   A) lose two protons

   B) gain two protons

   C) lose two electrons

   D) gain two electrons

   E) become electrically neutral

28) Which of the following correctly provides the name of the element, the symbol for the ion, and the name of the ion?

   A) fluorine, F^+, fluoride ion

   B) zinc, Zn^{2+}, zincate ion

   C) copper, Cu^+, cuprous ion

   D) barium, Ba^{3+}, barium ion

   E) sulfur, S^{2-}, sulfurous ion

29) Elements of Group 4A _____.

   A) form positive ions   B) form negative ions

   C) do not commonly form ions   D) do not combine with other elements

30) The metals in Groups 1A, 2A, and 3A _____.

   A) gain electrons when they form ions

   B) have a numerical charge that is found by subtracting the group number from 8

   C) all have ions with a 1^+ charge

   D) lose electrons when they form ions

31) In which of the following are the symbol and name for the ion given correctly?

   A) NH^{+4}: ammonia; H^+ : hydride

   B) $C_2H_3O_2^-$: acetate; $C_2O_4^-$: oxalite

   C) OH^- : hydroxide; O^{2-}: oxide

   D) HSO_3^-: bisulfate; HSO_4^-: bisulfite

   E) PO_3^{3-} : phosphate; PO_4^{3-} : phosphite

32) Polyatomic ions are tightly bound groups of _____.

   A) atoms   B) electrons   C) cations   D) metals   E) protons

33) Which of the following correctly provides the names and formulas of polyatomic ions?

A) carbonate: HCO_3^-; bicarbonate: CO_3^{2-}

B) nitrite: NO^-; nitrate: NO_2^-

C) sulfite: S^{2-}; sulfate: SO_3^{2-}

D) chlorate: ClO_2^-; chlorite: Cl^-

E) chromate: CrO_4^{2-}; dichromate: CrO_7^{2-}

34) An –ate or –ite at the end of a compound name usually indicates that the compound contains _____.
  A) fewer anions than cations
  B) neutral molecules
  C) only two elements
  D) hydroxide or cyanide ions
  E) a polyatomic ion

35) An –ite or –ate ending on the name of a compound indicates that the compound _____.
  A) is a binary ionic compound   B) is a binary molecular compound
  C) contains a polyatomic anion   D) contains a cyanide polyatomic ion

36) What is the ionic charge on the zirconium ion in the ionic compound zirconium oxide, ZrO_2?
  A) 2+   B) 2–   C) 4+   D) 4–   E) 0

37) What is the correct name for the N^{3-} ion?
  A) nitrate ion   B) nitrogen ion   C) nitride ion   D) nitrite ion

38) What is the correct formula for potassium sulfite?
  A) $KHSO_3$ B) $KHSO_4$ C) K_2SO_3 D) K_2SO_4 E) K_2S

39) What is the correct formula for barium chlorate?
  A) $Ba(ClO)_2$ B) $Ba(ClO_2)_2$ C) $Ba(ClO_3)_2$ D) $Ba(ClO_4)_2$ E) $BaCl_2$

40) Ternary ionic compounds contain three different _____.
  A) elements
  B) acids
  C) cations
  D) charges
  E) polyatomic ions

41) What is the correct formula for calcium dihydrogen phosphate?

A) CaH_2PO_4 B) $Ca_2H_2PO_4$ C) $Ca(H_2PO_4)_2$ D) $Ca(H_2HPO_4)_2$

42) Why are systematic names preferred over common names?

A) because common names do not provide information about the chemical composition of the compound

B) because common names are derived from the method used to obtain the compound

C) because common names were assigned by the scientist who discovered the compound

D) because common names are not very descriptive

E) because common names are too long

43) Which of the following shows correctly an ion pair and the ionic compound the two ions form?

A) Sn^{4+}, N^{3-}; Sn_4N_3

B) Cu^{2+}, O^{2-}; Cu_2O_2

C) Cr^{3+}, I^-; CrI

D) Au^{3+}, S^{2-}; Au_2S_3

E) Li^+, O^{2-}; LiO_2

44) In which of the following are the formula of the ionic compound and the charge on the metal ion shown correctly?

A) UCl_5, U^+

B) Y_2O_3, Y^{2-}

C) IrS_2, Ir^{2+}

D) NiO, Ni^0

E) ThO_2, Th^{4+}

45) Which of the following correctly represents an ion pair and the ionic compound the ions form?

A) Ca^{2-}, F^-; Ca_2F

B) Na^+, Cl^-; Na^+Cl^-

C) Sc^{3+}, S^{2-}; Sc_2S_3

D) Ba^{2+}, O^{2-}; Ba_2O_2

E) Pb^{4+}, O^{2-}; Pb_2O_4

46) In which of the following is the name and formula given correctly?

A) ammonium selenide, Al_2S_3

B) barium nitride, BaN

C) cobaltous chloride, $CoCl_3$

D) stannic fluoride, SnF_4

E) sodium oxide, NaO

47) Which of the following compounds contains the lead(IV) ion?

    A) PbO_2 B) $PbCl_2$ C) Pb_2O D) Pb_4O_3 E) PbO

48) Which of the following compounds contains the Mn^{3+} ion?

    A) MnS B) $MnBr_2$ C) Mn_2O_3 D) MnO E) Mn_3O_2

49) Which set of chemical name and chemical formula for the same compound is correct?

    A) iron(II) oxide, Fe_2O_3

    B) beryllium sulfide, BeS_2

    C) tin(IV) bromide, $SnBr_4$

    D) potassium chloride, K_2Cl_2

    E) aluminum fluorate, AlF_3

50) The procedure for writing formulas for ternary ionic compounds is the same as that for binary ionic compounds, with the exception that _____.

    A) the cation must be written first

    B) the cation and anion charges must be balanced

    C) parentheses may be used

    D) subscripts may be used

    E) the stock or classical name of a transition metal in the compound must be known

51) Which set of chemical name and chemical formula for the same compound is correct?

    A) ammonium sulfite, $(NH_4)_2S$

    B) iron(III) phosphate, $FePO_4$

    C) potassium chlorate, $K_2(ClO_3)_2$

    D) magnesium dichromate, $MgCrO_4$

    E) lithium carbonate, $LiCO_3$

52) When naming a transition metal that has more than one common ionic charge, the numerical value of the charge is indicated by a _____.

    A) prefix   B) suffix

    C) roman numeral following the name   D) superscript after the name

53) What do the names of all binary compounds, both ionic and molecular, end in?

    A) –ide   B) –ite   C) –ade   D) –ate   E) –en

54) What is the correct formula for sulfurous acid?

    A) H_2SO_4 B) H_2SO_3 C) H_2SO_2 D) H_2SO E) H_2S

55) What is the formula for hydrosulfuric acid?

    A) H_2S_2 B) H_2SO_2 C) HSO_2 D) H_2S

56) What are the components of binary molecular compounds?

   A) two oppositely-charged ions

   B) two polyatomic ions

   C) two nonmetallic elements

   D) two metallic elements

   E) one metallic element and one nonmetallic element

57) Which of the following correctly shows a prefix used in naming binary molecular compounds, with its corresponding number?

   A) deca–, 7   B) nona–, 9   C) hexa–, 8   D) octa–, 4   E) hepta–, 10

58) Binary molecular compounds are made of two _____.

   A) metallic elements

   B) nonmetallic elements

   C) polyatomic ions

   D) ternary compounds

   E) different ions

59) Which of the following is a binary molecular compound?

   A) $BeHCO_3$ B) PCl_5 C) AgI D) Cr_2O_3 E) MgS

60) In naming a binary molecular compound, the number of atoms of each element present in the molecule is indicated by _____.

   A) roman numerals   B) superscripts

   C) prefixes   D) suffixes

61) When dissolved in water, acids give off _____.

   A) negative ions

   B) polyatomic ions

   C) hydrogen ions

   D) oxide ions

   E) sulfide ions

62) When naming acids, the prefix hydro– is used when the name of the acid anion ends in

   _____.

   A) –ide   B) –ite   C) –ate   D) –ic   E) –ous

63) Which of the following shows both the correct formula and correct name of an acid?

   A) $HClO_2$, chloric acid

   B) HNO_2, hydronitrous acid

   C) H_3PO_4, phosphoric acid

   D) HI, iodic acid

   E) H_2CO_3, bicarbonic acid

64) What is the correct name for $Sn_3(PO_4)_2$?

    A) tritin diphosphate

    B) tin(II) phosphate

    C) tin(III) phosphate

    D) tin(IV) phosphate

    E) tin tetraphosphate

65) Consider a mystery compound having the formula M_xT_y. If the compound is not an acid, if it contains only two elements and if M is not a metal; which of the following is true about the compound?

    A) It contains a polyatomic ion.

    B) Its name ends in –ite or –ate.

    C) Its name ends in –ic.

    D) It is a binary molecular compound.

    E) It is a binary ionic compound.

Problems

1) Tin reacts with fluorine to form two different compounds, A and B. Compound A contains 23.7 g of tin for each 7.6 g of fluorine. Compound B contains 35.6 g of tin for each 22.8 g of fluorine. What is the lowest whole–number mass ratio of tin that combines with a given mass of fluorine?

2) Complete the following table by writing in the chemical formulas and names for the compounds formed by combining the indicated positive and negative ions.

	K^+	Mg^{2+}	Fe^{3+}	Sn^{4+}
Br^-	_____	_____	_____	_____
O^{2-}	_____	_____	_____	_____
PO_4^{3-}	_____	_____	_____	_____
CO_3^{2-}	_____	_____	_____	_____

3) Complete the following table by writing in the chemical formulas and names for the compounds formed by combining the indicated positive and negative ions.

	Fluoride ion	Sulfate ion	Nitrite ion
Hydrogen ion	_____	_____	_____
Cobalt(II) ion	_____	_____	_____
Lead(IV) ion	_____	_____	_____

4) Name the following compounds: $CoCl_2$, N_2O_5, and $K_2Cr_2O_7$.

5) Write the formulas for the following compounds: barium cyanide, sulfur hexafluoride, and mercury(II) chloride.

Essay Questions

1) Explain the terms molecular formula and formula unit. Give an example of each.

2) Why was it necessary for chemists to develop a system for naming chemical compounds?

3) Compare the characteristics of ionic and molecular compounds.

4) Explain how to write an ionic formula, given an anion and a cation. As an example, use phosphate anion. Write formulas for the compounds produced by the combinations of these ions. Name the compounds for which you have written formulas.

5) Name the compounds $CuBr_2$, SCl_2, and BaF_2. Explain the use or omission of the Roman numeral (II) and the prefix di–.

Chapter 6 Chemical Names and Formulas

Matching Questions

1) Answer: D

2) Answer: E

3) Answer: B

4) Answer: C

5) Answer: A

6) Answer: G

7) Answer: E

8) Answer: B

9) Answer: A

10) Answer: D

11) Answer: F

12) Answer: C

Multiple Choice and Bimodal Questions

1) Answer: B

2) Answer: A

3) Answer: D

4) Answer: E

5) Answer: B

6) Answer: C

7) Answer: D

8) Answer: B

9) Answer: A

10) Answer: D

11) Answer: A

12) Answer: D

13) Answer: B

14) Answer: C

15) Answer: C

16) Answer: A

17) Answer: B

18) Answer: A

19) Answer: D

20) Answer: A

21) Answer: C

22) Answer: D

23) Answer: A

24) Answer: B

25) Answer: A

26) Answer: B

27) Answer: C

28) Answer: C

29) Answer: C

30) Answer: D

31) Answer: C

32) Answer: A

33) Answer: E

34) Answer: E

35) Answer: C

36) Answer: C

37) Answer: C

38) Answer: C

39) Answer: C

40) Answer: A

41) Answer: C

42) Answer: A

43) Answer: D

44) Answer: E

45) Answer: C

46) Answer: D

47) Answer: A

48) Answer: C

49) Answer: C

50) Answer: C

51) Answer: B

52) Answer: C

53) Answer: A

54) Answer: B

55) Answer: D

56) Answer: C

57) Answer: B

58) Answer: B

59) Answer: B

60) Answer: C

61) Answer: C

62) Answer: A

63) Answer: C

64) Answer: B

65) Answer: D

Problems

1) Answer: Compound A   23.7 g Sn/7.6 g F = 3.12 g Sn/1.00 g F

            Compound B   35.6 g Sn/22.8 g F = 1.56 g Sn/1.00 g F

            The mass ratio of tin per gram of fluorine is 2:1.

            3.12 g Sn (in Compound A)/1.56 g Sn (in Compound B) = 2/1

2) Answer:

Column 1 (K^+)	Column 3 (Fe^{3+})
KBr	$FeBr_3$
potassium bromide	iron(III) bromide
K_2O	Fe_2O_3
potassium oxide	iron(III) oxide
K_3PO_4	$FePO_4$
potassium phosphate	iron(III) phosphate
K_2CO_3	$Fe_2(CO_3)_3$
potassium carbonate	iron(III) carbonate

Column 2 (Mg^{2+})	Column 4 (Sn^{4+})
$MgBr_2$	$SnBr_4$
magnesium bromide	tin(IV) bromide
MgO	SnO_2
magnesium oxide	tin(IV) oxide
$Mg_3(PO_4)_2$	$Sn_3(PO_4)_4$
magnesium phosphate	tin(IV) phosphate
$MgCO_3$	$Sn(CO_3)_2$
magnesium carbonate	tin(IV) carbonate

3) Answer:

Column 1 (fluoride)	Column 3 (nitrite)
HF	HNO_2
hydrofluoric acid	nitrous acid
CoF_2	$Co(NO_2)_2$
cobalt(II) fluoride	cobalt(II) nitrite,
PbF_4	$Pb(NO_2)_4$
lead(IV) fluoride	lead(IV) nitrite

Column 2 (sulfate)

H_2SO_4

sulfuric acid

$CoSO_4$

cobalt(II) sulfate

$Pb(SO_4)_2$

lead(IV) sulfate

4) Answer: cobalt(II) chloride, dinitrogen pentoxide, potassium dichromate

5) Answer: $Ba(CN)_2$, SF_6, $HgCl_2$

Essay Questions

1) Answer: A molecular formula shows the kinds and numbers of atoms present in a molecule of a compound. CO_2 is an example of a molecular formula. A formula unit is the lowest whole–number ratio of ions in an ionic compound. $BaCl_2$ is an example of a formula unit. The ratio of barium to chloride ions is 1:2. $BaCl_2$ is not a molecule.

2) Answer: Common names do not describe the chemical composition of a compound. They may give a physical or chemical property, but usually do not reveal what elements are in the compound. The systematic method that was adopted not only tells what atoms are in the compound, but gives the ratio in which they have combined to form the compound. Scientists in any country can tell what components are in a compound, and their relative amounts, when the systematic method for naming compounds is used.

3) Answer: Both are composed of at least two elements. Ionic compounds are made of oppositely charged ions. Molecular compounds are made of molecules. Ionic compounds are composed of metallic and nonmetallic elements. Molecular compounds are composed of nonmetallic elements only. Ionic compounds are solids with high melting points. Molecular compounds can be solids, liquids, or gases at room temperature, and have low melting points.

4) Answer: The cation is written first, the anion second. The resulting formula must indicate an electrically neutral substance. The charge of the anion becomes the subscript of the cation, and the charge of the cation becomes the subscript of the anion. When the charges of the two ions are the same, no subscripts are written.

Example: Cu^+, PO_4^{3-} copper(I) phosphate Cu_3PO_4

Cu^{2+}, PO_4^{3-} copper(II) phosphate $Cu_3(PO_4)_2$

Many other examples are possible.

5) Answer: $CuBr_2$ is copper(II) bromide. The name must include a Roman numeral because copper is a transition element. SCl_2 is sulfur dichloride. The compound is named with prefixes because sulfur is a nonmetal. BaF_2 is barium fluoride. Neither a Roman numeral nor a prefix is needed in this name because barium is a Group A metal.

Chapter 7 Chemical Quantities

Matching Questions

Chapter 7: Matching I

1) gram formula mass

2) molar mass

3) gram atomic mass

4) gram molecular mass

5) molar volume

A) the number of grams of an element that is numerically equal to the atomic mass of the element in an amu

B) the volume occupied by a mole of any gas at STP

C) the mass of a mole of an ionic compound

D) the mass of a mole of any element or compound

E) the mass of a mole of a molecular compound

Chapter 7: Matching II

6) representative particle

7) mole

8) Avogadro's number

9) percent composition

10) standard temperature

A) the percent by mass of each element in a compound

B) 0°C and 1 atm

C) the number of representative particles of a substance and pressure present in 1 mole of that substance

D) the SI unit used to measure amount of substance

E) an atom, an ion, or a molecule, depending upon the way a substance commonly exists

Multiple Choice and Bimodal Questions

1) What SI unit is used to measure the number of representative particles in a substance?

   A) kilogram   B) ampere   C) kelvin   D) mole   E) candela

2) How many moles of tungsten atoms are there in 4.8×10^{25} atoms of tungsten?

   A) 8.0 moles

   B) 8.0×10^1 moles

   C) 8.0×10^2 moles

   D) 1.3×10^{-2} moles

   E) 1.3×10^{-1} moles

3) How many moles of silver atoms are there in 1.8×10^{20} atoms of silver?

   A) 3.0×10^{-4} B) 3.3×10^{-3} C) 3.0×10^2 D) 1.1×10^{44}

4) How many atoms are there in 5.70 mol of hafnium?

   A) 6.02×10^{23} atoms

   B) 1.06×10^{22} atoms

   C) 3.43×10^{23} atoms

   D) 1.06×10^{23} atoms

   E) 3.43×10^{24} atoms

5) How many atoms are there in 0.075 mol of titanium?

   A) 1.2×10^{-25} B) 3.6   C) 6.4×10^2 D) 4.5×10^{22} E) 2.2×10^{24}

6) How many molecules are there in 2.10 mol CO_2?

   A) 2.53×10^{24} molecules

   B) 3.79×10^{24} molecules

   C) 3.49×10^{-24} molecules

   D) 1.05×10^{-23} molecules

   E) 1.26×10^{24} molecules

7) How many ammonium ions, NH_4^+, are there in 5.0 mol $(NH_4)_2S$?

   A) 3.4×10^2 B) 3.0×10^{24} C) 6.0×10^{24} D) 1.5×10^{25} E) 6.0×10^{25}

8) Butanol is composed of carbon, hydrogen, and oxygen. If 1.0 mol of butanol contains 6.0×10^{24} atoms of hydrogen, what is the subscript for the hydrogen atom in $C_4H_?O$?

   A) 1   B) 4   C) 6   D) 8   E) 10

9) How many moles of helium atoms are there in 2.4×10^{24} helium atoms?

   A) 2.4×10^{24} mol

   B) 4.0 mol

   C) 2.0 mol

   D) 6.0 mol

   E) 10.0 mol

10) How many atoms are there in 3.5 moles of arsenic atoms?

   A) 5.8×10^{-24} atoms

   B) 7.5×10^{1} atoms

   C) 2.6×10^{2} atoms

   D) 1.7×10^{23} atoms

   E) 2.1×10^{24} atoms

11) How many bromide ions are there in 1.5 moles of $MgBr_2$?

   A) 5.0×10^{-24} ions

   B) 3.0 ions

   C) 2.8×10^{2} ions

   D) 9.0×10^{23} ions

   E) 1.8×10^{24} ions

12) How many hydrogen atoms are in 5 molecules of isopropyl alcohol, C_3H_7O?

   A) $5 \times (6.02 \times 10^{23})$ B) 5

   C) 35   D) $35 \times (6.02 \times 10^{23})$

13) How many moles of SO_3 are in 2.4×10^{24} molecules of SO_3?

   A) 0.25   B) 3.4×10^{22} C) 4.0   D) 2.9×10^{-23}

14) What is the gram formula mass of $AuCl_3$?

   A) 96 g   B) 130 g   C) 232.5 g   D) 303.6 g   E) 626.5 g

15) What is the gram formula mass of chromic sulfate, $Cr_2(SO_4)_3$?

   A) 148.1 g   B) 200.0 g   C) 288.0 g   D) 344.2 g   E) 392.2 g

16) What is the gram formula mass of $(NH_4)_2CO_3$?

   A) 144 g   B) 138 g   C) 96 g   D) 78 g   E) 43 g

17) Which of the following is NOT a representative particle?

   A) atom   B) molecule   C) anion   D) cation   E) electron

18) Which of the following elements exists as a diatomic molecule?

   A) neon   B) lithium   C) nitrogen   D) sulfur   E) aluminum

19) Avogadro's number of representative particles is equal to one _____.

   A) kilogram   B) gram   C) liter   D) kelvin   E) mole

20) All of the following are equal to Avogadro's number EXCEPT _____.

   A) the number of molecules of nitrogen in 1 mol N_2

   B) the number of atoms of gold in 1 mol Au

   C) the number of formula units of sodium phosphate in 1 mol Na_3PO_4

   D) the number of molecules of carbon monoxide in 1 mol CO

   E) the number of atoms of bromine in 1 mol Br_2

21) Avogadro's number is _____.

   A) a dozen

   B) a mole

   C) 6.02×10^{23}

   D) the weight of a carbon atom

   E) dependent on what is measured

22) Which of the following is not a true statement concerning the gram atomic mass?

   A) The gram atomic mass is 12 g for magnesium.

   B) The gram atomic mass is the mass of one mole of atoms.

   C) The gram atomic mass is found by checking the periodic table.

   D) The gram atomic mass is the number of grams of an element that is numerically equal to the atomic mass in amu.

   E) The gram atomic mass is the mass of 6.02×10^{23} atoms of any monatomic element.

23) The gram atomic masses of any two elements contain the same number of _____.

   A) atoms   B) grams   C) ions   D) milliliters   E) anions

24) The gram formula mass of C_7H_{16} and the gram formula mass of $CaCO_3$ contain approximately the same number of _____.

   A) carbon atoms

   B) anions

   C) cations

   D) grams

   E) atoms

25) The gram molecular mass of oxygen is _____.

   A) 16.0 g

   B) 32.0 g

   C) equal to the mass of one mole of oxygen atoms

   D) none of the above

26) How many grams are in 0.900 mol Pd?

   A) 0.900 g   B) 106.4 g   C) 0.008 46 g   D) 95.8 g   E) 1.80 g

27) What is the mass in grams of 5.90 mol C_8H_{18}?

    A) 0.0512 g

    B) 19.4 g

    C) 389 g

    D) 673 g

    E) 3.55×10^{24} g

28) What is the number of moles in 432 g $Ba(NO_3)_2$?

    A) 0.237   B) 0.605   C) 1.65   D) 3.66   E) 113 000

29) What is the number of moles in 15.0 g AsH_3?

    A) 0.19   B) 0.44   C) 2.3   D) 5.2   E) 1200

30) What is the number of moles in 0.025 g $(NH_4)_2Cr_2O_7$?

    A) 4.2×10^{-26} B) 1.0×10^{-4} C) 6.3   D) 1.0×10^4 E) 1.5×10^{22}

31) What is the mass, in grams, of 0.450 moles of Sb?

    A) 2.02×10^1 g

    B) 3.55×10^1 g

    C) 5.48×10^1 g

    D) 0.450 g

    E) 2.71×10^{23} g

32) What is the number of moles of beryllium atoms in 36 g of Be?

    A) 0.25 mol

    B) 4.0 mol

    C) 45.0 mol

    D) 320 mol

    E) 2.2×10^{25} mol

33) How many moles of $CaBr_2$ are there in 5.0 grams of $CaBr_2$?

    A) 2.5×10^{-2} mol

    B) 4.2×10^{-2} mol

    C) 4.0×10^1 mol

    D) 1.0×10^3 mol

    E) 3.0×10^{24} mol

34) The chemical formula of aspirin is $C_9H_8O_4$. What is the mass of 0.40 mol of aspirin?

    A) 45 g   B) 10.8 g   C) 160 g   D) 72 g

35) What is the volume, in liters, of 0.500 mol of C_3H_8 gas at STP?

    A) 0.0335 L   B) 11.2 L   C) 16.8 L   D) 22.4 L   E) 5.60 L

36) What is the volume, in liters, of 6.8 mol of Kr gas at STP?

    A) 0.30 L   B) 3.3 L   C) 25 L   D) 150 L   E) 13 000 L

37) What is the number of moles in 500 L of He gas at STP?

    A) 0.05 mol   B) 0.2 mol   C) 20 mol   D) 90 mol   E) 10 000 mol

38) What is the number of moles in 9.63 L of H_2S gas at STP?

    A) 0.104 mol   B) 0.430 mol   C) 3.54 mol   D) 14.7 mol   E) 216 mol

39) What is the volume, in liters, of 2.8 moles of NO_2 gas at STP?

    A) 1500 L   B) 130 L   C) 63 L   D) 8.0 L   E) 0.13 L

40) How many moles of Ar atoms are there in 202 L of Ar gas at STP?

    A) 1.20×10^{24} mol

    B) 4.52×10^3 mol

    C) 9.02 mol

    D) 1.79 mol

    E) 1.11×10^{-1} mol

41) What is the volume (in liters at STP) of 2.50 mol of carbon monoxide?

    A) 70 L   B) 3.1 L   C) 56 L   D) 9.0 L

42) What is the density at STP of the gas sulfur hexafluoride, SF_6?

    A) 0.153 g/L

    B) 6.52 g/L

    C) 3270 g/L

    D) 3.93×10^{24} g/L

    E) Not enough information is given to make this calculation.

43) The gram formula mass of a certain gas is 49 g. What is the density of the gas in g/L at STP?

    A) 3.6×10^{-24} g/L

    B) 0.46 g/L

    C) 2.2 g/L

    D) 71 g/L

    E) 1100 g/L

44) The mass of a mole of NaCl is the _____.

    A) gram formula mass   B) gram atomic mass

    C) gram molecular mass   D) atomic mass

45) Select the correct statement.

   A) Molar mass refers to ternary ionic compounds only.

   B) Gram Avogadro mass refers to binary compounds only.

   C) Gram formula mass refers to all elements and compounds.

   D) Gram atomic mass refers to all elements.

   E) Gram molecular mass refers to all ionic compounds.

46) The volume of one mole of a substance is 22.4 L at STP for all _____.

   A) elements

   B) compounds

   C) solids

   D) liquids

   E) gases

47) A 22.4–L sample of which of the following substances, at STP, would contain 6.02×10^{23} representative particles?

   A) oxygen

   B) gold

   C) cesium iodide

   D) sulfur

   E) All would have the same number of representative particles.

48) Which of the following gas samples would have the largest number of representative particles at STP?

   A) 12.0 L He

   B) 7.0 L O_2

   C) 0.10 L Xe

   D) 0.007 L SO_3

   E) 5.5 L N_2O_4

49) The molar volume of a gas at STP occupies _____.

   A) 22.4 L

   B) 0°C

   C) 1 kilopascal

   D) 12 grams

   E) a volume that depends upon the nature of the gas

50) Which combination of temperature and pressure correctly describes standard temperature and pressure, STP?

   A) 0°C and 101 kPa

   B) 1°C and 0 kPa

   C) 0°C and 22.4 kPa

   D) 22.4°C and 6.02×10^{23} kPa

   E) 100°C and 100 kPa

51) Given 22.4 liters of each of the following gases at STP, which gas would be the lightest?
   A) Cl_2

   B) Ne

   C) C_4H_{10}

   D) NH_3

   E) All would have the same mass.

52) Given 1.00 mole of each of the following gases at STP, which gas would have the greatest volume?
   A) He

   B) O_2

   C) SO_3

   D) UF_6

   E) All would have the same volume.

53) The gram formula mass of a substance can be calculated from its density alone, if that substance is _____.
   A) an element

   B) a compound

   C) a solid

   D) a liquid

   E) a gas at STP

54) If the density of a gas is 0.902 g/L at STP, that gas is _____.
   A) H_2 B) He   C) Ne   D) F_2 E) SO_3

55) If the density of an unknown gas Z is 4.50 g/L at STP, what is the gram formula mass of gas Z?
   A) 0.201 g

   B) 5.00 g

   C) 26.9 g

   D) 101 g

   E) This cannot be determined without knowing the formula of the gas.

56) Given the following densities of five different gases, all measured at STP, which density indicates the gas with the greatest gram formula mass?
   A) 1.1 g/L   B) 2.7 g/L   C) 3.5 g/L   D) 4.9 g/L   E) 5.6 g/L

57) Which of the following gases has the greatest density at STP?
   A) F_2 B) CO_2 C) C_2H_6 D) Xe   E) PF_3

58) Which of the following statements is NOT true about 1 mol of each of these substances at STP: hydrogen, oxygen, nitrogen, fluorine?

    A) All have the same density.

    B) All occupy a volume of 22.4 L.

    C) All are diatomic elements.

    D) All contain Avogadro's number of representative particles.

59) The gram formula mass of a gas can be determined from _____.

    A) the density of the gas at STP   B) the volume of a mole of the gas

    C) Avogadro's number   D) none of the above

60) Which of the following conversion processes does NOT depend upon the gram formula mass of a substance? (volume refers to the volume of a gas at STP.)

    A) mass $\rightarrow$ mole $\rightarrow$ number of representative particles

    B) mass $\rightarrow$ mole $\rightarrow$ volume

    C) volume $\rightarrow$ mole $\rightarrow$ number of representative particles

    D) volume $\rightarrow$ mole $\rightarrow$ mass

    E) number of representative particles $\rightarrow$ mole $\rightarrow$ mass

61) For which of the following conversions does the value of the conversion factor depend upon the formula of the substance?

    A) volume of gas (STP) to moles

    B) density of gas (STP) to gram formula mass

    C) mass of any substance to moles

    D) moles of any substance to number of particles

    E) number of particles to moles of gas (STP)

62) A large weather balloon filled with helium has a volume of 7.00×10^2 L at STP. Which expression should be used to find the mass of helium in the balloon?

    A) $\dfrac{22.4 \text{ L}}{\text{mol}} \times \dfrac{4 \text{ g He}}{\text{mol}}$ B) $\dfrac{7.0 \times 10^2}{\text{L}} \times \dfrac{4 \text{ g He}}{\text{mol}}$

    C) $\dfrac{22.4 \text{ L/mol}}{7.00} \times 10^{-2} \text{ L} \times \dfrac{4 \text{ g He}}{\text{mol}}$ D) $\dfrac{7.00 \times 10^2 \text{ L}}{22.4 \text{ L/mol}} \times \dfrac{4 \text{ g He}}{\text{mol}}$

63) To determine the formula of a new substance, one of the first steps is to find the _____.

    A) gram formula mass

    B) percent composition

    C) volume at STP

    D) number of particles per mole

    E) value for Avogadro's number

64) If 60.2 grams of Hg combines completely with 24.0 grams of Br to form a compound, what is the percent composition of Hg in the compound?

    A) 28.5%   B) 39.9%   C) 71.5%   D) 60.1%   E) 251%

65) What is the percent composition of chromium in $BaCrO_4$?

    A) 4.87%   B) 9.47%   C) 20.5%   D) 25.2%   E) 54.2%

66) What is the mass of silver in 3.4 g $AgNO_3$?

    A) 0.025 g   B) 0.032 g   C) 0.64 g   D) 2.2 g   E) 3.0 g

67) What is the mass of oxygen in 250 g of sulfuric acid, H_2SO_4?

    A) 0.65 g   B) 3.9 g   C) 16 g   D) 41 g   E) 160 g

68) If 20.0 grams of Ca combines completely with 16.0 grams of S to form a compound, what is the percent composition of Ca in the compound?

    A) 1.25%   B) 20.0%   C) 44.4%   D) 55.6%   E) 80.0%

69) What information is needed to calculate the percent composition of a compound?

    A) the weight of the sample to be analyzed and its density

    B) the weight of the sample to be analyzed and its molar volume

    C) the formula of the compound and the gram atomic mass of its elements

    D) the formula of the compound and its density

    E) the density of the compound and Avogadro's number

70) What is the percent composition of carbon, in heptane, C_7H_{16}?

    A) 12%   B) 16%   C) 19%   D) 68%   E) 84%

71) What is the percent by mass of carbon in acetone, C_3H_6O?

    A) 20.7%   B) 62.1%   C) 1.61%   D) 30.0%

72) What is the empirical formula of a compound that is 40% sulfur and 60% oxygen by weight?

    A) SO   B) SO_2 C) SO_3 D) S_6O_4 E) S_2O_3

73) What is the empirical formula of a compound that is 50.7% antimony and 49.3% selenium by weight?

    A) SbSe   B) $SbSe_2$ C) Sb_2Se D) Sb_2Se_3 E) Sb_3Se_2

74) What is the empirical formula of a substance that is 53.5% C, 15.5% H, and 31.1% N by weight?

    A) $C_{4.5}H_{15.5}N_{2.2}$

    B) $C_4H_{14}N_2$

    C) C_2H_7N

    D) CH_4N_7

    E) C_3HN_2

75) The ratio of carbon atoms to hydrogen atoms to oxygen atoms in a molecule of dicyclohexyl maleate is 4 to 6 to 1. What is the molecular formula of this substance if its gram formula mass is 280 g?

A) $C_4H_6O_1$

B) $C_8H_{12}O_2$

C) $C_{12}H_{18}O_3$

D) $C_{16}H_{24}O_4$

E) $C_{20}H_{30}O_5$

76) Which of the following compounds has the lowest percent gold content by weight?

A) $AuOH$ B) $Au(OH)_3$ C) $AuCl_3$ D) AuI_3 E) $AuBr_3$

77) Which of the following compounds has the highest oxygen content, by weight?

A) Na_2O B) CO_2 C) BaO D) H_2O E) NO

78) All of the following are empirical formulas EXCEPT _____.

A) Na_2SO_4 B) C_6H_5Cl C) N_2O_4 D) $Sn_3(PO_4)_4$

79) Which expression represents the percent by mass of nitrogen in NH_4NO_3?

A) $\dfrac{14\text{ g N}}{80\text{ g NH}_4\text{NO}_3} \times 100\%$

B) $\dfrac{28\text{ g N}}{80\text{ g NH}_4\text{NO}_3} \times 100\%$

C) $\dfrac{80\text{ g NH}_4\text{NO}_3}{14\text{ g N}} \times 100\%$

D) $\dfrac{80\text{ g NH}_4\text{NO}_3}{28\text{ g N}} \times 100\%$

80) The lowest whole–number ratio of the elements in a compound is called the _____.

A) empirical formula

B) molecular formula

C) ionic compound

D) binary formula

E) representative formula

81) Which of the following is not an empirical formula?

A) $C_2N_2H_8$ B) C_3H_8O C) $BeCr_2O_7$ D) Sb_2S_3 E) MoO_2Cl_2

82) Which of the following is an empirical formula?

A) $C_3H_6O_2$ B) C_5H_{10} C) $C_2H_8N_2$ D) P_4O_{10} E) H_2O_2

83) Which of the following compounds have the same empirical formula?

A) NO and NO_2

B) CO_2 and SO_2

C) C_4H_{10} and $C_{10}H_4$

D) C_6H_{12} and C_6H_{14}

E) C_7H_{14} and $C_{10}H_{20}$

84) Which of the following is NOT a true statement concerning empirical and molecular formulas?

    A) The molecular formula of a compound can be the same as its empirical formula.

    B) The molecular formula of a compound can be some whole–number multiple of its empirical formula.

    C) Several compounds can have the same empirical formula, but have different molecular formulas.

    D) The empirical formula of a compound can be triple its molecular formula.

    E) If the molecular formula of hydrogen peroxide is H_2O_2, its empirical formula is HO.

85) Which of the following sets of empirical formula, gram formula mass, and molecular formula is correct?

    A) HO, 34 g, H_2O

    B) CH_4N, 90 g, $C_3H_{12}N_3$

    C) CaO, 56 g, Ca_2O_2

    D) C_3H_8O, 120 g, $C_3H_8O_2$

    E) CH, 78 g, $C_{13}H_{13}$

Problems

1) How many representative particles are there in 1.45 g of a molecular compound with a gram molecular mass of 237 g?

2) Find the mass in grams of 2.20×10^{23} molecules of F_2.

3) Find the number of moles of argon in 481 g of argon.

4) What mass of gold contains twice as many atoms as 2.74 g of silver?

5) Find the mass, in grams, of 1.40×10^{23} molecules of N_2.

6) How many kilograms of aluminum can be recovered from 429 kg of the ore, Al_2O_3?

7) What is the percent by mass of hydrogen in aspirin, $C_9H_8O_4$?

8) What is the percent composition of NiO, if a sample of NiO with a mass of 10.3 g contains 8.1 g Ni and 2.2 g O?

9) The percentage composition of a polymer used for the non– stick surfaces of cooking utensils, is 24.0% C and 76.0% F by mass. What is the empirical formula of the polymer?

10) What is the empirical formula of a compound that is 40.7% carbon, 54.2% oxygen, and 5.1% hydrogen?

11) What is the empirical formula of a compound formed by the reaction of 102.6 g of Ca and 97.4 g F?

12) The ratio of carbon to hydrogen to nitrogen atoms in nicotine is 5 to 7 to 1. What is the molecular formula of nicotine if its gram molecular mass is 162 g? The empirical formula is C_5H_7N.

13) The density of acetylene at STP is 1.17 g/L. What is the gram molecular mass of acetylene? The empirical formula of acetylene is CH. What is its molecular formula?

14) Calculate the molecular formulas of the compounds having the following empirical formulas and molecular weights: C_2H_5, 58 g/mol; CH, 78 g/mol; and HgCl, 236.1 g/mol.

Essay Questions

1) What is the advantage of using the specific term, gram molecular mass, instead of the general term, gram formula mass?

2) Why is it possible to calculate the density of a gas at STP, knowing only its gram formula mass, but it is not possible to make the same calculation for a solid or a liquid?

Chapter 7 Chemical Quantities

Matching Questions

1) Answer: C

2) Answer: D

3) Answer: A

4) Answer: E

5) Answer: B

6) Answer: E

7) Answer: D

8) Answer: C

9) Answer: A

10) Answer: B

Multiple Choice and Bimodal Questions

1) Answer: D

2) Answer: B

3) Answer: A

4) Answer: E

5) Answer: D

6) Answer: E

7) Answer: C

8) Answer: E

9) Answer: B

10) Answer: E

11) Answer: E

12) Answer: C

13) Answer: C

14) Answer: D

15) Answer: E

16) Answer: C

17) Answer: E

18) Answer: C

19) Answer: E

20) Answer: E

21) Answer: B

22) Answer: A

23) Answer: A

24) Answer: D

25) Answer: B

26) Answer: D

27) Answer: D

28) Answer: C

29) Answer: A

30) Answer: B

31) Answer: C

32) Answer: B

33) Answer: A

34) Answer: D

35) Answer: B

36) Answer: D

37) Answer: C

38) Answer: B

39) Answer: C

40) Answer: C

41) Answer: C

42) Answer: B

43) Answer: C

44) Answer: A

45) Answer: C

46) Answer: E

47) Answer: A

48) Answer: A

49) Answer: A

50) Answer: A

51) Answer: B

52) Answer: E

53) Answer: E

54) Answer: C

55) Answer: D

56) Answer: E

57) Answer: D

58) Answer: A

59) Answer: A

60) Answer: C

61) Answer: C

62) Answer: D

63) Answer: B

64) Answer: C

65) Answer: C

66) Answer: D

67) Answer: E

68) Answer: D

69) Answer: C

70) Answer: E

71) Answer: B

72) Answer: C

73) Answer: D

74) Answer: C

75) Answer: D

76) Answer: D

77) Answer: D

78) Answer: C

79) Answer: B

80) Answer: A

81) Answer: A

82) Answer: A

83) Answer: E

84) Answer: D

85) Answer: B

Problems

1) Answer: $1.45 \text{ g} \times \dfrac{1.00 \text{ mol}}{237 \text{ g}} \times \dfrac{6.02 \times 10^{23} \text{ molecules}}{1.00 \text{ mol}}$

$= 3.68 \times 10^{21} \text{ molecules}$

2) Answer: $2.20 \times 10^{23} \text{ molecules} \times \dfrac{1 \text{ mol } F_2}{6.02 \times 10^{23} \text{ molecules}} \times \dfrac{38.0 \text{ g } F_2}{1 \text{ mol } F_2}$

$= 13.9 \text{ g } F_2$

3) Answer: $481 \text{ g Ar} \times \dfrac{1 \text{ mol Ar}}{39.9 \text{ g Ar}} = 12.1 \text{ mol Ar}$

4) Answer: $2.74 \text{ g Ag} \times \dfrac{1 \text{ mol}}{108 \text{ g Ag}} \times \dfrac{197 \text{ g Au}}{1 \text{ mol}} = 5.00 \text{ g Au}$

$5.00 \text{ g Au} \times 2 = 10.0 \text{ g Au}$

5) Answer: $1.40 \times 10^{23} \text{ molecules } N_2 \times \dfrac{1.00 \text{ mol } N_2}{6.02 \times 10^{23} \text{ molecules } N_2} \times \dfrac{28.0 \text{ g } N_2}{1 \text{ mol } N_2}$

$= 6.51 \text{ g}$

6) Answer: $2 \text{ mol Al} \times \dfrac{27.0 \text{ g Al}}{1.00 \text{ mol Al}} = 54.0 \text{ g Al}$

$3 \text{ mol O} \times \dfrac{16.0 \text{ g O}}{1.00 \text{ mol O}} = 48.0 \text{ g O}$

gfm of Al_2O_3 is 102.0 g

$\%Al = \dfrac{\text{g Al}}{\text{gfm } Al_2O_3} \times 100\%$

$= \dfrac{54.0 \text{ g}}{102.0 \text{ g}} \times 100\%$

$= 52.9\%$

$429 \text{ kg } Al_2O_3 \times \dfrac{0.529 \text{ kg Al}}{1 \text{ kg } Al_2O_3} = 227 \text{ kg Al}$

7) Answer: $\dfrac{8.00 \text{ g } H_2}{180 \text{ g } C_9H_8O_4} \times 100\% = 4.44\% \, H_2$

8) Answer: $\dfrac{8.1 \text{ g Ni}}{10.3 \text{ g NiO}} \times 100\% = 79\%$ Ni

$\dfrac{2.2 \text{ g O}}{10.3 \text{ g NiO}} \times 100\% = 21\%$ O

9) Answer: $24.0 \text{ g C} \times \dfrac{1 \text{ mol C}}{12.0 \text{ g C}} = 2 \text{ mol C}$

$76 \text{ g F} \times \dfrac{1 \text{ mol F}}{19.0 \text{ g F}} = 4 \text{ mol F}$

The mole ratio of C to F is $\dfrac{2 \text{ mol C}}{4 \text{ mol F}}$.

The lowest whole–number ratio of C to F is CF_2.

10) Answer: $40.7 \text{ g C} \times \dfrac{1.00 \text{ mol C}}{12.0 \text{ g C}} = 3.39 \text{ mol C}$

$54.2 \text{ g O} \times \dfrac{1.00 \text{ mol O}}{16.0 \text{ g O}} = 3.39 \text{ mol O}$

$5.1 \text{ g H} \times \dfrac{1.00 \text{ mol H}}{1.0 \text{ g H}} = 5.1 \text{ mol H}$

$\dfrac{5.1}{3.39} = 1.5 \text{ mol H}$ $\dfrac{3.39}{3.39} = 1 \text{ mol C}$

$\dfrac{3.39}{3.39} = 1 \text{ mol O}$

1.5 mol H x 2 = 3 mol H
1 mol C x 2 = 2 mol C
1 mol O x 2 = 2 mol O
Empirical formula = $C_2H_3O_2$

11) Answer: $102.6 \text{ g Ca} \times \dfrac{1.00 \text{ mol Ca}}{40.1 \text{ g Ca}} = 2.56 \text{ mol Ca}$

$97.4 \text{ g F} \times \dfrac{1.00 \text{ mol F}}{19.0 \text{ g F}} = 5.13 \text{ mol F}$

$\dfrac{5.13 \text{ mol F}}{2.56} = 2 \text{ mol F}$

$\dfrac{2.56 \text{ mol Ca}}{2.56} = 1 \text{ mol Ca}$

Empirical formula = CaF_2

12) Answer: The empirical formula is C_5H_7N.

The empirical mass is:

$5 \text{ mol C} \times \dfrac{12 \text{ g C}}{1 \text{ mol C}} = 60 \text{ g C}$

$7 \text{ mol H} \times \dfrac{1 \text{ g H}}{1 \text{ mol H}} = 7 \text{ g H}$

$1 \text{ mol N} \times \dfrac{14 \text{ g N}}{1 \text{ mol N}} = 14 \text{ g N}$

Empirical formula mass = 81 g

$\dfrac{\text{gfm}}{\text{efm}} = \dfrac{162 \text{ g}}{81 \text{ g}} = 2$

The molecular formula is $C_{10}H_{14}N_2$.

13) Answer: $22.4 \text{ L} \times \dfrac{1.17 \text{ g}}{1 \text{ L}} = 26.2 \text{ g} = \text{gmm}$

$$1 \text{ mol C} \times \dfrac{12 \text{ g C}}{1 \text{ mol C}} = 12 \text{ g C}$$

$$1 \text{ mol H} \times \dfrac{1 \text{ g H}}{1 \text{ mol H}} = 1 \text{ g H}$$

Empirical formula mass = 13 g

$$\dfrac{\text{gfm}}{\text{efm}} = \dfrac{26.2 \text{ g}}{13 \text{ g}} = 2$$

Molecular formula = $2(CH) = C_2H_2$.

14) Answer: $\dfrac{58 \text{ g/mol}}{29 \text{ g/efm}} = 2 \dfrac{\text{efm}}{\text{mol}}; C_4H_{10}$

$$\dfrac{78 \text{ g/mol}}{13 \text{ g/efm}} = 6 \dfrac{\text{efm}}{\text{mol}}; C_6H_6$$

$$\dfrac{236.1 \text{ g/mol}}{236.1 \text{ g/efm}} = 1 \dfrac{\text{efm}}{\text{mol}}; HgCl$$

Essay Questions

1) Answer: There may be some confusion when the terms are applied to diatomic gases such as nitrogen and oxygen. For instance, the gram molecular mass of nitrogen is 28 g. The gram formula mass could be either 14 g or 28 g, depending upon whether the subject is nitrogen atoms or nitrogen molecules.

2) Answer: The molar volume of any gas is 22.4 L at STP. The density can be calculated in the following way:

$$\dfrac{\text{gfm of ANY gas (g)}}{1 \text{ mol}} \times \dfrac{1 \text{ mol}}{22.4 \text{ L}} = \text{density of gas (g/L)}$$

However, the molar volumes of different solids and liquids are not uniformly the same at any prescribed condition.

Chapter 8 Chemical Reactions

Matching Questions

Chapter 8: Matching I

1) product

2) reactant

3) chemical equation

4) balanced equation

5) skeleton equation

A) a concise representation of a chemical reaction

B) an equation in which each side has the same number of atoms of each element

C) a chemical equation that does not indicate relative amounts of reactants and products

D) a starting substance in a chemical reaction

E) a new substance formed in a chemical reaction

Chapter 8: Matching II

6) activity series of metals

7) single-replacement reaction

8) combustion reaction

9) decomposition reaction

A) a list of metals in order of decreasing reactivity

B) a reaction in which a single compound is broken down into simpler substances

C) a reaction in which oxygen reacts with another substance, often producing heat or light

D) a reaction in which the atoms of one element replace the atoms of a second element

Multiple Choice and Bimodal Questions

1) What are the missing coefficients for the skeleton equation below?

$Al_2(SO_4)_3(aq) + KOH(aq) \rightarrow Al(OH)_3(aq) + K_2SO_4(aq)$

   A) 1,3,2,3   B) 2,12,4,6   C) 4,6,2,3   D) 1,6,2,3   E) 2,3,1,1

2) What are the missing coefficients for the skeleton equation below?

$Cr(s) + Fe(NO_3)_2(aq) \rightarrow Fe(s) + Cr(NO_3)_3(aq)$

   A) 4,6,6,2   B) 2,3,2,3   C) 2,3,3,2   D) 1,3,3,1   E) 2,3,1,2

3) What are the missing coefficients for the skeleton equation below?

$NH_3(g) + O_2(g) \rightarrow N_2(g) + H_2O(l)$

   A) 4,3,2,6   B) 2,1,2,3   C) 1,3,1,3   D) 2,3,2,3   E) 3,4,6,2

4) If you rewrite the following word equation as a balanced chemical equation, what will the coefficient and symbol for iodine be?

bromine + potassium iodide $\rightarrow$ potassium bromide + iodine

   A) $2I^-$ B) I   C) 2I   D) I_2 E) $2I_2$

5) If you rewrite the following word equation as a balanced chemical equation, what will the coefficient and symbol for fluorine be?

nitrogen trifluoride $\rightarrow$ nitrogen + fluorine

   A) 3F   B) $6F_2$ C) F_3 D) 6F   E) $3F_2$

6) What are the missing coefficients for the skeleton equation below?

$AlCl_3 + NaOH \rightarrow Al(OH)_3 + NaCl$

   A) 1,3,1,3   B) 3,1,3,1   C) 1,1,1,3   D) 1,3,3,1   E) 3,1,1,1

7) What are the missing coefficients for the skeleton equation below?

$N_2 + H_2 \rightarrow NH_3$

   A) 1,1,2   B) 1,3,3   C) 3,1,2   D) 1,3,2   E) 2,6,6

8) Aluminum chloride and bubbles of hydrogen gas are produced when metallic aluminum is placed in hydrochloric acid. What is the balanced equation for this reaction?

   A) $H + AlCl \rightarrow Al + HCl$

   B) $2Al + 6HCl \rightarrow 2AlCl_3 + 3H_2$

   C) $Al + HCl_3 \rightarrow AlCl_3 + H$

   D) $Al + 2HCl \rightarrow AlCl_2 + H_2$

   E) $H_2 + AlCl_3 \rightarrow Al + 2HCl$

9) What does the symbol Δ in a chemical equation mean?

   A) heat is supplied to the reaction   B) a catalyst is needed

   C) yields   D) precipitate

10) When the equation, $Fe + Cl_2 \rightarrow FeCl_3$, is balanced, what is the coefficient for Cl_2?

    A) 1   B) 2   C) 3   D) 4

11) When the following equation is balanced, what is the coefficient for HCl?
$Mg(s) + HCl(aq) \rightarrow MgCl_2(aq) + H_2\uparrow$

    A) 6   B) 3   C) 1   D) 2

12) Chemical reactions _____.

    A) occur only in living organisms   B) create and destroy atoms

    C) only occur outside living organisms   D) produce new substances

13) Which of the following is NOT a true statement concerning what happens in all chemical reactions?

    A) The ways in which atoms are joined together are changed.

    B) New atoms are formed as products.

    C) The starting materials are named reactants.

    D) The bonds of the reactants are broken and new bonds of the products are formed.

    E) In a word equation representing a chemical reaction, the reactants are written on the left and the products on the right.

14) Chemical equations _____.

    A) describe chemical reactions

    B) show how to write chemical formulas

    C) give directions for naming chemical compounds

    D) describe only biological changes

15) A skeleton equation does NOT show which of the following?

    A) the correct formulas of the reactants and products

    B) the reactants on the left, the products on the right

    C) an arrow connecting the reactants to the products

    D) the physical states of the substances

    E) the relative amounts of reactants and products

16) Everyday equations describe _____.

    A) thermonuclear reactions   B) everyday processes

    C) chemical reactions   D) biological chemistry

17) Chemical equations must be balanced to satisfy the _____.

    A) law of definite proportions   B) law of multiple proportions

    C) law of conservation of mass   D) principle of Avogadro

18) Symbols used in equations, together with the explanations of the symbols, are shown below. Which set is correct?

   A) (g), grams
   B) (l), liters
   C) (aq), dissolved in water
   D) ↑, solid product
   E) $\xrightarrow{Pt}$ is formed

19) In the chemical equation, $H_2O_2(aq) \rightarrow H_2O(l) + O_2(g)$, the H_2O_2 is a _____.

   A) product   B) reactant   C) catalyst   D) solid   E) gas

20) A catalyst is _____.

   A) the product of a combustion reaction
   B) not used up in a reaction
   C) one of the reactants in single–replacement reactions
   D) a solid product of a reaction

21) When the following equation is balanced, $KClO_3(s) \rightarrow KCl(s) + O_2(g,)$ the coefficient of $KClO_3$ is _____.

   A) 1   B) 2   C) 3   D) 4   E) 6

22) Which of the following is the correct skeleton equation for the reaction that takes place when solid phosphorus combines with oxygen gas to form diphosphorus pentoxide?

   A) $P(s) + O_2(g) \rightarrow PO_2(g)$
   B) $P(s) + O(g) \rightarrow P_5O_2(g)$
   C) $P(s) + O_2(g) \rightarrow P_2O_5$
   D) $P_2O_5 \rightarrow P_2(s) + O_2(g)$
   E) $P_2(s) + O_5(g) \rightarrow P_2O_5(g)$

23) In every balanced chemical equation, each side of the equation has the same number of _____.

   A) atoms
   B) molecules
   C) moles
   D) coefficients
   E) subscripts

24) When potassium hydroxide and barium chloride react, potassium chloride and barium hydroxide are formed. The balanced equation for this reaction is _____.

  A) $KH + BaCl \rightarrow KCl + BaH$

  B) $KOH + BaCl \rightarrow KCl + BaOH$

  C) $2KOH + BaCl_2 \rightarrow 2KCl + Ba(OH)_2$

  D) $KOH + BaCl_2 \rightarrow KCl_2 + BaOH$

  E) $2KOH + 2BaCl_2 \rightarrow 2KCl_2 + 2Ba(OH)_2$

25) This symbol $\rightleftharpoons$ indicates _____.

  A) that heat must be applied   B) an incomplete combustion reaction

  C) that a gas is formed by the reaction   D) that the reaction is reversible

26) If a combination reaction takes place between potassium and chlorine, what is the product?

  A) KCl B) KCl_2 C) K_2Cl D) PCl E) PCl_2

27) The product of a combination reaction is $Ba(OH)_2$. If one of the reactants was H_2O, what was the other reactant?

  A) Ba_2O B) BaO C) BaH D) BaO_2 E) Ba_2O_7

28) Write a balanced equation for the combination reaction that takes place when iron(III) oxide is formed from its constituent elements.

  A) $Fe_2 + O_3 \rightarrow Fe_2O_3$

  B) $2Fe + 3O \rightarrow Fe_2O_3$

  C) $4Fe + 3O_2 \rightarrow 2Fe_2O_3$

  D) $3Fe + O \rightarrow Fe_3O$

  E) $Fe + O_3 \rightarrow FeO_3$

29) The reaction, $2Fe + 3Cl_2 \rightarrow 2FeCl_3$, is an example of which type of reaction?

  A) combustion reaction   B) single–replacement reaction

  C) combination reaction   D) decomposition reaction

30) Write a balanced equation to represent the decomposition of lead(IV) oxide.

  A) $PbO_2 \rightarrow Pb + 2O$

  B) $PbO_2 \rightarrow Pb + O_2$

  C) $Pb_2O \rightarrow 2Pb + O$

  D) $PbO \rightarrow Pb + O_2$

  E) $2PbO \rightarrow 2Pb + O_2$

31) What is the balanced chemical equation for the reaction that takes place between bromine and sodium iodide?

    A) $Br_2 + NaI \rightarrow NaBr_2 + I$

    B) $Br_2 + 2NaI \rightarrow 2NaBr + I_2$

    C) $Br^-_2 + 2NaI \rightarrow 2NaBr + 2I^-$

    D) $Br + NaI_2 \rightarrow NaBrI_2$

    E) $Br + NaI_2 \rightarrow NaBr + I_2$

32) The equation $Mg(s) + 2HCl(aq) \rightarrow MgCl_2(aq) + H_2\uparrow$ is an example of which type of reaction?

    A) combination   B) single–replacement

    C) decomposition   D) double–replacement

33) What are the correct formulas and coefficients for the products of this double–replacement reaction?

    $RbOH + H_3PO_4 \rightarrow$

    A) $Rb(PO_4)_3 + H_2O$

    B) $RbPO_4 + 2H_2O$

    C) $Rb_3PO_4 + 3H_2O$

    D) $H_3Rb + PO_4OH$

    E) $3RbH + H_2OPO_4$

34) The equation $H_3PO_4 + 3KOH \rightarrow K_3PO_4 + 3H_2O$ is an example of which type of reaction?

    A) double–replacement   B) combination

    C) decomposition   D) single–replacement

35) When the equation for the complete combustion of ethanol, C_2H_5OH, is balanced, what is the coefficient for oxygen?

    A) 1   B) 3   C) 6   D) 7   E) 14

36) The equation $2C_3H_7OH + 9O_2 \rightarrow 6CO_2\uparrow + 8H_2O\uparrow$ is an example of which type of reaction?

    A) combustion   B) single–replacement

    C) double–replacement   D) decomposition

37) Which of the following statements is NOT true concerning the decomposition of a simple binary compound?

    A) The products are unpredictable.

    B) The products are the constituent elements.

    C) The reactant is a single substance.

    D) The reactant could be an ionic or a molecular compound.

    E) Energy is usually required.

38) Which of the following statements is true concerning single-replacement reactions?

    A) They are restricted to metals.

    B) They involve a single product.

    C) They involve a single reactant.

    D) Any metal replaces any other metal.

    E) They are also called displacement reactions.

39) In order to predict whether or not a single–replacement reaction takes place, we need to consult a chart which shows the _____.

    A) periodic table

    B) activity series of metals

    C) common polyatomic ions

    D) ionic charges of representative elements

    E) formulas and names of common metal ions having an ionic charge greater than 1.

40) In the activity series of metals, which metal(s) will displace hydrogen from an acid?

    A) any metal

    B) only metals above hydrogen

    C) only metals below hydrogen

    D) only metals from Li to Na

    E) only gold

41) Which of the following reactions will NOT take place spontaneously in the direction written?

    A) $Cu + HCl \rightarrow$

    B) $Ca + Pb(NO_3)_2 \rightarrow$

    C) $Ag + AuCl_3 \rightarrow$

    D) $Zn + HNO_3 \rightarrow$

    E) $K + H_2SO_4 \rightarrow$

42) Use the activity series of metals to write a balanced chemical equation for the following single replacement reaction:

    $Ag(s) + KNO_3(aq) \rightarrow$

    A) $Ag(s) + KNO_3(aq) \rightarrow AgNO_3 + K$

    B) $Ag(s) + KNO_3(aq) \rightarrow AgK + NO_3$

    C) $Ag(s) + KNO_3(aq) \rightarrow AgKNO_3$

    D) $Ag(s) + KNO_3(aq) \rightarrow Ag + K + NO_3$

    E) No reaction takes place because silver is less reactive than potassium.

43) In order for the reaction 2Al + 6HCl → 2AlCl$_3$ + 3H$_2$↑ to occur, which of the following must be true?

    A) Al must be above Cl on the activity series.

    B) Al must be above H on the activity series.

    C) Heat must be supplied for the reaction.

    D) A gas must be formed.

44) Which of the following statements is NOT true concerning double–replacement reactions?

    A) The product may precipitate from solution.

    B) The product may be a gas.

    C) The product may be a molecular compound.

    D) The reactant may be a solid metal.

    E) The reactant may be a binary ionic compound.

45) A double–replacement reaction takes place when aqueous cobalt(III) chloride reacts with aqueous lithium hydroxide. One of the products of this reaction would be _____.

    A) Co(OH)$_3$ B) Co(OH)$_2$ C) LiCo$_3$ D) LiCl$_3$ E) Cl$_3$OH

46) What is the driving force in the following reaction?

Ni(NO$_3$)$_2$(aq) + K$_2$S(aq) → NiS↓ + 2KNO$_3$(aq)

    A) A gas is formed.

    B) A precipitate is formed.

    C) Ionic compounds are reactants.

    D) Ionic compounds are products.

    E) Heat is required.

47) In a double–replacement reaction _____.

    A) the reactants are usually a metal and a nonmetal

    B) one of the reactants is often water

    C) the reactants are generally two ionic compounds in aqueous solution

    D) energy in the form of heat or light is often produced

48) A double–replacement reaction takes place when aqueous Na$_2$CO$_3$ reacts with aqueous Sn(NO$_3$)$_2$. You would expect one of the products of this reaction to be _____.

    A) NaNO$_3$ B) NaSn   C) Sn(CO$_3$)$_2$ D) CNO$_3$

49) In a combustion reaction, one of the reactants is _____.

    A) hydrogen

    B) nitrogen

    C) oxygen

    D) a metal

    E) a binary ionic compound

50) The products of a combustion reaction do NOT include _____.

A) water

B) carbon dioxide

C) carbon monoxide

D) heat

E) hydrogen

51) The complete combustion of which of the following substances produces carbon dioxide and water?

A) C_8H_{18} B) K_2CO_3 C) $CaHCO_3$ D) NO   E) H_2S

52) Which of the following is the correctly balanced equation for the incomplete combustion of heptene, C_7H_{14}?

A) $C_7H_{14} + 14O \rightarrow 7CO + 7H_2O$

B) $C_7H_{14} + 7O_2 \rightarrow 7CO + 7H_2O$

C) $2C_7H_{14} + 21O_2 \rightarrow 14CO_2 + 14H_2O$

D) $C_7H_{14} + O_2 \rightarrow C_7O_2 + 7H_2$

E) $C_7H_{14} + 7O_2 \rightarrow 7CO_2 + 7H_2O$

53) The type of reaction that takes place when one element reacts with a compound to form a new compound and a different element is a _____.

A) combination reaction

B) decomposition reaction

C) single-replacement reaction

D) double-replacement reaction

E) combustion reaction

54) In a double-replacement reaction, _____.

A) the products are always molecular

B) the reactants are two ionic compounds

C) the reactant is always oxygen

D) the reactants are two elements

E) the products are a new element and a new compound

55) Which of the following statements is incorrect?

A) The only way to determine the products of a reaction is to carry out the reaction.

B) All chemical reactions can be classified as one of five general types.

C) Complete combustion has occurred when all the carbon in the product is in the form of carbon dioxide.

D) A single reactant is the identifying characteristic of a decomposition reaction.

Problems

1) Balance the everyday equation described in the following sentence. "A wagon is made of a handle, body, four wheels, and two axles."

$H + B + W + A \rightarrow HBW_4A_2$

2) Complete and balance the following equation:

$K_3PO_4 + BaCl_2 \rightarrow$

3) Complete and balance the following equation:

cadmium nitrate plus ammonium chloride goes to _____ .

4) Balance the following equation.

$NaClO_3 \rightarrow NaCl + O_2\uparrow$

5) Balance the following equation.

$Mg + H_3PO_4 \rightarrow Mg_3(PO_4)_2\downarrow + H_2\uparrow$

6) Balance the following equation.

$(NH_4)_2CO_3 + NaOH \rightarrow Na_2CO_3 + NH_3 + H_2O$

7) Balance the following equation. Complete the equation first, if necessary.

$C_3H_6 + O_2 \xrightarrow{\Delta} CO\uparrow + H_2O\uparrow$

8) Balance the following equation. Complete the equation first, if necessary.

$Ba + H_2O \rightarrow Ba(OH)_2 + H_2\uparrow$

9) Balance the following equation. Complete the equation first, if necessary.

$Au_2O_3 \rightarrow Au + O_2\uparrow$

10) Balance the following equation. Complete the equation first, if necessary.

$Na_3PO_4 + ZnSO_4 \rightarrow Na_2SO_4 + Zn_3(PO_4)_2\downarrow$

11) Balance the following equation. Complete the equation first, if necessary.

$Al + Cl_2 \rightarrow$

12) Balance the following equation. Complete the equation first, if necessary.

$CH_4 + O_2 \xrightarrow{\Delta} CO_2 +$

13) Balance the following equation. Complete the equation first, if necessary.

$Fe_2(SO_4)_3 + Ba(OH)_2 \rightarrow$

14) Balance the following equation. Indicate whether combustion is complete or incomplete.

$C_3H_8 + O_2 \rightarrow CO\uparrow + H_2O\uparrow$

15) Balance the following equation. Indicate whether combustion is complete or incomplete.

$$C_2H_5OH + O_2 \rightarrow CO_2\uparrow + H_2O\uparrow$$

16) Write a balanced net ionic equation for the following reaction.

$$H_3PO_4(aq) + Ca(OH)_2(aq) \rightarrow Ca_3(PO_4)_2(aq) + H_2O(l)$$

Essay Questions

1) What determines whether one metal will replace another metal from a compound in a single–replacement reaction?

Chapter 8 Chemical Reactions

Matching Questions

 1) Answer: E

 2) Answer: D

 3) Answer: A

 4) Answer: B

 5) Answer: C

 6) Answer: A

 7) Answer: D

 8) Answer: C

 9) Answer: B

Multiple Choice and Bimodal Questions

 1) Answer: D

 2) Answer: C

 3) Answer: A

 4) Answer: D

 5) Answer: E

 6) Answer: A

 7) Answer: D

 8) Answer: B

 9) Answer: A

 10) Answer: C

 11) Answer: D

 12) Answer: D

 13) Answer: B

 14) Answer: A

 15) Answer: E

 16) Answer: B

 17) Answer: C

 18) Answer: C

 19) Answer: B

 20) Answer: B

 21) Answer: B

 22) Answer: C

 23) Answer: A

 24) Answer: C

 25) Answer: D

 26) Answer: A

 27) Answer: B

 28) Answer: C

 29) Answer: C

 30) Answer: B

31) Answer: B

32) Answer: B

33) Answer: C

34) Answer: A

35) Answer: B

36) Answer: A

37) Answer: A

38) Answer: E

39) Answer: B

40) Answer: B

41) Answer: A

42) Answer: E

43) Answer: B

44) Answer: D

45) Answer: A

46) Answer: B

47) Answer: C

48) Answer: A

49) Answer: C

50) Answer: E

51) Answer: A

52) Answer: B

53) Answer: C

54) Answer: B

55) Answer: B

Problems

1) Answer: $H + B + 4W + 2A \rightarrow HBW_4A_2$

2) Answer: $2K_3PO_4 + 3BaCl_2 \rightarrow Ba_3(PO_4)_2\downarrow + 6KCl$

3) Answer: $Cd(NO_3)_2 + 2NH_4Cl \rightarrow CdCl_2 + 2\,NH_4NO_3$

4) Answer: $2NaClO_3 \rightarrow 2NaCl + 3O_2\uparrow$

5) Answer: $3Mg + 2H_3PO_4 \rightarrow Mg_3(PO_4)_2\downarrow + 3H_2\uparrow$

6) Answer: $(NH_4)_2CO_3 + 2NaOH \rightarrow Na_2CO_3 + 2NH_3 + 2H_2O$

7) Answer: $C_3H_6 + 3O_2 \xrightarrow{\Delta} 3CO\uparrow + 3H_2O\uparrow$

8) Answer: $Ba + 2H_2O \rightarrow Ba(OH)_2 + H_2\uparrow$

9) Answer: $2Au_2O_3 \rightarrow 4Au + 3O_2\uparrow$

10) Answer: $2Na_3PO_4 + 3ZnSO_4 \rightarrow 3Na_2SO_4 + Zn_3(PO_4)_2\downarrow$

11) Answer: $2Al + 3Cl_2 \rightarrow 2AlCl_3$

12) Answer: $CH_4 + 2O_2 \xrightarrow{\Delta} CO_2\uparrow + 2H_2O\uparrow$

13) Answer: $Fe_2(SO_4)_3 + 3Ba(OH)_2 \rightarrow 2Fe(OH)_3\downarrow + 3BaSO_4$

14) Answer: $2C_3H_8 + 7O_2 \rightarrow 6CO\uparrow + 8H_2O\uparrow$ (incomplete)

15) Answer: $C_2H_5OH + 3O_2 \rightarrow 2CO_2\uparrow + 3H_2O\uparrow$ (complete)

16) Answer: $2PO_4^{3-}(aq) + 3Ca^{2+}(aq) \rightarrow 3Ca^{2+}(aq) + 2PO_4^{3-}(aq)$

Essay Questions

1) Answer: Whether one metal will replace another is determined by the relative reactivity of the two metals. The activity series of metals lists metals in order of decreasing reactivity. A reactive metal will replace any metal found below it in the activity series.

Chapter 9 Stoichiometry
Matching Questions
Chapter 9: Matching I

1) actual yield

2) percent yield

3) theoretical yield

4) excess reagent

5) limiting reagent

A) the ratio of the actual yield to the theoretical yield

B) quantity of a reactant that is more than enough to react with a limiting reagent

C) the reactant that determines the amount of product that can be formed in a reaction

D) the calculated amount of product formed during a reaction

E) the amount of product formed when a reaction is carried out in the laboratory

Multiple Choice and Bimodal Questions

1) The calculation of quantities in chemical equations is called _____.

   A) accuracy and precision
   B) dimensional analysis
   C) percent composition
   D) percent yield
   E) stoichiometry

2) What is conserved in the reaction shown below?
   $H_2(g) + Cl_2(g) \rightarrow 2HCl(g)$

   A) only mass
   B) only mass and moles
   C) only mass, moles, and molecules
   D) only mass, moles, molecules and volume

3) What is conserved in the reaction shown below?
   $N_2(g) + 3F_2(g) \rightarrow 2NF_3(g)$

   A) only atoms

   B) only mass

   C) only mass and atoms

   D) only moles

   E) only mass, atoms, moles, and molecules

4) In every chemical reaction, _____.

   A) mass and molecules are conserved

   B) moles and liters are conserved

   C) mass and atoms are conserved

   D) moles and molecules are conserved

   E) mass and liters are conserved

5) Which of the following statements is true about the total number of reactants and the total number of products in this reaction?
   $C_5H_{12}(l) + 8O_2(g) \rightarrow 5CO_2(g) + 6H_2O(g)$

   A) 9 moles of reactants regroup to form 11 moles of product

   B) 9 grams of reactants regroup to form 11 grams of product

   C) 9 liters of reactants regroup to form 11 liters of product

   D) 9 atoms of reactants regroup to form 11 atoms of product

   E) 22.4 liters of reactants regroup to form 22.4 liters of product

6) Which of these is an INCORRECT interpretation of this balanced equation?
   $2S(s) + 3O_2(g) \rightarrow 2SO_3(g)$

   A) 2 atoms S + 3 molecules $O_2 \rightarrow$ 2 molecules SO_3

   B) 2 g S + 3 g $O_2 \rightarrow$ 2 g SO_3

   C) 2 mol S + 3 mol $O_2 \rightarrow$ 2 mol SO_3

   D) none of the above

7) In a chemical reaction the mass of the products _____.

   A) is less than the mass of the reactants

   B) is greater than the mass of the reactants

   C) is equal to the mass of the reactants

   D) has no relationship to the mass of the reactants

8) In any chemical reaction the quantities that are preserved are _____.

   A) the number of moles and the volumes

   B) the number of molecules and the volumes

   C) mass and number of atoms

   D) mass and moles

9) How many liters of oxygen are required to react completely with 3.6 liters of hydrogen to form water?

$2H_2(g) + O_2(g) \rightarrow 2H_2O(g)$

   A) 1.8 L   B) 3.6 L   C) 2.0 L   D) 2.4 L

10) How many moles of aluminum are needed to react completely with 1.2 mol of FeO?

$2Al(s) + 3FeO(s) \rightarrow 3Fe(s) + Al_2O_3(s)$

   A) 1.2 mol   B) 0.8 mol   C) 1.6 mol   D) 2.4 mol   E) 4.8 mol

11) Calculate the number of moles of Al_2O_3 that are produced when 0.60 mol of Fe is produced in the following reaction.

$2Al(s) + 3FeO(s) \rightarrow 3Fe(s) + Al_2O_3(s)$

   A) 0.20 mol   B) 0.40 mol   C) 0.60 mol   D) 0.90 mol   E) 1.8 mol

12) How many moles of glucose, $C_6H_{12}O_6$, can be "burned" biologically when 10.0 mol of oxygen is available?

$C_6H_{12}O_6(s) + 6O_2(g) \rightarrow 6CO_2(g) + 6H_2O(l)$

   A) 0.938 mol   B) 1.67 mol   C) 53.3 mol   D) 60.0 mol   E) 301 mol

13) Hydrogen gas can be produced by reacting aluminum with sulfuric acid. How many moles of sulfuric acid are needed to completely react with 15.0 mol of aluminum?

$2Al(s) + 3H_2SO_4(aq) \rightarrow Al_2(SO_4)_3(aq) + 3H_2(g)$

   A) 0.100 mol   B) 10.0 mol   C) 15.0 mol   D) 22.5 mol   E) 2710 mol

14) When iron rusts in air, iron(III) oxide is produced. How many moles of oxygen react with 2.4 mol of iron in the rusting reaction?

$4Fe(s) + 3O_2(g) \rightarrow 2Fe_2O_3(s)$

   A) 1.2 mol   B) 1.8 mol   C) 2.4 mol   D) 3.2 mol   E) 4.8 mol

15) Iron(III) oxide is formed when iron combines with oxygen in the air. How many grams of Fe_2O_3 are formed when 16.7 g of Fe reacts completely with oxygen?

$4Fe(s) + 3O_2(g) \rightarrow 2Fe_2O_3(s)$

   A) 12.0 g   B) 23.9 g   C) 47.8 g   D) 95.6 g   E) 267 g

16) When glucose is consumed it reacts with oxygen in the body to produce carbon dioxide, water, and energy. How many grams of carbon dioxide would be produced if 45 g of $C_6H_{12}O_6$ completely reacted with oxygen?

   A) 1.5 g   B) 1.8 g   C) 11 g   D) 66 g   E) 12 000 g

17) Aluminum reacts with sulfuric acid to produce aluminum sulfate and hydrogen gas. How many grams of aluminum sulfate would be formed if 250 g H_2SO_4 completely reacted with aluminum?

$2Al(s) + 3H_2SO_4(aq) \rightarrow Al_2(SO_4)_3(aq) + 3H_2(g)$

   A) 0.85 g   B) 290 g   C) 450 g   D) 870 g   E) 2600 g

18) Mercury can be obtained by reacting mercury(II) sulfide with calcium oxide. How many grams of calcium oxide are needed to produce 36.0 g of Hg?

$4HgS(s) + 4CaO(s) \rightarrow 4Hg(l) + 3CaS(s) + CaSO_4$

  A) 1.80 g   B) 7.56 g   C) 10.1 g   D) 13.4 g   E) 36.0 g

19) How many moles of H_3PO_4 are produced when 71.0 g P_4O_{10} reacts completely to form H_3PO_4?

$P_4O_{10}(s) + 6H_2O(l) \rightarrow 4H_3PO_4(aq)$

  A) 0.063 5 mol

  B) 1.00 mol

  C) 4.00 mol

  D) 16.0 mol

  E) 98.0 mol

20) How many grams of H_3PO_4 are produced when 10.0 moles of water react with an excess of P_4O_{10}?

$P_4O_{10}(s) + 6H_2O(l) \rightarrow 4H_3PO_4(aq)$

  A) 1.22 g   B) 6.7 g   C) 147 g   D) 653 g   E) 1180 g

21) How many grams of chromium are needed to react with an excess of $CuSO_4$ to produce 27.0 g Cu?

$2Cr(s) + 3CuSO_4(aq) \rightarrow Cr_2(SO_4)_3(aq) + 3Cu(s)$

  A) 0.005 48 g   B) 14.7 g   C) 18.0 g   D) 33.2 g   E) 81.5 g

22) The equation below shows the decomposition of lead nitrate. How many grams of oxygen are produced when 11.5 g NO_2 is formed?

$2Pb(NO_3)_2(s) \rightarrow 2PbO(s) + 4NO_2(g) + O_2(g)$

  A) 1.00 g   B) 2.00 g   C) 2.88 g   D) 32.0 g   E) 46.0 g

23) How many grams of beryllium are needed to produce 36.0 g of hydrogen? (Assume an excess of water.)

$Be(s) + 2H_2O(l) \rightarrow Be(OH)_2 (aq) + H_2(g)$

  A) 4.00 g   B) 36.0 g   C) 162 g   D) 324 g   E) 648 g

24) How many liters of NH_3, at STP, will react with 5.3 g O_2 to form NO_2 and water?

$4NH_3(g) + 7O_2(g) \rightarrow 4NO_2 + 6H_2O(g)$

  A) 0.004 23 L   B) 2.12 L   C) 3.03 L   D) 6.49 L   E) 77.3 L

25) How many liters of hydrogen gas are needed to react with CS_2 to produce 2.50 L of CH_4, at STP?

$4H_2(g) + CS_2(l) \rightarrow CH_4(g) + 2H_2S(g)$

  A) 2.50 L   B) 0.625 L   C) 5.00 L   D) 7.50 L   E) 10.0 L

26) How many liters of chlorine gas can be produced when 0.98 L of HCl react with excess O_2, at STP?
$$4HCl(g) + O_2(g) \rightarrow 2Cl_2(g) + 2H_2O(g)$$

A) 0.98 L B) 0.49 L C) 3.9 L D) 2.0 L E) 0.25 L

27) Which conversion factor do you use first to calculate the number of grams of CO_2 produced by the reaction of 50.6 g of CH_4 with O_2? The equation for the complete combustion of methane is:
$$CH_4(g) + 2O_2(g) \rightarrow CO_2(g) + 2H_2O(l)$$

A) $\dfrac{1 \text{ mol } CH_4}{16.0 \text{ g } CH_4}$ B) $\dfrac{2 \text{ mol } O_2}{1 \text{ mol } CO_2}$ C) $\dfrac{16.0 \text{ g } CH_4}{1 \text{ mol } CO_4}$ D) $\dfrac{44.0 \text{ g } CO_2}{2 \text{ mol } CO_2}$

28) Which type of stoichiometric calculation does not require the use of the gram formula mass?

A) mass–mass problems   B) mass–volume problems

C) mass–particle problems   D) volume–volume problems

29) The first step in most stoichiometry problems is to

A) add the coefficients of the reagents.   B) convert given quantities to moles.

C) convert given quantities to volumes.   D) convert given quantities to masses.

30) Which of the following statements is true about the following reaction?
$$3NaHCO_3(aq) + C_6H_8O_7(aq) \rightarrow 3CO_2(g) + 3H_2O(s) + Na_3C_6H_5O_7(aq)$$

A) 22.4 L of CO_2(g) are produced for every liter of $C_6H_8O_7$(aq) reacted

B) 1 mole of water is produced for every mole of carbon dioxide produced

C) 6.02 x 10^{23} molecules of $Na_3C_6H_5O_7$(aq) are produced for every mole of $NaHCO_3$(aq) used

D) 54 g of water is produced for every mole of $NaHCO_3$(aq) produced

31) How many liters of NH_3 are needed to react completely with 30.0 L of NO (at STP)?
$$4NH_3(g) + 6NO(g) \rightarrow 5N_2(g) + 6H_2O(g)$$

A) 5.0 L B) 20.0 L C) 7.5 L D) 120.0 L E) 180.0 L

32) When 0.2 mol of calcium reacts with 880 g of water, 2.24 L of hydrogen gas form (at STP). How would the amount of hydrogen produced change if the volume of water was decreased to 440 mL (440 g)?

A) Only one half the volume of hydrogen would be produced.

B) The volume of hydrogen produced would be the same.

C) The volume of hydrogen produced would double.

D) No hydrogen would be produced.

33) Identify the limiting reagent and the volume of product formed when 11 L CS_2 reacts with 18 L O_2 to produce CO_2 gas and SO_2 gas.

$$CS_2(g) + 3O_2(g) \rightarrow CO_2(g) + 2SO_2(g)$$

  A) CS_2; 5.5 L CO_2
  B) O_2; 6.0 L CO_2
  C) CS_2; 11 L CO_2
  D) O_2; 27 L SO_2
  E) O_2; 54 L CO_2

34) What is the maximum number of grams of PH_3 that can be formed when 6.2 g of phosphorus reacts with 4.0 g of hydrogen to form PH_3?

$$P_4(g) + 6H_2(g) \rightarrow 4PH_3(g)$$

  A) 0.43 g   B) 6.8 g   C) 270 g   D) 45 g   E) 99 g

35) Methane and hydrogen sulfide form when hydrogen reacts with carbon disulfide. Identify the excess reagent and calculate how much remains after 36 L of H_2 reacts with 12 L of CS_2.

$$4H_2(g) + CS_2(g) \rightarrow CH_4(g) + 2H_2S(g)$$

  A) 3 L CS_2 B) 6 L CS_2 C) 9 L CS_2 D) 12 L H_2 E) 24 L H_2

36) Metallic copper is formed when aluminum reacts with copper(II) sulfate. How many grams of metallic copper can be obtained when 54.0 g of Al reacts with 319 g of $CuSO_4$?

$$2Al + 3CuSO_4 \rightarrow Al_2(SO_4)_3 + 3Cu$$

  A) 21.2 g   B) 127 g   C) 162 g   D) 381 g   E) 957 g

37) Lead nitrate can be decomposed by heating. What is the percent yield of the decomposition reaction if 9.9 g $Pb(NO_3)_2$ is heated to give 5.5 g of PbO?

$$2Pb(NO_3)_2(s) \rightarrow 2PbO(s) + 4NO_2(g) + O_2(g)$$

  A) 18%   B) 44%   C) 56%   D) 67%   E) 82%

38) Hydrogen gas is produced when zinc reacts with hydrochloric acid. If the actual yield of this reaction is 85%, how many grams of zinc are needed to produce 112 L of H_2 at STP?

$$Zn(s) + 2HCl(aq) \rightarrow ZnCl_2(s) + H_2(g)$$

  A) 2.2 g   B) 95 g   C) 180 g   D) 280 g   E) 380 g

39) In a particular reaction between copper metal and silver nitrate, 12.7 g Cu produced 38.1 g Ag. What is the percent yield of silver in this reaction?

$$Cu + 2AgNO_3 \rightarrow Cu(NO_3)_2 + 2Ag$$

  A) 29.4%   B) 56.7%   C) 77.3%   D) 88.2%   E) 176%

40) In the reaction $2CO(g) + O_2(g) \rightarrow 2CO_2(g)$, what is the ratio of moles of oxygen used to moles of CO_2 produced?

  A) 1:1   B) 2:1   C) 1:2   D) 2:2

41) Glucose, $C_6H_{12}O_6$, is a good source of food energy. When it reacts with oxygen, carbon dioxide, and water are formed. How many liters of CO_2 are produced when 126 g of glucose completely reacts with oxygen?
$C_6H_{12}O_6(s) + 6O_2(g) \rightarrow 6CO_2(g) + 6H_2O(l) + 673$ kcal

   A) 4.21 L   B) 5.33 L   C) 15.7 L   D) 94.1 L   E) 185 L

42) Calcium oxide, or lime, is produced by the thermal decomposition of limestone in the reaction:

$CaCO_3(s) \xrightarrow{\Delta} CaO(s) + CO_2(g)$.

What mass of lime can be produced from 1.5×10^3 kg of limestone?
   A) 8.4×10^5 kg   B) 8.4×10^2 kg
   C) 8.4 kg   D) Not enough information given.

43) When two substances react to form products, the reactant which is used up is called the
_____.

   A) determining reagent

   B) limiting reagent

   C) excess reagent

   D) catalytic reagent

   E) reactive reagent

44) Which of the following is NOT a true statement concerning limiting and excess reagents?

   A) The amount of product obtained is determined by the limiting reagent.

   B) A balanced equation is necessary to determine which reactant is the limiting reagent.

   C) Some of the excess reagent is left over after the reaction is complete.

   D) The reactant that has the smallest given mass is the limiting reagent.

   E) Adding more of the limiting reagent to the reaction chamber will cause more product to be produced.

45) Which statement is true if 12 mol CO and 12 mol Fe_2O_3 are allowed to react?
$3CO(g) + Fe_2O_3(s) \rightarrow 2Fe(s) + 3CO_2(g)$

   A) The limiting reagent is CO and 8.0 mol Fe will be formed.

   B) The limiting reagent is CO and 3.0 mol CO_2 will be formed.

   C) The limiting reagent is Fe_2O_3 and 24 mol Fe will be formed.

   D) The limiting reagent is Fe_2O_3 and 36 mol CO_2 will be formed.

   E) The limiting reagent is Fe and 18 mol CO_2 will be formed.

46) When an equation is used to calculate the amount of product that will form during a reaction, then the value obtained is called the _____.

   A) actual yield

   B) percent yield

   C) theoretical yield

   D) minimum yield

   E) percent composition

47) Which of the following is NOT a true statement about "yield"?

    A) The value of the actual yield must be given in order for the percent yield to be calculated.

    B) The actual yield is often less than the theoretical yield.

    C) The percent yield is the ratio of the actual yield to the theoretical yield.

    D) The actual yield may be different from the theoretical yield because reactions do not always go to completion.

    E) The actual yield may be different from the theoretical yield because insufficient limiting reagent was used.

48) Which of the following would be the limiting reagent in the reaction:
$$2H_2(g) + O_2(g) \rightarrow 2H_2O(g)$$

    A) 50 molecules of H_2

    B) 50 molecules of O_2

    C) Neither a nor b is limiting.

49) For a given chemical reaction, the theoretical yield is _____ greater than the actual yield.

    A) sometimes   B) always   C) never

50) The reagent present in the smallest amount is _____ the limiting reagent.

    A) always   B) sometimes   C) never

51) Which of the following is not a reason why actual yield is less than theoretical yield?

    A) impure reactants present   B) competing side reactions

    C) loss of product during purification   D) conservation of mass

Problems

1) How many grams of CO are needed to react with an excess of Fe_2O_3 to produce 591 g Fe?
$$Fe_2O_3(s) + 3CO(g) \rightarrow 3CO_2(g) + 2Fe(s)$$

2) What is the limiting reagent when 150 0 g of nitrogen reacts with 32.1 g of hydrogen?
$$N_2(g) + 3H_2(g) \rightarrow 2NH_3(g)$$

3) A 500 g sample of $Al_2(SO_4)_3$ is reacted with 450 g of $Ca(OH)_2$. A total of 596 g of $CaSO_4$ is produced. What is the limiting reagent in this reaction, and how many moles of excess reagent are unreacted?
$$Al_2(SO_4)_3(aq) + 3Ca(OH)_2(aq) \rightarrow 2Al(OH)_3(s) + 3CaSO_4(s)$$

4) How many liters of O_2 are needed to react completely with 45.0 L of H_2S at STP?
$$2H_2S(g) + 3O_2(g) \rightarrow 2SO_2(g) + 2H_2O(g)$$

5) If 5.0 g of H_2 are reacted with excess CO, how many grams of CH_3OH are produced, based on a yield of 86%?
$$CO(g) + 2H_2(g) \rightarrow CH_3OH(l)$$

6) The decomposition of potassium chlorate yields oxygen gas. If the yield is 95%, how many grams of $KClO_3$ are needed to produce 10.0 L of O_2?

$$2KClO_3(s) \rightarrow 2KCl(s) + 3O_2(g)$$

7) When a mixture of sulfur and metallic silver is heated, silver sulfide is produced. What mass of silver sulfide is produced from a mixture of 3.0 g Ag and 3.0 g S_8?

$$16Ag(s) + S_8(s) \rightarrow 8Ag_2S(s)$$

8) For the reaction $2Na + Cl_2 \rightarrow 2NaCl$, how many grams of NaCl could be produced from 103.0 g of Na and 13.0 L of Cl_2 (at STP)?

9) Solid sodium reacts violently with water, producing heat, hydrogen gas, and sodium hydroxide. How many molecules of hydrogen gas are formed when 11.3 g of sodium are added to water?

$$2Na + 2H_2O \rightarrow 2NaOH + H_2$$

Essay Questions

1) What is the importance of the coefficients in a balanced chemical reaction?

2) In which kind of stoichiometric calculation can the steps involving conversion to and from moles be omitted? Explain why it is possible to do so.

Chapter 9 Stoichiometry

Matching Questions

    1) Answer: E

    2) Answer: A

    3) Answer: D

    4) Answer: B

    5) Answer: C

Multiple Choice and Bimodal Questions

    1) Answer: E

    2) Answer: D

    3) Answer: C

    4) Answer: C

    5) Answer: A

    6) Answer: B

    7) Answer: C

    8) Answer: C

    9) Answer: A

  10) Answer: B

  11) Answer: A

  12) Answer: B

  13) Answer: D

  14) Answer: B

  15) Answer: B

  16) Answer: D

  17) Answer: B

  18) Answer: C

  19) Answer: B

  20) Answer: D

  21) Answer: B

  22) Answer: B

  23) Answer: C

  24) Answer: B

  25) Answer: E

  26) Answer: B

  27) Answer: A

  28) Answer: D

  29) Answer: B

  30) Answer: B

  31) Answer: B

  32) Answer: B

  33) Answer: B

  34) Answer: B

  35) Answer: A

36) Answer: B

37) Answer: E

38) Answer: E

39) Answer: D

40) Answer: C

41) Answer: D

42) Answer: B

43) Answer: B

44) Answer: D

45) Answer: A

46) Answer: C

47) Answer: E

48) Answer: B

49) Answer: B

50) Answer: B

51) Answer: D

Problems

1) Answer: $591 \text{ g Fe} \times \dfrac{1 \text{ mol Fe}}{55.8 \text{ g Fe}} \times \dfrac{3 \text{ mol CO}}{2 \text{ mol Fe}} \times \dfrac{28 \text{ g CO}}{1 \text{ mol CO}} = 445 \text{ g CO}$

2) Answer: $150.0 \text{ g N}_2 \times \dfrac{1 \text{ mol N}_2}{28 \text{ g N}_2} = 5.36 \text{ mol N}_2$

$32.1 \text{ g H}_2 \times \dfrac{1 \text{ mol H}_2}{2 \text{ g H}_2} = 16.1 \text{ mol H}_2$

$\dfrac{5.36 \text{ mol N}_2}{16.1 \text{ mol H}_2} = \dfrac{1 \text{ mol N}_2}{3 \text{ mol H}_2}$

There is no limiting reagent because the mole ratio of the reactants is 1 mol N_2 to 3 mol H_2.

3) Answer: $500 \text{ g Al}_2(\text{SO}_4)_3 \times \dfrac{1 \text{ mol Al}_2(\text{SO}_4)_3}{342 \text{ g Al}_2(\text{SO}_4)_3} \times \dfrac{3 \text{ mol Ca(OH)}_2}{1 \text{ mol Al}_2(\text{SO}_4)_3} \times \dfrac{74 \text{ g Ca(OH)}_2}{1 \text{ mol Ca(OH)}_2}$

$= 325 \text{ g Ca(OH)}_2$

$450 \text{ g} - 325 \text{ g} = 125 \text{ g excess Ca(OH)}_2.$

$\text{Al}_2(\text{SO}_4)_3$ is the limiting reagent.

$125 \text{ g Ca(OH)}_2 \times \dfrac{1 \text{ mol Ca(OH)}_2}{74 \text{ g Ca(OH)}_2} = 1.69 \text{ mol Ca(OH)}_2 \text{ remaining}$

4) Answer: $45.0 \text{ L H}_2\text{S} \times \dfrac{1 \text{ mol H}_2\text{S}}{22.4 \text{ L H}_2\text{S}} \times \dfrac{3 \text{ mol O}_2}{2 \text{ mol H}_2\text{S}} \times \dfrac{22.4 \text{ L O}_2}{1 \text{ mol O}_2} = 67.5 \text{ L O}_2$

5) Answer: Theoretical yield:

$5.0 \text{ g H}_2 \times \dfrac{1 \text{ mol H}_2}{2.0 \text{ g H}_2} \times \dfrac{1 \text{ mol CH}_3\text{OH}}{2 \text{ mol H}_2} \times \dfrac{32 \text{ g CH}_3\text{OH}}{1 \text{ mol CH}_3\text{OH}}$

$= 40 \text{ g CH}_3\text{OH}$

$40 \text{ g CH}_3\text{OH} \times 86\% = 34 \text{ g CH}_3\text{OH}$

6) Answer: $10.0 \text{ L} \times \dfrac{100\%}{95\%} = 10.5 \text{ L}$ theoretical yield

$$10.5 \text{ L O}_2 \times \frac{1 \text{ mol O}_2}{22.4 \text{ L O}_2} \times \frac{2 \text{ mol KClO}_3}{3 \text{ mol O}_2} \times \frac{122.6 \text{ g KClO}_3}{1 \text{mol KClO}_3}$$

$$= 38.4 \text{ g KClO}_3$$

7) Answer: Limiting reagent is silver:

$$3.0 \text{ g Ag} \times \frac{1 \text{ mol Ag}}{108 \text{ g Ag}} = 0.03 \text{ mol Ag}$$

$$3.0 \text{ g S}_8 \times \frac{1 \text{ mol S}_8}{256 \text{ g S}_8} = 0.01 \text{ mol S}_8$$

$$0.03 \text{ mol Ag} \times \frac{8 \text{ mol Ag}_2\text{S}}{16 \text{ mol Ag}} \times \frac{248 \text{ g Ag}_2\text{S}}{1 \text{ mol Ag}_2\text{S}} = 3.72 \text{ g Ag}_2\text{S}$$

8) Answer: $13.0 \text{ L Cl}_2 \times \dfrac{1 \text{ mol Cl}_2}{22.4 \text{ L Cl}_2} = 0.580 \text{ mol Cl}_2$

$$103.0 \text{ g Na} \times \frac{1 \text{ mol Na}}{23 \text{ g Na}} = 4.48 \text{ mol Na}$$

Cl_2 is limiting reagent: $0.580 \text{ mol Cl}_2 \times \dfrac{2 \text{ mol NaCl}}{1 \text{ mol Cl}_2} = 1.16 \text{ mol NaCl}$

$$1.16 \text{ mol NaCl} \times \frac{58 \text{ g NaCl}}{1 \text{ mol NaCl}} = 67.3 \text{ g NaCl}$$

9) Answer: Assume the sodium is limiting:

$$11.3 \text{ g Na} \times \frac{1 \text{ mol H}_2}{2 \text{ mol Na}} \times \frac{6.02 \times 10^{23} \text{ molecules H}_2}{1 \text{ mol H}_2}$$

$$= 2.1 \times 10^{17} \text{ molecules H}_2$$

Essay Questions

1) Answer: The coefficients in a balanced chemical equation indicate the relative number of moles of reactants and products. From this information the amounts of reactants and products can be calculated. The number of moles may be converted to mass, volume, or number of representative particles.

2) Answer: Volume–volume conversions between gases do not require mole conversions. Molar volumes of all gases at STP are the same. The coefficients in a balanced equation indicate the relative number of moles and the relative volumes of interacting gases.

Chapter 10 States of Matter

Matching Questions
Chapter 10: Matching I

1) unit cell

2) crystal

3) allotropes

4) amorphous solid

A) a solid that lacks an ordered internal structure

B) two or more different molecular forms of an element in the same state

C) the smallest group of particles within a crystal that retains the shape of the crystal

D) a solid in which the atoms, ions, or molecules are arranged in an orderly pattern

Chapter 10: Matching II

5) melting point

6) boiling point

7) phase change

8) evaporation

9) vaporization

10) normal boiling point

A) the temperature at which a solid turns into a liquid

B) the conversion of a liquid to a gas below the boiling point

C) the temperature at which the vapor pressure of a liquid is equal to 1 atmosphere

D) the term for a change in the physical state of a substance

E) the vaporization of an uncontained liquid

F) the temperature at which the vapor pressure of a liquid is just equal to the external pressure

11) kinetic theory

12) atmospheric pressure

13) vapor pressure

14) barometer

15) kinetic energy

A) the pressure above a liquid in a sealed container caused by collision of vaporized particles with the walls of the container

B) the energy an object has due to its motion

C) the pressure resulting from the collision of air molecules with objects

D) a device used to measure atmospheric pressure

E) the assertion that the tiny particles in all forms of matter are in constant motion

Multiple Choice and Bimodal Questions

1) What happens to the range of energies of the molecules in matter when the temperature is increased?

   A) It becomes narrower.   B) It becomes broader.   C) It does not change.

2) What happens to the average kinetic energy of the particles in a sample of matter as the temperature of the sample is increased?

   A) It decreases.   B) It increases.   C) It does not change.

3) Consider an iron ball and an aluminum ball. If the two balls were at the same temperature, how would the average kinetic energy of the iron atoms compare with the average kinetic energy of the aluminum atoms?

   A) The average kinetic energy of the iron atoms would be greater.

   B) The average kinetic energy of the aluminum atoms would be greater.

   C) There would be no difference in the average kinetic energies.

   D) No determination can be made on the basis of the information given.

4) Which temperature scale provides a direct measure of the average kinetic energy of a substance?

   A) Celsius   B) Fahrenheit   C) Kelvin

5) What instrument is normally used to measure atmospheric pressure?

   A) thermistor   B) barometer   C) hydrometer   D) spectrometer

6) What is the SI unit of pressure?

   A) candela   B) mole   C) pascal   D) newton   E) joule

7) How does the atmospheric pressure at altitudes below sea level compare with atmospheric pressure at sea level?

   A) The atmospheric pressure below sea level is higher.

   B) The atmospheric pressure below sea level is lower.

   C) The pressures are the same.

8) What volume does 3.00 moles of gas particles occupy at STP?

   A) 3.00 L

   B) 3.40 L

   C) 33.6 L

   D) 67.2 L

   E) 1.00×10^2 L

9) What is the volume occupied by 2.20 mol of hydrogen at STP?

   A) 2.20 L   B) 24.6 L   C) 49.3 L   D) 98.6 L   E) 2.60 L

10) What is the number of moles of gas in 20.0 L of oxygen at STP?

   A) 30.0 mol   B) 20.0 mol   C) 3.57 mol   D) 1.79 mol   E) 0.893 mol

11) What is the number of molecules of nitrogen in 11.2 L at STP?

   A) 1×10^{23} molecules

   B) 3×10^{23} molecules

   C) 6×10^{23} molecules

   D) 12×10^{23} molecules

   E) 18×10^{23} molecules

12) What is the volume occupied by 14.0×10^{23} molecules of fluorine at STP?

   A) 13.0 L   B) 26.0 L   C) 39.1 L   D) 52.1 L   E) 104 L

13) What is the volume occupied by 71 g of chlorine gas at STP?

   A) 22.4 L   B) 44.8 L   C) 56.0 L   D) 67.2 L   E) 78.4 L

14) What is the number of grams of neon present in 78.4 L of neon at STP?

   A) 20 g   B) 35 g   C) 70 g   D) 105 g   E) 140 g

15) Which of the following best describes the motion of iron atoms in a piece of steel?

   A) All are at rest.   B) A few are moving.   C) All are moving.

16) Collisions between gas molecules are _____.

    A) elastic   B) inelastic   C) never observed

17) The average speed of oxygen molecules in air is approximately _____.

    A) 0 km/hr   B) 170 km/hr   C) 1700 km/hr   D) 17 000 km/hr

18) How far can a molecule travel in air before it collides with another molecule?

    A) much less than a meter

    B) about a meter

    C) much more than a meter

19) The average kinetic energy of water molecules is greatest in _____.

    A) steam at 200°C   B) water at 90°C   C) water at 373 K   D) ice at 0°C

20) According to the kinetic theory of gases _____.

    A) the particles of a gas move independently of each other

    B) the particles in a gas move rapidly

    C) the particles in a gas are far apart

    D) all of the above

21) Which of these statements is NOT true, according to the kinetic theory?

    A) There is no attraction between particles of a gas.

    B) Only particles of matter in the gaseous state are in constant motion.

    C) The particles of a gas collide with each other and with other objects.

22) When a gas is heated _____.

    A) all of the absorbed thermal energy is converted to kinetic energy

    B) some of the absorbed thermal energy is converted to the internal energy of the gas particles, and some is converted to kinetic energy

    C) all of the absorbed thermal energy is converted to potential energy

    D) one–half the absorbed thermal energy is converted to potential energy and the other half is converted to kinetic energy

23) The average kinetic energy of the particles of a substance is _____.

    A) not affected by the temperature of the substance

    B) raised as the temperature of the substance is lowered

    C) proportional to the temperature of the substance

    D) equal to the total thermal energy absorbed by the substance

24) The temperature at which the motion of particles theoretically ceases is _____.

    A) –273 K   B) 0 K   C) 0°C   D) 273°C

25) What is the pressure of one standard atmosphere?

    A) 0 kPa   B) 10.1 kPa   C) 101 kPa   D) 1010 kPa

26) Standard conditions when working with gases are defined as _____.

    A) 0 K and 101 kPa   B) 0 K and 10 kPa

    C) 0°C and 101 kPa   D) 0°C and 10 kPa

27) The pressure of a gas in a container is 152 mm Hg. This is equivalent to _____.

    A) 0.2 atm   B) 2 atm   C) 0.3 atm   D) 0.4 atm

28) Compared with 1 mole of chlorine gas at STP, 1 mole of hydrogen gas at STP occupies _____.

    A) more volume   B) less volume   C) the same volume

29) It is possible for equal volumes of gases, at the same temperature and pressure, to contain equal numbers of particles because _____.

    A) gas particles are far apart

    B) gas molecules are large

    C) the volume of a gas molecule is inversely proportional to its mass

    D) This is not actually possible.

30) Equal volumes of nitrogen and oxygen, at the same temperature and pressure, would _____.

    A) have the same mass   B) contain the same number of particles

    C) contain different numbers of particles   D) have different average kinetic energies

31) Which states of matter can flow?

    A) gases only   B) liquids only

    C) gases and liquids only   D) gases, liquids, and solids

32) What happens to the temperature of a liquid as it evaporates?

    A) It increases.   B) It decreases.   C) It does not change.

33) What happens to the evaporation rate of a liquid as the liquid is cooled?

    A) It increases.   B) It decreases.   C) It is unchanged.

34) Why does a liquid's evaporation rate increase when the liquid is heated?

    A) because more surface molecules have enough energy to overcome the attractive forces holding them in the liquid

    B) because the average kinetic energy of the liquid decreases

    C) because the surface area of the liquid is reduced

    D) because the potential energy of the liquid increases

35) When the external pressure is 505 kPa, what is the vapor pressure of water at its boiling point?

    A) 0 kPa   B) 101 kPa   C) 505 kPa   D) 1010 kPa

36) If heat is added to a boiling liquid, what happens to the temperature of the liquid?

    A) It increases.   B) It decreases.   C) It does not change.

37) What types of forces exist between particles of a liquid?

    A) weak attractive forces   B) strong attractive forces

    C) weak repulsive forces   D) strong repulsive forces

38) What are the condensed states of matter?

    A) solid only   B) solid and liquid only   C) solid, liquid, and gas

39) The first particles to evaporate from a liquid are _____.

    A) those with the lowest kinetic energy

    B) those with the highest kinetic energy

    C) those farthest from the surface of the liquid

40) Which of the following will evaporate the fastest?

    A) water at 0°C

    B) water at 20°C

    C) water at 40°C

    D) all of the above evaporate at the same rate.

41) If a liquid is sealed in a container and kept at constant temperature, how does its vapor pressure change over time?

    A) It rises continuously.

    B) It rises at first, then remains constant.

    C) It rises at first, then falls.

42) In a dynamic equilibrium between the liquid state and the gas state, the rate of evaporation is _____.

    A) greater than the rate of condensation

    B) less than the rate of condensation

    C) equal to the rate of condensation

43) An increase in the temperature of a contained liquid _____.

    A) has no effect on the kinetic energy of the liquid

    B) decreases the vapor pressure of the liquid

    C) causes fewer particles to escape the surface of the liquid

    D) causes the vapor pressure above the liquid to increase

44) The escape of gas molecules from the surface of an uncontained liquid is known as _____.

    A) boiling   B) sublimation   C) evaporation   D) condensation

45) What is the pressure when a liquid is boiling at its normal boiling point?

    A) 0 kPa   B) 101 kPa   C) 202 kPa   D) 505 kPa

46) When the vapor pressure of a liquid is equal to the atmospheric pressure, the liquid _____.

    A) condenses   B) freezes

    C) boils   D) No change is observed.

47) Water could be made to boil at 105°C instead of 100°C by _____.
   A) applying a great deal of heat
   B) increasing the air pressure on the water
   C) decreasing the pressure on the water
   D) decreasing the air pressure above the water

48) Crystals are classified into how many different crystal systems?
   A) 3   B) 4   C) 5   D) 6   E) 7

49) The boiling points of ionic solids tend to be _____.
   A) low   B) high   C) average

50) Crystals are characterized by particular patterns that repeat _____.
   A) in one dimension only
   B) in two dimensions only
   C) in three dimensions only

51) Different crystal systems differ in the _____.
   A) angles between faces only
   B) number of equal edges of the faces only
   C) angles between faces and the number of equal edges of the faces

52) The repeating group of a crystal is called the _____.
   A) nucleus   B) unit cell   C) net   D) crystal system

53) Which of the following forms of carbon is an amorphous solid?
   A) diamond   B) graphite   C) soot

54) Glasses are sometimes called _____.
   A) supersaturated liquids   B) supercooled liquids
   C) superconductive liquids   D) transparent liquids

55) Most solids _____.
   A) are dense and incompressible   B) have high melting points
   C) are amorphous in nature   D) consist of particles in chaotic motion

56) Which of the following elements is characterized by its ability to undergo sublimation?
   A) oxygen   B) carbon   C) chlorine   D) sodium   E) iodine

57) Which of the following is NOT a phase change?
   A) sublimation   B) melting   C) diffusion   D) vaporization

58) The direct change of a substance from a solid to a gas is called _____.
   A) evaporation   B) sublimation   C) condensation   D) boiling

Problems

1) What is a pressure of 8.00 atm equal to in mm Hg?

2) What is a pressure of 555 mm Hg equal to in atm?

3) What is the volume of 0.060 mol of neon gas at STP?

4) How many moles of argon atoms are present in 11.7 L of argon gas at STP?

5) How many molecules are present in 33.0 L of nitrogen gas at STP?

6) What is the volume occupied by 3.00×10^{23} molecules of oxygen gas at STP?

7) How many nitrogen molecules are in 7.02 L of nitrogen gas at STP?

8) Determine the volume in liters occupied by 22.6 g of Cl_2 gas at STP.

Essay Questions

1) Name the three basic assumptions of the kinetic theory.

2) Explain why the pressure exerted by a gas does not depend on the size of the gas particles.

3) Explain why a liquid will eventually evaporate completely if held at a constant temperature below its boiling point.

Chapter 10 States of Matter

Matching Questions

1) Answer: C
2) Answer: D
3) Answer: B
4) Answer: A
5) Answer: A
6) Answer: F
7) Answer: D
8) Answer: E
9) Answer: B
10) Answer: C
11) Answer: E
12) Answer: C
13) Answer: A
14) Answer: D
15) Answer: B

Multiple Choice and Bimodal Questions

1) Answer: B
2) Answer: B
3) Answer: C
4) Answer: C
5) Answer: B
6) Answer: C
7) Answer: A
8) Answer: D
9) Answer: C
10) Answer: E
11) Answer: B
12) Answer: D
13) Answer: A
14) Answer: C
15) Answer: C
16) Answer: A
17) Answer: C
18) Answer: A
19) Answer: A
20) Answer: D
21) Answer: B
22) Answer: B
23) Answer: C
24) Answer: B

25) Answer: C

26) Answer: C

27) Answer: A

28) Answer: C

29) Answer: A

30) Answer: B

31) Answer: C

32) Answer: B

33) Answer: B

34) Answer: A

35) Answer: C

36) Answer: C

37) Answer: A

38) Answer: B

39) Answer: B

40) Answer: C

41) Answer: B

42) Answer: C

43) Answer: D

44) Answer: C

45) Answer: B

46) Answer: C

47) Answer: B

48) Answer: E

49) Answer: B

50) Answer: C

51) Answer: C

52) Answer: B

53) Answer: C

54) Answer: B

55) Answer: A

56) Answer: E

57) Answer: C

58) Answer: B

Problems

1) Answer: $8.00 \text{ atm} \times \dfrac{760 \text{ mm Hg}}{1 \text{ atm}} = 6080 \text{ mm Hg}$

2) Answer: $253 \text{ mm Hg} \times \dfrac{1 \text{ atm}}{760 \text{ mm Hg}} = 0.730 \text{ atm}$

3) Answer: $0.060 \text{ mol Ne} \times \dfrac{22.4 \text{ L}}{1 \text{ mol}} = 1.3 \text{ L Ne}$

4) Answer: $11.9 \text{ L Ar} \times \dfrac{1 \text{ mol}}{22.4 \text{ L}} = 0.522 \text{ mol}$

5) Answer: $33.0 \text{ L} \times \dfrac{1 \text{ mol}}{22.4 \text{ L}} \times \dfrac{6.02 \times 10^{23} \text{ molecules}}{1 \text{ mol}}$

$= 8.87 \times 10^{23}$ molecules

6) Answer: $3.00 \times 10^{23} \text{ molecules} \times \dfrac{1 \text{ mol}}{6.02 \times 10^{23} \text{ molecules}} \times \dfrac{22.4 \text{ L}}{1 \text{ mol}}$

$= 11.2 \text{ L}$

7) Answer: $7.02 \text{ L N}_2 \times \dfrac{1 \text{ mol N}_2}{22.4 \text{ L N}_2} \times \dfrac{6.02 \times 10^{23} \text{ molecules N}_2}{1 \text{ mol N}_2}$

$= 1.89 \times 10^{23}$ molecules N_2

8) Answer: $22.6 \text{ g Cl}_2 \times \dfrac{1 \text{ mol Cl}_2}{71.0 \text{ g Cl}_2} \times \dfrac{22.4 \text{ L Cl}_2}{1.00 \text{ mol Cl}_2} = 7.13 \text{ L Cl}_2$

Essay Questions

1) Answer: The kinetic theory is based upon the assumptions that a gas is composed of particles, that these particles are in constant random motion, and that all collisions between particles are elastic.

2) Answer: Gas particles at the same temperature have the same average kinetic energy. When the same number of particles with the same average kinetic energy are contained in the same amount of space, they should exert the same pressure, regardless of their size. Also keep in mind that the particles of a gas are very far apart with nothing but space between them. No matter how large the particles are, they are still small when compared to the volume of space occupied by the gas.

3) Answer: The particles in a liquid have a range of energies. At any particular temperature, some particles of the liquid have enough energy to overcome the attractive forces at the surface of the liquid and escape to the vapor state. As the high energy particles leave, the temperature of the liquid would normally go down. However, when exposed to the environment, the liquid will absorb heat from the environment to maintain a constant temperature. As a result, additional particles of the liquid will gain enough energy to escape the liquid. This process of escape, absorption of heat, and more escape is repeated until the liquid has evaporated completely.

Chapter 11 Thermochemistry––Heat and Chemical Change

Matching Questions

Chapter 11: Matching I

1) calorimeter

2) calorie

3) joule

4) kilogram

5) liter

6) gram

A) the mass of 1 mL of water at 4°C

B) the volume of a cube 10 cm on each edge

C) SI unit of energy

D) quantity of heat needed to raise the temperature of 1 g of water by 1°C

E) the mass of 1 L of water at 4°C

F) used to measure the heat involved in a chemical process

Chapter 11: Matching II

7) enthalpy

8) specific heat

9) specific gravity

10) density

11) heat capacity

A) quantity of heat needed to change the temperature of an object by 1°C

B) ratio of mass to volume for an object

C) ratio between the density of a substance and the density of water

D) quantity of heat needed to change the temperature of 1 g of a substance by 1°C

E) heat content of a system at standard pressure

12) heat of reaction

13) heat of formation

14) Hess's Law

15) heat of fusion

16) heat of solution

A) the energy involved in the creation of a compound from its elements

B) the energy involved in dissolving a solid

C) the energy change involved in a chemical reaction

D) used to find ΔH for complicated reactions

E) the energy required to melt a solid at its melting point

Multiple Choice and Bimodal Questions

1) How many joules are there in 148 calories? (1 cal = 4.18 J)

A) 6.61 J   B) 35.4 J   C) 148 J   D) 619 J   E) 3320 J

2) What is the amount of heat required to raise the temperature of 200.0 g of aluminum by 10°C? (specific heat of aluminum = $0.21 \frac{cal}{g \times °C}$)

A) 420 cal

B) 4200 cal

C) 42 000 cal

D) 420 000 cal

E) none of the above

3) What is the specific heat of a substance if 1560 cal is required to raise the temperature of a 312–g sample by 15°C?

A) $0.033 \frac{cal}{g \times °C}$ B) $0.33 \frac{cal}{g \times °C}$ C) $0.99 \frac{cal}{g \times °C}$ D) $1.33 \frac{cal}{g \times °C}$

4) How many kilocalories of heat are required to raise the temperature of 225 g of aluminum from 20°C to 100°C? (specific heat of aluminum = $0.21 \frac{cal}{g \times °C}$)

A) 0.59 kcal   B) 3.8 kcal

C) 85 kcal   D) none of the above

5) How much heat does it take to warm 16.0 g of pure water from 90.0°C to 100.0°C? (specific heat of water = 4.18 J/g x °C)

  A) 66.9 joules   B) 669 joules   C) 160 joules   D) 16.0 joules

6) As the temperature of a sample of matter is increased, what happens to the average kinetic energy of the particles in the sample?

  A) It decreases.   B) It increases.   C) It does not change.

7) When 45 g of an alloy is dropped into 100.0 g of water at 25°C, the final temperature is 37°C. What is the specific heat of the alloy?

  A) 0.423   B) 1.77   C) 9.88   D) 48.8

8) A piece of candy has 5 Calories (or 5000 calories). If it could be burned, leaving nothing but carbon dioxide and water, how much heat would it give off?

  A) 500 calories   B) 5000 calories

  C) 5000 joules   D) Not enough information is given.

9) What is the specific heat of olive oil if it takes approximately 420 J of heat to raise the temperature of 7 g of olive oil by 30°C?

  A) greater than the specific heat of water   B) less than the specific heat of water

  C) equal to the specific heat of water   D) Not enough information given.

10) The specific heat capacity of silver is $0.24 \frac{J}{g \times °C}$. How many joules of energy are needed to warm 0.500 g of silver from 25.0°C to 27.5°C?

  A) 2.62 J   B) 0.83 J   C) 3.24 J   D) 0.192 J

11) As an object becomes hotter, the rate of heat transfer from the object to a cooler body with which it is in contact would become _____.

  A) slower

  B) faster

  C) There would be no change.

  D) No determination can be made from the information given.

12) Which of the following has the greatest heat capacity?

  A) 1000 g of water   B) 1000 g of steel   C) 1 g of water   D) 1 g of steel

13) Which of the following substances has the highest specific heat?

  A) steel   B) water   C) alcohol   D) chloroform

14) By what quantity must the heat capacity of an object be divided to obtain the specific heat of that material?

A) its mass

B) its volume

C) its temperature

D) its energy

E) its density

15) The heat capacity of an object depends in part on its _____.

A) mass   B) enthalpy

C) shape   D) potential energy

16) The amount of heat transferred from an object depends on all of the following except _____.

A) the specific heat of the object

B) the change in temperature the object undergoes

C) the initial temperature of the object

D) the mass of the object

17) When cooking food with natural gas, the energy comes from _____.

A) kinetic energy in the gas

B) chemical potential energy of the gas molecules

C) the pressure of the gas

D) the volume of the gas

18) The energy produced by burning gasoline in a car engine _____.

A) is lost as heat in the exhaust

B) is transformed into work to move the car

C) heats the parts of the engine

D) all of the above

19) A piece of metal is heated, then submerged in cool water. Which statement below describes what happens?

A) The temperature of the metal will increase.

B) The temperature of the water will increase.

C) The temperature of the water will decrease.

D) The temperature of the water will increase and the temperature of the metal will decrease.

E) The temperature of the water will decrease and the temperature of the metal will increase.

20) A calorie is _____ a joule.

A) smaller than   B) larger than   C) the same size as

21) Two objects are sitting next to each other in direct sunlight. Object A gets hotter than object B.
    A) Object A has a higher specific heat than object B.
    B) Object A has a lower specific heat than object B.
    C) Both objects have the same specific heat.

22) In an exothermic reaction, the energy stored in the chemical bonds of the reactants is _____.
    A) equal to the energy stored in the bonds of the products
    B) greater than the energy stored in the bonds of the products
    C) less than the energy stored in the bonds of the products
    D) less than the heat released
    E) less than the heat absorbed

23) Compared to 100 g of iron, a 10-g sample of iron has _____.
    A) a higher specific heat   B) a lower specific heat   C) the same specific heat

24) A process that absorbs heat is a(n) _____ process.
    A) exothermic   B) endothermic   C) polythermic   D) ectothermic

25) If you were to touch the flask in which an endothermic reaction were occurring, _____.
    A) the flask would probably feel cooler than before the reaction started
    B) the flask would probably feel warmer than before the reaction started
    C) the flask would feel the same as before the reaction started
    D) none of the above.

26) Which of the following is not a form of energy?
    A) light   B) pressure   C) heat   D) electricity

27) When gasoline is burned in an automobile engine, _____.
    A) energy is created
    B) heat energy is converted to chemical energy
    C) energy is destroyed
    D) potential energy is transformed into kinetic energy

28) Approximately how much energy must be put into a very efficient process that gives out 500 calories each second?
    A) much less than 500 calories
    B) a little less than 500 calories
    C) 500 calories
    D) a little more than 500 calories
    E) much more than 500 calories

29) In a steam turbine, not all the energy used to heat the water is converted to the kinetic energy of the moving turbine. Some energy escapes in the form of _____.

    A) electrical energy

    B) heat

    C) potential energy

    D) chemical energy

    E) mechanical energy

30) When energy is changed from one form to another, _____.

    A) some of the energy is lost entirely

    B) all of the energy can be accounted for

    C) a physical change occurs

    D) all of the energy is changed to a useful form

31) If heat is produced by a chemical system, _____.

    A) an equal amount of heat will be absorbed by the surroundings

    B) an equal amount will be absorbed by the universe

    C) an equal amount will be produced by the surroundings

    D) an equal amount will be produced by the universe

32) When your body breaks down sugar completely, it releases _____ if you burned the same amount of sugar in a flame.

    A) more heat than

    B) less heat than

    C) the same amount of heat as

33) Which of the following equations correctly represents an endothermic reaction?

    A) A + B → C + D + heat   B) A + B + heat → C + D

34) The quantity of heat required to change the temperature of 1 g of a substance by 1°C is defined as _____.

    A) a joule   B) specific heat capacity

    C) a calorie   D) density

35) Which of the following are valid units for specific heat (or specific heat capacity):

    A) $\dfrac{cal}{g \times °C}$ B) cal   C) $\dfrac{cal}{g}$ D) °C   E) $\dfrac{g \times °C}{cal}$

36) If you want to cool a hot drink, it is best to use a spoon with a relatively _____ specific heat.

    A) low

    B) high

    C) The specific heat of the spoon does not matter.

37) Calculate the energy required to produce 7.00 mol Cl_2O_7 on the basis of the following balanced equation:
$$2Cl_2(g) + 7O_2(g) + 130 \text{ kcal} \rightarrow 2Cl_2O_7(g)$$

    A) 7.00 kcal   B) 65 kcal   C) 130 kcal   D) 910 kcal   E) 455 kcal

38) What does the symbol "ΔH" stand for?
    A) the specific heat of a substance
    B) the heat capacity of a substance
    C) the heat of reaction for a chemical reaction
    D) one Calorie given off by a reaction

39) What is the standard heat of reaction for this reaction:
$$Zn(s) + Cu^{2+}(aq) \rightarrow Zn^{2+}(aq) + Cu(s)$$

(ΔH_f° for Cu^{2+} = +64.4 kJ/mol; ΔH_f° for Zn^{2+} = –152.4 kJ/mol)

    A) 216.8 kJ created per mole   B) 88.0 kJ created per mole
    C) 88.0 kJ absorbed per mole   D) 216.8 kJ absorbed per mole

40) Calculate ΔH for this reaction:
$$C_2H_4(g) + H_2(g) \rightarrow C_2H_6(g)$$

(ΔH_f° for $C_2H_4(g)$ = 52.5 kJ/mol; ΔH_f° for $C_2H_6(g)$ = –84.7 kJ/mol)

    A) –137.2 kJ   B) –32.2 kJ   C) 32.2 kJ   D) 137.2 kJ

41) If the heat involved in a chemical reaction has a negative sign, _____.
    A) heat is lost to the surroundings
    B) heat is gained from the surroundings
    C) no heat is exchanged in the process

42) Standard conditions of temperature and pressure for a thermochemical equation are _____.
    A) 0°C and 101 kPa
    B) 25°C and 101 kPa
    C) 0°C and 0 kPa
    D) 25°C and 22.4 kPa
    E) 100°C and 1000 kPa

43) The amount of heat released by the complete burning of 1 mole of a substance is the _____.
    A) specific heat   B) heat of combustion
    C) heat capacity   D) system heat

44) The following equation shows the reaction that occurs when nitroglycerine explodes.
$$4C_3H_5O_9N_3 \rightarrow 12CO_2 + 6N_2 + O_2 + 10H_2O + 1725 \text{ kcal}$$
This reaction is _____.

A) endothermic

B) exothermic

C) a combination reaction

D) a combustion reaction

45) Using the chart that gives the standard heats of formation, you can calculate the change in enthalpy for a given chemical reaction. The change in enthalpy is equal to _____.

A) ΔH_f° of products minus ΔH_f° of reactants

B) ΔH_f° of products plus ΔH_f° of reactants

C) ΔH_f° of reactants minus ΔH_f° of products

D) ΔH_f° of products divided by ΔH_f° of reactants

E) ΔH_f° of reactants divided by ΔH_f° of products

46) On what principle does calorimetry depend?

A) Hess's Law

B) Law of Conservation of Energy

C) Law of Enthalpy

D) Law of Multiple Proportions

47) The heat content of a substance is equal to the enthalpy only for a system that is at _____.

A) constant temperature

B) constant volume

C) constant pressure

D) constant mass

48) To determine the heat change for a reaction in an aqueous solution, _____.

A) you need to know the specific heat of the reactants

B) you can mix the reactants in a calorimeter and measure the temperature change

C) you need to know the mass of the reactants

D) You cannot determine the heat change for this type of reaction

49) What is the amount of heat needed to melt one mole of a solid called?

A) molar heat of fusion

B) molar heat of solidification

C) heat of reaction

D) enthalpy

50) What is the heat of solution?

A) the amount of heat required to change a solid into a liquid

B) the amount of heat absorbed or released when a solid dissolves

C) the amount of heat required to change a vapor into a liquid

D) the amount of heat released when a vapor changes into a liquid

51) When 1.0g of solid NaOH (ΔH_{soln} = –445.1 kJ/mol) dissolves in 10 L of water, how much heat is released?

   A) 445.1 kJ   B) 405.1 kJ   C) 11.1 J   D) 11.1 kJ

52) The amount of heat absorbed by a melting solid _____ the amount of heat lost by a solidifying liquid.

   A) is the same as   B) is less than   C) is greater than

53) During a phase change, the temperature of a substance _____.

   A) increases   B) decreases
   C) remains constant   D) may increase or decrease

54) The vaporization of a liquid is an _____.

   A) exothermic process   B) endothermic process

55) Heat changes can occur when _____.

   A) a substance dissolves
   B) a substance melts
   C) a substance solidifies
   D) a substance vaporizes
   E) all of the above.

56) The ΔH_{soln} is _____.

   A) always negative
   B) always positive
   C) sometimes positive, sometimes negative

57) To calculate the amount of heat absorbed as a substance melts, which of the following information is not needed?

   A) the mass of the substance   B) the specific heat of the substance
   C) the change in temperature   D) the density of the sample

58) Which of the following is transferred due to a temperature difference?

   A) chemical energy   B) mechanical energy
   C) electrical energy   D) heat

59) How much heat does it take to make the water in a teakettle boil if the water starts at 22°C?

   A) 22 calories   B) 22 joules
   C) 22 Calories   D) Not enough information given.

60) For a given substance, the molar heat of fusion _____ the molar heat of vaporization.

   A) always equals   B) is less than   C) is greater than

61) For a given substance, the molar heat of vaporization _____ the molar heat of condensation.

   A) always equals   B) is less than   C) is greater than

62) When 10 g of diethyl ether is converted to vapor at its boiling point, about how much heat is absorbed? ($C_4H_{10}O$, ΔH_{vap} = 15.7 kJ/mol, boiling point: 34.6°C)

   A) 2 kJ   B) 2 J
   C) 0.2 kJ   D) Not enough information given

63) When heat is added to boiling water, its temperature _____.

   A) increases   B) decreases
   C) stays the same   D) depends on the amount of water

64) Compared to a glass of ice water with ice in it, a glass of ice–cold water without ice will warm up _____.

   A) faster   B) slower   C) at the same rate

65) When snow melts, what happens to the surrounding air?

   A) It gets warmer.
   B) It gets cooler.
   C) Nothing happens to the surrounding air.

66) A chunk of ice whose temperature is –20°C is added to an insulated cup filled with water at 0°C. What happens in the cup?

   A) The ice melts until it reaches the temperature of the water.
   B) The water cools until it reaches the temperature of the ice.
   C) Some of the water freezes, so the chunk of ice gets larger.
   D) none of the above

67) A person tries to heat up a bath by adding 5 L of water at 80°C to 60 L of water at 30°C. The final temperature of the water is _____.

   A) greater than 80°C   B) less then 30°C   C) between 30°C and 80°C

68) What is the amount of heat involved in the creation of 1 mole of a substance from its elements called?

   A) enthalpy   B) heat of reaction
   C) standard heat of formation   D) heat of solidification

69) Calculate the energy released when 24.8 g Na_2O reacts in the following reaction.

   $Na_2O(s) + 2HI(g) \rightarrow 2NaI(s) + H_2O(l)$ ΔH = –120.00 kcal

   A) 0.207 kcal
   B) 2.42 kcal
   C) 48.0 kcal
   D) 3.00×10^2 kcal
   E) 2980 kcal

©Prentice-Hall, Inc.

70) What does the symbol ΔH°_f stand for?

    A) the specific heat of a substance
    B) the heat capacity of a substance
    C) the heat of reaction for a chemical reaction
    D) the heat of formation for a compound

71) ΔH°_f for the formation of rust (Fe_2O_3) is –826 kJ/mol. How much energy is involved in the

formation of 5 grams of rust?
    A) 25.9 kJ   B) 25.9 J   C) 66 kJ   D) 66 J

72) Calculate ΔH for the reaction of sulfur dioxide in oxygen.
    $2SO_2(g) + O_2(g) \rightarrow 2SO_3(g)$

    (ΔH°_f $SO_2(g)$ = –296.8 kJ/mol; ΔH°_f $SO_3(g)$ = –395.7 kJ/mol)

    A) –98.9 kJ   B) –197.8 kJ
    C) 197.8 kJ   D) Not enough information given

73) Hess's Law _____.
    A) makes it possible to calculate ΔH for complicated chemical reactions
    B) states that when you reverse a chemical equation, you must change the sign of ΔH
    C) determines the way a calorimeter works
    D) describes the vaporization of solids

74) For ammonia, (NH_3), ΔH°_f = –46 kJ/mol. This means that _____.

    A) it takes 46 kJ to vaporize 1 mole of liquid ammonia
    B) 46 kJ of heat is released when 1 mole of ammonia gas condenses
    C) it takes 46 kJ to form 1 mole of ammonia from nitrogen and hydrogen
    D) 46 kJ is released when 1 mole of ammonia is formed from nitrogen and hydrogen

75) Which of the following statements about ΔH° and ΔH°_f is true?

    A) ΔH° refers to a reaction while ΔH°_f refers to a compound.

    B) ΔH°_f refers to a reaction while ΔH° refers to a compound.

    C) ΔH°_f refers to the temperature at which fusion occurs.

    D) ΔH° is zero for a free element.

76) The heat of formation for an element in its standard state is _____.

    A) always zero   B) sometimes zero   C) never zero

Problems

1) The specific heat capacity of graphite is 0.71 J/(g x °C). Calculate the energy required to raise the temperature of 750 g of graphite by 160°C.

2) It takes 770 joules of energy to raise the temperature of 50.0 g of mercury by 110°C. What is the specific heat capacity of mercury?

3) Calculate the heat absorbed by the water in a calorimeter when 172 grams of copper cools from 166.0°C to 23.0°C. The specific heat capacity of copper is 0.385 J/(g x °C).

4) Assume 372 joules of heat are added to 4.00 g of water originally at 23.0°C. What would be the final temperature of the water? The specific heat capacity of water = 4.184 J/(g x °C).

5) How many joules are there in 162 calories? (1 cal = 4.18 J)

6) How many calories are there in 164 joules? (1 cal = 4.18 J)

7) How much heat is required to raise the temperature of 2.0×10^2 g of aluminum by 38.0°C? (specific heat of aluminum = 0.21 cal/(g x °C))

8) If 500 g of iron absorbs 22 000 cal of heat, what will be the change in temperature? (specific heat of iron = 0.11 cal/(g x °C))

9) What is the specific heat of a substance for which 1000.0 cal are required to raise the temperature of 100.0 g by 50.0°C?

10) A 55.0 g piece of copper wire is heated, and the temperature of the wire changes from 19.0°C to 86.0°C. The amount of heat absorbed is 343 cal. What is the specific heat of copper?

11) Analyze the reaction:

$$H_2(g) + \frac{1}{2}O_2(g) \rightarrow H_2O(l) \quad \Delta H° = -286 \text{ kJ}$$

Then calculate how much heat is produced when 70.0 L of H_2 (at STP) is reacted with excess O_2.

12) When 64.0 g of methanol (CH_3OH) is burned, 1454 kJ of energy is produced. What is the heat of combustion for methanol?

13) How much energy does it take to convert 0.75 kg of ice at –15°C to liquid water at 40°C? Specific heats: ice = 2.1 J/(g x °C); liquid = 4.2 J/(g x °C); ΔH_{fus} = 6.0 kJ/mol

14) How much heat is required to melt 1.6 moles of NaCl (ΔH_{fus} = 30.2 kJ/mol) at its melting point?

15) Consider a 32–g chunk of ice (ΔH_{fus} = 6.0 kJ/mol) in a beaker immersed in a water bath. To produce just enough heat to melt the ice, how many moles of solid NaOH (ΔH_{soln} = –445.1 kJ/mol) must you dissolve in the water bath?

16) A substance releases 496 kJ of heat as 2.60 moles condense from a gas into a liquid. What is the substance's heat of vaporization?

17) If you add 6.5 kJ of heat, how many moles of ice at 0°C can be melted, heated to its boiling point, and completely boiled away? ΔH_{vap} = 40.5 kJ/mol; ΔH_{fus} = 6.0 kJ/mol; specific heat = 0.075 6 kJ/(mol x °C)

18) A certain substance with a formula mass of 43 amu has a heat of fusion of 48 cal/g. How many calories are needed to melt 7.2 kg of the substance?

19) Suppose a substance has a heat of fusion equal to 45 cal/g and a specific heat of 0.75 cal/(g x °C) in the liquid state. If 5.0 kcal of heat are applied to a 50 g sample of the substance at a temperature of 24°C, what will its new temperature be? What state will the sample be in? (melting point is 27°C; specific heat of the solid is 0.48 cal/(g x °C); boiling point is 700°C)

20) Use the information below to calculate $\Delta H°$ for the following reaction.
$$2NO_2(g) \rightarrow N_2O_4(g)$$

$$N_2(g) + 2O_2(g) \rightarrow 2NO_2(g) \quad \Delta H° = 67.7 \text{ kJ}$$

$$N_2(g) + 2O_2(g) \rightarrow N_2O_4(g) \quad \Delta H° = 9.7 \text{ kJ}$$

Essay Questions

1) When steam is used to drive a turbine, the kinetic energy of the moving turbine will be less than the energy used initially to heat the water to steam. Explain why this is not a violation of the law of conservation of energy.

2) Outline the energy transformations that are associated with the use of petroleum as an energy source.

3) Explain the difference between temperature and heat. Also, state what determines the direction of heat transfer.

4) Explain the distinction between heat capacity and specific heat capacity. Provide an example to illustrate this distinction.

5) Explain how you could determine the number of Calories in a sample of sugar.

6) Describe the parts of a calorimeter and the function of each part.

7) A 100–g sample of water is heated from 50°C to 100°C. At 100°C, although heat is still applied, the temperature does not rise. Explain.

8) Using what you know about phase changes, why does steam at 100°C produce a more harmful burn than boiling water?

Chapter 11 Thermochemistry--Heat and Chemical Change

Matching Questions

1) Answer: F
2) Answer: D
3) Answer: C
4) Answer: E
5) Answer: B
6) Answer: A
7) Answer: E
8) Answer: D
9) Answer: C
10) Answer: B
11) Answer: A
12) Answer: C
13) Answer: A
14) Answer: D
15) Answer: E
16) Answer: B

Multiple Choice and Bimodal Questions

1) Answer: D
2) Answer: A
3) Answer: B
4) Answer: B
5) Answer: B
6) Answer: B
7) Answer: B
8) Answer: B
9) Answer: B
10) Answer: A
11) Answer: B
12) Answer: A
13) Answer: B
14) Answer: A
15) Answer: A
16) Answer: B
17) Answer: B
18) Answer: D
19) Answer: D
20) Answer: B
21) Answer: B
22) Answer: B
23) Answer: C
24) Answer: B

25) Answer: A

26) Answer: B

27) Answer: D

28) Answer: D

29) Answer: B

30) Answer: B

31) Answer: A

32) Answer: C

33) Answer: B

34) Answer: C

35) Answer: A

36) Answer: A

37) Answer: E

38) Answer: C

39) Answer: A

40) Answer: A

41) Answer: A

42) Answer: B

43) Answer: B

44) Answer: B

45) Answer: A

46) Answer: B

47) Answer: C

48) Answer: B

49) Answer: A

50) Answer: B

51) Answer: D

52) Answer: A

53) Answer: C

54) Answer: B

55) Answer: E

56) Answer: C

57) Answer: D

58) Answer: D

59) Answer: D

60) Answer: B

61) Answer: A

62) Answer: A

63) Answer: C

64) Answer: A

65) Answer: B

66) Answer: C

67) Answer: C

68) Answer: C

69) Answer: C

70) Answer: D

71) Answer: A

72) Answer: B

73) Answer: A

74) Answer: D

75) Answer: A

76) Answer: A

Problems

1) Answer: $\Delta H = 750 \text{ g} \times \dfrac{0.71 \text{ J}}{\text{g} \times {}^\circ\text{C}} \times 160{}^\circ\text{C} = 85\,000 \text{ J}$

2) Answer: Specific heat capacity $= \dfrac{770 \text{ J}}{50 \text{ g} \times 110{}^\circ\text{C}} = 0.14 \text{ J}/(\text{g} \times {}^\circ\text{C})$

3) Answer: Heat gained by water = heat lost by copper

$\Delta H = mc\Delta T = 172 \text{ g} \times \dfrac{0.385 \text{ J}}{\text{g} \times {}^\circ\text{C}} \times (166.0 - 23.0){}^\circ\text{C} = 9470 \text{ J}$

4) Answer: $\Delta H = mc\Delta T$

$\dfrac{\Delta H}{mc} = \Delta T$

$\Delta T = \dfrac{\Delta H}{mc} = \dfrac{372 \text{ J}}{4.00 \text{ g}} \times \dfrac{\text{g} \times {}^\circ\text{C}}{4.184 \text{ J}} = 22.2{}^\circ\text{C}$

$23.0{}^\circ\text{C} + 22.2{}^\circ\text{C} = 45.2{}^\circ\text{C}$

5) Answer: $162 \text{ cal} \times \dfrac{4.184 \text{ J}}{1 \text{ cal}} = 6.78 \times 10^2 \text{ J}$

6) Answer: $\dfrac{164 \text{ J}}{4.184 \text{ J/cal}} = 39.2 \text{ cal}$

7) Answer: Heat energy = mass x specific heat x temperature change

$= 200 \text{ g} \times \dfrac{0.21 \text{ cal}}{\text{g} \times {}^\circ\text{C}} \times 38.0{}^\circ\text{C}$

$= 1600 \text{ cal}$

8) Answer: Temperature change $= \dfrac{\text{heat energy absorbed}}{\text{specific heat x mass}}$

$= \dfrac{22\,000 \text{ cal}}{0.11 \text{ cal}/(\text{g} \times {}^\circ\text{C}) \times 500 \text{ g}} = 400{}^\circ\text{C}$

9) Answer: Specific heat $= \dfrac{\text{energy absorbed}}{\text{mass x temperature change}}$

$\dfrac{1000.0 \text{ cal}}{100.0 \text{ g} \times 50.0{}^\circ\text{C}} = 0.200 \text{ cal}/(\text{g} \times {}^\circ\text{C})$

10) Answer: $86.0{}^\circ\text{C} - 19.0{}^\circ\text{C} = 67.0{}^\circ\text{C}$ change

Specific heat $= \dfrac{\text{energy absorbed}}{\text{mass x temperature change}} = \dfrac{343 \text{ cal}}{55.0 \text{ g} \times 67.0{}^\circ\text{C}}$

$= 9.31 \times 10^{-2} \text{ cal}/(\text{g} \times {}^\circ\text{C})$

11) Answer: $70.0 \text{ L H}_2 \times \dfrac{1 \text{ mol H}_2}{22.4 \text{ L H}_2} \times \dfrac{-286 \text{ kJ}}{\text{mol H}_2} = -894 \text{ kJ}$

12) Answer: $\Delta H_{comb} = \dfrac{1454 \text{ kJ}}{64.0 \text{ g methanol}} \times \dfrac{32 \text{ g methanol}}{\text{mol methanol}} = 727 \text{ kj/mol}$

13) Answer: Warm ice to 0°C:

$$\Delta H = mc\Delta T = 750 \text{ g} \times \frac{2.1 \text{ J}}{\text{g} \times °\text{C}} \times 15°\text{C} = 24\,000 \text{ J}$$

Melt ice:

$$750 \text{ g } H_2O \times \frac{1 \text{ mol}}{18 \text{ g}} \times \frac{6.0 \text{ kJ}}{\text{mol}} = 250 \text{ J}$$

Total energy = 24 000 J + 250 J
= 24 000 J

14) Answer: $1.6 \text{ mol} \times \dfrac{30.2 \text{ kJ}}{\text{mol}} = 48 \text{ kJ}$

15) Answer: Heat to melt ice comes from heat released by the dissolving of NaOH:

$$\text{Heat to melt ice} = \frac{6.0 \text{ kJ}}{\text{mol}} \times 32 \text{ g } H_2O \times \frac{1 \text{ mol}}{18 \text{ g } H_2O} = 10 \text{ kJ}$$

$$10 \text{ kJ} \times \frac{1 \text{ mol NaOH}}{445.1 \text{ kJ}} = 0.023 \text{ mol NaOH}$$

16) Answer: $\Delta H_{vap} = \dfrac{496 \text{ kJ}}{2.60 \text{ mol}} = 191 \text{ kJ/mol}$

17) Answer: Total heat = heat to melt ice + heat to warm water to 100°C + heat to evaporate water
Total heat = (moles ice x ΔH_{fus}) + (moles water x CΔT) + (moles water x ΔH_{vap})

$$6.5 \text{ kJ} = (\text{moles of } H_2O \times \frac{6.0 \text{ kJ}}{\text{mol}}) + (\text{moles of } H_2O \times \frac{0.0756 \text{ kJ}}{\text{mol} \times °\text{C}} \times 100°\text{C})$$

$$+ (\text{moles of } H_2O \times 40.5 \frac{\text{kJ}}{\text{mol}})$$

$$6.5 \text{ kJ} = \text{moles } H_2O \,(6.0 \frac{\text{kJ}}{\text{mol}} + \frac{0.0756 \text{ kJ}}{\text{mol} \times °\text{C}} \times 100°\text{C} + 40.5 \frac{\text{kJ}}{\text{mol}})$$

$$6.5 \text{ kJ} = \text{moles } H_2O \,(\frac{54.1 \text{ kJ}}{\text{mol}})$$

$$\frac{6.5 \text{ kJ}}{54.1 \text{ kJ/mol}} = \text{moles } H_2O$$

moles H_2O = 0.12 mol

18) Answer: $\dfrac{48 \text{ cal}}{\text{g}} \times 7.2 \text{ kg} \times \dfrac{1000 \text{ g}}{\text{kg}} = 350\,000 \text{ cal}$

19) Answer: $50 \text{ g} \times \dfrac{0.48 \text{ cal}}{\text{g} \times °\text{C}} \times 3.0°\text{C}$

= 72 cal to raise the temperature of the solid to 27°C

$50 \text{ g} \times \dfrac{45 \text{ cal}}{\text{g}} = 2250$ cal to melt the sample

2250 cal + 72 cal = 2322 cal
5000 cal – 2322 cal = 2678 cal remaining

$2678 \text{ cal} \times \dfrac{\text{g} \times °\text{C}}{50 \text{ g} \times 0.75 \text{ cal}} = 71°\text{C}$

71°C + 27°C = 98°C
The substance is in a liquid state.

20) Answer: $2NO_2(g) \rightarrow N_2(g) + 2O_2(g) \quad \Delta H° = -67.7 \text{ kJ}$

$N_2(g) + 2O_2(g) \rightarrow N_2O_4(g) \quad \Delta H° = 9.7 \text{ kJ}$

_____

$2NO_2(g) \rightarrow N_2O_4(g) \qquad \Delta H° = -58 \text{ kJ}$

Essay Questions

1) Answer: The energy that is not converted to kinetic energy is not "lost." Rather, it escapes as heat. The connections between moving parts of the turbine become hot from friction and the air surrounding the turbine becomes warm. When this thermal energy is considered, it can be shown that the energy input equals the energy output and that the law of conservation of energy is obeyed.

2) Answer: Petroleum is removed from the ground, refined, and stored. It is then burned (chemical energy) to produce heat (thermal energy) which is used to generate electricity (electrical energy). The electricity (electrical energy) is used in a light bulb to produce light (light energy) and heat (thermal energy). The heat and light leave the bulb and are absorbed by the surroundings, raising their temperature (thermal energy).

3) Answer: Temperature is a measure of the hotness or coldness of an object. Heat is the energy that is transferred between two objects, of different temperature, that are in contact with each other. Temperature determines the direction of heat transfer. Heat always flows from the object of higher temperature to the object of lower temperature.

4) Answer: Heat capacity is the quantity of heat required to change an object's temperature by 1°C. The heat capacity of any particular object varies with the mass of that object (as well as with the type of material in the object). The heat capacity of a steel girder is much greater than the heat capacity of a steel nail, for instance. Specific heat capacity, on the other hand, does not vary with the mass of the object, but rather, depends only on the nature of the material in the object. Specific heat capacity is the quantity of heat required to raise the temperature of 1 gram of a substance by 1°C. The specific heat capacities of the steel in the steel girder and the steel in the steel nail are identical (assuming the two steels are of the same composition). Specific heat capacity is a property of a particular material; heat capacity is a property of a particular object.

5) Answer: The sugar could be burned and the heat given off used to heat a sample of water having a known mass. The temperature change of the water could be measured. The number of Calories in the sugar could then be calculated on the basis of this relationship: 1 calorie (0.001 Calorie) is the amount of heat required to raise the temperature of 1 gram of water 1°C.

6) Answer: Generally a calorimeter consists of an insulated container, water, and a temperature-measuring instrument. The insulated container prevents heat from entering or leaving the system from the outside. There is water in the container to absorb heat. The temperature-measuring device is often a thermometer. Some calorimeters have a stirrer to distribute the heat evenly through the water. A bomb calorimeter may contain a set of ignition wires.

7) Answer: The additional heat energy is being used to change the liquid water to a gas. The temperature will not rise until all of the water is in the gaseous state.

8) Answer: Steam at 100°C gives up more heat to your skin both because it contains more energy than boiling water at 100°C and because it releases more heat when it condenses into a liquid on contact with your skin.

Chapter 12 The Behavior of Gases
Matching Questions

1) Which of the following is NOT one of the assumptions of kinetic theory?

Chapter 12: Matching I

2) Boyle's law

3) Charles' law

4) Dalton's law

5) Graham's law

6) Gay-Lussac's law

7) ideal gas law

A) $P \times V = n \times R \times T$

B) The volume of a fixed mass of gas is directly proportional to its Kelvin temperature, if the pressure is kept constant.

C) For a given mass of gas at constant temperature, the volume of the gas varies inversely with pressure.

D) At constant volume and temperature, the total pressure exerted by a mixture of gases is equal to the sum of the partial pressures.

E) The rate at which a gas will escape through a small hole in a container is inversely proportional to the square root of the formula mass of the gas.

F) The pressure of a gas is directly proportional to its Kelvin temperature if the volume is kept constant.

Chapter 12: Matching II

8) diffusion

9) partial pressure

10) effusion

11) liquefaction

12) cryostat

A) a process in which the volume of a gas is decreased significantly

B) Dewar flask

C) the escape of gas through a small hole in a container

D) movement to regions of lower concentration

E) the pressure exerted by each gas in a mixture

Multiple Choice and Bimodal Questions

1) Which of the following is NOT one of the assumptions of kinetic theory?

   A) Gases consist of hard spherical particles.

   B) Particles in a gas are assumed to have an insignificant volume.

   C) All gas particles move in constant random motion.

   D) Only small attractive and repulsive forces exists between gas particles.

   E) none of the above

2) Why does the pressure inside a container of gas increase if more gas is added to the container?

   A) because there is a corresponding increase in the number of particles striking an area of the wall of the container per unit time

   B) because there is a corresponding increase in the temperature

   C) because there is a corresponding decrease in volume

   D) because there is a corresponding increase in the force of the collisions between the particles and the walls of the container

3) Why does air leave a tire when the tire valve is opened?

   A) because the pressure outside the tire is lower than the pressure inside the tire

   B) because the pressure outside the tire is greater than the pressure inside the tire

   C) because the temperature is higher outside the tire than inside the tire

   D) because there are more gas particles outside the tire than inside the tire

4) If 4 moles of gas are added to a container that already holds 1 mole of gas, how will the pressure change within the container?

   A) The pressure will be five times as great.   B) The pressure will be twice as great.

   C) The pressure will be four times as great.   D) The pressure will not change.

5) Increasing the volume of a given amount of gas at constant temperature causes the pressure to decrease because _____.

   A) the molecules are striking a larger area with the same force

   B) there are fewer molecules

   C) the molecules are moving more slowly

   D) there are more molecules

6) If the volume of a container holding a gas is reduced, what will happen to the pressure within the container?

   A) The pressure will increase.

   B) The pressure will not change.

   C) The pressure will decrease.

7) What happens to the temperature of a gas when it is compressed?

   A) The temperature increases.

   B) The temperature does not change.

   C) The temperature increases.

8) What happens to the pressure of a gas inside a container if the temperature of the gas is lowered?

   A) The pressure increases.

   B) The pressure does not change.

   C) The pressure decreases.

9) If a balloon is squeezed, what happens to the air pressure within the balloon?

   A) It increases.   B) It stays the same.   C) It decreases.

10) The volume of a gas is doubled while the temperature is held constant. How does the gas pressure change?

    A) is reduced by one–half

    B) remains unchanged

    C) is doubled

    D) varies depending on the nature of the gas

11) The volume of a gas is reduced from 4 L to 0.5 L while the temperature is held constant. How does the gas pressure change?

    A) increases by a factor of four   B) decreases by a factor of eight

    C) increases by a factor of eight   D) increases by a factor of two

12) A gas occupies a volume of 0.7 L at 10.1 kPa. What volume will the gas occupy at 101 kPa?

    A) 7 L   B) 4 L   C) 0.7 L   D) 0.07 L

13) A sample of gas occupies 40.0 mL at –123°C. What volume does the sample occupy at 27°C?

    A) 182 mL   B) 8.80 mL   C) 80.0 mL   D) 20.0 mL

14) Which of these changes would NOT cause an increase in the pressure of a gaseous system?
    A) The container is made larger.
    B) Additional amounts of the same gas are added to the container.
    C) The temperature is increased.
    D) Another gas is added to the container.

15) Why does an aerosol can become cooler when gas is released?
    A) because the propellant expands
    B) because the propellant contracts
    C) because the product expands within the can
    D) because the volume of the can decreases

16) As the temperature of a fixed volume of a gas increases, the pressure will _____.
    A) vary inversely   B) decrease   C) be unchanged   D) increase

17) As the temperature of the gas in a balloon decreases _____.
    A) the volume increases
    B) the average kinetic energy of the gas decreases
    C) the pressure increases
    D) all of the above

18) Boyle's law states that _____.
    A) the volume of a gas varies inversely with pressure
    B) the volume of a gas varies directly with pressure
    C) the temperature of a gas varies inversely with pressure
    D) the temperature of a gas varies directly with pressure

19) When the temperature and number of particles are kept constant for a sample of gas, which of the following is also constant for the sample?
    A) the sum of the pressure and volume
    B) the difference of the pressure and volume
    C) the product of the pressure and volume
    D) the quotient of the pressure and volume

20) If a balloon is rubbed vigorously, what happens to the volume of the air in the balloon if the pressure is constant?
    A) It increases.   B) It stays the same.   C) It decreases.

21) Charles' law states that _____.
    A) the pressure of a gas is inversely proportional to its temperature in kelvins
    B) the volume of a gas is directly proportional to its temperature in kelvins
    C) the pressure of a gas is directly proportional to its temperature in kelvins
    D) the volume of a gas is inversely proportional to its temperature in kelvins

22) When the pressure and number of particles are kept constant for a sample of gas, which of the following is also constant for the sample?

    A) the sum of the volume and temperature (in kelvins)

    B) the difference of the volume and temperature (in kelvins)

    C) the product of the volume and temperature (in kelvins)

    D) the quotient of the volume and temperature (in kelvins)

23) If a capped syringe is plunged into cold water, in which direction will the syringe piston slide?

    A) in   B) out   C) No sliding will occur.

24) If a balloon is rubbed vigorously, what happens to the pressure of the air inside the balloon if the volume remains constant?

    A) It increases.   B) It stays the same.   C) It decreases.

25) Generally, for a gas at a constant volume _____.

    A) the pressure of a gas is inversely proportional to its temperature in kelvins

    B) the volume of a gas is inversely proportional to its temperature in kelvins

    C) the volume of a gas is directly proportional to its temperature in kelvins

    D) the pressure of a gas is directly proportional to its temperature in kelvins

26) If a capped syringe is heated, in which direction will the syringe plunger move?

    A) out

    B) in

    C) The plunger will not move.

27) The combined gas law relates which of these?

    A) pressure and volume only   B) temperature and pressure only

    C) volume and temperature only   D) temperature, pressure, and volume

28) If a balloon containing 1000 L of gas at 50°C and 101 kPa rises to an altitude where the pressure is 50.5 kPa and the temperature is 10°C, the volume of the balloon under these new conditions would be _____.

    A) $1000 \text{ L} \times \dfrac{101 \text{ kPa}}{50.5 \text{ kPa}} \times \dfrac{10°C}{50°C}$ B) $1000 \text{ L} \times \dfrac{323 \text{ K}}{283 \text{ K}} \times \dfrac{50.5 \text{ kPa}}{101 \text{ kPa}}$

    C) $1000 \text{ L} \times \dfrac{101 \text{ kPa}}{50.5 \text{ kPa}} \times \dfrac{283 \text{ K}}{323 \text{ K}}$ D) $1000 \text{ L} \times \dfrac{50°C}{10°C} \times \dfrac{50.5 \text{ kPa}}{101 \text{ kPa}}$

29) At very high pressures, how does the volume of a real gas compare with the volume that would be predicted for an ideal gas under the same conditions?

    A) It is much greater.   B) It is much less.   C) There is no difference.

30) At low temperatures and pressures, how does the volume of a real gas compare with the volume that would be predicted for an ideal gas under the same conditions?

    A) It is greater.   B) It is less.   C) There is no difference.

31) An ideal gas CANNOT be _____.

A) liquefied   B) cooled   C) heated   D) pressurized

32) When the volume and number of particles are held constant for a sample of gas, which of the following is also constant for the sample?

A) the sum of the pressure and temperature in kelvins

B) the difference of the pressure and temperature in kelvins

C) the product of the pressure and temperature in kelvins

D) the quotient of the pressure and temperature in kelvins

33) Which of the following is constant for 1 mole of any ideal gas?

A) PVT   B) $\frac{PV}{T}$ C) $\frac{PT}{V}$ D) $\frac{VT}{P}$

34) What does the ideal gas law allow a scientist to calculate that the other laws do not?

A) number of moles

B) pressure

C) volume

D) temperature

E) energy

35) What is the normal form of the ideal gas law?

A) $\frac{PV}{nT} = R$ B) $\frac{PV}{T} = nR$ C) $PV = nRT$ D) $P = \frac{nRT}{V}$

36) At a certain temperature and pressure, 0.20 mol of CO_2 has a volume of 3.1 L. A 3.1–L sample of hydrogen at the same temperature and pressure _____.

A) has the same mass   B) contains the same number of atoms

C) has a higher density   D) contains the same number of molecules

37) Under what conditions of temperature and pressure is the behavior of real gases most like that of ideal gases?

A) low temperature and low pressure   B) low temperature and high pressure

C) high temperature and low pressure   D) high temperature and high pressure

38) If oxygen is removed from the air in the process of rusting, what happens to the partial pressure of oxygen in the air?

A) It increases.   B) It stays the same.   C) It decreases.

39) If oxygen is removed from the air by the process of rusting, what happens to the total pressure of the air?

A) It increases.   B) It stays the same.   C) It decreases.

40) What happens to the partial pressure of oxygen in the air if the air temperature is increased?

A) It increases.   B) It stays the same.   C) It decreases.

41) If the volume of a container of air is reduced by one-half, what happens to the partial pressure of oxygen within the container?

   A) It is reduced by one-half.

   B) It is unchanged.

   C) It is doubled.

42) A breathing mixture used by deep-sea divers contains helium, oxygen, and carbon dioxide. What is the partial pressure of oxygen at 101 kPa if P_{He} = 84 kPa and P_{CO_2} = 0.1 kPa?

   A) 101.1 kPa   B) 100.9 kPa   C) 16.9 kPa   D) 80%

43) When a container is filled with 3 moles of H_2, 2 moles of O_2, and 1 mole of N_2, the pressure in the container is 8787 kPa. What Is the partial pressure of O_2?

   A) 2929 kPa   B) 202 kPa

   C) 404 kPa   D) impossible to calculate

44) If the atmospheric pressure on Mt. Everest is one-third the atmospheric pressure at sea level, the partial pressure of oxygen on Everest is _____.

   A) one-sixth that at sea level   B) one-third that at sea level

   C) one-half that at sea level   D) equal to that at sea level

45) A box with a volume of 22.4 L contains 1.0 mol of nitrogen and 2.0 mol of hydrogen at 0°C. Which of the following statements is true?

   A) The total pressure in the box is 101 kPa.

   B) The partial pressures of N_2 and H_2 are equal.

   C) The total pressure is 202 kPa

   D) The partial pressure of N_2 is 101 kPa.

46) The tendency of molecules to move toward areas of lower concentration is called _____.

   A) effusion   B) suffusion   C) diffusion   D) suspension

47) Which of the following gases will effuse the most rapidly?

   A) bromine   B) chlorine   C) ammonia   D) hydrogen   E) argon

48) Which of the following atoms would have the greatest velocity if each atom had the same kinetic energy?

   A) bromine   B) chlorine   C) ammonia   D) hydrogen   E) argon

49) Which of the following gases is the best choice to serve as the inflating gas of a balloon that must remain inflated for a long period of time.

   A) nitrogen   B) oxygen   C) hydrogen   D) neon   E) argon

Problems

1) The volume of a gas is 250 mL at 340.0 kPa pressure. What will the volume be when the pressure is reduced to 50.0 kPa, assuming the temperature remains constant?

2) A 10–g mass of krypton occupies 15.0 L at a pressure of 210 kPa. Find the volume of the krypton when the pressure is increased to 790 kPa.

3) A balloon filled with helium has a volume of 30.0 L at a pressure of 100 kPa and a temperature of 15.0°C. What will the volume of the balloon be if the temperature is increased to 80.0°C and the pressure remains constant?

4) A gas has a volume of 590 mL at a temperature of –55.0°C. What volume will the gas occupy at 30.0°C?

5) A rigid container of O_2 has a pressure of 340 kPa at a temperature of 713 K. What is the pressure at 273 K?

6) A gas has a pressure of 710 kPa at 227°C. What will its pressure be at 27°C, if the volume does not change?

7) A gas occupies a volume of 140 mL at 35.0°C and 97 kPa. What is the volume of the gas at conditions of STP?

8) A gas storage tank has a volume of 3.5×10^5 m^3 when the temperature is 27°C and the pressure is 101 kPa. What is the new volume of the tank if the temperature drops to –10°C and the pressure drops to 95 kPa?

9) How many moles of N_2 are in a flask with a volume of 250 mL at a pressure of 300.0 kPa and a temperature of 300.0 K?

10) The gaseous product of a reaction is collected in a 25.0–L container at 27°C. The pressure in the container is 300.0 kPa and the gas has a mass of 96.0 g. What is the formula mass of the gas?

11) A mixture of gases at a total pressure of 95 kPa contains N_2, CO_2, and O_2. The partial pressure of the CO_2 is 24 kPa and the partial pressure of the N_2 is 48 kPa. What is the partial pressure of the O_2?

12) What is the pressure exerted by 32 g of O_2 in a 22.0–L container at 30.0°C?

13) The separation of uranium–235 from uranium–238 has been carried out using gaseous diffusion. Calculate the relative rates of diffusion of gaseous UF_6 containing these isotopes. Formula mass of UF_6 containing uranium–235 = 349 amu. Formula mass of UF_6 containing uranium–238 = 352 amu.

Essay Questions

1) Explain how pumping air into a bicycle tire increases the pressure within the tire.

2) How does the air pressure in a balloon change when the balloon is squeezed? Explain why this change occurs.

3) How does the pressure of an enclosed gas change when the gas is heated? Explain why this change occurs.

4) What are some of the differences between a real gas and an ideal gas?

5) What is Dalton's law of partial pressures? Explain how this law relates to the fact that mountaineers must carry their own oxygen when scaling high peaks.

6) Explain why the rates of diffusion and effusion, for any particular gas at constant temperature, are proportional to the square root of the formula mass of the gas.

Chapter 12 The Behavior of Gases

Matching Questions

    1) Answer:

    2) Answer: C

    3) Answer: B

    4) Answer: D

    5) Answer: E

    6) Answer: F

    7) Answer: A

    8) Answer: D

    9) Answer: E

    10) Answer: C

    11) Answer: A

    12) Answer: B

Multiple Choice and Bimodal Questions

    1) Answer: D

    2) Answer: A

    3) Answer: A

    4) Answer: A

    5) Answer: A

    6) Answer: A

    7) Answer: A

    8) Answer: C

    9) Answer: A

    10) Answer: A

    11) Answer: C

    12) Answer: D

    13) Answer: C

    14) Answer: A

    15) Answer: A

    16) Answer: D

    17) Answer: B

    18) Answer: A

    19) Answer: C

    20) Answer: A

    21) Answer: B

    22) Answer: D

    23) Answer: A

    24) Answer: A

    25) Answer: D

26) Answer: A

27) Answer: D

28) Answer: C

29) Answer: A

30) Answer: B

31) Answer: A

32) Answer: D

33) Answer: B

34) Answer: A

35) Answer: C

36) Answer: D

37) Answer: C

38) Answer: C

39) Answer: C

40) Answer: A

41) Answer: C

42) Answer: C

43) Answer: A

44) Answer: B

45) Answer: D

46) Answer: C

47) Answer: D

48) Answer: D

49) Answer: E

Problems

1) Answer: $V_2 = V_1 \times \dfrac{P_1}{P_2} = 250 \text{ mL} \times \dfrac{340.0 \text{ kPa}}{50.0 \text{ kPa}} = 1700 \text{ mL}$

2) Answer: $P_1 \times V_1 = P_2 \times V_2$

$210 \text{ kPa} \times 15.0 \text{ L} = 790 \text{ kPa} \times V_2$

$\dfrac{210 \text{ kPa} \times 15.0 \text{ L}}{790 \text{ kPa}} = V_2$

$V_2 = 4.0 \text{ L}$

3) Answer: $V_2 = V_1 \times \dfrac{T_2}{T_1} = 30.0 \text{ L} \times \dfrac{353 \text{ K}}{288 \text{K}} = 34.3 \text{ L}$

4) Answer: $T_1 = -55°\text{C} + 273 = 218 \text{ K}$

$T_2 = 30.0°\text{C} + 273 = 303 \text{ K}$

$V_2 = V_1 \times \dfrac{T_2}{T_1} = 590 \text{ mL} \times \dfrac{303 \text{ K}}{218 \text{ K}} = 820 \text{ mL}$

5) Answer: $P_2 = P_1 \times \dfrac{T_2}{T_1} = 340 \text{ kPa} \times \dfrac{273 \text{ K}}{713 \text{ K}} = 140 \text{ kPa}$

6) Answer: $227°C + 273 = 500 \text{ K}$

$27°C + 273 = 300 \text{ K}$

$$\frac{P_1}{T_1} = \frac{P_2}{T_2} \; ; \; \frac{710 \text{ kPa}}{500 \text{ K}} = \frac{P_2}{300 \text{ K}}$$

$$710 \text{ kPa} \times \frac{300 \text{ K}}{500 \text{ K}} = P_2$$

$P_2 = 470 \text{ kPa}$

7) Answer: $T_1 = 35.0°C + 273 = 308 \text{ K}$

$T_2 = 0.0°C + 273 = 273 \text{ K}$

$$V_2 = P_1 \times V_1 \times \frac{T_2}{T_1 \times P_2}$$

$$V_2 = 97 \text{ kPa} \times 140 \text{ mL} \times \frac{273 \text{ K}}{308 \text{ K} \times 101 \text{ kPa}} = 120 \text{ mL}$$

8) Answer: $T_1 = 27°C + 273 = 300 \text{ K}; \; P_1 = 101 \text{ kPa}$

$T_2 = -10°C + 273 = 263 \text{ K}; \; P_2 = 95 \text{ kPa}$

$$V_2 = P_1 \times V_1 \times \frac{T_2}{T_1 \times P_2} = (101 \text{ kPa}) \times (3.5 \times 10^5 \text{ m}^3) \times \frac{263 \text{ K}}{300 \text{ K} \times 95 \text{ kPa}}$$

$V_2 = 3.26 \times 10^5 \text{ m}^3$

9) Answer: $250 \text{ mL} \times \dfrac{1 \text{ L}}{1000 \text{ mL}} = 0.25 \text{ L}$

$$n = \frac{PV}{RT} = \frac{300.0 \text{ kPa} \times 0.25 \text{ L}}{8.31 (\text{L} \times \text{kPa})/(\text{K} \times \text{mol}) \times 300.0 \text{ K}} = 0.030 \text{ mol}$$

10) Answer: $n = \dfrac{PV}{RT} = \dfrac{300.0 \text{ kPa} \times 25 \text{ L}}{8.31 (\text{L} \times \text{kPa})/(\text{K} \times \text{mol}) \times 300 \text{ K}} = 3.0 \text{ mol}$

$96 \text{ g}/3.0 \text{ mol} = 32 \text{ g}/\text{mol}$ formula mass

11) Answer: $P_{O_2} = P_{total} - (P_{CO_2} + P_{N_2}) = 95 \text{ kPa} - (48 \text{ kPa} + 24 \text{ kPa}) = 23 \text{ kPa}$

12) Answer: $32 \text{ g O}_2 \times \dfrac{1 \text{ mol O}_2}{32 \text{ g O}_2} = 1 \text{ mol O}_2$

$$P = \frac{nRT}{V} = \frac{1.0 \text{ mol} \times 8.31 (\text{L} \times \text{kPa})/(\text{K} \times \text{mol}) \times 303 \text{ K}}{22.0 \text{ L}} = 110 \text{ kPa}$$

13) Answer: $\dfrac{Rate_{235}}{Rate_{238}} = \dfrac{\sqrt{352}}{\sqrt{349}} = 1.004$

UF_6 containing U–235 diffuses 1.004 times faster.

Essay Questions

1) Answer: The pressure exerted by an enclosed gas is caused by collisions of gas particles with the walls of the container, which is the tire in this case. As more gas particles are added into the tire by pumping, there is a corresponding increase in the number of collisions of gas particles with a unit area of the tire wall per unit time. The more particles that are moving with the same average kinetic energy (i.e. at the same temperature) in the same enclosed volume, the greater the pressure. Pumping air into a tire increases the pressure in the tire because more air particles have been added to the enclosed volume of the tire, at constant temperature.

2) Answer: The air pressure increases. This happens because the act of squeezing reduces the enclosed volume of the balloon without changing the number of gas particles enclosed in the balloon, and without significantly changing the temperature. Consequently, the number of collisions between the gas particles and a unit area of the balloon per unit time increases.

3) Answer: The pressure of an enclosed gas increases when the gas is heated. The reason for this is that when the temperature of the gas is raised there is a corresponding increase in the average kinetic energy of the particles of the gas. The average kinetic energy can only go up if the average speed of the particles increases. And if the speed increases, while the enclosed volume remains the same, there will be an increase in the number of collisions between gas particles and a unit area of the container wall per unit time. In addition, because the particles are moving faster, on average, the collisions will occur with greater force. Both factors, the increased frequency of collision and the increased force of collision, contribute to the increase in pressure associated with the heating of an enclosed gas.

4) Answer: An ideal gas is one that follows the gas laws at all conditions of pressure and temperature. The behavior of a real gas deviates from the behavior of an ideal gas at various temperatures and pressures. Also, kinetic theory assumes that the particles of an ideal gas have no volume and are not attracted to each other. This is not true for real gases. Real gases can be liquefied and sometimes solidified by cooling and applying pressure, while ideal gases cannot.

5) Answer: Dalton's law of partial pressures states that, at constant volume and temperature, the total pressure exerted by a mixture of gases is equal to the sum of the partial pressures of the individual gases in the mixture. The reason mountaineers must carry their own oxygen is that, at high altitudes, the total air pressure is much lower than it is at sea level and the partial pressure of oxygen in the air is correspondingly lower also. For instance, if the partial pressure of oxygen is 0.20 atm at sea level where the total pressure is 1.0 atm, then on a mountain peak where the total air pressure is only 0.3 atm the partial pressure of oxygen would be 0.3 x 0.2 atm or 0.06 atm. This low partial pressure of oxygen is not sufficient to support normal metabolism and must be supplemented by oxygen from a tank if the mountaineer is to survive the climb.

6) Answer: At constant temperature, particles all have the same average kinetic energy. The formula for kinetic energy is $KE = (1/2)mv^2$. At constant temperature, the KE is constant and the velocity is proportional to the square root of $1/m$. Because the diffusion and effusion rates are directly proportional to the velocity at which a particle is moving, these rates are also proportional to the square root of $1/m$. This implies that the more mass a particle has, the more slowly it will diffuse or effuse.

Chapter 13 Electrons in Atoms
Matching Questions
Chapter 13: Matching I

1) orbital

2) Aufbau principle

3) electron configuration

4) ground state

5) exclusion principle

6) photoelectric effect

A) arrangement of electrons around atomic nucleus

B) each orbital has at most two electrons

C) region of high probability of finding an electron

D) lowest energy level

E) tendency of electrons to enter orbitals of lowest energy first

F) ejection of electrons from metals by light

Chapter 13: Matching II

7) Heisenberg uncertainty principle

8) speed of electromagnetic waves traveling in a vacuum

9) Planck's constant

10) mass of an electron

11) a frequency in the range of red light

12) de Broglie's equation

A) 3×10^{10} cm/s

B) $6.626\ 2 \times 10^{-34}$ J s

C) states the impossibility of knowing both the velocity and position of a moving particle at the same time

D) predicts that all matter will exhibit wave-like motion

E) 9.11×10^{-28} g

F) 6.0×10^{14} s^{-1}

13) amplitude

14) frequency

15) wavelength

16) photon

17) quantum

18) spectrum

A) height of a wave from origin to crest

B) separation of light into different wavelengths

C) energy needed to move an electron from one energy level to another

D) discrete bundle of electromagnetic energy

E) distance between wave crests

F) number of wave cycles passing a point per unit of time

Multiple Choice and Bimodal Questions

1) Which scientist developed an atomic theory in the early 1800s?

A) Isaac Newton

B) Antoine Lavoisier

C) Francis Bacon

D) Roger Bacon

E) John Dalton

2) Who discovered the electron?

A) Joseph Thomson

B) Niels Bohr

C) Ernest Rutherford

D) John Dalton

E) Albert Einstein

3) How does the energy of an electron change when the electron moves closer to the nucleus?

A) It decreases.   B) It increases.   C) It stays the same.

4) Which scientist developed the quantum mechanical model of the atom?
   A) Albert Einstein
   B) Erwin Schrodinger
   C) Niels Bohr
   D) Ernest Rutherford
   E) Joseph Thomson

5) The principal quantum number indicates what property of an electron?
   A) position
   B) speed
   C) energy level
   D) electron cloud shape
   E) spin

6) What is the shape of the 3p atomic orbital?
   A) a sphere
   B) a dumbbell
   C) a bar
   D) two perpendicular dumbbells
   E) an egg

7) How many energy sublevels are there in the second principal energy level?
   A) 1   B) 2   C) 3   D) 4   E) 5

8) How many f orbitals can there be in one atom?
   A) 1   B) 3   C) 5   D) 7   E) 9

9) What is the maximum number of d orbitals in a principal energy level?
   A) 1   B) 2   C) 3   D) 5   E) 10

10) What is the maximum number of orbitals in the p sublevel?
   A) 2   B) 3   C) 4   D) 5   E) 6

11) What is the maximum number of electrons in the second principal energy level?
   A) 2   B) 8   C) 18   D) 32

12) Which of the following is an accurate description of Thomson's model of the atom?
   A) The electrons orbit the protons, which are at the center of the atom.
   B) The electrons and protons move throughout the atom.
   C) Electrons occupy fixed positions around the protons, which are at the center of the atom.
   D) The electrons, like "raisins," are stuck into a lump of protons, like "dough," in a "plum pudding" atom.

13) In Rutherford's model of the atom, where are the electrons and protons located?

    A) The electrons orbit the protons, which are at the center of the atom.

    B) The electrons and protons move throughout the atom.

    C) The electrons occupy fixed positions around the protons, which are at the center of the atom.

    D) The electrons and protons are located throughout the atom, but they are not free to move.

14) In Bohr's model of the atom, where are the electrons and protons located?

    A) The electrons orbit the protons, which are at the center of the atom.

    B) The electrons and protons move throughout the atom.

    C) The electrons occupy fixed positions around the protons, which are at the center of the atom.

    D) The electrons and protons are located throughout the atom, but they are not free to move.

15) In the Bohr model of the atom, an electron in an orbit has a fixed _____.

    A) position   B) color   C) energy

16) When an electron moves from a lower to a higher energy level, the electron _____.

    A) always doubles its energy

    B) absorbs a continuously variable amount of energy

    C) absorbs a quantum of energy

    D) moves closer to the nucleus

17) What did Rutherford's experiment demonstrate?

    A) that electrons orbit the nucleus

    B) that all neutrons are located in the nucleus

    C) that most of an atom's mass is concentrated in a relatively small portion of the atom's entire volume

    D) that atoms are made of positively and negatively charged particles

18) The quantum mechanical model exactly predicts which characteristic of electrons in an atom?

    A) position

    B) energy

    C) orbit

    D) charge

    E) none of the above

19) What is the probability of finding an electron within the region indicated by the drawn electron cloud?

    A) 50%   B) 67%   C) 75%   D) 90%   E) 100%

20) The quantum mechanical model of the atom _____.

    A) defines the exact path of an electron around the nucleus

    B) was proposed by Niels Bohr

    C) is concerned with the probability of finding an electron in a certain position

    D) has many analogies in the visible world

21) The shape (not the size) of an electron cloud is determined by the electron's _____.

    A) energy sublevel

    B) spin

    C) position

    D) speed

    E) principal quantum number

22) What types of atomic orbitals are in the third principal energy level?

    A) s and p only

    B) p and d only

    C) s, p, and d only

    D) p, d, and f only

    E) s, p, d, and f

23) The formula $2n^2$ represents _____.

    A) the number of orbitals in a sublevel

    B) the maximum number of electrons that can occupy an energy level

    C) the number of sublevels in any energy level

    D) none of the above

24) Which of the following energy levels has the lowest energy?

    A) 3d   B) 4s   C) 4p   D) 4f

25) The letter "p" in the symbol $4p^3$ indicates the _____.

    A) spin of an electron   B) orbital shape

    C) principle energy level   D) speed of an electron

26) If three electrons are available to fill three empty 2p atomic orbitals, how will the electrons be distributed in the three orbitals?

    A) one electron in each orbital

    B) two electrons in one orbital, one in another, none in the third

    C) three in one orbital, none in the other two

27) If only two electrons occupy two p orbitals, what is the direction of the spins of these two electrons?

   A) Both are always clockwise.

   B) Both are always counterclockwise.

   C) They are either both clockwise or both counterclockwise.

   D) One is clockwise and the other is counterclockwise.

28) What is the next atomic orbital in the series 1s, 2s, 2p, 3s, 3p?

   A) 2d   B) 2f   C) 3d   D) 3f   E) 4s

29) How many unpaired electrons are there in a sulfur atom (atomic number 32)?

   A) 0   B) 1   C) 2   D) 3   E) 4

30) What is the number of electrons in the outermost energy level of an oxygen atom?

   A) 2   B) 4   C) 6   D) 8   E) 10

31) How many half–filled orbitals are there in a bromine atom?

   A) 1   B) 2   C) 3   D) 4   E) 5

32) What is the electron configuration of potassium?

   A) $1s^2 2s^2 2p^2 3s^2 3p^2 4s^1$ B) $1s^2 2s^2 2p^{10} 3s^2 3p^3$

   C) $1s^2 2s^2 3s^2 3p^6 3d^1$ D) $1s^2 2s^2 2p^6 3s^2 3p^6 4s^1$

33) If the spin of one electron in an orbital is clockwise, what is the spin of the other electron in that orbital?

   A) zero   B) clockwise   C) counterclockwise

34) Which of the following states that no more than two electrons can occupy an atomic orbital and that two electrons in the same orbital must have opposite spins?

   A) Hund's rule   B) Dalton's theory

   C) the Aufbau principle   D) the Pauli exclusion principle

35) In order to occupy the same orbital, two electrons must have _____.

   A) the same direction of spin   B) low energy

   C) a high quantum number   D) opposite spin

36) According to the Aufbau principle _____.

   A) an orbital may be occupied by only two electrons

   B) electrons in the same orbital must have opposite spins

   C) electrons enter orbitals of highest energy first

   D) electrons enter orbitals of lowest energy first

37) What is the basis for exceptions to the Aufbau diagram?

    A) Filled and half-filled energy sublevels are more stable than partially-filled ones.

    B) Electron configurations are only probable.

    C) Electron spins are more important than energy levels in determining electron configuration.

    D) Some elements have unusual atomic orbitals.

38) Which of the following electron configurations is the most stable?

    A) $4d^5 5s^1$ B) $4d^4 5s^2$ C) $4d^3 5s^3$ D) $4d^2 5s^4$

39) Which electron configuration of the 4f energy sublevel is the most stable?

    A) $4f^6$ B) $4f^7$ C) $4f$ D) $4f^{13}$ E) $4f^{14}$

40) Stable electron configurations are likely to contain _____.

    A) filled energy sublevels

    B) fewer electrons than unstable configurations

    C) unfilled s orbitals

    D) electrons with a clockwise spin

41) How does the speed of visible light compare with the speed of gamma rays, when both speeds are measured in a vacuum?

    A) The speed of visible light is greater.

    B) The speed of gamma rays is greater.

    C) The speeds are the same.

    D) No definite statement can be made on this question.

42) How does the speed of light change as light moves from a distant star toward earth in the vacuum of space?

    A) The speed decreases.

    B) The speed increases.

    C) The speed remains constant.

43) Which color of visible light has the shortest wavelength?

    A) orange   B) yellow   C) green   D) blue   E) violet

44) What are quanta of light called?

    A) charms   B) excitons   C) muons   D) photons   E) solitons

45) Who predicted that all matter can behave as waves as well as particles?

    A) Niels Bohr

    B) Albert Einstein

    C) Erwin Schrodinger

    D) Max Planck

    E) Louis de Broglie

46) Who developed the uncertainty principle?

    A) Albert Einstein

    B) Niels Bohr

    C) Werner Heisenberg

    D) Erwin Schrodinger

    E) Louis de Broglie

47) The amplitude of a wave is the measure of the _____.

    A) distance between crests   B) number of cycles per unit time

    C) height from origin to crest   D) number of particles in a wave front

48) Which of the following electromagnetic waves have the highest frequencies?

    A) ultraviolet light waves

    B) x-rays

    C) microwaves

    D) gamma rays

    E) infrared light waves

49) What is the wavelength of an electromagnetic wave that travels at 3×10^8 m/s and has a frequency of 60 Hz?

    A) $\dfrac{60 \text{ Hz}}{300\,000\,000 \text{ m/s}}$

    B) 60 Hz x 300 000 000 m/s

    C) $\dfrac{300\,000\,000 \text{ m/s}}{60 \text{ Hz}}$

    D) No answer can be determined from the information given.

50) Which type of electromagnetic radiation includes the wavelength 10^{-7} m?

    A) gamma ray

    B) microwave

    C) radio wave

    D) visible light

    E) x-ray

51) The light given off by an electric discharge through a sodium vapor is _____.

    A) a continuous spectrum   B) an emission spectrum

    C) of a single wavelength   D) white light

52) The atomic emission spectra of a sodium atom on earth and of a sodium atom in the sun would be _____.

    A) the same

    B) different from each other

    C) the same as those of several other elements

    D) the same as each other only in the ultraviolet range

53) In classical physics, energy changes were thought to be _____.
  A) continuous
  B) quantized
  C) always small
  D) always large
  E) unpredictable

54) What is the approximate energy of a photon having a frequency of 4×10^7 Hz?
  ($h = 6.6 \times 10^{-34}$ J s)
  A) 3×10^{-26} J
  B) 3×10^{-27} J
  C) 2×10^{-41} J
  D) 3×10^{42} J
  E) 1×10^{-18} J

55) What is the approximate frequency of a photon having an energy 5×10^{-24} J?
  ($h = 6.6 \times 10^{-34}$ J s)
  A) 7×10^9 Hz
  B) 3×10^{-57} Hz
  C) 3×10^{-58} Hz
  D) 1×10^{-10} Hz
  E) 1×10^{-11} Hz

56) Which of the following metals is particularly sensitive to the photoelectric effect?
  A) potassium
  B) aluminum
  C) iron
  D) zinc
  E) copper

57) When light below a specific wavelength shines on lithium, which particle can be ejected from the metal?
  A) proton
  B) electron
  C) photon
  D) neutron
  E) pion

58) Red light CANNOT cause an electron to be ejected from a potassium atom because which of the following is too low?
  A) the frequency of red light
  B) the wavelength of red light
  C) the intensity of red light
  D) the amplitude of red light

59) If there is an increase in the intensity of incident light with energy above the threshold for the photoelectric effect, _____.
  A) more electrons are ejected
  B) the ejected electrons move faster
  C) fewer electrons are ejected
  D) the ejected electrons move more slowly

60) According to classical physics, an electron was ejected from an atom as the result of _____.
  A) a fast particle of light colliding with the electron
  B) energy accumulating in the electron
  C) nuclear repulsion
  D) other electrons repelling the electron

61) The lowest energy state of an atom is called the _____.

    A) excited state

    B) ground state

    C) independent state

    D) dependent state

    E) configurational state

62) Emission of light from an atom occurs when the electron _____.

    A) drops from a higher to a lower energy level

    B) jumps from a lower to a higher energy level

    C) moves within its atomic orbital

    D) falls into the nucleus

63) How do the energy differences between the higher energy levels of an atom compare with the energy differences between the lower energy levels of the atom?

    A) They are greater in magnitude.

    B) They are smaller in magnitude.

    C) There is no significant difference in the magnitudes of these differences.

64) Which of the following quantum leaps would be associated with the greatest energy of emitted light?

    A) $n = 5$ to $n = 1$

    B) $n = 1$ to $n = 5$

    C) $n = 2$ to $n = 5$

    D) $n = 5$ to $n = 2$

    E) $n = 5$ to $n = 3$

65) Bohr's model could only explain the spectra of which type of atoms?

    A) single atoms with one electron

    B) bonded atoms with one electron

    C) single atoms with more than one electron

    D) bonded atoms with more than one electron

66) To which variable of an object is the object's wavelength directly proportional?

    A) mass

    B) velocity

    C) temperature

    D) position

    E) none of the above

67) To which variable of an object is the object's mass directly proportional?

    A) wavelength

    B) velocity

    C) temperature

    D) position

    E) frequency

68) What is the approximate mass of a particle having a wavelength of 10^{-7} m and a speed of 1 m/s? ($h = 6.6 \times 10^{-34}$ J s)

    A) 7×10^{-27} kg   B) 7×10^{-41} kg   C) 7×10^{-20} kg   D) 7×10^{-48} kg

69) According to the uncertainty principle, if the position of a moving particle is known, what other quantity cannot be known?

    A) mass

    B) temperature

    C) charge

    D) spin

    E) velocity

70) How can the position of a particle be determined?

    A) by analyzing its interactions with another particle

    B) by measuring its velocity

    C) by measuring its mass

    D) by determining its charge

Problems

1) Give the electron configuration for a neutral atom of chlorine.

2) Give the electron configuration for a neutral atom of beryllium.

3) Give the electron configuration for a neutral atom of selenium.

4) How many electrons are in the highest occupied energy level of a neutral chlorine atom?

5) How many electrons are in the highest occupied energy level of a neutral strontium atom?

6) Write the electron configuration for chromium.

7) How many electrons are in the highest occupied energy level of copper?

8) What is the frequency of light with wavelength 1.0×10^{-8} m? ($c = 3.0 \times 10^8$ m/s)

9) What is the wavelength of light with a frequency of 1.0×10^{20} Hz? ($c = 3.0 \times 10^8$ m/s)

10) What is the frequency of a photon with energy 1.0×10^{-25} J? ($h = 6.6 \times 10^{-34}$ J s)

11) What is the energy of a photon of light with frequency 1.0×10^{12} Hz? ($h = 6.6 \times 10^{-34}$ J s)

12) What is the velocity of a particle that has a mass of 1.4 kg and a wavelength of 1.0×10^{-20} m? ($h = 6.6 \times 10^{-34}$ J s)

13) What is the wavelength of a particle if its mass is 1.0 kg and its velocity is 500.0 m/s? ($h = 6.6 \times 10^{-34}$ J s)

14) What is the mass of a particle if its velocity is 1.9 m/s and its wavelength is 1.0×10^{-10} m? ($h = 6.6 \times 10^{-34}$ J s)

Essay Questions

1) Describe the shapes and relative energies of the s, p, d, and f atomic orbitals.

2) Describe the different principles that govern the building of an electron configuration.

3) Explain why the 4s sublevel fills before the 3d sublevel begins to fill as electrons are added.

4) What is the quantum mechanical model?

5) What happens in the photoelectric effect?

6) What is the explanation for the discrete lines in atomic emission spectra?

7) Explain what is meant by the Heisenberg uncertainty principle.

Chapter 13 Electrons in Atoms

Matching Questions

1) Answer: C
2) Answer: E
3) Answer: A
4) Answer: D
5) Answer: B
6) Answer: F
7) Answer: C
8) Answer: A
9) Answer: B
10) Answer: E
11) Answer: F
12) Answer: D
13) Answer: A
14) Answer: F
15) Answer: E
16) Answer: D
17) Answer: C
18) Answer: B

Multiple Choice and Bimodal Questions

1) Answer: E
2) Answer: A
3) Answer: A
4) Answer: B
5) Answer: C
6) Answer: B
7) Answer: B
8) Answer: D
9) Answer: D
10) Answer: B
11) Answer: B
12) Answer: D
13) Answer: C
14) Answer: A
15) Answer: C
16) Answer: C
17) Answer: C
18) Answer: E
19) Answer: D
20) Answer: C
21) Answer: A

22) Answer: C

23) Answer: B

24) Answer: B

25) Answer: B

26) Answer: A

27) Answer: C

28) Answer: E

29) Answer: C

30) Answer: C

31) Answer: A

32) Answer: D

33) Answer: C

34) Answer: D

35) Answer: D

36) Answer: D

37) Answer: A

38) Answer: A

39) Answer: E

40) Answer: A

41) Answer: C

42) Answer: C

43) Answer: E

44) Answer: D

45) Answer: E

46) Answer: C

47) Answer: C

48) Answer: D

49) Answer: C

50) Answer: D

51) Answer: B

52) Answer: A

53) Answer: A

54) Answer: A

55) Answer: A

56) Answer: A

57) Answer: B

58) Answer: A

59) Answer: A

60) Answer: B

61) Answer: B

62) Answer: A

63) Answer: B

64) Answer: A

65) Answer: A

66) Answer: E

67) Answer: E

68) Answer: A

69) Answer: E

70) Answer: A

Problems

1) Answer: $1s^2 2s^2 2p^6 3s^2 3p^5$

2) Answer: $1s^2 2s^2$

3) Answer: $1s^2 2s^2 2p^6 3s^2 3p^6 3d^{10} 4s^2 4p^4$

4) Answer: 7

5) Answer: 2

6) Answer: $1s^2 2s^2 2p^6 3s^2 3p^6 3d^5 4s^1$

7) Answer: 1

8) Answer: $\nu = c/\lambda = \dfrac{3.0 \times 10^8 \text{ m/s}}{1.0 \times 10^{-8} \text{ m}} = 3.0 \times 10^{16} \text{ s}^{-1}$

$3.0 \times 10^{16} \text{ s}^{-1} \times \dfrac{1 \text{ Hz}}{\text{s}^{-1}} = 3.0 \times 10^{16} \text{ Hz}$

9) Answer: $\lambda = c/\nu = \dfrac{3.0 \times 10^8 \text{ m/s}}{1.0 \times 10^{20} \text{ s}^{-1}} = 3.0 \times 10^{-12} \text{ m}$

10) Answer: $\nu = E/h$

$\nu = \dfrac{1.0 \times 10^{-25} \text{ J}}{6.6 \times 10^{-34} \text{ J s}}$

$= 1.5 \times 10^8 \text{ s}^{-1}$

$= 1.5 \times 10^8 \text{ Hz}$

11) Answer: $E = h \times \nu$

$= (6.6 \times 10^{-34} \text{ J s}) \times (1.0 \times 10^{12} \text{ s}^{-1})$

$= 6.6 \times 10^{-22} \text{ J}$

12) Answer: $1 \text{ J} = 1 \text{ N m}$

$1 \text{ N} = 1 \text{ kg m s}^{-2}$

$\nu = \dfrac{h}{m\lambda}$

$= \dfrac{6.6 \times 10^{-34} \text{ J s}}{(1.4 \text{ kg}) \times (1.0 \times 10^{-20} \text{ m})}$

$= \dfrac{4.7 \times 10^{-14} \text{ J s}}{\text{kg} \times \text{m}}$

$= \dfrac{4.7 \times 10^{-14} \text{ J s}}{\text{kg} \times \text{m}} \times \dfrac{1 \text{ N m}}{1 \text{ J}} \times \dfrac{1 \text{ kg m s}^{-2}}{1 \text{N}}$

$= 4.7 \times 10^{-14} \text{ m/s}$

13) Answer: $1\,J = 1\,N\,m$

$$1\,N = 1\,kg\,m\,s^{-2}$$

$$\lambda = \frac{h}{mv}$$

$$= \frac{6.6 \times 10^{-34}\,J\,s}{1.0\,kg \times 500.0\,ms^{-1}}$$

$$= \frac{6.6 \times 10^{-36}\,J\,s^2}{kg \times ms^{-1}}$$

$$= \frac{6.6 \times 10^{-36}\,J\,s^2}{kg \times m} \times \frac{1\,N\,m}{1\,J} \times \frac{1\,kg\,m\,s^{-2}}{1N}$$

$$= 1.3 \times 10^{-36}\,m$$

14) Answer: $1\,J = 1\,N\,m$

$$1\,N = 1\,kg\,m\,s^{-2}$$

$$m = \frac{h}{v\lambda}$$

$$= \frac{6.6 \times 10^{-34}\,J\,s}{(1.9\,m/s) \times (1.0 \times 10^{-10}\,m)}$$

$$= \frac{3.5 \times 10^{-24}\,J\,s^2}{m^2}$$

$$= \frac{3.5 \times 10^{-24}\,J\,s^2}{m^2} \times \frac{1\,N\,m}{1\,J} \times \frac{1\,kg\,m\,s^{-2}}{1N}$$

$$= 3.5 \times 10^{-24}\,kg$$

Essay Questions

1) Answer: An s orbital has the shape of a sphere and is the orbital having the lowest energy. A p orbital is dumbbell–shaped and has the next highest energy. A d orbital has a more complex shape and a higher energy than either an s orbital or a p orbital. An f orbital has the highest energy of these four orbital types; this orbital has a very complex shape.

2) Answer: The Aufbau principle states that electrons enter the orbitals of lowest energy first. The Pauli exclusion principle states that each orbital can hold only two electrons. Hund's rule states that electrons first enter separate orbitals of the same energy, with each electron having the same spin, before sharing an orbital or having different spins.

3) Answer: Electrons occupy orbitals in a definite sequence, filling orbitals with lower energies first. Generally, orbitals in a lower energy level have lower energies that those in a higher energy level, but in the third level the energy ranges of the principal energy levels begin to overlap. As a result, the 4s sublevel is lower in energy than the 3d sublevel, so it fills first.

4) Answer: It is a model that describes the motions of electrons in atoms as probabilistic motions within a certain region. It is depicted as electron clouds, the density of which represents the probability of finding the electron in that region. The electron cloud of the quantum mechanical model is centered on the atomic orbital as proposed by Bohr.

5) Answer: In the photoelectric effect, electrons are ejected by metals when light shines on them. The effect is only observed if the frequency of the incident light is above a certain threshold frequency.

6) Answer: Electrons absorb energy and leap from one orbital in an atom to an orbital of higher energy. When these excited electrons fall back down to lower energy levels, they emit light. The lines result from the fact that the electrons can move only between discrete energy levels; they cannot have intermediate energies. Electron energies are quantized, not continuous.

7) Answer: The measurement of the speed or position of a moving particle necessarily involves an interaction with the particle. Therefore, the position and motion must be disturbed from what they were before the measurement. As a consequence, accurate measurements of both these variables cannot be made simultaneously.

Chapter 14 Chemical Periodicity

Matching Questions
Chapter 14: Matching I

1) electronegativity

2) ionization energy

3) period

4) periodic law

5) atomic radius

A) energy required to remove an electron from an atom

B) a repeating pattern of physical and chemical properties occurs when elements are arranged in order of increasing atomic number

C) one–half the distance between nuclei in a diatomic element

D) horizontal row of the periodic table

E) tendency of an atom to attract electrons in a chemical bond

Multiple Choice and Bimodal Questions

1) How many electrons are present in the d sublevel of a neutral atom of nickel?

   A) 0   B) 2   C) 4   D) 6   E) 8

2) What is the electron configuration of sulfur?

   A) $1s^2 2s^2 2p^6 3s^2 3p^3$ B) $1s^2 2s^2 2p^6 3s^2 3p^4$

   C) $1s^2 2s^2 2p^6 3s^2 3p^5$ D) $1s^2 2s^2 2p^6 3s^2 3p^6$

3) What orbital is filled when iodine gains an electron to become a negative ion?

   A) 4d   B) 4p   C) 5p   D) 6s

4) What element has the electron configuration $1s^2 2s^2 2p^6 3s^2 3p^2$?

   A) nitrogen   B) selenium   C) silicon   D) silver

5) What is true of the electron configurations of the noble gases?

   A) The outermost s and p sublevels are filled.

   B) The outermost s and p sublevels are partially filled.

   C) The outermost s and d sublevels are very close in energy and have electrons in them.

   D) The outermost s and f sublevels are very close in energy and have electrons in them.

6) What is true of the electron configurations of the representative elements?

   A) The outermost s and p sublevels are filled.

   B) The outermost s and p sublevels are partially filled.

   C) The outermost s and d sublevels are very close in energy and have electrons in them.

   D) The outermost s and f sublevels are very close in energy and have electrons in them.

7) What is another name for the representative elements?

   A) noble gases

   B) Group A elements

   C) Group B elements

   D) Group C elements

   E) transition elements

8) What is another name for the transition metals?

   A) noble gases

   B) Group A elements

   C) Group B elements

   D) Group C elements

   E) representative elements

9) Each period number in the periodic table corresponds to _____.

   A) a principal energy level   B) an energy sublevel

   C) an atomic mass   D) an atomic number

10) The representative elements are usually called _____.

    A) noble gases   B) Group A elements

    C) Group B elements   D) halogens

11) The category of elements that is characterized by the filling of f orbitals is the _____.

    A) inner transition metals   B) alkali metals

    C) alkaline earth metals   D) transition metals

12) Which element is a transition metal?

    A) cesium   B) copper   C) tellurium   D) tin

13) Which of the following groupings contains only representative elements?

    A) Cu, Co, Cd   B) Ni, Fe, Zn   C) Al, Mg, Li   D) Hg, Cr, Ag

14) How does atomic radius change from left to right across a period in the periodic table?

    A) It tends to decrease.

    B) It tends to increase.

    C) It does not change.

    D) It first increases, then decreases.

    E) It first decreases, then increases.

15) How does atomic radius change down a group in the periodic table?

   A) It tends to decrease.

   B) It tends to increase.

   C) It does not change.

   D) It first increases, then decreases.

   E) It first decreases, then increases.

16) Why is the radius of a positive ion always less than the radius of its neutral atom?

   A) The nucleus pulls the remaining electrons in closer.

   B) The number of principal energy levels is always reduced.

   C) The atomic orbitals contract all by themselves.

   D) Electron speeds are reduced.

17) Why is the radius of a negative ion always greater than the radius of its neutral atom?

   A) because the number of principal energy levels is always reduced

   B) because atomic orbitals contract all by themselves

   C) because electron speeds are reduced

   D) because repulsion between electrons increases

18) Which group of the periodic table has the highest electronegativity?

   A) 1A   B) 2A   C) 3A   D) 6A   E) 7A

19) Which of the following factors contributes to the relatively greater atomic size of the higher-atomic-number elements within a particular family of the periodic table?

   A) more shielding of the outer electrons by the inner electrons

   B) larger nuclei

   C) greater number of protons

   D) smaller number of valence electrons

20) How does the shielding phenomenon affect the relative atomic sizes of elements in the same period?

   A) An increase in the degree of shielding causes an increase in atomic size.

   B) An increase in the degree of shielding causes a decrease in atomic size.

   C) Shielding has no effect on relative atomic size within a period.

21) Which of the following elements has the smallest atomic radius?

   A) chlorine   B) sulfur   C) selenium   D) bromine

22) Atomic size generally _____.

   A) increases as you move from left to right across a period

   B) decreases as you move down a group

   C) remains constant within a period

   D) decreases as you move from left to right across a period

23) Which of the following elements has the smallest atomic radius?

    A) Li   B) K   C) O   D) S

24) The energy required to remove an electron from a gaseous atom is called the _____.

    A) excitation energy

    B) ionization energy

    C) polarization energy

    D) heat of vaporization

    E) electrolytic energy

25) Which of the following electron configurations is particularly stable?

    A) a half-filled energy sublevel

    B) a filled energy sublevel

    C) one empty and one filled energy sublevel

    D) a filled principal energy level

26) For Group 2A metals, which electron is the most difficult to remove from a neutral atom?

    A) the first

    B) the second

    C) the third

    D) All the electrons are equally difficult to remove.

27) Which of the following factors contributes to the lower ionization energy of the higher-atomic-number elements in a family in the periodic table?

    A) greater distance from nucleus   B) larger nuclei

    C) greater number of protons in nuclei   D) smaller number of valence electrons

28) Which of the following factors contributes to the greater ionization energy of the elements on the right side of a period in the periodic table?

    A) more shielding by inner electrons   B) larger nuclei

    C) greater number of protons in nuclei   D) smaller number of valence electrons

29) Which of the following elements has the smallest first ionization energy?

    A) sodium   B) calcium   C) potassium   D) magnesium

30) As you move from left to right across the second period of the periodic table _____.

    A) the ionization energy increases   B) the atomic radii increase

    C) the electron affinity decreases   D) the atomic mass decreases

31) Of the following atoms, which one has the smallest first ionization energy?

    A) boron   B) carbon   C) aluminum   D) silicon

32) Which of the following elements has the lowest electronegativity?

    A) lithium   B) carbon   C) bromine   D) fluorine

33) Electronegativity _____.

    A) is the electrical attraction of a negative ion to another negative ion

    B) generally increases as you move down a group

    C) is generally higher for metals than for nonmetals

    D) generally increases from left to right across a period

34) What term is used to describe an atom's tendency to attract electrons to itself when it is chemically combined with another element?

    A) electronation

    B) electron affinity

    C) electronegativity

    D) electrolysis

    E) electrochemical attraction

35) Which of the following elements, when ionically bound to sulfur, attracts electrons less strongly than the sulfur?

    A) chlorine   B) cesium   C) oxygen   D) fluorine

36) Compared with the electronegativities of the elements at the left end of a particular period, the electronegativities of the elements at the right side of that same period tend to be

_____.

    A) lower   B) higher   C) the same   D) unpredictable

37) Which of the following increases with increasing atomic number in Group 2A?

    A) atomic radius   B) electron affinity

    C) first ionization energy   D) number of outermost electrons

Problems

1) What is the electron configuration of oxygen?

2) Which element in the second principal energy level has the greatest atomic radius?

3) Which element has the lowest electronegativity?

4) Which element has the greatest electronegativity?

Essay Questions

1) Describe the periodic trends in atomic radii that can be observed in the periodic table. Provide examples.

2) Describe the periodic trends in first ionization energies that can be observed in the periodic table. Provide examples.

3) Positive ions are smaller than the neutral atoms from which they are formed, whereas negative ions are bigger. Explain why this is so.

4) Describe the periodic trends in electronegativity that can be observed in the periodic table. Provide examples.

Chapter 14 Chemical Periodicity
Matching Questions
1) Answer: E
2) Answer: A
3) Answer: D
4) Answer: B
5) Answer: C

Multiple Choice and Bimodal Questions
1) Answer: E
2) Answer: B
3) Answer: C
4) Answer: C
5) Answer: A
6) Answer: B
7) Answer: B
8) Answer: C
9) Answer: A
10) Answer: B
11) Answer: A
12) Answer: B
13) Answer: C
14) Answer: A
15) Answer: B
16) Answer: A
17) Answer: D
18) Answer: E
19) Answer: A
20) Answer: C
21) Answer: A
22) Answer: D
23) Answer: C
24) Answer: B
25) Answer: D
26) Answer: C
27) Answer: A
28) Answer: C
29) Answer: C
30) Answer: A
31) Answer: C
32) Answer: A
33) Answer: D
34) Answer: C

35) Answer: B

36) Answer: B

37) Answer: A

Problems

1) Answer: $1s^2 2s^2 2p^4$

2) Answer: lithium

3) Answer: cesium

4) Answer: fluorine

Essay Questions

1) Answer: Atomic radii increase with increasing atomic number down a column or family--sodium is bigger than lithium; potassium is bigger than sodium; rubidium is bigger than potassium, for example. Atomic radii decrease with increasing atomic number across a period--lithium is bigger than beryllium; beryllium is bigger than boron; and boron is bigger than carbon, etc., for example.

2) Answer: First ionization energies decrease down a family and across a period from right to left. The first ionization energy of rubidium is less than that of lithium and the first ionization energy of iodine is much greater than that of lithium, for example.

3) Answer: When an electron is added to a neutral atom to form a negative ion there is a resulting increase in electronic repulsion. This increase causes the electron cloud to expand and thereby increases the atomic radius. There is also a reduction in the average nuclear attraction experienced by each electron and this contributes to the increased atomic radius. When an electron is removed to form a positive ion, the remaining electrons are drawn closer to the nucleus because of an increase in the average nuclear attraction experienced by the electrons as well as reduced electronic repulsion.

4) Answer: Electronegativities decrease down a column or family and from right to left across a period. Rubidium is less electronegative than lithium, for instance, and lithium is less electronegative than fluorine.

Chapter 15 Ionic Bonding and Ionic Compounds
Matching Questions
Chapter 15: Matching I

1) halide ion

2) octet rule

3) ionic bond

4) electron dot structure

5) valence electron

6) coordination number

7) metallic bond

A) the number of ions of opposite charge surrounding each ion in a crystal

B) an electron in the highest occupied energy level of an atom

C) atoms react so as to acquire the stable electron structure of a noble gas

D) the attraction of valence electrons for metal ions

E) a depiction of valence electrons around the symbol of an element

F) the force of attraction binding oppositely charged ions together

G) an anion of chlorine or other halogen

Multiple Choice and Bimodal Questions

1) How many valence electrons are there in an atom of phosphorus?

    A) 2   B) 3   C) 4   D) 5   E) 6

2) How many valence electrons are there in an atom of magnesium?

    A) 2   B) 3   C) 4   D) 5   E) 6

3) How many valence electrons does a helium atom have?

    A) 2   B) 3   C) 4   D) 5   E) 6

4) How many valence electrons does an atom of any halogen have?

    A) 7   B) 4   C) 6   D) 8

5) How many valence electrons are there in a silicon atom?

A) 2   B) 4   C) 6   D) 8

6) What is the electron configuration of the calcium ion?

A) $1s^2 2s^2 2p^6 3s^2 3p^6$

B) $1s^2 2s^2 2p^6 3s^2 3p^4 4s^2$

C) $1s^2 2s^2 2p^6 3s^2 3p^5 4s^1$

D) $1s^2 2s^2 2p^6 3s^2$

E) $1s^2 2s^2 2p^6 3s^2 3p^{10}$

7) What is the electron configuration of the gallium ion?

A) $1s^2 2s^2 2p^6 3s^2 3p^3$

B) $1s^2 2s^2 2p^6 3s^2 3p^6$

C) $1s^2 2s^2 2p^6 3s^2 3p^5 4s^1$

D) $1s^2 2s^2 2p^6 3s^2 3p^6 4s^2 4p^6$

E) $1s^2 2s^2 2p^6 3s^2 3p^6 3d^{10}$

8) What is the charge on the strontium ion?

A) 2–   B) 1–   C) 1+   D) 2+   E) 3+

9) What is the electron configuration of the oxide ion (O^{2-})?

A) $1s^2 2s^2 2p^4$ B) $1s^2 2s^2 2p^6$ C) $1s^2 2s^2$ D) $1s^2 2s^2 2p^2$ E) $1s^2 2s^2 2p^5$

10) What is the electron configuration of the iodide ion (I^-)?

A) $1s^2 2s^2 2p^6 3s^2 3p^6 3d^{10} 4s^2 4p^6 4d^{10} 5s^2 5p^6$

B) $1s^2 2s^2 2p^6 3s^2 3p^6 3d^{10} 4s^2 4p^6 4d^{10}$

C) $1s^2 2s^2 2p^6 3s^2 3p^6 3d^{10} 4s^2 4p^6 4d^{10} 5s^2$

D) $1s^2 2s^2 2p^6 3s^2 3p^6 3d^{10} 4s^2 4p^6$

E) $1s^2 2s^2 2p^6 3s^2 3p^6 3d^{10} 4s^2 4p^6 4d^{10} 4f^{14}$

11) How many electrons does nitrogen have to gain in order to achieve a noble–gas electron configuration?

A) 1   B) 2   C) 3   D) 4   E) 5

12) How many electrons does boron have to give up in order to achieve a noble–gas electron configuration?

A) 1   B) 2   C) 3   D) 4   E) 5

13) How many electrons does silver have to give up in order to achieve a pseudo–noble–gas electron configuration?

A) 1   B) 2   C) 3   D) 4   E) 5

14) How many electrons does barium have to give up to achieve a noble–gas electron configuration?

A) 1   B) 2   C) 3   D) 4   E) 5

15) What is the formula of the ion formed when phosphorus achieves a noble-gas electron configuration?

    A) P^{3+} B) P^{2+} C) P^{-} D) P^{2-} E) P^{3-}

16) What is the formula of the ion formed when potassium achieves noble-gas electron configuration?

    A) K^{2+} B) K^{+} C) K^{1-} D) K^{2-} E) K^{3-}

17) What is the formula of the ion formed when tin achieves a stable electron configuration?

    A) Sn^{4+}

    B) Sn^{3+}

    C) Sn^{2-}

    D) Sn^{4-}

    E) none of the above

18) What is the formula of the ion formed when cadmium achieves a pseudo-noble-gas electron configuration?

    A) Cd^{3+} B) Cd^{2+} C) Cd^{+} D) Cd^{-} E) Cd^{2-}

19) What is the charge of a particle having 9 protons and 10 electrons?

    A) 2-   B) 1-   C) 0   D) 1+   E) 2+

20) What is the name given to the electrons in the highest occupied energy level of an atom?

    A) affinity electrons

    B) orbital electrons

    C) valence electrons

    D) anions

    E) cations

21) The octet rule states that, in chemical compounds, atoms tend to have _____.

    A) the electron configuration of a noble gas

    B) more protons than electrons

    C) eight electrons in their principal energy level

    D) more electrons than protons

22) How does calcium obey the octet rule when reacting to form compounds?

    A) It gains electrons.

    B) It gives up electrons.

    C) It does not change its number of electrons.

23) What is the maximum charge an ion is likely to have?

    A) 2   B) 3   C) 4   D) 5   E) 6

24) Which of the following is a pseudo-noble-gas electron configuration?

  A) $1s^22s^22p^63s^23d^5$

  B) $1s^22s^22p^63s^23d^6$

  C) $1s^22s^22p^63s^23d^{10}$

  D) $1s^22s^22p^63s^23d^{10}4s^2$

  E) $1s^22s^22p^63s^23d^{10}3f^{14}$

25) Which of the following ions has a pseudo-noble-gas electron configuration?

  A) Fe^{2+} B) Mn^{2+} C) Cu^+ D) Ni^+

26) How does oxygen obey the octet rule when reacting to form compounds?

  A) It gains electrons.

  B) It gives up electrons.

  C) It does not change its number of electrons.

27) Which kind of ion does sulfur become when it combines with a metal?

  A) anion

  B) cation

  C) It does not become an ion.

28) The electron configuration of a fluoride ion, F^-, is _____.

  A) $1s^22s^22p^5$ B) the same as that of a neon atom

  C) $1s^22s^22p^63s^1$ D) the same as that of a potassium ion

29) What is the charge on the cation in the ionic compound, sodium sulfide?

  A) 0   B) 1+   C) 2+   D) 3+   E) 4+

30) How many valence electrons are transferred from the nitrogen atom to potassium in the formation of the compound, potassium nitride?

  A) 0   B) 1   C) 2   D) 3   E) 4

31) How many valence electrons are transferred from the calcium atom to iodine in the formation of the compound, calcium iodide?

  A) 0   B) 1   C) 2   D) 3   E) 4

32) What is the formula unit of sodium nitride?

  A) NaN   B) Na_2N C) Na_3N D) NaN_3 E) Na_2N_3

33) What is the formula unit of aluminum oxide?

  A) AlO   B) Al_2O C) Al_3O D) AlO_3 E) Al_2O_3

34) What is the name of the ionic compound formed from strontium and phosphorus?
    A) strontium phosphorus
    B) strontium phosphoride
    C) strontium phosphate
    D) strontium phosphide
    E) strontide phosphate

35) What is the name of the ionic compound formed from lithium and bromine?
    A) lithium bromine
    B) lithium bromide
    C) lithium bromium
    D) lithium bromate
    E) lithium brominide

36) What is the formula for sodium sulfate?
    A) $NaSO_4$ B) Na_2SO_4 C) $Na(SO_4)_2$ D) $Na_2(SO_4)_2$

37) What is the formula for potassium sulfide?
    A) KS B) K_2S C) KS_2 D) K_2S_2

38) What is the formula for magnesium sulfide?
    A) MgS B) Mg_2S C) MgS_2 D) Mg_2S_2

39) Which of the following occurs in an ionic bond?
    A) Oppositely–charged ions attract.
    B) Two atoms share two electrons.
    C) Two atoms share more than two electrons.
    D) Like–charged ions attract.

40) What is the net charge of the ionic compound, calcium fluoride?
    A) 2–   B) 1–   C) 0   D) 1+   E) 2+

41) A compound held together by ionic bonds is called a _____.
    A) diatomic molecule
    B) triatomic molecule
    C) polar compound
    D) covalent molecule
    E) salt

42) Which of the following elements does NOT have an ionic charge of 1+?
    A) fluorine   B) hydrogen   C) potassium   D) sodium

43) Which of the following pairs of elements is most likely to form an ionic compound?

    A) magnesium and fluorine   B) nitrogen and sulfur

    C) oxygen and chlorine   D) sodium and aluminum

44) Which of the following compounds has the formula KNO_3?

    A) potassium nitrate   B) potassium nitride

    C) potassium nitrite   D) potassium nitrogen oxide

45) An ionic compound is _____.

    A) a salt   B) held together by ionic bonds

    C) composed of anions and cations   D) all of the above

46) Ionic compounds are normally in which physical state at room temperature?

    A) solid   B) liquid   C) gas   D) plasma

47) The melting temperature of potassium chloride is relatively _____.

    A) high   B) variable

    C) low   D) Potassium chloride does not melt.

48) What does the term "coordination number" refer to?

    A) the number of charges floating free in a crystal

    B) the total number of valence electrons in an atom

    C) the number of oppositely–charged ions surrounding a particular ion

    D) the number of atoms in a particular formula unit

    E) the number of like–charged ions surrounding a particular ion

49) What is the coordination number of both ions in the cesium chloride crystal?

    A) 2   B) 4   C) 6   D) 8   E) 12

50) How was the coordination number determined for the oxide ion in rutile (titanium oxide)?

    A) by ultraviolet spectroscopy

    B) by infrared spectroscopy

    C) by x–ray diffraction

    D) by gamma ray diffraction

    E) by ultrasound refractometry

51) Under what conditions can potassium bromide conduct electricity?

    A) only when melted

    B) only when dissolved

    C) only when it is in crystal form

    D) only when melted, or dissolved in water

    E) all of the above

52) Which of these is NOT a characteristic of most ionic compounds?

  A) They are solids.

  B) They have low melting points.

  C) When melted they conduct an electric current.

  D) They are composed of metallic and nonmetallic elements.

53) Which of the following particles are free to drift in metals?

  A) protons   B) electrons   C) neutrons   D) pions   E) cations

54) What is the basis of a metallic bond?

  A) the attraction of metal ions for mobile electrons

  B) the attraction between neutral metal atoms

  C) the neutralization of protons by electrons

  D) the attraction of oppositely-charged ions

  E) the sharing of two valence electrons between two atoms

55) What characteristic of metals makes them good electrical conductors?

  A) They have mobile valence electrons.

  B) They have mobile protons.

  C) They have mobile cations.

  D) Their crystal structures can be rearranged easily.

56) Which of the following crystals is the most malleable?

  A) sodium iodide   B) copper

  C) ammonium nitrate   D) aluminum phosphate

57) What is the coordination number of a body-centered cubic crystal?

  A) 6   B) 8   C) 10   D) 12   E) 16

58) Which metallic crystal structure has a coordination number of 8?

  A) body-centered cube

  B) face-centered cube

  C) hexagonal close-packing

  D) tetragonal

  E) trigonal

59) A metallic bond is a bond between _____.

  A) valence electrons and positively charged metal ions

  B) the ions of two different metals

  C) a metal and a nonmetal

  D) none of the above

Problems

  1) How many valence electrons are there in rubidium?

2) How many valence electrons are there in selenium?

3) Give the electron configurations for strontium and its ion.

4) Give the electron configurations for boron and its ion.

5) Give the electron configurations for mercury and its 2+ ion.

6) Give the electron configurations for sulfur and its 2– ion.

7) Give the electron configurations for iodine and its 1– ion.

8) How many electrons does a gallium atom give up when it becomes an ion?

9) What is the formula for the oxide ion?

10) Give the electron configuration for the chloride ion.

11) Give the electron configuration for calcium ion.

12) Give the electron configuration for the lithium ion.

13) Give the electron configuration for the oxide ion.

14) Write the formula for the compound, barium oxide.

15) Write the formula for the compound, boron nitride.

16) Write the formula for the compound, rubidium phosphide.

17) Write the formula for the compound, aluminum iodide.

18) Write the electron configuration diagram that shows the transfer of electrons that takes place to form the compound sodium fluoride. Include the electron configurations of the ions formed. Which noble gas configuration does each ion have?

Essay Questions

1) Explain the octet rule and give an example of how it is used.

2) Explain what a pseudo–noble-gas electron configuration is. Give examples of ions that have this type of configuration.

3) Explain how atoms (ions) are held together in an ionic bond. Give an example of an ionic compound.

4) Why must each cation in an ionic solid be surrounded by anions?

5) Why are there different coordination numbers for different crystals?

6) Explain how a pure metal is held together. Include a definition of a metallic bond in your explanation.

7) Explain how scientists have used metallic bonding to account for many of the physical properties of metals, such as electrical conductivity and malleability.

Chapter 15 Ionic Bonding and Ionic Compounds
Matching Questions
    1) Answer: G

    2) Answer: C

    3) Answer: F

    4) Answer: E

    5) Answer: B

    6) Answer: A

    7) Answer: D

Multiple Choice and Bimodal Questions
    1) Answer: D

    2) Answer: A

    3) Answer: A

    4) Answer: A

    5) Answer: B

    6) Answer: A

    7) Answer: E

    8) Answer: D

    9) Answer: B

    10) Answer: A

    11) Answer: C

    12) Answer: C

    13) Answer: A

    14) Answer: B

    15) Answer: E

    16) Answer: B

    17) Answer: A

    18) Answer: B

    19) Answer: B

    20) Answer: C

    21) Answer: A

    22) Answer: B

    23) Answer: B

    24) Answer: C

    25) Answer: C

    26) Answer: A

    27) Answer: A

    28) Answer: B

    29) Answer: B

    30) Answer: A

    31) Answer: C

    32) Answer: C

    33) Answer: E

34) Answer: D

35) Answer: B

36) Answer: B

37) Answer: B

38) Answer: A

39) Answer: A

40) Answer: C

41) Answer: E

42) Answer: A

43) Answer: A

44) Answer: A

45) Answer: D

46) Answer: A

47) Answer: A

48) Answer: C

49) Answer: D

50) Answer: C

51) Answer: D

52) Answer: B

53) Answer: B

54) Answer: A

55) Answer: A

56) Answer: B

57) Answer: B

58) Answer: A

59) Answer: A

Problems

1) Answer: 1

2) Answer: 6

3) Answer: Sr $\quad 1s^22s^22p^63s^23p^63d^{10}4s^24p^65s^2$

         Sr^{2+} $\quad 1s^22s^22p^63s^23p^63d^{10}4s^24p^6$

4) Answer: B $\quad 1s^22s^22p^1$

         B^{3+} $\quad 1s^2$

5) Answer: Hg $\quad 1s^22s^22p^63s^23p^63d^{10}4s^24p^64d^{10}4f^{14}5s^25p^65d^{10}6s^2$

         Hg^{2+} $\quad 1s^22s^22p^63s^23p^63d^{10}4s^24p^64d^{10}4f^{14}5s^25p^65d^{10}$

6) Answer: S $\quad 1s^22s^22p^63s^23p^4$

         S^{2-} $\quad 1s^22s^22p^63s^23p^6$

7) Answer: I $\quad 1s^22s^22p^63s^23p^63d^{10}4s^24p^64d^{10}4f^{14}5s^25p^5$

         I^- $\quad 1s^22s^22p^63s^23p^63d^{10}4s^24p^64d^{10}4f^{14}5s^25p^6$

8) Answer: 3

9) Answer: O^{2-}

10) Answer: $1s^22s^22p^63s^23p^6$

11) Answer: $1s^22s^22p^63s^23p^6$

12) Answer: $1s^2$

13) Answer: $1s^22s^22p^6$

14) Answer: BaO

15) Answer: BN

16) Answer: Rb_3P

17) Answer: AlI_3

18) Answer: $Na(1s^22s^22p^63s^1) + F(1s^22s^22p^5) \rightarrow Na^+(1s^22s^22p^6) + F^-(1s^22s^22p^6)$
    Both ions have the configuration of neon.

Essay Questions

1) Answer: The electron configuration (filled s and p orbitals s^2p^6) of the noble gases is extremely stable. In this configuration, repulsion between electrons is minimized and the energy state is, therefore, relatively low. The octet rule states that, in chemical reactions, elements gain or lose electrons to achieve the stable electron configuration of a noble gas. This stable configuration is called an octet because it includes a total of 8 valence electrons (s^2p^6): 2 from the outermost s orbital and 6 from the outermost p orbital. An example of use of the octet rule is the following. Oxygen has the electron configuration $1s^22s^22p^4$. When oxygen reacts to form ionic compounds, it completes its octet ($2s^22p^4$) by gaining two electrons from the element it reacts with. These two elements add to the p orbital of oxygen, giving it the electron configuration ($1s^22s^22p^6$) of the noble gas, neon. Oxygen's incomplete octet is thus completed by the gain of two additional electrons to give the stable octet of the noble gas ($2s^22p^6$).

2) Answer: A pseudo–noble–gas configuration has the form $s^2p^6d^{10}$. It has 18 electrons in the outer energy level and is a relatively stable configuration. Examples of ions with this configuration are Ag^+, Cu^+, Cd^{2+}, and Hg^{2+}.

3) Answer: In an ionic bond, oppositely–charged ions are held together by the electronic force of attraction that exists between oppositely–charged particles. In the ionic compound, anions and cartons are present in a specific ratio that causes the total charge on the compound to be zero. An example of an ionic compound is sodium phosphide, Na_3P, which has three sodium ions for each phosphide ion. This ratio insures a zero total charge given the charges on the two individual ions (Na = 1+, P = 3–).

4) Answer: In this arrangement, like–charged ions are shielded from each other and electronic repulsion is reduced. Also, the force of attraction between oppositely–charged ions is maximized in this arrangement. Each of these events contributes to a general lowering of energy and increase in stability for the ionic compound.

5) Answer: Differences in atomic radii, and in charge, dictate that atoms fit together in different ways. Also, several different arrangements of atoms (with each arrangement similar in energy content) are often possible in a solid, because of the simple ratios between numbers of cations and anions.

6) Answer: Scientists believe that a piece of pure metal, such as copper or iron, consists not of metal atoms, but of closely packed cations. The cations are surrounded by mobile valence electrons that are free to drift from one part of the metal to another. Metallic bonds result from the attraction between the free-floating valence electrons and the positively–charged metal ions.

7) Answer: Metallic bonds are the result of the attraction of free-floating valence electrons for positively–charged metal ions. An electric current is a flow of electrons. As electrons enter one end of a piece of metal, some of the free-floating electrons leave the other end. Thus metals are good conductors of electricity. The cations in a piece of metal are insulated from each other by the free electrons. Thus when the metal is struck, the cations slide past each other easily. This makes the metal malleable and ductile.

Chapter 16 Covalent Bonding

Matching Questions

Chapter 16: Matching I

1) coordinate covalent bond

2) double covalent bond

3) structural formula

4) single covalent bond

5) polar bond

6) hydrogen bond

A) a covalent bond in which the shared electron pair comes from only one of the atoms

B) a covalent bond in which only one pair of electrons is shared

C) a covalent bond in which only two pairs of electrons are shared

D) a depiction of the arrangement of atoms in molecules and polyatomic ions

E) a covalent bond between two atoms of significantly different electronegativities

F) a type of bond that is very important in determining the properties of water and of important biological molecules such as proteins and DNA

Chapter 16: Matching II

7) network solid

8) bonding orbital

9) dipole interaction

10) bond dissociation energy

11) tetrahedral angle

12) VSEPR theory

13) sigma bond

A) symmetrical bond along the axis between the two nuclei

B) crystal in which all the atoms are covalently bonded to each other

C) shapes adjust so valence electron pairs are as far apart as possible

D) energy needed to break a single bond

E) molecular orbital with energy lower than either of its atomic orbitals

F) 109.5°

G) attraction between polar molecules

Multiple Choice and Bimodal Questions

1) How many electrons are shared in a single covalent bond?

   A) 1   B) 2   C) 3   D) 4   E) 8

2) How many valence electrons does an atom of any halogen have?

   A) 1   B) 2   C) 4   D) 7

3) How many electrons are shared in a double covalent bond?

   A) 2   B) 3   C) 4   D) 6   E) 8

4) How many electrons does a nitrogen atom need to gain to attain a noble–gas electron configuration?

   A) 1   B) 2   C) 3   D) 4   E) 5

5) How many unshared pairs of electrons does the nitrogen atom in ammonia possess?

   A) 1   B) 2   C) 3   D) 4   E) 5

6) How many electrons does carbon need to gain to obtain a noble–gas electron configuration?

   A) 1   B) 2   C) 3   D) 4   E) 8

7) What is the total number of covalent bonds normally associated with a single carbon atom in a compound.

   A) 1   B) 2   C) 3   D) 4   E) 8

8) How many unshared pairs of electrons are there in a molecule of hydrogen iodide?

   A) 1   B) 2   C) 3   D) 4   E) 8

9) How many covalent bonds are there in a covalently bonded molecule containing 1 phosphorus atom and 3 chlorine atoms?

   A) 1   B) 2   C) 3   D) 4   E) 6

10) What is the name given to the energy required to break a single bond?
  A) ionization energy
  B) bond dissociation energy
  C) polarization energy
  D) electronegativity
  E) electron affinity

11) How do atoms achieve noble–gas electron configurations in single covalent bonds?
  A) One atom completely loses two electrons to the other atom in the bond.
  B) Two atoms share two pairs of electrons.
  C) Two atoms share two electrons.
  D) Two atoms share one electron.

12) Why do atoms share electrons in covalent bonds?
  A) to become ions and attract each other
  B) to attain a noble–gas electron configuration
  C) to become more polar
  D) to increase their atomic numbers

13) What is shown by the structural formula of a molecule or polyatomic ion?
  A) the arrangement of bonded atoms   B) the number of ionic bonds
  C) the number of metallic bonds   D) the shapes of molecular orbitals

14) Which of the following is the name given to the pairs of valence electrons that do not participate in bonding in diatomic oxygen molecules?
  A) unvalenced pair
  B) outer pair
  C) inner pair
  D) unshared pair
  E) bound pair

15) Which elements can form diatomic molecules joined by a single covalent bond?
  A) hydrogen only
  B) halogens only
  C) halogens and members of the oxygen group only
  D) hydrogen and the halogens only
  E) hydrogen, halogens, and members of the oxygen group

16) Which of these elements does not exist as a diatomic molecule?
  A) Ne   B) F   C) H   D) I

17) Which of the following elements can form diatomic molecules held together by triple covalent bonds?
  A) hydrogen   B) carbon   C) oxygen   D) fluorine   E) nitrogen

18) Which of the following elements can form diatomic molecules held together by double covalent bonds?

    A) hydrogen   B) carbon   C) oxygen   D) fluorine   E) nitrogen

19) A covalent bond in which each atom contributes two electrons is a _____.

    A) double covalent bond   B) four electron bond

    C) polar covalent bond   D) coordinate covalent bond

20) A diatomic molecule with a triple covalent bond is _____.

    A) N_2 B) F_2 C) H_2 D) O_2

21) A molecule with a single covalent bond is _____.

    A) CO_2 B) Cl_2 C) CO D) N_2

22) Which noble gas has the same electron configuration as the oxygen in a water molecule?

    A) helium   B) neon   C) argon   D) xenon

23) Which of the following electron configurations gives the correct arrangement of the four valence electrons of the carbon atom in the molecule methane (CH_4)?

    A) $2s^2 2p^2$ B) $2s^1 2p^1 3s^1$ C) $2s^1 2p^2 3s^1$ D) $2s^1 2p^3$

24) Which of the following diatomic molecules is joined by a double covalent bond?

    A) Cl_2 B) H_2 C) N_2 D) O_2

25) When one atom contributes both bonding electrons in a single covalent bond, the bond is called a(n) _____.

    A) one–sided covalent bond

    B) unequal covalent bond

    C) coordinate covalent bond

    D) ionic covalent bond

    E) ordinary covalent bond

26) Once formed, how are coordinate covalent bonds different from normally formed covalent bonds?

    A) They are stronger.   B) They are more ionic in character.

    C) They are weaker.   D) There is no difference.

27) When H^+ forms a bond with H_2O to form the hydronium ion H_3O^+, this bond is called a coordinate covalent bond because _____.

    A) both bonding electrons come from the oxygen atom

    B) it forms an especially strong bond

    C) the electrons are equally shared

    D) the oxygen no longer has eight valence electrons

28) Consider a set of different molecules having the numbers of resonance structures indicated below. Which number of resonance structures would be associated with the most stable molecule in the group?

A) 0   B) 1   C) 2   D) 3   E) 4

29) Which of the following is a true statement concerning the resonant molecule dinitrogen tetraoxide?

A) It alternates between its resonance forms.

B) It remains in one resonance form most of the time.

C) It has a structure that is intermediate between its drawn resonance forms.

D) It breaks down readily because resonant molecules are inherently unstable.

30) When do exceptions to the octet rule occur?

A) when the total number of valence electrons is zero

B) when the total number of valence electrons is even

C) when the total number of valence electrons is odd

D) when the total number of valence electrons is a multiple of eight

31) Substances in which all of the electrons are paired are said to be _____.

A) diamagnetic   B) electromagnetic

C) ferromagnetic   D) paramagnetic

32) How many unpaired electrons are present in each molecule of a para–magnetic substance?

A) 0   B) 1

C) 1 or more   D) 2 or more (not 1)

33) Which of the following types of magnetism is the strongest?

A) diamagnetic   B) ferromagnetic   C) paramagnetic

34) Which of the following diatomic molecules fails to follow the octet rule?

A) hydrogen   B) nitrogen   C) oxygen   D) fluorine

35) In which of the following compounds is the octet expanded to include 12 electrons.

A) H_2S B) SO_3 C) SO_3^{2-} D) SO_4^{2-} E) SCl_6

36) What is one way in which compounds that do not follow the octet rule can achieve stability?

A) by adding an electron

B) by alternating between different resonance forms

C) by absorbing light energy

D) by gaining mass

37) Which of the following pairs of elements can be joined by a covalent bond?

A) Na and C   B) Mg and C   C) Li and Cl   D) N and C

38) Which of the following bond types is the most stable?
   A) nonpolar covalent bond between small atoms
   B) nonpolar covalent bond between large atoms
   C) polar covalent bond between small atoms
   D) polar covalent bond between large atoms

39) Which of the following bonds is the least reactive?
   A) C—C   B) N—N   C) O—O   D) C—Cl   E) Br—Br

40) Which of the following bonds will break without the addition of energy?
   A) C—C
   B) N—N
   C) O—O
   D) Cl—Cl
   E) none of the above

41) How many electrons can occupy a single molecular orbital?
   A) 0   B) 1   C) 2   D) 4   E) 8

42) The side–by–side overlap of p orbitals produces what kind of bond?
   A) alpha bond
   B) beta bond
   C) pi bond
   D) sigma bond
   E) zeta bond

43) Molecular orbital theory is based upon which of the following models of the atom?
   A) classical mechanical model   B) Bohr model
   C) quantum mechanical model   D) Democritus model

44) How is a pair of molecular orbitals formed?
   A) by the splitting of a single atomic orbital
   B) by the reproduction of a single atomic orbital
   C) by the overlap of two atomic orbitals from the same atom
   D) by the overlap of two atomic orbitals from different atoms
   E) by the overlap of four atomic orbitals from two different atoms

45) Which of the following types of orbital has the highest energy?
   A) bonding orbital   B) antibonding orbital   C) atomic orbital

46) According to molecular orbital theory, why does a covalent bond form?
   A) because electrons have a lower energy in a bonding orbital than they do in their atomic orbitals and, therefore, the bonded structure is more stable
   B) because electrons have a lower energy in an antibonding orbital than in their atomic orbitals and, therefore, the bonded structure is more stable
   C) because electrons have a higher energy in a bonding orbital than in their atomic orbitals and, therefore, the bonded structure is more stable
   D) because electrons have a higher energy in an antibonding orbital than in their atomic orbitals and, therefore, the bonded structure is more stable

47) Where are the electrons most probably located in a molecular bonding orbital?
   A) anywhere in the orbital
   B) between the two atomic nuclei
   C) in stationary positions between the two atomic nuclei
   D) in circular orbits around each nucleus

48) A bond that is symmetrical along the axis between two atomic nuclei is a(n) _____.
   A) alpha bond
   B) beta bond
   C) pi bond
   D) sigma bond
   E) zeta bond

49) A molecular antibonding orbital is unfavorable to bonding between atoms because _____.
   A) electrons are not located between nuclei and, therefore, repulsive forces are increased
   B) electrons are not located between nuclei and, therefore, repulsive forces are decreased
   C) electrons are located between nuclei and, therefore, repulsive forces are decreased
   D) electrons are located between nuclei and, therefore, repulsive forces are increased

50) Sigma bonds are formed as a result of the overlapping of which type(s) of atomic orbital(s)?
   A) s only   B) p only   C) d only   D) s and p   E) p and d

51) Which of the following bond types is normally the weakest?
   A) sigma bond formed by the overlap of two s orbitals
   B) sigma bond formed by the overlap of two p orbitals
   C) sigma bond formed by the overlap of one s and one p orbital
   D) pi bond formed by the overlap of two p orbitals

52) According to VSEPR theory, molecules adjust their shapes to keep which of the following as far apart as possible?
   A) pairs of valence electrons   B) inner shell electrons
   C) mobile electrons   D) the electrons closest to the nuclei

53) What causes water molecules to have a bent shape, according to VSEPR theory?
  A) repulsive forces between specific electrons
  B) interaction between the fixed orbitals of the unshared pairs of oxygen
  C) ionic attraction and repulsion
  D) the unusual location of the free electrons

54) What is the measure of the tetrahedral bond angle?
  A) 90.0°   B) 109.5°   C) 120.0°   D) 180°

55) Which of the following structures is characterized by a bond angle of 107°?
  A) tetrahedral structure   B) pyramidal structure
  C) bent structure   D) linear structure

56) What is the bond angle in a water molecule?
  A) 90°   B) 105°   C) 109.5°   D) 120°   E) 180°

57) The shape of the carbon tetrachloride molecule is called _____.
  A) tetrahedral   B) square   C) four–cornered   D) planar

58) Which of the following theories provides information concerning both molecular shape and molecular bonding?
  A) molecular orbital theory   B) VSEPR theory
  C) orbital hybridization theory   D) Bohr atomic theory

59) What type of hybrid orbital exists in the methane molecule?
  A) sp   B) sp^2 C) sp^3 D) sp^3d^2

60) What is the measure of the angle between the carbon–carbon double bond and each carbon–hydrogen single bond in a molecule of ethene C_2H_4?
  A) 90°   B) 109.5°   C) 120°   D) 180°

61) How many hybrid orbitals surround a carbon atom that participates in only one double bond?
  A) 0   B) 1   C) 2   D) 3   E) 4

62) What is the shape of a molecule with a triple bond?
  A) tetrahedral   B) pyramidal   C) bent   D) linear

63) What type of hybridization occurs in the orbitals of a carbon atom participating in a triple bond with another carbon atom?
  A) sp^2 B) sp^3 C) sp

64) How many pi bonds are formed when sp^2 hybridization occurs in ethene, C_2H_4?
  A) 0   B) 1   C) 2   D) 3   E) 4

65) Which of the following covalent bonds is the most polar?

    A) C—C   B) C—H   C) C—Cl   D) C—Br   E) C—S

66) Which of the following atoms would acquire the most negative charge in a polar covalent bond with hydrogen?

    A) C   B) F   C) O   D) S

67) Which of the following pairs of elements can be joined by a polar bond?

    A) Na and C   B) C and C   C) N and C

68) We would expect a bond formed between a silicon atom and an oxygen atom to be _____.

    A) an ionic bond   B) a coordinate covalent bond

    C) a polar covalent bond   D) a nonpolar covalent bond

69) In an electric field, which region of the water molecule is attracted to the positive pole?

    A) the oxygen region of the molecule

    B) the hydrogen region of the molecule

    C) No part of the water molecule is attracted to the positive pole.

70) Which of the following compounds is the most polar?

    A) CBr_4 B) CO   C) I_2 D) NH_3

71) What is thought to cause the dispersion forces?

    A) attraction between ions

    B) motion of electrons

    C) sharing of electron pairs

    D) differences in electronegativity

    E) attraction between polar molecules

72) Which of the forces of molecular attraction is the weakest?

    A) dipole interaction   B) dispersion   C) hydrogen bond

73) What causes dipole interactions?

    A) attraction between ions

    B) motion of electrons

    C) sharing of electron pairs

    D) bonding of a covalently–bonded hydrogen to an unshared electron pair

    E) attraction between polar molecules

74) What causes hydrogen–bonding?

    A) attraction between ions

    B) motion of electrons

    C) sharing of electron pairs

    D) bonding of a covalently–bonded hydrogen to an unshared electron pair

    E) attraction between polar molecules

75) Why is hydrogen–bonding only possible with hydrogen?

    A) because hydrogen is the only atom whose nucleus is not shielded by electrons when it is involved in a covalent bond

    B) because hydrogen is the only atom that is the same size as an oxygen atom

    C) because hydrogen has the highest electronegativity of any element in the periodic table

76) Which of the forces of molecular attraction is the strongest?

    A) dipole interaction   B) dispersion forces   C) hydrogen bonds

77) Which of the following causes the boiling point of HF to be much higher than that of HCl or HBr?

    A) hydrogen bonds   B) van der Waals forces

    C) covalent bonds   D) coordinate covalent bonds

78) Which of the following is the weakest "bond"?

    A) hydrogen bond   B) dipole interaction

    C) polar covalent bond   D) ionic bond

79) Which type of solid has the highest melting point?

    A) ionic solid   B) network solid

    C) metal   D) nonmetallic solid

Problems

1) Calculate the total bond energy in one mole of methyl alcohol, CH_3OH. (Assume that the total bond energy in a molecule is the sum of the individual bond energies.)

Bond	Energy (kJ/mol)
H—H	435
C—H	393
C—O	356
O—H	464

Essay Questions

1) Explain what an unshared pair of electrons is. Give an example.

2) Explain what a coordinate covalent bond is. Give an example of a molecule having this type of bond.

3) What is resonance? Give an example.

4) Describe what the difference is between diamagnetic, paramagnetic, and ferromagnetic substances. Include a discussion of how these substances behave in the presence of an external magnetic field.

5) Can some atoms exceed the limits of the octet rule in bonding? If so, give an example.

6) What is the bond dissociation energy and how does it affect stability?

7) Indicate how bonding is explained in terms of molecular orbitals. Include definitions of bonding and antibonding orbitals in your discussion.

8) Explain what a pi bond is and what a sigma bond is. Which of these bond types tends to be the weaker? Why?

9) Explain what is meant by VSEPR theory. Give an example of how VSEPR theory can be applied to predict the shape of a molecule.

10) Explain what is meant by orbital hybridization. Give an example of a molecule in which orbital hybridization occurs.

11) What determines the degree of polarity in a bond? Distinguish between nonpolar covalent, polar covalent, and ionic bonds in terms of relative polarity.

12) Explain what a polar molecule is. Provide an example.

13) What are dispersion forces? How is the strength of dispersion forces related to the number of electrons in a molecule? Give an example of molecules that are attracted to each other by dispersion forces.

14) Describe a network solid and give two examples.

Chapter 16 Covalent Bonding

Matching Questions

1) Answer: A
2) Answer: C
3) Answer: D
4) Answer: B
5) Answer: E
6) Answer: F
7) Answer: B
8) Answer: E
9) Answer: G
10) Answer: D
11) Answer: F
12) Answer: C
13) Answer: A

Multiple Choice and Bimodal Questions

1) Answer: B
2) Answer: D
3) Answer: C
4) Answer: C
5) Answer: A
6) Answer: D
7) Answer: D
8) Answer: C
9) Answer: C
10) Answer: B
11) Answer: C
12) Answer: B
13) Answer: A
14) Answer: D
15) Answer: D
16) Answer: A
17) Answer: E
18) Answer: C
19) Answer: A
20) Answer: A
21) Answer: B
22) Answer: B
23) Answer: D
24) Answer: D
25) Answer: C
26) Answer: D

27) Answer: A

28) Answer: E

29) Answer: C

30) Answer: C

31) Answer: A

32) Answer: C

33) Answer: B

34) Answer: C

35) Answer: E

36) Answer: B

37) Answer: D

38) Answer: A

39) Answer: A

40) Answer: E

41) Answer: C

42) Answer: C

43) Answer: C

44) Answer: D

45) Answer: B

46) Answer: A

47) Answer: B

48) Answer: D

49) Answer: A

50) Answer: D

51) Answer: D

52) Answer: A

53) Answer: A

54) Answer: B

55) Answer: B

56) Answer: B

57) Answer: A

58) Answer: C

59) Answer: C

60) Answer: C

61) Answer: D

62) Answer: D

63) Answer: C

64) Answer: B

65) Answer: C

66) Answer: B

67) Answer: C

68) Answer: C

69) Answer: A

70) Answer: B

71) Answer: B

72) Answer: B

73) Answer: E

74) Answer: D

75) Answer: A

76) Answer: C

77) Answer: A

78) Answer: B

79) Answer: B

Problems

1) Answer: C——H   3 mol x 393 kJ/1 mol = 1179 kJ

           C——O   1 mol x 356 kJ/1 mol = 356 kJ

           O——H   1 mol x 464 kJ/1 mol = 464 kJ

           Total bond energy   = 1999 kJ

Essay Questions

1) Answer: An unshared pair of electrons is two valence electrons that are not shared between atoms. Each fluorine atom in a molecule of fluorine has three unshared electron pairs, for example.

2) Answer: A coordinate covalent bond is formed when one atom provides both shared electrons. An example is the carbon monoxide molecule in which the oxygen atom supplies two electrons to the carbon.

3) Answer: When two or more equally valid electron dot structures can be written for a compound, that compound is said to have resonance. The actual resonance structure is intermediate between the ones that can be drawn. The ozone molecule (0_3) has the following resonance structures: 0——0══0 and 0══0——0.

4) Answer: Diamagnetic substances are those in which all of the electrons are paired. Diamagnetic substances are weakly repelled by an external magnetic field. Paramagnetic substances are substances having one or more unpaired electrons. Paramagnetic substances exhibit a relatively strong attraction to an external magnetic field. Ferromagnetic substances are substances, such as iron, that have unpaired electrons and large groups of randomly dispersed ions. In a magnetic field, these groups of ions line up with the magnetic field in an orderly fashion. This creates a strong magnetic attraction. Ferromagnetic attraction is much stronger than either paramagnetic attraction or diamagnetic repulsion.

5) Answer: Yes. Sulfur and phosphorus can have 12 or 10 valence electrons, respectively, when combined with small halogens. In PCl_5, for instance, phosphorus has 10 valence electrons.

6) Answer: Bond dissociation energy is the energy required to break a single bond. The greater the bond dissociation energy is, the more stable the compound.

7) Answer: Two atomic orbitals overlap to form molecular orbitals. The overlap of two atomic orbitals produces two molecular orbitals. One is a bonding orbital——a molecular orbital whose energy is lower than that of the atomic orbitals from which it was formed. The other is an antibonding orbital——a molecular orbital whose energy is higher than that of the atomic orbital from which it was formed. An atomic orbital belongs to a particular atom; a molecular orbital belongs to a molecule as a whole. The number of molecular orbitals is equal to the number of atomic orbitals that overlap.

8) Answer: A pi bond is the bond formed as a result of the side–by–side overlap of two p orbitals. A sigma bond is the bond that results from the end–to–end overlap of two s orbitals, two p orbitals, or a p and an s orbital. Orbital overlap in pi bonding is not as extensive as it is in sigma bonding. Therefore, pi bonds tend to be weaker than sigma bonds.

9) Answer: VSEPR (valence–shell electron–pair repulsion) theory states that because electron pairs repel, molecules adjust their shapes so that the valence–electron pairs are as far apart as possible. In methane (CH_4), for example, there are four bonding electron pairs and no unshared pairs. The bonding pairs are farthest apart when the angle between the central carbon and each of its attached hydrogens is 109.5°. This turns out to be the angle that is actually observed experimentally.

10) Answer: In orbital hybridization, several atomic orbitals mix to form the same number of equivalent hybrid orbitals. For instance, the s and p orbitals of a valence shell may be modified to make hybrid orbitals having the character of both the s orbital and the p orbital. These hybrid orbitals are equivalent. Orbital hybridization occurs in the methane molecule in which one 2s orbital and three 2p orbitals hybridize to form four sp^3 orbitals.

11) Answer: The relative electronegativity of the two bonded atoms determines the polarity of a bond. If the difference in electronegativities between the two atoms is less than 0.4, the bond is nonpolar covalent. If the difference is 0.4 to 1.0, the bond is moderately polar covalent. If the difference is 1.0 to 2.0, the bond is highly polar covalent. If it is more than 2.0, the bond is ionic.

12) Answer: A polar molecule is one in which one end of the molecule is slightly negative in electric charge and the other end is slightly positive. An example of a polar molecule is water. The oxygen atom in water develops a slightly negative charge and the hydrogen atoms develop slightly positive charges as the result of the difference in electronegativity between the oxygen and hydrogen atoms.

13) Answer: Dispersion forces are the weakest of all molecular interactions, and are thought to be caused by the motion of electrons. Generally, the strength of dispersion forces increases as the number of electrons in a molecule increases. Diatomic molecules of halogen elements are an example of molecules whose attraction for one another is caused by dispersion forces.

14) Answer: Network solids are substances in which all of the atoms are covalently bonded to each other. Samples of these solids are thought of as single molecules. Two examples are diamond and silicon carbide.

Chapter 17 Water and Aqueous Systems

Matching Questions

Chapter 17: Matching I

1) solvation

2) weak electrolyte

3) aqueous solution

4) solvent

5) electrolyte

A) solute ions or molecules are surrounded by solvent molecules

B) dissolving medium

C) compound that ionizes incompletely in aqueous solution

D) compound that will conduct current in the liquid state or in aqueous solution

E) homogeneous mixture of water and dissolved substances

Chapter 17: Matching II

6) colloid

7) desiccant

8) water of hydration

9) hygroscopic

10) surfactant

A) takes water from the air

B) wetting agent

C) water of crystallization

D) mixture in which particle size averages between 1 nm and 100 nm in diameter

E) drying agent

Chapter 17: Matching III

11) efflorescent

12) deliquescent

13) emulsion

14) suspension

15) solute

A) gives off water of hydration

B) colloid of a liquid in a liquid

C) absorbs water from air to form solution

D) mixture in which particle size averages greater than 100 nm in diameter

E) dissolved particle

Chapter 17: Matching IV

16) dispersed phase

17) surface tension

18) Brownian motion

19) dispersion medium

20) Tyndall effect

A) chaotic movement of colloidal particles

B) colloidal particles in a suspension

C) phenomenon observed when beam of light passes through colloidal dispersion or suspension

D) inward force tending to minimize surface area

E) non–colloidal material in a colloidal suspension

Multiple Choice and Bimodal Questions

1) How many hydrogen bonds can be formed between one hydrogen atom in a water molecule and oxygen atoms of surrounding water molecules?

A) 0   B) 1   C) 2   D) 3   E) 4

2) How does the surface tension of water compare with the surface tensions of most other liquids?

A) It is lower.   B) It is about the same.   C) It is higher.

3) What is the effect of a wetting agent on surface tension?

    A) It increases surface tension.

    B) It decreases surface tension.

    C) It has no effect on surface tension.

4) How many calories are needed to raise the temperature of 10 g of water from 25°C to 35°C?

    A) 10 cal   B) 20 cal   C) 100 cal   D) 1000 cal

5) How many nonbonding pairs of electrons are in a water molecule?

    A) 1   B) 2   C) 3   D) 4

6) What is the shape of the water molecule?

    A) linear

    B) tetrahedral

    C) trigonal planar

    D) pyramidal

    E) bent

7) What is the angle between the bonds of a water molecule?

    A) 90°   B) 105°   C) 120°   D) 180°

8) Which of the following is primarily responsible for holding water molecules together in the liquid state?

    A) dispersion forces   B) hydrogen bonds

    C) ionic bonds   D) polar covalent bonds

9) Which atom in a water molecule has the greatest electronegativity?

    A) one of the hydrogen atoms

    B) both hydrogen atoms

    C) the oxygen atom

    D) There is no difference in the electronegativities of the atoms in a water molecule.

10) The bonds between the hydrogen and oxygen atoms in a water molecule are _____.

    A) hydrogen bonds   B) ionic bonds

    C) nonpolar covalent bonds   D) polar covalent bonds

11) The bonds between adjacent water molecules are called _____.

    A) hydrogen bonds   B) ionic bonds

    C) nonpolar covalent bonds   D) polar covalent bonds

12) What is primarily responsible for the surface tension of water?

    A) dispersion forces   B) hydrogen-bonding

    C) ionic attractions   D) covalent bonding

13) Which of the following is NOT a result of surface tension in water?

    A) Surface area is maximized.

    B) Water has an unusually low vapor pressure.

    C) Surface appears to have a "skin."

    D) Drops tend to become spherical.

14) How does a surfactant reduce surface tension?

    A) by increasing dispersion forces

    B) by decreasing the distances between water molecules

    C) by interfering with hydrogen–bonding

    D) by increasing dipole interaction

15) What causes water's low vapor pressure?

    A) dispersion forces   B) covalent bonding

    C) hydrogen–bonding   D) ionic attractions

16) Surface tension _____.

    A) is the inward force which tends to minimize the surface area of a liquid

    B) may be decreased by detergents

    C) is increased by hydrogen–bonding

    D) all of the above

17) The high surface tension of water is due to the _____.

    A) small size of water molecules

    B) high kinetic energy of water molecules

    C) hydrogen bonding between water molecules

    D) covalent bonds in water molecules

18) At what temperature does liquid water have its maximum density?

    A) 0°C   B) 4°C   C) 37°C   D) 100°C

19) Which of the following is NOT a result of water's high heat capacity?

    A) The temperature of water goes up rapidly as it absorbs solar energy.

    B) The temperatures of cities near large bodies of water are moderated.

    C) For the same increase in temperature, iron needs to absorb only about one–tenth as much energy as water.

    D) Water is an excellent medium for the storage of solar energy.

20) How does the boiling point of water compare with the boiling points of other molecules of similar size?

    A) It is lower.   B) It is about the same.   C) It is higher.

21) How does the heat of vaporization of water compare with the heats of vaporization of other liquids?

    A) It is lower.   B) It is about the same.   C) It is higher.

22) As a result of water's high heat of vaporization, differences in temperature extremes on earth are _____.
   A) less than they would otherwise be
   B) greater than they would otherwise be
   C) There is no effect on temperature extremes.

23) Which of the following is most directly responsible for water's high heat of vaporization?
   A) dispersion forces   B) covalent bonding
   C) hydrogen–bonding   D) ionic attractions

24) Which of the following is most directly responsible for water's high boiling point?
   A) dispersion forces   B) covalent bonding
   C) hydrogen–bonding   D) ionic attractions

25) Which of the following is responsible for the relatively high boiling point of ammonia?
   A) polar covalent bonding   B) hydrogen–bonding
   C) ionic bonding   D) metallic bonding

26) The condensation of steam is a(n) _____.
   A) endothermic process   B) exothermic process
   C) electrolytic process   D) catalytic process

27) What energy change occurs when 100 g of ice melts to form 100 g of water at 0°C?
   A) 8 kcal is absorbed by the ice.
   B) 8 kcal is released by the ice.
   C) No energy change occurs.

28) Approximately what percent of an ice cube's volume is above the water level when the cube is floating in water at 0 degrees Celsius?
   A) 0%   B) 10%   C) 20%   D) 50%   E) 90%

29) The fact that ice is less dense than water is related to the fact that _____.
   A) the molecular structure of ice is much less orderly than that of water
   B) the molecules of ice are held to each other by covalent bonding
   C) ice has a molecular structure in which water molecules are arranged randomly
   D) ice has a molecular structure that is an open framework held together by hydrogen-bonding

30) Which of the following is responsible for the high heat of melting of ice?
   A) covalent bonding   B) dispersion forces
   C) hydrogen–bonding   D) ionic attractions

31) How many water molecules are in four formula units of calcium chloride dihydrate (CaCl$_2$ • 2H$_2$O)?
   A) 2   B) 4   C) 6   D) 8

32) What is the term for the dissolving medium in a solution?

    A) solvent   B) solute   C) solvator   D) emulsifier

33) A solution has which of the following properties?

    A) Gravity separates its parts.

    B) The top layer is different in composition than the bottom layer.

    C) The average diameter of its solute particles is usually less than 1.0 nm.

    D) A filter can remove the solute.

    E) The solvent is always a liquid.

34) Which of the following substances is the most soluble in water?

    A) sodium chloride

    B) methane

    C) bromine

    D) oxygen

    E) carbon

35) A solution is a mixture _____.

    A) from which the solute can be filtered

    B) that has the same properties throughout

    C) that is heterogeneous

    D) in which a solid solute is always dissolved in a liquid solvent

36) Predict which one of the following compounds would be insoluble in water.

    A) NaCl   B) HCl   C) CF_4 D) $CuSO_4$

37) What occurs in solvation?

    A) Solute ions separate from solvent molecules.

    B) Solvent molecules surround solute ions.

    C) Solvent molecules bind covalently to solute molecules.

    D) Ionic compounds are formed.

38) Why are two nonpolar substances able to dissolve in each other?

    A) There is no repulsive force between them.

    B) They combine to produce a polar substance.

    C) There is no attractive force between them.

    D) Nonpolar substances cannot dissolve in each other.

39) Which of the following substances dissolves most readily in gasoline?

    A) CH_4 B) HCl   C) NH_3 D) NaBr   E) $BaSO_4$

40) Which of the following substances dissolves most readily in water?

    A) $BaSO_4$ B) $CaCO_3$ C) NH_3 D) CH_4

41) Which of these would you expect to be soluble in the nonpolar solvent carbon disulfide, CS_2?

A) H_2O B) CI_4 C) $CaCO_3$ D) SnS_2

42) Which of the following compounds is an electrolyte?

A) rubbing alcohol

B) sugar

C) carbon tetrachloride

D) silicon dioxide

E) sodium hydroxide

43) Which of the following compounds conducts electricity only in the molten state?

A) sodium bromide

B) magnesium sulfate

C) calcium hydroxide

D) barium sulfate

E) copper chloride

44) Which of the following compounds is a nonelectrolyte?

A) sodium bromide

B) magnesium sulfate

C) calcium hydroxide

D) carbon tetrachloride

E) copper chloride

45) Which of the following compounds is a nonelectrolyte when pure, but an electrolyte when dissolved in water?

A) rubbing alcohol

B) sugar

C) carbon tetrachloride

D) ammonia

E) silicon dioxide

46) What type of compound is always an electrolyte?

A) polar covalent   B) nonpolar covalent

C) ionic   D) network solid

47) Which of the following are weak electrolytes in water?

A) ionic compounds that are slightly soluble

B) ionic compounds that are soluble

C) polar compounds that ionize

D) nonpolar compounds that do not ionize

48) Which of the following compounds is a weak electrolyte?

A) NaBr B) HBr C) KOH D) $PbCl_2$ E) $C_6H_{12}O_6$

49) Which of the following compounds is a strong electrolyte?

A) ammonia

B) acetic acid

C) sugar

D) lead(II) chloride

E) magnesium sulfate

50) Which of the following substances is NOT an electrolyte?

A) $AlCl_3$ B) CCl_4 C) LiCl D) Na_2SO_4

51) An electric current is conducted by _____.

A) a salt solution   B) a sugar solution

C) methane gas   D) none of the above

52) What is another term for the water of hydration?

A) water of solvation

B) water of crystallization

C) water of sublimation

D) water of efflorescence

E) water of deliquescence

53) A hydrated crystal that has a water vapor pressure greater than the water vapor pressure of air is called _____.

A) a desiccant   B) deliquescent   C) hygroscopic   D) efflorescent

54) A crystal that absorbs water vapor from the air is called _____.

A) aqueous   B) deliquescent   C) hygroscopic   D) efflorescent

55) A crystal that absorbs water vapor from the air and then dissolves in the water is _____.

A) a desiccant   B) deliquescent   C) hygroscopic   D) efflorescent

56) Which of the following is a true statement concerning the result of a deliquescent substance dissolving in the water it absorbs from the air?

A) The water vapor pressure of the resulting solution is lower than the water vapor pressure of the air.

B) The water vapor pressure of the resulting solution is greater than the water vapor pressure of the air.

C) There is no difference between the water vapor pressure of the resulting solution and the water vapor pressure of the air.

57) Which of the following is a true statement concerning efflorescent hydrates?
   A) The water vapor pressure of the hydrate is lower than the water vapor pressure of the air.
   B) The water vapor pressure of the hydrate is higher than the water vapor pressure of the air.
   C) There is no difference between the water vapor pressure of the hydrate and the water vapor pressure of the air.

58) How many phases are present in a colloid?
   A) 1   B) 2   C) 1 or 2

59) Which of the following mixture types is characterized by the settling of particles?
   A) solution   B) suspension   C) colloid   D) hydrate

60) What is the average diameter of particles in a suspension?
   A) over 10 000 nm
   B) between 1000 nm and 10 000 nm
   C) between 100 nm and 1000 nm
   D) between 10 nm and 100 nm
   E) between 1 nm and 10 nm

61) Which of the following types of mixture can be filtered to remove solute?
   A) suspensions only
   B) colloids only
   C) suspensions and colloids
   D) suspensions and solutions
   E) colloids and solutions

62) Which of the following materials is NOT a colloid?
   A) glue
   B) smoke
   C) paint
   D) aerosol spray
   E) alloy

63) The solute in a colloidal suspension is called the _____.
   A) dissolving phase   B) dispersed phase
   C) dispensing phase   D) dispersion medium

64) Which of the following types of mixtures exhibit the Tyndall effect?
   A) suspensions and colloids
   B) suspensions and solutions
   C) colloids and solutions

65) What causes Brownian motion in colloidal suspensions?

    A) molecules of the dispersion medium colliding with particles of the dispersed phase

    B) particles of the dispersed phase colliding with molecules of the dispersion medium

    C) There is no Brownian motion in colloidal suspensions.

66) An emulsion is which type of mixture?

    A) suspension   B) colloid   C) solution

67) An emulsion is a colloidal dispersion of _____.

    A) solids in liquids   B) liquids in liquids

    C) gases in liquids   D) liquids in gases

68) An emulsifying agent is typically characterized by having _____.

    A) one polar end

    B) one nonpolar end

    C) two polar ends

    D) two nonpolar ends

    E) one polar end and one nonpolar end

69) Which of the following mixtures is NOT a colloid?

    A) fog   B) milk   C) paint   D) sugar water

70) Which of these statements is correct?

    A) Particles can be filtered from a suspension.

    B) A solution is heterogeneous.

    C) A colloidal system does not give the Tyndall effect.

    D) The particles in a colloidal system are affected by gravity.

71) Which of the following mixtures exhibits the Tyndall effect?

    A) colloids   B) solutions   C) suspensions   D) both A. and C.

72) Emulsions are _____.

    A) a form of colloid   B) dispersions of liquids in liquids

    C) both A. and B.   D) none of the above

Problems

1) How many calories are required to heat 354 grams of water from 19°C to 87°C?

2) How many calories are released when 15 grams of steam at 100°C condense to 15 grams of water at 100°C?

3) How many grams of copper sulfate pentahydrate ($CuSO_4 \bullet 5H_2O$) would you heat to produce 18 grams of water?

4) What is the percentage of water in the hydrate $CoCl_2 \bullet 6H_2O$?

Essay Questions

1) Describe the structure of the water molecule and indicate how this structure is responsible for many of the unique properties of this vital compound.

2) Why will a needle float on the surface of water but sink immediately if it breaks through the surface?

3) What does a surfactant do? Give an example of a surfactant and explain the origin of the word.

4) How is water's high heat capacity related to the ability of a large body of water to moderate temperature changes in its vicinity?

5) Explain why water has a relatively high heat of vaporization.

6) Why is ice less dense than water?

7) Define the terms solute, solvent, and aqueous solution. Provide an example of each.

8) Describe the process of solvation.

9) What is an electrolyte? Give examples and distinguish between a strong electrolyte and a weak electrolyte.

10) Distinguish among efflorescent, hygroscopic, and deliquescent substances. Provide examples.

11) Distinguish among a suspension, a colloid, and a solution. Give an example of each.

Chapter 17 Water and Aqueous Systems

Matching Questions

1) Answer: A
2) Answer: C
3) Answer: E
4) Answer: B
5) Answer: D
6) Answer: D
7) Answer: E
8) Answer: C
9) Answer: A
10) Answer: B
11) Answer: A
12) Answer: C
13) Answer: B
14) Answer: D
15) Answer: E
16) Answer: B
17) Answer: D
18) Answer: A
19) Answer: E
20) Answer: C

Multiple Choice and Bimodal Questions

1) Answer: B
2) Answer: C
3) Answer: B
4) Answer: C
5) Answer: B
6) Answer: E
7) Answer: B
8) Answer: B
9) Answer: C
10) Answer: D
11) Answer: A
12) Answer: B
13) Answer: A
14) Answer: C
15) Answer: C
16) Answer: D
17) Answer: C
18) Answer: B
19) Answer: A

20) Answer: C

21) Answer: C

22) Answer: A

23) Answer: C

24) Answer: C

25) Answer: B

26) Answer: B

27) Answer: A

28) Answer: B

29) Answer: D

30) Answer: C

31) Answer: D

32) Answer: A

33) Answer: C

34) Answer: A

35) Answer: B

36) Answer: C

37) Answer: B

38) Answer: A

39) Answer: A

40) Answer: C

41) Answer: B

42) Answer: E

43) Answer: D

44) Answer: D

45) Answer: D

46) Answer: C

47) Answer: A

48) Answer: D

49) Answer: E

50) Answer: B

51) Answer: A

52) Answer: B

53) Answer: D

54) Answer: C

55) Answer: B

56) Answer: A

57) Answer: B

58) Answer: B

59) Answer: B

60) Answer: C

61) Answer: A

62) Answer: E

63) Answer: B

64) Answer: A

65) Answer: A

66) Answer: B

67) Answer: B

68) Answer: E

69) Answer: D

70) Answer: A

71) Answer: D

72) Answer: C

Problems

1) Answer: $\Delta T = 87°C - 19°C = 68°C$

$$354 \text{ g } H_2O \times 1\frac{cal}{g \times °C} \times 68°C$$

$$= 2.4 \times 10^4 \text{ cal}$$

2) Answer: $15 \text{ g} \times \dfrac{540 \text{ cal}}{1 \text{ g}} = 8.1 \times 10^3 \text{ cal}$

3) Answer: $18 \text{ g } H_2O = 1 \text{ mol } H_2O$

Gram formula mass $CuSO_4 \bullet 5H_2O = 249.6$ g

$1 \text{ mol } CuSO_4 \bullet 5H_2O \rightarrow 5 \text{ mol } H_2O$

$$\frac{1 \text{ mol } CuSO_4 \bullet 5H_2O}{5 \text{ mol } H_2O} \times \frac{249.6 \text{ g } CuSO_4 \bullet 5H_2O}{1 \text{ mol } CuSO_4 \bullet 5H_2O}$$

$$= \frac{49.9 \text{ g } CuSO_4 \bullet 5H_2O}{1 \text{ mol } H_2O} = 50 \text{ g } CuSO_4 \bullet 5H_2O$$

4) Answer: Gram formula mass $CoCl_2 \bullet 6H_2O = 237.9$ g

$1 \text{ mol } CoCl_2 \bullet 6H_2O \rightarrow 6 \text{ mol } H_2O$

$6 \text{ mol } H_2O \times \dfrac{18 \text{ g}}{1 \text{ mol}} = 108.0 \text{ g } H_2O$

Essay Questions

1) Answer: Water is a simple, triatomic molecule. Each O—H covalent bond in the water molecule is highly polar. Because of its greater electronegativity, the oxygen atom attracts the electron pair of the covalent O—H bond and acquires a slightly negative charge. The hydrogen atoms, being less electronegative than the oxygen, acquire a slightly positive charge. The atoms of the water molecule are joined in a 105° angle. As a result, the slight charges on the individual atoms do not cancel each other out and the molecule itself is polar. There is a slight negative charge in the region around the oxygen and a slight positive charge in the region around the hydrogens. Because water molecules are polar, they attract each other. The hydrogen of one molecule is attracted to the oxygen of another molecule. This attraction is termed hydrogen-bonding and it is stronger than other polar attractions because of the fact that the hydrogen nucleus is not shielded by an electron cloud in the way that other nuclei would be (hydrogen atoms have only 1 electron). It is the strong intermolecular attraction associated with hydrogen-bonding that is responsible for many of the unusual properties of water, including its high surface tension, low vapor pressure, high specific heat, high heat of vaporization, and high boiling point.

2) Answer: The surface of the water presents greater resistance (surface tension) to the needle than does the rest of the water. This is because water molecules are packed more closely at the surface than elsewhere. This closer packing results from the one-sided intermolecular attraction that exists at the surface of the water. The water molecules at the surface are attracted to the water molecules below them. But, unlike in the rest of the liquid, there are no water molecules above them to pull them in the opposite direction. The closer-packed water molecules at the surface form a "skin" that is denser than the water below. Objects denser than water (e.g. the needle) can float upon this skin. All liquids will exhibit surface tension, but this phenomenon is more pronounced in water because of its hydrogen-bonding.

3) Answer: Surfactants are surface active agents used to decrease surface tension. Detergents and soaps are examples of surfactants. When added to beads of water on a greasy surface, for example, the detergent molecules interfere with the hydrogen-bonding between water molecules and cause the water to spread out.

4) Answer: As a result of its high heat capacity, water can absorb and release significant amounts of energy with only relatively small changes in temperature. Consequently, large bodies of water act to moderate temperature changes in their vicinities. As the temperature of the surroundings goes up, water absorbs heat energy, but its temperature goes up only relatively slightly. This has the effect of moderating the temperature in the area around the water. In cold weather, a similar phenomenon takes place. As the temperature of the surroundings drops, water will give off energy to the surroundings, but the temperature of the water will go down only slightly. In this way, cold temperatures also are moderated in areas near bodies of water.

5) Answer: Water has a high heat of vaporization as a result of its hydrogen-bonding. Because of its extensive network of hydrogen-bonds, the molecules of water are held together more tightly than are the molecules of many other liquids. The attractive force of these hydrogen-bonds must be overcome in order for water to vaporize.

6) Answer: The structure of ice is a very regular, open framework in which the water molecules are farther apart from each other than they are in liquid water. When ice melts, this open framework collapses and the water molecules move closer together. As a result, the water is denser than the ice.

7) Answer: An aqueous solution is any sample of water that contains one or more dissolved substances. A solvent is the dissolving medium in a solution. A solute is the dissolved material in a solution. Salt (NaCl) in water is an example of an aqueous solution. In this solution, water is the solvent and salt is the solute.

8) Answer: Solvent molecules collide with solute particles and exert attractive forces on them. Whenever these forces are greater than the attractive forces within the solute, the solute particles separate from the bulk of the solute. The particles of solute then become surrounded by particles of solvent.

9) Answer: An electrolyte is any substance that will conduct an electric current in aqueous solution or in the molten state. Strong electrolytes are substances that are completely, or almost completely, ionized in water. Examples of strong electrolytes are sodium chloride, hydrochloric acid, and sodium hydroxide. Weak electrolytes are substances that are only slightly ionized in water. Examples of weak electrolytes are mercuric chloride and acetic acid.

10) Answer: Efflorescent substances are hydrates that spontaneously give off the water of hydration. A hydrate will effloresce if it has a water vapor pressure higher than that of the water vapor in the air. An example of an efflorescent compound is copper sulfate pentahydrate, $CuSO_4 \bullet 5H_2O$. Hygroscopic substances are substances that absorb moisture from the air to form hydrates or solutions. Examples of hygroscopic substances are phosphorus pentoxide, P_2O_5; sodium hydroxide, NaOH; and calcium chloride monohydrate, $CaCl_2 \bullet H_2O$. Deliquescent substances are substances that can absorb so much moisture from the air as to actually dissolve in the absorbed water. For deliquescent substances, the water vapor pressure of the solution formed when the substance absorbs water from the air is lower than that of the water vapor in the air. An example of a deliquescent substance is sodium hydroxide.

11) Answer: Suspensions are mixtures out of which some particles will settle upon standing. Particles in a typical suspension have an average diameter greater than 1000 nm. Suspensions are heterogeneous mixtures. An example of a suspension is a sand–water mixture. Colloids are mixtures containing particles that are intermediate in size between the particles in suspensions and the particles in true solutions. The average diameter of a particle in colloidal suspension is between 1 nm and 100 nm. Colloids exhibit the Tyndall effect, which is the scattering of light in all directions by the particles in the suspension. (Note: Suspensions also exhibit the Tyndall effect, but solutions do not.) A solution is a homogeneous mixture. The particles in a solution have an average diameter of 1 nm. Solutions do not exhibit the Tyndall effect.

Chapter 18 Solutions
Matching Questions
Chapter 18: Matching I

1) Henry's law

2) immiscible

3) saturated solution

4) supersaturated solution

5) concentration

A) describes liquids that are insoluble in one another

B) measure of the amount of solute dissolved in a specified quantity of solvent

C) solution containing more solute than can theoretically dissolve at a given temperature

D) at a given temperature, the solubility of a gas in a liquid is directly proportional to the pressure of the gas above the liquid

E) solution containing maximum amount of solute

Chapter 18: Matching II

6) boiling point elevation

7) molality

8) mole fraction

9) molarity

10) freezing point depression

A) ratio of moles of solute in solution to total number of moles of both solvent and solute

B) number of moles of solute dissolved in 1000 g of solvent

C) number of moles of solute dissolved in 1 L of solution

D) a colligative property related to a decrease in the vapor pressure of a solution

E) a colligative property related to the fact that ice will form at higher temperatures in the Great Lakes than in the ocean

Chapter 18: Matching III

11) colligative property

12) dilute solution

13) miscible

14) unsaturated solution

15) concentrated solution

A) describes liquids that are soluble in one another

B) solution containing a small amount of solute

C) solution containing a large amount of solute

D) solution containing less than the maximum amount of dissolved solute

E) depends on the number of particles a solute yields in solution

Multiple Choice and Bimodal Questions

1) How does solubility generally vary as the temperature increases?
   A) solubility decreases
   B) solubility increases
   C) solubility remains the same

2) What is the maximum amount of KCl that can dissolve in 200 g of water? (solubility of KCl is 34 g/100 g H_2O at 20°C)

   A) 17 g   B) 34 g   C) 68 g   D) 6800 g   E) 0.34 g

3) What is the solubility of silver nitrate if only 11.1 g can dissolve in 5.0 g of water at 20°C?

A) $\dfrac{2.2 \text{ g}}{100 \text{ g H}_2\text{O}}$ at 20°C

B) $\dfrac{45 \text{ g}}{100 \text{ g H}_2\text{O}}$ at 20°C

C) $\dfrac{22.2 \text{ g}}{100 \text{ g H}_2\text{O}}$ at 20°C

D) $\dfrac{222 \text{ g}}{100 \text{ g H}_2\text{O}}$ at 20°C

E) $\dfrac{0.45 \text{ g}}{100 \text{ g H}_2\text{O}}$ at 20°C

4) What happens to the solubility of a gas, in a liquid, if the partial pressure of the gas above the liquid decreases?

A) The solubility decreases.

B) The solubility increases.

C) The solubility remains the same.

5) If the solubility of a gas in water is 4.0 g/L when the pressure of the gas above the water is 3.0 atm, what is the pressure of the gas above the water when the solubility of the gas is 1.0 g/L?

A) 0.75 atm   B) 1.3 atm   C) 4.0 atm   D) 12 atm

6) Which of the following factors both affect the solubility of a particular substance?

A) temperature and the nature of solute and solvent

B) temperature and degree of mixing

C) particle size and degree of mixing

D) particle size and temperature

7) Which of the following operations usually makes a substance dissolve faster in a solvent?

A) agitation   B) raising the temperature

C) crushing the substance to a powder   D) all of the above

8) Increasing the temperature of a solution will generally _____.

A) increase the rate at which a solute dissolves

B) increase the amount of solute that dissolves

C) both A. and B.

D) neither A. nor B.

9) Which of the following expressions is generally used for solubility?

A) grams of solute per 100 grams of solvent

B) grams of solute per 100 milliliters of solvent

C) grams of solute per 100 grams of solution

D) grams of solute per 100 milliliters of solution

10) Which of the following pairs of substances are miscible?

    A) water and ethanol   B) water and sodium chloride

    C) water and oxygen   D) water and gasoline

11) If a crystal added to an aqueous solution causes many particles to come out of the solution, the original solution was _____.

    A) saturated   B) unsaturated   C) supersaturated   D) an emulsion

12) Which of the following are immiscible liquids?

    A) ethanol and water   B) acetic acid (vinegar) and water

    C) gasoline and water   D) sulfuric acid and water

13) Holding the temperature constant while adding more solute to a solution that already has solute crystals at the bottom of the container _____.

    A) makes the solution more concentrated

    B) causes the solution to become supersaturated

    C) causes more solute crystals to appear at the bottom of the container

    D) none of the above

14) Which of the following substances is less soluble in hot water than in cold water?

    A) CO_2 B) NaCl   C) $NaNO_3$ D) KBr

15) If the solubility of a particular solute is $\frac{10 \text{ g}}{100 \text{ g H}_2\text{O}}$ at 20°C, which of the following solution concentrations would represent a supersaturated aqueous solution of that solute?

    A) $\frac{10 \text{ g}}{100 \text{ g H}_2\text{O}}$ at 25°C   B) $\frac{10 \text{ g}}{100 \text{ g H}_2\text{O}}$ at 15°C

    C) $\frac{9 \text{ g}}{100 \text{ g H}_2\text{O}}$ at 20°C   D) $\frac{11 \text{ g}}{100 \text{ g H}_2\text{O}}$ at 20°C

16) What does not exist in a supersaturated solution?

    A) undissolved solute   B) dissolved solute   C) solvent vapors

17) What can be done to crystallize a supersaturated solution?

    A) add almost any type of crystal

    B) add a crystal of the solute only

    C) add a crystal of the solute or scratch the glass

    D) add almost any type of crystal or scratch the glass

18) To increase the solubility of a gas at constant temperature from 0.85 g/mL, at 1.0 atm, to 5.1 g/mL, the pressure would have to be increased to _____.

    A) 0.17 atm   B) 5.0 atm   C) 6.0 atm   D) 4.3 atm

19) If the pressure of a gas above a liquid is increased (at constant temperature), the solubility of the gas in the liquid _____.

A) remains unchanged   B) increases

C) decreases   D) would be impossible to calculate

20) The solubility of a gas in a liquid is _____.

A) proportional to the square root of the pressure of the gas above the liquid

B) directly proportional to the pressure of the gas above the liquid

C) inversely proportional to the pressure of the gas above the liquid

D) unrelated to the pressure of the gas above the liquid

21) In general, as the temperature of a solution composed of a gas in a liquid is increased, the solubility of the gas _____.

A) increases   B) decreases   C) remains the same

22) In a concentrated solution there is _____.

A) no solvent   B) a large amount of solute

C) a small amount of solute   D) no solute

23) What is the molarity of a solution containing 9.0 moles of solute in 500.0 mL of solution?

A) 4.5M   B) 18M   C) 0.45M   D) 1.8M   E) 0.18M

24) What is the number of moles of solute in 250 mL of a 0.4M solution?

A) 0.1 mol   B) 0.16 mol   C) 0.62 mol   D) 1.6 mol   E) 1 mol

25) What is the molarity of a solution containing 8 grams of solute in 500 mL of solution? (gram formula mass of solute = 24 g)

A) 1M   B) 0.67M   C) 0.1M   D) 0.5M   E) 0.05M

26) What mass of Na_2SO_4 is needed to make 2.5 L of 2.0M solution? (Na = 23 amu; S = 32 amu; O = 16 amu)

A) 178 g   B) 284 g   C) 356 g   D) 710 g

27) What is the molarity of 200 mL of solution in which 2.0 moles of sodium bromide is dissolved?

A) 2.0M   B) 10M   C) 0.40M   D) 4.0M

28) How many mL of 3M HCl are needed to make 300 mL of 0.1M HCl?

A) 10 mL   B) 100 mL   C) 90 mL   D) 9 mL   E) 30 mL

29) If 2.0 mL of 6.0M HCl is used to make a 500.0–mL aqueous solution, what is the molarity of the dilute solution?

A) 0.024M   B) 0.24M   C) 0.30M   D) 0.83M   E) 2.4M

30) How many mL of a 2.0M NaBr solution are needed to make 200.0 mL of 0.50M NaBr?

A) 25 mL   B) 50 mL   C) 100 mL   D) 150 mL

31) What is the molarity of a solution that contains 6 moles of solute in 2 liters of solution?

A) 6M   B) 12M   C) 7M   D) 3M

32) What mass of sucrose, $C_{12}H_{22}O_{11}$, is needed to make 500.0 mL of a 0.200M solution?

A) 34.2 g   B) 100 g   C) 17.1 g   D) 68.4 g

33) To 225 mL of a 0.80M solution of KI, a student adds enough water to make 1.0 L of a more dilute KI solution. What is the molarity of the new solution?

A) 180M   B) 2.8M   C) 0.35M   D) 0.18M

34) If the percent by volume is 2.0% and the volume of solution is 250 mL, what is the volume of solute in solution?

A) 0.5 mL   B) 1.25 mL   C) 5.0 mL   D) 12.5 mL

35) If the percent (mass/volume) for the solute is 4% and the volume of the solution is 750 mL, what is the mass of solute in solution?

A) 3.0 g   B) 7.5 g   C) 30 g   D) 75 g

36) What is the volume of alcohol present in 200.0 mL of a 55% (v/v) solution of alcohol?

A) 28 mL   B) 36 mL   C) 110 mL   D) 145 mL

37) How many milliliters of alcohol are in 167 mL of a 85.0% (v/v) alcohol solution?

A) 252 mL   B) 228 mL   C) 145 mL   D) 142 mL

38) What is the percent (m/v) of 400.0 mL of a solution that contains 60.0 g of calcium chloride, $CaCl_2$?

A) 1.35%   B) 15.0%   C) 24.0%   D) 6.70%

39) How many mL of alcohol are in 240.0 mL of a 93.0% (v/v) alcohol solution?

A) 252 mL   B) 223 mL   C) 145 mL   D) 142 mL

40) In which of the following is the solution concentration expressed in terms of molarity?

A) $\dfrac{10 \text{ g of solute}}{1000 \text{ g of solution}}$

B) $\dfrac{10 \text{ g of solute}}{1000 \text{ mL of solution}}$

C) $\dfrac{10 \text{ mL of solute}}{1 \text{ L of solution}}$

D) $\dfrac{10 \text{ mol of solute}}{1 \text{ L of solution}}$

E) $\dfrac{10 \text{ mol of solute}}{1 \text{ kg of solution}}$

41) A dilute solution is one in which there is a _____.

    A) large amount of solvent

    B) large amount of solute

    C) small amount of solute in a small amount of solvent

    D) small amount of solute in a large amount of solvent

42) What does not change when a solution is diluted by the addition of solvent?

    A) volume of solvent

    B) mass of solvent

    C) number of moles of solute

    D) molarity of solution

    E) mass of solution

43) Which of the following operations yields the number of moles of solute?

    A) molarity x moles of solution

    B) molarity x volume of solution

    C) molarity x mass of solution

    D) moles of solution ÷ volume of solution

    E) mass of solution ÷ volume of solution

44) If more solvent is added to a solution _____.

    A) its molarity decreases   B) it becomes more dilute

    C) its percent (v/v) decreases   D) all of the above

45) In which of the following is concentration expressed in percent by volume?

    A) 10% (v/v)   B) 10% (m/v)   C) 10% (m/m)   D) 10%

46) In which of the following is concentration expressed in percent by volume?

    A) $\dfrac{10\text{ mL of solute}}{100\text{ mL of solvent}} \times 100\%$ B) $\dfrac{10\text{ mL of solute}}{100\text{ mL of solution}} \times 100\%$

    C) $\dfrac{10\text{ g of solute}}{100\text{ mL of solvent}} \times 100\%$ D) $\dfrac{10\text{ g of solute}}{100\text{ mL of solution}} \times 100\%$

47) In which of the following is concentration expressed in percent (mass/volume)?

    A) $\dfrac{10\text{ mL of solute}}{100\text{ mL of solvent}} \times 100\%$ B) $\dfrac{10\text{ mL of solute}}{100\text{ mL of solution}} \times 100\%$

    C) $\dfrac{10\text{ g of solute}}{100\text{ mL of solvent}} \times 100\%$ D) $\dfrac{10\text{ g of solute}}{100\text{ mL of solution}} \times 100\%$

48) What is the mole fraction of ethanol in a solution of 3.00 moles of ethanol and 5.00 moles of water?

    A) 0.375   B) 0.6   C) 1.67   D) 15

49) Colligative properties depend upon _____.

   A) the nature of the solute

   B) the nature of the solvent

   C) the number of particles dissolved in a given mass of solvent

   D) none of the above

50) Which of the following solutes is most effective in lowering the vapor pressure of water?

   A) NaCl   B) $MgCl_2$ C) $AlCl_3$ D) CCl_4

51) Why does a solute depress the freezing point?

   A) because the solute is colder than the solvent

   B) because the solute disrupts crystal formation by the solvent

   C) because the solute tends to sink to the bottom of the solution

   D) because the solute has bigger molecules than the solvent

52) If one mole of each of these solutes is added to the same amount of water, which solution has the highest boiling point?

   A) glucose, $C_6H_{12}O_6$ B) aluminum sulfate, $Al_2(SO_4)_3$

   C) magnesium acetate, $Mg(C_2H_3O_2)_2$ D) copper(I) chloride, CuCl

53) Which of the following is NOT a colligative property of a solution?

   A) boiling point elevation   B) supersaturation

   C) vapor pressure lowering   D) freezing point depression

54) Colligative properties are _____.

   A) chemical properties   B) physical properties

   C) biological properties   D) none of the above

55) What is the molality of a solution containing 9.0 moles of solute in 2.4 kg of solvent?

   A) 0.38m   B) 3.8m   C) 2.4m   D) 22m

56) What is the molality of a solution containing 8.0 grams of solute in 0.50 kg of solvent? (gram formula mass of solute = 24 g)

   A) 0.67m   B) 4m   C) 1.67m   D) 0.17m   E) 6.7m

57) What is the number of kilograms of solvent in a 0.70 molal solution containing 5.0 grams of solute? (gram formula mass of solute = 30 g)

   A) 0.24 kg   B) 2.4 kg   C) 0.11 kg   D) 1.1 kg   E) 11 kg

58) What is the boiling point of a solution that contains 3 moles of KBr in 2000 g of water? (K_b = 0.512°C/m; gram formula mass of water = 18 g)

   A) 97°C   B) 99.7°C   C) 100°C   D) 101.5°C   E) 103°C

59) What is the freezing point of a solution that contains 0.5 moles of NaI in 500 g of water? (K_f = 1.86°C/m; gram formula mass of water = 18 g)

   A) –3.72°C   B) –1.86°C   C) –0.002°C   D) +1.86°C   E) +3.72°C

60) What is the molality of a solution of water and KCl if the freezing point of the solution is –3°C? (K_f = 1.86°C/m; gram formula mass of water = 18 g)

   A) 0.6m   B) 1.2m   C) 0.8m   D) 6m   E) 16m

61) What is the freezing point of a solution of 0.5 mol of LiBr in 500 mL of water? (K_f = 1.86°C/m)

   A) –1.86°C   B) –3.72°C   C) –5.58°C   D) –7.44°C

62) What is the boiling point of a solution of 0.1 mole of glucose in 200 mL of water? (K_b = 0.50°C/m)

   A) 100.06°C   B) 100.13°C   C) 100.25°C   D) 100.5°C

63) Which of the following is an expression of molality?

   A) $\dfrac{10 \text{ mol of solute}}{1 \text{ kg of solvent}}$

   B) $\dfrac{10 \text{ mol of solute}}{1 \text{ L of solution}}$

   C) $\dfrac{10 \text{ mol of solute}}{1 \text{ L of solvent}}$

   D) $\dfrac{10 \text{ mol of solute}}{1 \text{ g of solution}}$

   E) $\dfrac{10 \text{ mol of solute}}{1 \text{ kg of solution}}$

64) To which of the following variables is change in boiling point directly proportional?

   A) molarity of solution   B) molality of solution
   C) percent by volume of solution   D) percent (mass/volume) of solution

65) What is the approximate molecular mass of a solute if 300 g of the solute in 1000 g of water causes the solution to have a boiling point of 101°C? (K_b = 0.512°C/m; K_f = 1.86°C/m; gram formula mass of water = 18 g)

   A) 3 amu   B) 15 amu   C) 30 amu   D) 150 amu   E) 300 amu

Problems

1) What mass of KCl (solubility = $\dfrac{34 \text{ g KCl}}{100 \text{ g of water}}$ at 20°C) can dissolve in 3.30 x 10^2 g of water?

2) What is the solubility of silver nitrate if 11.1 g can dissolve in 5.0 g of water at 20°C? Express the solubility in $\dfrac{\text{g}}{100 \text{ g of water}}$.

3) If the solubility of a gas is 7.5 g/L at 404 kPa of pressure, what is the solubility of the gas when the pressure is 202 kPa?

4) A gas has a solubility in water of 16.8 g/L at 15°C and 505 kPa of pressure. What is its solubility in water at 15°C and 303 kPa of pressure?

5) What is the molarity of a solution containing 9.0 moles of solute in 2500 mL of solution?

6) What is the number of moles of solute in 650 mL of a 0.40M solution?

7) How many liters of a 0.30M solution are needed to give 2.7 moles of solute?

8) What is the molarity of a solution containing 1.2 grams of solute in 450 mL of solution? (gram formula mass of solute = 24 g)

9) How many liters of a 1.5M solution are required to yield 5.0 grams of solute? (gram formula mass of solute = 30.0 g)

10) Calculate the molarity of a solution prepared by dissolving 175 g of KNO_3 in 750 mL of water.

11) How many mL of 3.0M HCl are needed to make 300.0 mL of 0.10M HCl?

12) If 1.0 mL of 6.0M HCl is added to 499 mL of water to give exactly a 500–mL solution, what is the molarity of the dilute solution?

13) If 5.0 mL of 15M HCl is added to 195 mL of water to give exactly a 200–mL solution, what is the molarity of the dilute solution?

14) How would you prepare 250 mL of 0.60M $Al_2(SO_4)_3$ solution from a 2.00M $Al_2(SO_4)_3$ stock solution?

15) If the volume of solute is 6.0 mL and the volume of solution is 300.0 mL, what is the solute's percent by volume?

16) If the percent (mass/volume) is 4% and the volume of solution is 1500 mL, what is the mass of the solute?

17) If the mass of solute is 9.0 g and the volume of solution is 250 mL, what is the solute's percent (mass/volume)?

18) What is the molality of a solution containing 5.0 moles of solute in 3.2 kg of solvent?

19) What is the number of moles of solute in a 0.3 molal solution containing 0.10 kg of solvent?

20) How many kilograms of solvent are there in a sample of 0.30 molal solution if the sample contains 13 moles of solute?

21) What is the molality of a solution containing 15 grams of solute in 0.50 kilograms of solvent? (gram formula mass of solute = 24 g)

22) What is the mole fraction of ethanol in a solution of 2.0 moles of ethanol and 7.0 moles of water?

23) What is the mole fraction of KCl in a 0.20 molal solution of KCl? (gram formula mass of KCl = 75 g; gram formula mass of water = 18 g)

24) Calculate the molality of a solution prepared by dissolving 175 g of KNO_3 in 750 g of water.

25) What is the boiling point of a solution that has 3.0 moles of KBr in 1500 g of water? (K_b = 0.512°C/m; gram formula mass of water = 18.0 g)

26) What is the freezing point of a solution that has 5.0 moles of NaI in 1250 g of water? (K_f = 1.86°C/m; gram formula mass of water = 18.0 g)

27) What is the molality of a solution of water and KCl, if the boiling point of the solution is 103.0°C? (K_b = 0.512°C/m; gram formula mass of water = 18.0 g)

28) Calculate the boiling point of a solution that contains 1.80 mol of H_3PO_4 dissolved in 2750 g of water.

29) What is the molecular mass of a solute if a solution containing 150 g of that solute and 1.0 kg of water has a boiling point of 102.0°C? (K_b = 0.512°C/m)

30) A solution of 10.6 g of a nonvolatile compound in 55.0 g of water freezes at –3.26°C. What is the molecular mass of the solute? (Assume the solute exists as molecules in the solution.)

Essay Questions

1) Explain what a saturated solution is. Give a specific example.

2) Discuss the different factors that can affect the solubility of a substance. Include specific examples in your discussion.

3) Discuss the phenomenon of supersaturation. Indicate how crystallization can be initiated in a supersaturated solution.

4) Explain on a particle basis how the addition of a solute affects the boiling point, the freezing point, and the vapor pressure of the solvent.

Chapter 18 Solutions

Matching Questions

    1) Answer: D

    2) Answer: A

    3) Answer: E

    4) Answer: C

    5) Answer: B

    6) Answer: D

    7) Answer: B

    8) Answer: A

    9) Answer: C

    10) Answer: E

    11) Answer: E

    12) Answer: B

    13) Answer: A

    14) Answer: D

    15) Answer: C

Multiple Choice and Bimodal Questions

    1) Answer: B

    2) Answer: C

    3) Answer: D

    4) Answer: A

    5) Answer: A

    6) Answer: A

    7) Answer: D

    8) Answer: C

    9) Answer: A

    10) Answer: A

    11) Answer: C

    12) Answer: C

    13) Answer: C

    14) Answer: A

    15) Answer: D

    16) Answer: A

    17) Answer: C

    18) Answer: C

    19) Answer: B

    20) Answer: B

    21) Answer: B

    22) Answer: B

23) Answer: B

24) Answer: A

25) Answer: B

26) Answer: D

27) Answer: B

28) Answer: A

29) Answer: A

30) Answer: B

31) Answer: D

32) Answer: A

33) Answer: D

34) Answer: C

35) Answer: C

36) Answer: C

37) Answer: D

38) Answer: B

39) Answer: B

40) Answer: D

41) Answer: D

42) Answer: C

43) Answer: B

44) Answer: D

45) Answer: A

46) Answer: B

47) Answer: D

48) Answer: A

49) Answer: C

50) Answer: C

51) Answer: B

52) Answer: B

53) Answer: B

54) Answer: B

55) Answer: B

56) Answer: A

57) Answer: A

58) Answer: D

59) Answer: A

60) Answer: C

61) Answer: B

62) Answer: C

63) Answer: A

64) Answer: B

65) Answer: D

Problems

1) Answer: $3.30 \times 10^2 \text{ g H}_2\text{O} \times \dfrac{34 \text{ g KCl}}{100 \text{ g H}_2\text{O}} = 112 \text{ g KCl}$

2) Answer: $\text{g AgNO}_3 = 11.1 \text{ g AgNO}_3 \times \dfrac{100 \text{ g H}_2\text{O}}{5 \text{ g H}_2\text{O}} = 220 \text{ g}$

AgNO_3 solubility is $\dfrac{200 \text{ g}}{100 \text{ g H}_2\text{O}}$

3) Answer: $S_2 = S_1 \times \dfrac{P_2}{P_1} = 7.5 \text{ g/L} \times \dfrac{202 \text{ kPa}}{404 \text{ kPa}} = 3.8 \text{ g/L}$

4) Answer: $\dfrac{S_1}{P_1} = \dfrac{S_2}{P_2}$

$S_2 = S_1 \times \dfrac{P_2}{P_1} = 16.8 \text{ g/L} \times \dfrac{303 \text{ kPa}}{505 \text{ kPa}}$

$= 10.1 \text{ g/L}$

5) Answer: $\dfrac{9.0 \text{ mol}}{2500 \text{ mL}} \times \dfrac{1000 \text{ mL}}{1 \text{ L}}$

$= \dfrac{9.0 \text{ mol}}{2 \, 5 \text{ L}} = 3.6 \text{ mol/L}$

6) Answer: $650 \text{ mL} \times \dfrac{0.4 \text{ mol}}{1000 \text{ mL}} = 0.26 \text{ mol}$

7) Answer: $\dfrac{2.7 \text{ mol}}{0.30 \text{ mol/L}} = 9.0 \text{ L}$

8) Answer: $\dfrac{1.2 \text{ g}}{450 \text{ mL}} \times \dfrac{1 \text{ mol}}{24 \text{ g}} \times \dfrac{1000 \text{ mL}}{1 \text{ L}} = 0.11 \text{ M}$

9) Answer: $5.0 \text{ g} \times \dfrac{1 \text{ L}}{1.5 \text{ mol}} \times \dfrac{1 \text{ mol}}{30.0 \text{ g}} = 0.11 \text{ L}$

10) Answer: Gram formula mass KNO_3:

K: $1 \times 39.1 \text{ g} = 39.1 \text{ g}$
N: $1 \times 14.0 \text{ g} = 14.0 \text{ g}$
O: $3 \times 16.0 \text{ g} = 48.0 \text{ g}$
gfm $= 101.1 \text{ g}$

$\dfrac{\text{Mass KNO}_3}{\text{gfm}} = \dfrac{175 \text{ g KNO}_3}{101.1 \text{ g/mol}}$

$= 1.73 \text{ mol KNO}_3$

$\dfrac{1.73 \text{ mol KNO}_3}{0.750 \text{ L}} = 2.31 \text{ M}$

11) Answer: $V_1 = \dfrac{V_2 \times M_2}{M_1} = \dfrac{300 \text{ mL} \times 0.10 \text{ M}}{3.0 \text{ M}} = 10 \text{ mL}$

12) Answer: $M_2 = \dfrac{M_1 \times V_1}{V_2} = \dfrac{6.0 \text{ M} \times 1.0 \text{ mL}}{500 \text{ mL}} = 0.012 \text{ M}$

13) Answer: $M_2 = \dfrac{M_1 \times V_1}{V_2} = \dfrac{15 \text{ M} \times 5.0 \text{ mL}}{200.0 \text{ mL}} = 0.38 \text{ M}$

14) Answer: $M_1 = 0.60M$

$V_1 = 250$ mL

$M_2 = 2.00M$

$M_1V_1 = M_2V_2$

$0.60M \times 250$ mL $= 2.00M \times V_2$

$V_2 = \dfrac{0.60M \times 250 \text{ mL}}{2.00M}$

$V_2 = 75$ mL

Mix 75 mL of 2.0M $Al_2(SO_4)_3$ with 175 mL of water.

15) Answer: Percent by volume $= \dfrac{6.0 \text{ mL}}{300.0 \text{ mL}} \times 100\%$

$= 0.020 \times 100\%$

$= 2.0\%$

16) Answer: Mass = percent (mass/volume) x volume

$= \dfrac{0.04 \text{ g}}{\text{mL}} \times 1500$ mL $= 60$ g

17) Answer: Percent (mass/volume) = mass/volume x 100%

$= \dfrac{9.0 \text{ g}}{250 \text{ mL}} \times 100\%$

$= 0.036$ g/mL x 100%

$= 3.6\%$ g/mL

18) Answer: $\dfrac{5.0 \text{ mol}}{3.2 \text{ kg}} = \dfrac{1.6 \text{ mol}}{1 \text{ kg}} = 1.6m$

19) Answer: Number of moles = mass of solvent x molality

$= 0.10$ kg x 0.3 mol/kg $= 0.03$ mol

20) Answer: $\dfrac{1 \text{ kg}}{0.30 \text{ mol}} \times 13$ mol $= 43$ kg

21) Answer: $\dfrac{15 \text{ g}}{0.50 \text{ kg}} \times \dfrac{1 \text{ mol}}{24 \text{ g}} = 1.3$ m

22) Answer: $X_{\text{ethanol}} = \dfrac{n_{\text{ethanol}}}{n_{\text{ethanol}} + n_{\text{water}}}$

$= \dfrac{2.0 \text{ mol}}{2.0 \text{ mol} + 7.0 \text{ mol}}$

$= \dfrac{2.0 \text{ mol}}{9.0 \text{ mol}} = 0.22$

23) Answer: $n_{\text{water}} = \dfrac{1000 \text{ g}}{18 \text{ g/mol}} = 55.5$ mol

$X_{\text{KCl}} = \dfrac{n_{\text{KCl}}}{n_{\text{KCl}} + n_{\text{water}}}$

$= \dfrac{0.20 \text{ mol}}{0.20 \text{ mol} + 55.5 \text{ mol}}$

$= \dfrac{0.20 \text{ mol}}{55.7 \text{ mol}} = 0.003\ 6$

24) Answer: gfm KNO_3:

K: $1 \times 39.1 \text{ g} = 39.1 \text{ g}$

N: $1 \times 14.0 \text{ g} = 14.0 \text{ g}$

O: $3 \times 16.0 \text{ g} = 48.0 \text{ g}$

gfm = 101.1 g

$$\text{Molarity} = \frac{\text{mol solute}}{1 \text{ L solution}}$$

$$= \frac{\dfrac{\text{mass } KNO_3}{\text{gfm}}}{750 \text{ mL } H_2O \times \dfrac{1 \text{ L}}{1000 \text{ mL } H_2O}}$$

$$= \frac{175 \text{ g } KNO_3}{101.1 \text{ g/mol}} \times \frac{1}{0.750 \text{ L}} = 2.31M$$

25) Answer: $\Delta T_b = K_b \times m$

$1 \text{ mol } KBr \rightarrow 1 \text{ mol } K^+ + 1 \text{ mol } Br^-$

$$= \frac{0.512°C}{m} \times \frac{6.0 \text{ mol}}{1.5 \text{ kg}}$$

$$= \frac{0.512°C}{m} \times \frac{4.0 \text{ mol}}{kg}$$

$$= \frac{0.512°C}{m} \times 4.0m$$

$$= 2.0°C$$

Boiling point = normal boiling point + ΔT_b

$$= 100.0°C + 2.0°C$$

$$= 102.0°C$$

26) Answer: $\Delta T_f = K_f \times m$

$1 \text{ mol } NaI \rightarrow 1 \text{ mol } Na^+ + 1 \text{ mol } I^-$

$$= \frac{1.86°C}{m} \times \frac{10.0 \text{ mol}}{1250 \text{ g}} \times \frac{1000 \text{ g}}{1 \text{ kg}}$$

$$= \frac{1.86°C}{m} \times \frac{10\,000 \text{ mol}}{1250 \text{ kg}}$$

$$= \frac{1.86°C}{m} \times \frac{8.0 \text{ mol}}{kg}$$

$$= \frac{1.86°C}{m} \times 8.0m$$

$$= 15°C$$

Freezing point = normal freezing point − ΔT_f

$$= 0°C - 15°C$$

$$= -15°C$$

27) Answer: $\Delta T_b = K_b \times m$

$$m = \frac{\Delta T_b}{K_b} = \frac{3.0°C}{0.512°C/m} = 5.86m$$

$1 \text{ mol } KCl \rightarrow 2 \text{ mol particles } (K^+ + Cl^-)$

$$\frac{5.86 \text{ mol}}{2} = 2.9m \text{ } KCl$$

28) Answer: $\dfrac{1 \text{ mol } H_3PO_4}{1000 \text{ g } H_2O} = m$

$\dfrac{1.8 \text{ mol } H_3PO_4}{2750 \text{ g } H_2O} \times \dfrac{1000 \text{ g } H_2O}{1 \text{ kg}} = 0.655m$

$H_3PO_4 \rightarrow 3H^+ + PO_4^{3-} = 4 \text{ particles}$

$4 \text{ particles} \times 0.655m = 2.62m$

$\Delta T_b = K_b \times m = \dfrac{0.512°C}{m} \times 2.62m = 1.34°C$

Boiling point of the solution is 101.34°C.

29) Answer: $\Delta T_b = K_b \times m$

$m = \dfrac{\Delta T_b}{K_b} = \dfrac{2.0°C}{0.512°C/m} = 3.9m$

$\dfrac{3.9 \text{ mol solute}}{\text{kg of water}} \times \dfrac{1 \text{ kg}}{1000g} \times 1000 \text{ g water}$

$= 3.9 \text{ mol solute}$

$\text{Molecular mass of solute} = \dfrac{\text{mass of solute}}{\text{moles of solute}}$

$= 150g/3.9 \text{ mol} = 38 \text{ g/mol}$

30) Answer: $\Delta T_f = K_f \times m$

$3.26°C = 1.86°C/m \times m$

$m = \dfrac{3.26°C}{1.86°C/m} = 1.75m$

mol solute = Molality x mass solvent

$= \dfrac{1.75 \text{ mol solute}}{\text{kg } H_2O} \times \dfrac{1 \text{ kg}}{1000 \text{ g}} \times 55.0 \text{ g } H_2O$

$= 0.095\ 7 \text{ mol solute}$

$\text{Molecular mass} = \dfrac{\text{mass solute}}{\text{mol solute}} = \dfrac{10.6 \text{ g}}{0.095\ 7 \text{ mol}}$

$= 111 \text{ g/mol}$

Essay Questions

1) Answer: A saturated solution contains the maximum amount of solute for a given amount of solvent at a constant temperature. For example, no more than 36.2 g of sodium chloride will go into solution in 100 g of water. Above this concentration, there is a dynamic equilibrium between the solid and its dissolved ions. In this equilibrium, just as many ions are going out of the solution as are going in per unit time, and solid will, therefore, always be present.

2) Answer: The factors are temperature, pressure, and the nature of the substances. Specific examples include the following: Sodium chloride is more soluble in water at high temperature than at low temperature. Gases are less soluble at high temperatures than at low temperatures. The solubility of a particular gas increases as the partial pressure of that gas increases above the solution. Sodium nitrate is much more soluble in water than is barium sulfate, regardless of temperature. Polar substances tend to be soluble in water, whereas nonpolar substances tend to not be soluble in water.

3) Answer: A solution that contains more solute than it can theoretically hold at a given temperature is a supersaturated solution. A dynamic equilibrium between solid and dissolved particles does not exist because there is no solid. Crystallization can be initiated by adding a seed crystal to the solution or by exposing the solution to a rough surface. The latter can be done by scratching the inside of the container holding the solution.

4) Answer: Boiling point elevation, and freezing point and vapor pressure lowering are colligative properties. They depend on the number of particles in solution and not on the chemical nature of the solute or solvent. Boiling point elevation: Additional attractive forces exist between solute and solvent; they must be overcome for the solution to boil. Kinetic energy must be added to overcome these forces. Freezing point lowering: More kinetic energy must be withdrawn from a solution because the solute is surrounded by shells of solvent. This interferes with the formation of the orderly pattern that the particles assume as the solvent changes from liquid to solid. Vapor pressure lowering: The formation of solvent shells around the solute particles reduces the number of solvent particles that have sufficient kinetic energy to vaporize.

Chapter 19 Reaction Rates and Equilibrium
Matching Questions
Chapter 19: Matching I

1) activated complex

2) reaction rate

3) inhibitor

4) activation energy

5) free energy

A) a substance that interferes with catalysis

B) energy available to do work

C) arrangement of atoms at the peak of an energy barrier

D) the number of atoms, ions or molecules that react in a given time to form products

E) the minimum energy colliding particles must have in order to react

Chapter 19: Matching II

6) endothermic reaction

7) entropy

8) chemical equilibrium

9) reaction mechanism

10) elementary reaction

A) the measure of disorder

B) when the forward and reverse reactions take place at the same rate

C) includes all elementary reactions of a complex reaction

D) a reaction that absorbs energy

E) reactants are converted to products in a single step

Multiple Choice and Bimodal Questions

1) Which expression represents a reaction rate?

A) $\dfrac{time}{mass}$
B) $\dfrac{number}{time}$
C) $\dfrac{energy}{time}$
D) $\dfrac{time}{energy}$

2) Which set of units represents a reaction rate?

A) $\dfrac{s}{g}$ B) $\dfrac{mol}{s}$ C) $\dfrac{s}{(no\ units)}$ D) $\dfrac{J}{s}$ E) $\dfrac{s}{J}$

3) At what stage of a reaction does the activated complex exist?

A) beginning   B) middle   C) end

4) What is another name for the activated complex?

A) energy barrier
B) transition state
C) rate limiter
D) collision group
E) reactant/product

5) At what stage of a reaction do atoms have the highest energy?

A) reactant stage   B) product stage   C) transition state stage

6) Which of the following factors affects the reaction rate the most?

A) relative masses of reactant and product molecules
B) relative energy in reactant and product molecules
C) activation energy
D) whether one or two reactant molecules is required

7) Activation energy is _____.

A) the heat released in a reaction
B) an energy barrier between reactants and products
C) the energy given off when reactants collide
D) generally very high for a reaction that takes place rapidly

8) Why does a higher temperature cause a reaction to go faster?

A) There are more collisions per second only.
B) Collisions occur with greater energy only.
C) There are more collisions per second and the collisions are of greater energy.

9) Why does a higher concentration make a reaction faster?

A) There are more collisions per second only.
B) Collisions occur with greater energy.
C) There are more collisions per second and the collisions are of greater energy.

10) Why does a small particle size generally cause a reaction to proceed faster?

A) There are more collisions per second only.
B) The collisions occur with greater energy.
C) There are more collisions per second and the collisions are of greater energy.

11) Why does a catalyst cause a reaction to proceed faster?
   A) There are more collisions per second only.
   B) The collisions occur with greater energy only.
   C) The activation energy is lowered only.
   D) There are more collisions per second and the collisions are of greater energy.

12) What happens to a catalyst in a reaction?
   A) It is unchanged.
   B) It is incorporated into the products.
   C) It is incorporated into the reactants.
   D) It evaporates away.
   E) It becomes slag.

13) Which of the following substances act as catalysts in the body?
   A) carbohydrates
   B) nucleic acids
   C) lipids
   D) enzymes
   E) water

14) A catalyst works by _____.
   A) lowering the activation energy barrier
   B) shifting the equilibrium position toward the products
   C) changing the temperature of the reactants
   D) changing the particle size of the reactants

15) The rate of a chemical reaction normally _____.
   A) decreases as temperature increases
   B) is slowed down by a catalyst
   C) increases as reactant concentration increases
   D) decreases as reactant concentration increases

16) If a catalyst is used in a reaction _____.
   A) the energy of activation increases
   B) different reaction products are obtained
   C) the reaction rate increases
   D) the reaction rate does not change

17) If sulfur dioxide and oxygen can be made into sulfur trioxide, what is the reverse reaction?
   A) $2SO_3 \rightarrow 2SO_2 + O_2$ B) $SO_3 + O_2 \rightarrow SO_5$
   C) $2SO_2 + O_2 \rightarrow 2SO_3$ D) $SO_2 + 2SO_3 \rightarrow 3S + 4O_2$

18) At equilibrium, what is the rate of production of reactants compared with the rate of production of products?

   A) much higher
   B) higher
   C) the same
   D) lower
   E) much lower

19) What is the equilibrium constant for the following reaction?
   $C + O_2 \rightleftharpoons CO_2$

   A) $\dfrac{[C][O_2]}{[CO_2]}$

   B) $\dfrac{[CO_2]}{[C][O_2]}$

   C) $\dfrac{[C]^2 [O_2]^2}{[CO_2]^2}$

   D) $\dfrac{[CO_2]^2}{[C]^2 [O_2]^2}$

20) What is the equilibrium constant for the following reaction?
   $4Na + O_2 \rightleftharpoons 2Na_2O$

   A) $\dfrac{[Na] [O_2]}{[Na_2O]}$

   B) $\dfrac{[NaO_2]}{[Na] [O_2]}$

   C) $\dfrac{[Na]^4 [O_2]}{[Na_2O]^2}$

   D) $\dfrac{[Na_2O]^2}{[Na]^4 [O_2]}$

21) Calculate the equilibrium constant for the production of MgO when the equilibrium concentrations are 0.01M for Mg, 0.01M for O_2, and 2M for MgO.

   A) 4×10^{-6} B) 2×10^2 C) 2×10^4 D) 2×10^6 E) 4×10^6

22) What is the expression for K_{eq} for this reaction?
   $2H_2O(g) \rightleftharpoons 2H_2(g) + O_2(g)$

   A) $K_{eq} = \dfrac{[2H_2O]}{2[H_2] \times [O_2]}$

   B) $K_{eq} = \dfrac{[H_2]^2 \times [O_2]}{[H_2O]^2}$

   C) $K_{eq} = \dfrac{[2H_2] \times [O_2]}{[2H_2O]}$

   D) $K_{eq} = \dfrac{[H_2O]^2}{[H_2]^2 \times [O_2]}$

23) If the temperature of a reaction increases, what happens to the value of the equilibrium constant?

   A) It increases.   B) It decreases.
   C) It stays the same.   D) It increases or decreases.

24) Which of the following does NOT affect the rate of a chemical reaction?

   A) the equilibrium position   B) the temperature
   C) the concentration of reactants   D) the presence of a catalyst

25) If a reaction is reversible, what are the relative amounts of reactant and product at the end of the reaction?

    A) no reactant; all product

    B) no product; all reactant

    C) some product; some reactant

26) Two opposing reactions (A + B ⇌ C + D) occurring simultaneously at the same rate is an example of a _____.

    A) dynamic equilibrium   B) chemical equilibrium

    C) both A. and B.   D) neither A. nor B.

27) What happens to a reaction at equilibrium when a product is removed from the reaction system?

    A) The reaction makes more products.

    B) The reaction makes more reactants.

    C) The reaction is unchanged.

28) What happens to a reaction at equilibrium when more reactant is added to the system?

    A) The reaction makes more products.

    B) The reaction makes more reactants.

    C) The reaction is unchanged.

29) In an endothermic reaction at equilibrium, what is the effect of raising the temperature?

    A) The reaction makes more products.

    B) The reaction makes more reactants.

    C) The reaction is unchanged.

30) In an exothermic reaction at equilibrium, what is the effect of lowering the temperature?

    A) The reaction makes more products.

    B) The reaction makes more reactants.

    C) The reaction is unchanged.

31) In a reaction (at equilibrium) that makes more moles of gas than it consumes, what is the effect of increasing the pressure?

    A) The reaction makes more products.

    B) The reaction makes more reactants.

    C) The reaction is unchanged.

32) In a reaction (at equilibrium) that makes fewer moles of gas than it consumes, what is the effect of lowering the pressure?

    A) The reaction makes more products.

    B) The reaction makes more reactants.

    C) The reaction is unchanged.

33) How does an increase in pressure affect the following reaction?
$C_2H_2(g) + H_2(g) \rightleftharpoons C_2H_4(g)$

A) The equilibrium shifts to the right.

B) The equilibrium shifts to the left.

C) There is no effect.

34) Which of the changes listed below would shift the following reaction to the right?
$4HCl(g) + O_2(g) \rightleftharpoons 2Cl_2(g) + 2H_2O(g)$

A) addition of Cl_2 B) removal of O_2 C) increase of pressure

35) What is the effect of adding more water to the following equilibrium reaction?
$CO_2 + H_2O \rightleftharpoons H_2CO_3$

A) More H_2CO_3 is produced.

B) CO_2 concentration increases.

C) The equilibrium is pushed in the direction of reactants.

D) Nothing

36) If a reaction has an equilibrium constant just greater than 1, what type of reaction is it?

A) irreversible   B) spontaneous

C) reversible, favoring products   D) reversible, favoring reactants

37) In an equilibrium reaction with a K_{eq} of 1×10^8, the _____.

A) reactants are favored   B) reaction is spontaneous

C) the products are favored   D) reaction is exothermic

38) The K_{eq} of a reaction is 4×10^{-7}. At equilibrium _____.

A) the reactants are favored

B) the products are favored

C) the reactants and products are present in equal amounts

D) the rate of the forward reaction is much greater than the rate of the reverse reaction

39) The formula HCl indicates _____.

A) the equilibrium concentration of hydrochloric acid

B) the concentration of hydrochloric acid in moles/liter

C) that HCl is a catalyst

D) that HCl is activated

40) What is the term for the energy that is available to do work in a reaction?

A) heat

B) enthalpy

C) entropy

D) free energy

E) activation energy

41) Exergonic reactions _____.
   A) are spontaneous
   B) release free energy
   C) produce energy that can be used to do useful work
   D) all of the above

42) The melting of ice at STP is _____.
   A) exergonic   B) endergonic   C) exothermic   D) endobaric

43) If a system is left to change spontaneously, in what state will it end?
   A) the same state in which it began
   B) the state with lowest possible energy
   C) the state with the maximum disorder
   D) the state with the lowest possible energy consistent with the state of maximum disorder

44) What does entropy measure?
   A) energy
   B) heat transferred
   C) disorder
   D) force
   E) number of particles

45) Which physical state of nitrogen has the highest entropy?
   A) solid   B) liquid   C) gas

46) At room temperature and standard pressure, in which direction will the following reaction go? $Hg(l) \rightarrow Hg(g)$
   A) to the right
   B) to the left
   C) There will be no reaction.

47) Which reaction results in the greatest increase in entropy?
   A) $A \rightarrow B$ B) $A \rightarrow 2B$ C) $2A \rightarrow B$

48) The amount of disorder in a system is measured by its _____.
   A) activation energy   B) entropy
   C) equilibrium position   D) K_{eq}

49) Which one of the following systems has the highest entropy?
   A) 10 mL of water at 10°C
   B) 10 mL of water at 50°C
   C) 10 mL of water at 100°C
   D) All have the same entropy because all are water.

50) In which of these systems is the entropy decreasing?

   A) air escaping from a tire   B) snow melting

   C) salt dissolving in water   D) a liquid cooling

51) Which one of the following systems has the highest entropy?

   A) water at 100°C   B) water at 95°C   C) steam at 105°C   D) steam at 100°C

52) Which of the following is responsible for the fact that the melting of ice is a spontaneous reaction at room temperature and pressure?

   A) Melting is accompanied by a decrease of entropy.

   B) Melting is accompanied by an increase of entropy.

   C) Melting is accompanied by a decrease of energy.

   D) Melting is accompanied by an increase of energy.

53) Which of the following is responsible for the fact that the freezing of water is a spontaneous reaction at a temperature below 0°C and at 1 atmosphere of pressure?

   A) The freezing of water is accompanied by a decrease of entropy.

   B) The freezing of water is accompanied by an increase of entropy.

   C) The freezing of water is accompanied by a decrease of energy.

   D) The freezing of water is accompanied by an increase of energy.

54) The two factors that determine whether a reaction is spontaneous or nonspontaneous are
   _____.

   A) entropy and disorder   B) entropy and energy

   C) electron configuration and ionic charge   D) energy and heat of reaction

55) The favorability or spontaneity of a reaction increases when, during the course of a reaction, _____.

   A) the energy content increases

   B) the entropy increases

   C) the activation energy decreases

   D) the energy content and entropy both decrease

56) Spontaneous reactions _____.

   A) are always exothermic

   B) always take place at a rapid rate

   C) always result in increased disorder of the system

   D) always give off free energy

57) An exergonic reaction _____.

   A) must be exothermic

   B) is nonspontaneous

   C) must correspond to an increase in entropy

   D) is spontaneous

58) Which statement is true?

    A) All spontaneous processes are exothermic.

    B) All nonspontaneous processes are endothermic.

    C) All spontaneous processes release free energy.

    D) Entropy always increases in a spontaneous process.

59) What is the rate law for the following reaction? $A + 2B \rightarrow C + D$

    A) rate = $k[A][B]$ B) rate = $k[A]^2[B]$ C) rate = $k[A][B]^2$ D) rate = $k[A]^2[B]^2$

60) What is the order of the following reaction? $A + 2B \rightarrow C + D$

    A) zero   B) first   C) second   D) third   E) fourth

61) In a first-order reaction, how does the rate change if the concentration of the reactant decreases to one-third its original value?

    A) decreases by a factor of one-ninth

    B) decreases by a factor of one-third

    C) decreases by a factor of one-half

    D) stays the same

    E) increases by a factor of one-third

62) As a first-order reaction proceeds, how does its rate change?

    A) increases   B) decreases   C) stays the same

63) If a reaction rate decreases by a factor of one-fourth when a reactant concentration is decreased by one-half, what is the order of the reaction with respect to that reactant?

    A) zero   B) first   C) second   D) third   E) fourth

64) What is the rate of a first-order reaction that has a reactant concentration of 0.1M and a rate constant of 0.1/s?

    A) 0.001M/s   B) 0.01M/s   C) 0.1M/s   D) 1M/s   E) 10M/s

65) In a first-order reaction, what is the reactant concentration if the rate constant is 0.1/s and the rate is 0.001M/s?

    A) 0.001M   B) 0.01M   C) 0.1M   D) 1M   E) 10M

66) In a first-order reaction, what is the rate constant if the rate is 0.01M/s and the reactant concentration is 0.01M?

    A) 0.01/s   B) 0.1/s   C) 1/s   D) 10/s   E) 100/s

67) In a two-step reaction mechanism, how many elementary reactions occur?

    A) 0   B) 1   C) 2   D) 3

68) When nitrous oxide is converted to nitrogen and oxygen, what is the term used to describe the oxygen atoms formed?

A) reactants

B) products

C) activated complexes

D) intermediates

E) elementary reactants

69) What information is NOT given by an overall equation for a chemical reaction?

A) the relative numbers of molecules used

B) the probable order of the reaction

C) the number of atoms participating in the reaction

D) the reaction mechanism

70) An elementary reaction _____.

A) has only elements as reactants

B) has only elements as products

C) never needs a catalyst

D) converts reactants to products in a single step

71) For a complex reaction, the reaction progress curve:

A) is a flat line.

B) has only one peak.

C) has several hills and valleys.

D) shows energy versus pressure.

E) is a rectangular curve.

Problems

1) What is the equilibrium constant for the following reaction?
$$Si + O_2 \rightleftharpoons SiO_2$$

2) What is the equilibrium constant for the following reaction?
$$4K + O_2 \rightleftharpoons 2K_2O$$

3) A mixture of hydrogen and iodine are in equilibrium with hydrogen iodide, as shown in the following equation.

$$H_2 + I_2 \rightleftharpoons 2HI.$$

Calculate the concentration of HI when the equilibrium constant is 10^5 and the equilibrium concentration of H_2 is 0.01M, and the equilibrium concentration of I_2 is 0.001M.

4) Carbon monoxide and hydrogen are combined in the commercial preparation of methyl alcohol.

$CO(g) + 2H_2(g) \rightleftharpoons CH_3OH(g)$

At a certain set of conditions, the equilibrium mixture contains 0.020 mol of CO, 0.30 mol of H_2, and the equilibrium constant is $2.4 \times 10^3 / mol^2$. How many moles of CH_3OH are present in the equilibrium mixture?

5) Calculate the value of K_{eq} for this reaction at equilibrium.

$2NOCl(g) \rightleftharpoons 2NO(g) + Cl_2(g)$

An analysis of the equilibrium mixture in a 1–L flask gives the following results:
NOCl, 0.30 mol; NO, 1.2 mol; Cl_2, 0.60 mol

6) What is the standard change in entropy for the following reaction when all reactants and products are in the specified states at 25°C and 101.3 kPa?

$2H_2O_2(l) \rightarrow 2H_2O(l) + O_2(g)$

Standard Entropies S^0 (J/K–mol): $H_2O(l)$ = 69.94, $H_2O_2(l)$ = 92.0, $O_2(g)$ = 205.0

7) What is the standard change in entropy for the following reaction when all reactants and products are in the specified states at 25°C and 101.3 kPa?

$2CO(g) + O_2(g) \rightarrow 2CO_2(g)$

Standard Entropies S^0 (J/K–mol): $CO(g)$ = 197.9, $CO_2(g)$ = 213.6, $O_2(g)$ = 205.0

8) The following reaction has a ΔH^0 of 89 kJ/mol and a ΔS^0 of 0.070 kJ/K–mol at 25°C.

$2A + B \rightarrow 2C$

Is this reaction spontaneous?

9) The following reaction has a ΔH^0 of 579 kJ/mol and a ΔS^0 of 73.6 kJ/K–mol at 25°C.

$2A \rightarrow B + 2C$

Is this reaction spontaneous?

10) What is the rate of a first–order reaction that has a reactant concentration of 0.1M and a rate constant of 0.2/s?

11) In a first–order reaction, what is the reactant concentration if the rate constant is 0.2/s and the rate is 0.004 M/s?

12) In a first–order reaction, what is the rate constant if the rate is 0.050 M/s and the reactant concentration is 0.030M?

13) The rate law for the following reaction is: Rate = $k[A]^a[B]^b$

aA + bB → cC + dD

From the data in the following chart, find the kinetic order of the reaction with respect to A and B, as well as the overall order.

Initial Concentration A(mol/L)	Initial Concentration of B(mol/L)	Initial Rate (mol/L x s)
0.05	0.05	2×10^{-3}
0.10	0.05	4×10^{-3}
0.20	0.05	8×10^{-3}
0.01	0.05	0.4×10^{-3}
0.01	0.10	3.2×10^{-3}
0.01	0.20	25.6×10^{-3}

Essay Questions

1) Explain the effects of reactant concentration and particle size on the rate of a reaction.

2) What is the effect of a catalyst on the rate of a reaction? Use an example.

3) Why are some reactions reversible?

4) What is free energy, and how is it related to spontaneity in a reaction?

5) What causes a reaction to be spontaneous? Give an example.

6) Characterize spontaneous and nonspontaneous reactions.

7) What is entropy? Give several examples.

Chapter 19 Reaction Rates and Equilibrium

Matching Questions

1) Answer: C

2) Answer: D

3) Answer: A

4) Answer: E

5) Answer: B

6) Answer: D

7) Answer: A

8) Answer: B

9) Answer: C

10) Answer: E

Multiple Choice and Bimodal Questions

1) Answer: B

2) Answer: B

3) Answer: B

4) Answer: B

5) Answer: C

6) Answer: C

7) Answer: B

8) Answer: C

9) Answer: A

10) Answer: A

11) Answer: C

12) Answer: A

13) Answer: D

14) Answer: A

15) Answer: C

16) Answer: C

17) Answer: A

18) Answer: C

19) Answer: B

20) Answer: D

21) Answer: E

22) Answer: B

23) Answer: D

24) Answer: A

25) Answer: C

26) Answer: C

27) Answer: A

28) Answer: A

29) Answer: A

30) Answer: A

31) Answer: B

32) Answer: B

33) Answer: A

34) Answer: C

35) Answer: A

36) Answer: C

37) Answer: C

38) Answer: A

39) Answer: B

40) Answer: D

41) Answer: D

42) Answer: A

43) Answer: D

44) Answer: C

45) Answer: C

46) Answer: A

47) Answer: B

48) Answer: B

49) Answer: C

50) Answer: D

51) Answer: C

52) Answer: B

53) Answer: C

54) Answer: B

55) Answer: B

56) Answer: D

57) Answer: D

58) Answer: C

59) Answer: C

60) Answer: D

61) Answer: B

62) Answer: B

63) Answer: C

64) Answer: B

65) Answer: B

66) Answer: C

67) Answer: C

68) Answer: D

69) Answer: D

70) Answer: D

71) Answer: C

Problems

1) Answer: $\dfrac{[SiO_2]}{[Si]\,[O_2]}$

2) Answer: $\dfrac{[K_2O]^2}{[K]^4\,[O_2]}$

3) Answer: $K_{eq} = \dfrac{[HI]^2}{[H_2] \times [I_2]}$

$[HI] = \sqrt{K_{eq} \times [H_2] \times [I_2]}$

$[HI] = \sqrt{10^5 \times 0.01M \times 0.001M}$

$[HI] = 1M$

4) Answer: $\dfrac{2.4 \times 10^3}{mol^2} = \dfrac{[CH_3OH]}{(0.020\ mol)(0.30\ mol)^2}$

$[CH_3OH] = \dfrac{(2.4 \times 10^3) \times (0.020\ mol) \times (0.30\ mol)^2}{mol^2}$

$= 4.3\ mol$

5) Answer: $K_{eq} = \dfrac{[NO]^2\,[Cl_2]}{[NOCl]^2}$

$= (1.2M)^2 \times \dfrac{(0.60M)}{(0.30M)^2} = 9.6M$

6) Answer: $2H_2O_2(l) \rightarrow 2H_2O(l) + O_2(g)$

$\Delta S^0 = S^0(products) - S^0(reactants)$

$\Delta S^0 = \left[2\ mol\ H_2O \times \dfrac{69.94\ \frac{J}{K\text{--}mol}}{mol\ H_2O} + 1\ mol\ O_2 \times \dfrac{205.0\ \frac{J}{K\text{--}mol}}{mol\ O_2} \right.$

$\left. - 2\ mol\ H_2O_2 \times \dfrac{92\ \frac{J}{K\text{--}mol}}{mol\ H_2O_2} \right]$

$= (139.88\ J/K\text{--}mol + 205.0\ J/K\text{--}mol) - 184\ J/K\text{--}mol$

$= 160.88\ J/K\text{--}mol = 161\ J/K\text{--}mol$

7) Answer: $\Delta S^0 = S^0(products) - S^0(reactants)$

$\Delta S^0 = \left[2\ mol\ CO_2 \times \dfrac{213.6\ \frac{J}{K\text{--}mol}}{mol\ CO_2} \right]$

$- \left[1\ mol\ O_2 \times \dfrac{205.0\ \frac{J}{K\text{--}mol}}{mol\ O_2} + 2\ mol\ CO \times \dfrac{197.9\ \frac{J}{K\text{--}mol}}{mol\ CO} \right]$

$= (427.2\ J/K\text{--}mol) - (205.0\ J/K\text{--}mol + 395.8\ J/K\text{--}mol)$

$= -173.6\ J/K\text{--}mol = -174\ J/K\text{--}mol$

8) Answer: $273 + 25°C = 298K$

$$\Delta G^0 = \Delta H^0 - T\Delta S^0$$

$$= 89\ kJ/mol - 298\ K \times \frac{0.070\ kJ}{K-mol}$$

$$= 89\ kJ/mol - 20.86\ kJ/mol$$
$$= 68\ kJ/mol$$

The reaction is not spontaneous.

9) Answer: $273 + 25°C = 298K$

$$\Delta G^0 = \Delta H^0 - T\Delta S^0$$

$$= 579\ kJ/mol - 298\ K \times \frac{73.6\ kJ}{K-mol}$$

$$= 579\ kJ/mol - 21\ 933\ kJ/mol$$
$$= -21\ 400\ kJ/mol$$

The reaction is spontaneous.

10) Answer: $Rate = 0.1M \times 0.2/s = 0.02M/s$

11) Answer: $[Reactant] = \dfrac{0.004\ M/s}{0.2/s} = 0.02M$

12) Answer: $k = \dfrac{0.050\ M/s}{0.030M} = 1.7\ s^{-1}$

13) Answer: Doubling the concentration of A doubles the rate; first order in A.
Doubling the concentration of B increases the rate 8 times;
$(2^3 = 8)$; third order in B.
First order + third order = fourth order overall.

Essay Questions

1) Answer: A small particle size increases the rate of a reaction because there is more surface area for a given mass of particles and so more collisions are possible per second. A high concentration of reactants increases the reaction rate because more molecules are present to collide each second.

2) Answer: A catalyst increases the reaction rate, by permitting the formation of a less energetic activated complex. Platinum is a catalyst for certain reactions of gases.

3) Answer: Reversible reactions have a small change in free energy, and so can easily proceed in either direction. Most reactions are reversible to some extent.

4) Answer: Free energy is a measure of the ability of a reaction to do work. Spontaneous reactions release free energy. Nonspontaneous reactions absorb free energy.

5) Answer: A reaction, such as sodium with water, is spontaneous because it can result in a lower energy state or a more disordered state for the system. Sometimes the energy and the disorder both increase, and sometimes the energy and the disorder both decrease. An example of the former is the dissolution of ammonium nitrate. This reaction is spontaneous even though it is endothermic. It occurs because the favored increase in disorder that accompanies dissolution outweighs the unfavored increase in energy.

6) Answer: Spontaneous reactions are reactions that, under the conditions specified, are known to produce the written products. Nonspontaneous reactions do not give products under the specified conditions. Some spontaneous reactions go so slowly that they appear to be nonspontaneous.

7) Answer: Entropy is the degree of disorder in a system. A gas has more entropy than a liquid. A chemical reaction in which there are more molecules of product than of reactant will cause an increase in entropy. A solution of sodium chloride in water has more entropy than a sodium chloride crystal.

Chapter 20 Acids and Bases

Matching Questions

Chapter 20: Matching I

1) acid dissociation constant

2) diprotic acid

3) hydrogen–ion donor

4) Lewis acid

5) pH

A) can accept an electron pair

B) ratio of the concentration of the dissociated to the undissociated form

C) Bronsted–Lowry acid

D) negative logarithm of the hydrogen ion concentration

E) acid with two ionizable protons

Chapter 20: Matching II

6) strong acid

7) amphoteric

8) basic

9) conjugate acid

10) hydronium ion

11) neutral

A) base that has gained a proton

B) H_3O^+

C) hydrogen ion concentration is less than $10^{-7}M$

D) hydrogen ion concentration is $10^{-7}M$

E) able to act as both an acid and a base

F) ionizes completely in water

12) acid

13) alkaline

14) conjugate base

15) hydrogen–ion acceptor

16) Lewis base

17) weak acid

A) Bronsted–Lowry base

B) hydrogen ion concentration is less than $10^{-7}M$

C) acid that has lost a proton

D) hydrogen ion concentration is greater than $10^{-7}M$

E) can donate an electron pair

F) ionizes only slightly in water

Multiple Choice and Bimodal Questions

1) When an acid reacts with a base what compounds are formed?
   A) a salt only
   B) water only
   C) metal oxides only
   D) a salt and water

2) What is the name of H_2SO_3?
   A) hyposulfuric acid
   B) hydrosulfuric acid
   C) sulfuric acid
   D) sulfurous acid
   E) hydrosulfite acid

3) What is the formula for phosphoric acid?
   A) H_2PO_3 B) H_3PO_4 C) HPO_2 D) HPO_4 E) HPO_3

4) Which of the following is a property of an acid?
   A) sour taste
   B) nonelectrolyte
   C) strong color
   D) unreactive
   E) slippery feel

5) What is a property of a base?
   A) bitter taste
   B) watery feel
   C) strong color
   D) unreactive
   E) nonelectrolyte

6) What is the charge on the hydronium ion?

   A) 2–   B) 2–   C) 0   D) 1+   E) 2+

7) If the hydrogen ion concentration is 10^{-10}M, is the solution acidic, alkaline, or neutral?

   A) acidic   B) alkaline   C) neutral

8) If the [H^+] in a solution is 1×10^{-1} mol/L, what is the [OH^-]?

   A) is 1×10^{-1} mol/L   B) is 1×10^{-15} mol/L

   C) is 1×10^{-13} mol/L   D) cannot be determined

9) If the hydrogen ion concentration is 10^{-7}M, what is the pH of the solution?

   A) 1   B) 4   C) 7   D) 11   E) 14

10) If the hydroxide ion concentration is 10^{-10}M, what is the pH of the solution?

   A) 1   B) 4   C) 7   D) 10   E) 14

11) If the pH is 9, what is the concentration of hydroxide ion?

   A) 10^{-1}M   B) 10^{-5}M   C) 10^{-7}M   D) 10^{-9}M   E) 10^{-14}M

12) If the pH is 6, what is the concentration of hydrogen ion?

   A) 10^{-1}M   B) 10^{-6}M   C) 10^{-7}M   D) 10^{-8}M   E) 10^{-14}M

13) If [OH^-] = 1×10^{-4}M, what is the pH of the solution?

   A) 4.0   B) 10.0   C) –4.0   D) –10.0

14) If [H^+] = 1×10^{-11}M, what is the pH of the solution?

   A) –1.0   B) –3.0   C) 3.0   D) 11.0

15) How many free hydrogen ions are there in one liter of water?

   A) none; they are all hydrated   B) approximately 10^{-7} mol
   C) approximately 10^{-1} mol   D) approximately 10^{0} mol

16) A liter of impure water has 10^{-4} mol of hydroxide ions. What is the concentration of hydronium ions in this sample of water?

   A) 10^{-4}M

   B) 10^{-10}M

   C) 10^{-7}M

   D) No determination can be made from the information given.

17) What is the concentration of hydronium ions in a neutral solution?

   A) 10M

   B) 10^{-10}M

   C) 10^{-7}M

   D) No determination can be made from the information given.

18) What is the ion–product constant for water?

A) $10^{-1}M^2$ B) $10^{-7}M^2$ C) $10^{-10}M^2$ D) $10^{-14}M^2$

19) For a solution to be classified as acidic, the _____.

A) hydrogen–ion concentration must be $10^{-7}M$

B) hydrogen–ion and hydroxide–ion concentrations must be equal

C) hydrogen–ion concentration must be greater than the hydroxide–ion concentration

D) the hydrogen–ion concentration must be 7M or greater

20) A solution in which the hydroxide–ion concentration is $1 \times 10^{-4}M$ is _____.

A) acidic   B) basic

C) neutral   D) none of the above

21) A solution in which the hydroxide–ion concentration is $1 \times 10^{-8}M$ is _____.

A) acidic   B) basic

C) neutral   D) none of the above

22) The formula of the hydrogen ion is often written as _____.

A) H_2O^+ B) OH^+ C) H^+ D) H_4N^+

23) The products of self–ionization of water are _____.

A) H_3O^+ and H_2O B) HO^- and OH^+

C) HO^+ and H^- D) HO^- and H^+

24) Which of these solutions is the most basic?

A) $[H^+] = 1 \times 10^{-2}M$ B) $[OH^-] = 1 \times 10^{-4}M$

C) $[H^+] = 1 \times 10^{-11}M$ D) $[OH^-] = 1 \times 10^{-13}M$

25) In a neutral solution, the $[H^+]$ is _____.

A) $10^{-14}M$ B) zero   C) 1×10^7M D) equal to $[OH^-]$

26) What is pH?

A) the negative logarithm of the hydrogen ion concentration

B) the positive logarithm of the hydrogen ion concentration

C) the negative logarithm of the hydroxide ion concentration

D) the positive logarithm of the hydroxide ion concentration

27) Which type of solution is one with a pH of 8?

A) acidic   B) basic   C) neutral

28) The pH of a solution with a concentration of 0.01M hydrochloric acid is _____.

A) 10^{-2} B) 12.0   C) 2.0   D) 10^{-12}

29) What is the pH when the hydrogen ion concentration is 7.0×10^{-3}M?

    A) 1.9   B) 2.2   C) 3   D) 3.3   E) 4

30) A solution with a pH of 5.0 _____.

    A) is basic

    B) has a hydrogen–ion concentration of 5.0M

    C) is neutral

    D) has a hydroxide–ion concentration of 1×10^{-9}M

31) What is the pH of a solution with a $[H^+] = 4.5 \times 10^{-9}$?

    A) 9.3   B) 8.3   C) 8.6   D) 8.0

32) An indicator is what type of compound?

    A) oxidizing agent

    B) weak base or acid

    C) strong base or acid

    D) salt

    E) reducing agent

33) In the reaction of aluminum bromide with ionized sodium bromide, which compound is the Lewis acid?

    A) aluminum bromide   B) bromide ion

    C) sodium ion   D) None are Lewis acids.

34) In the reaction of water with hydroxide ion, which compound is the Lewis base?

    A) water   B) hydroxide ion   C) Neither is a Lewis base.

35) What is an acid according to Arrhenius?

    A) a substance that ionizes to yield protons in aqueous solution

    B) a substance that is a hydrogen ion donor

    C) a substance that accepts an electron pair

    D) a substance that is a hydrogen ion acceptor

    E) a substance that donates an electron pair

36) What type of acid is sulfuric acid?

    A) monoprotic   B) diprotic   C) triprotic

37) Which hydrogens can ionize in a compound?

    A) those bonded to highly electronegative atoms

    B) those bonded to low electronegativity atoms

    C) those bonded to water molecules

    D) those participating in hydrogen bonds

38) Which hydroxides can ionize in a compound?

   A) those bonded to metal ions

   B) those bonded to nonmetal atoms

   C) those bonded to water molecules

   D) those participating in hydrated crystals

39) Which hydroxide compound yields the lowest concentration of hydroxide ions in aqueous solution?

   A) sodium hydroxide   B) potassium hydroxide

   C) calcium hydroxide   D) magnesium hydroxide

40) Which of the following equations represents the dissociation of a metal hydroxide in water? (Note: no charges are shown and the reactions are not balanced.)

   A) $XOH \rightarrow XO + OH$ B) $XOH \rightarrow X + OH$ C) $XOH \rightarrow XH + OH$

41) Which of these acids is monoprotic?

   A) CH_3COOH B) $H_2PO_4^-$ C) H_2SO_4 D) H_3PO_4

42) Which of these is an Arrhenius base?

   A) $LiOH$ B) NH_3 C) $H_2PO_4^-$ D) CH_3COOH

43) What is an acid according to Bronsted?

   A) A substance that ionizes to yield protons in aqueous solution

   B) A substance that is a hydrogen ion donor

   C) A substance that accepts an electron pair

   D) A substance that is a hydrogen ion acceptor

   E) A substance that donates an electron pair

44) Which of the following is a Bronsted–Lowry base, but not an Arrhenius base?

   A) sodium hydroxide   B) calcium hydroxide   C) ammonia

45) Which compound can act as both a Bronsted–Lowry acid and a Bronsted–Lowry base?

   A) water

   B) ammonia

   C) sodium hydroxide

   D) hydrochloric acid

   E) sodium chloride

46) What type of acid or base is the ammonium ion?

   A) conjugate acid   B) conjugate base   C) Arrhenius base

47) What is a conjugate acid made from?
   A) a Bronsted–Lowry acid   B) a Bronsted–Lowry base
   C) an Arrhenius acid   D) an Arrhenius base

48) What is transferred between a conjugate acid–base pair?
   A) an electron   B) a proton
   C) a hydroxide ion   D) a hydronium ion

49) What is the term used to describe a substance that can be both an acid and a base?
   A) amphoteric   B) amphiprotic
   C) Bronsted acid/base   D) Arrhenius acid/base

50) In the reaction, $NH_4^+ + H_2O \rightleftharpoons NH_3 + H_3O^+$, water is acting as a(n) _____.

   A) Arrhenius acid   B) Arrhenius base
   C) Bronsted–Lowry acid   D) Bronsted–Lowry base

51) In the reaction, $CO_3^{2-} + H_2O \rightleftharpoons HCO_3^- + OH^-$, the carbonate ion is acting as a(n) _____.

   A) Arrhenius base   B) Arrhenius acid
   C) Bronsted–Lowry base   D) Bronsted–Lowry acid

52) Which of the following reactions illustrates amphoterism?
   A) $H_2O + H_2O \rightleftharpoons H_3O^+ + OH^-$ B) $NaCl \rightleftharpoons Na^+ + OH^-$
   C) $HCl + H_2O \rightleftharpoons H_3O^+ + Cl^-$ D) $NaOH \rightleftharpoons Na^+ + OH^-$

53) Identify the Bronsted–Lowry bases in this reaction:
   $H_2S + H_2O \rightleftharpoons H_3O^+ + HS^-$
   A) H_2S and H_2O B) H_2S and H_3O^+ C) HS^- and H_2O D) HS^- and H_3O^+

54) Which of the following represents a Bronsted–Lowry conjugate acid–base pair?
   A) SO_3^{2-} and SO_2 B) CO_3^{2-} and CO

   C) H_3O and H_2 D) NH_4^+ and NH_3

55) According to the Bronsted–Lowry theory, water _____.
   A) acts as a base when it accepts a hydrogen ion
   B) can be neither an acid nor a base
   C) can act as an acid by accepting hydrogen ions
   D) can accept but not donate hydrogen ions

56) What are the acids in this equilibrium reaction?

$CN^- + H_2O \rightleftharpoons HCN + OH^-$

A) CN^-, H_2O B) H_2O, HCN   C) CN^-, OH^- D) H_2O, OH^-

57) What is an acid, according to Lewis?

A) a substance that ionizes to yield protons in aqueous solution

B) a substance that is a hydrogen ion donor

C) a substance that accepts an electron pair

D) a substance that is a hydrogen ion acceptor

E) a substance that donates an electron pair

58) Which of the following acids is only a Lewis acid and not any other kind?

A) hydrochloric acid   B) sulfuric acid

C) water   D) boron trifluoride

59) A hydrogen ion is what type of acid?

A) Arrhenius only

B) Bronsted–Lowry only

C) Lewis only

D) Lewis and Bronsted–Lowry only

E) Arrhenius, Bronsted–Lowry, and Lewis

60) A Lewis acid is a substance that can _____.

A) donate a pair of electrons   B) accept a pair of electrons

C) donate a hydrogen ion   D) accept a hydrogen ion

61) What is the acid dissociation constant of a weak acid if a concentration of 0.3M gives a hydrogen ion concentration of 0.001M?

A) 3×10^{-9} B) 3×10^{-6} C) 3×10^{-3}

62) What is the hydrogen ion concentration if the acid dissociation constant is 0.000 001 and the acid concentration is 0.01M?

A) 10^{-6}M   B) 10^{-5}M   C) 10^{-4}M   D) 10^{-3}M   E) 10^{-2}M

63) What is the concentration of acid if the hydrogen-ion concentration is 0.000 1M and the acid dissociation constant is 0.000 000 1?

A) 10^{-7}M   B) 10^{-5}M   C) 10^{-3}M   D) 10^{-1}M   E) 10^{1}M

64) What characterizes a strong acid or base?

A) polar covalent bonding

B) complete ionization in water

C) ionic bonding

D) presence of a hydroxide or hydrogen ion

65) The acid dissociation constant for an acid dissolved in water is equal to the _____.
   A) equilibrium constant
   B) equilibrium constant times the concentration of water
   C) equilibrium constant divided by the concentration of water
   D) equilibrium constant times the equilibrium constant of water

66) What is another name for the acid dissociation constant?
   A) equilibrium constant
   B) ionization constant
   C) rate constant
   D) mole fraction
   E) proportionality constant

67) What is the value of the acid dissociation constant for a weak acid?
   A) less than 0.001
   B) less than 0.1
   C) 1
   D) more than 10
   E) more than 1000

68) How many ionization constants are associated with sulfuric acid?
   A) 0   B) 1   C) 2   D) 3   E) 4

69) Which ionization constant is the largest for phosphoric acid?
   A) the first   B) the second   C) the third

70) Which acid has the greatest acid dissociation constant?
   A) nitric acid   B) acetic acid   C) carbonic acid   D) boric acid

71) Which base has the smallest base dissociation constant?
   A) potassium hydroxide   B) sodium hydroxide
   C) calcium hydroxide   D) ammonia

72) Which base is strong, but never concentrated?
   A) magnesium hydroxide   B) sodium hydroxide
   C) ammonia   D) water

73) Which acid can be concentrated but is always weak?
   A) acetic acid   B) hydrochloric acid
   C) nitric acid   D) sulfuric acid

74) The ionization constant (K_a) of HF is 6.7×10^{-4}. Which of the following is true in a 0.1M solution of this acid?

A) [HF] is greater than [H^+][F^-].
B) [HF] is less than [H^+][F^-].
C) [HF] is equal to [H^+][F^-].
D) [HF] is equal to [H^+][F^-].

75) A base has a K_b of 2.5×10^{-11}. Which of the following statements is true?

A) This is a concentrated base.

B) This base ionizes slightly in aqueous solution.

C) This is a strong base.

D) An aqueous solution of this base would be acidic.

76) A 0.12M solution of an acid that ionizes only slightly in solution would be termed _____.

A) concentrated and weak
B) strong and dilute
C) dilute and weak
D) concentrated and strong

77) Which of the following pairs consists of a weak acid and a strong base?

A) sulfuric acid, sodium hydroxide
B) acetic acid, ammonia
C) acetic acid, sodium hydroxide
D) nitric acid, calcium hydroxide

78) With solutions of "strong" acids and "strong" bases, the word "strong" refers to _____.

A) normality
B) molarity
C) solubility
D) degree of ionization

79) Acetic acid ionizes in water as follows:

$$1\%$$
$$CH_3COOH + H_2O \rightleftharpoons CH_3COO^- + H_3O^+$$
$$99\%$$

The acetate ion (CH_3COO^-) is therefore _____.

A) a poor hydrogen–ion acceptor
B) a good hydrogen–ion acceptor
C) a poor hydrogen–ion donor
D) a good hydrogen–ion donor

80) A 12.0M solution of an acid that ionizes completely in solution would be termed _____.

A) concentrated and weak
B) strong and dilute
C) dilute and weak
D) concentrated and strong

81) If an acid has a $K_a = 1.6 \times 10^{-10}$, what is the acidity of the solution?

A) acidic

B) basic

C) neutral

D) No determination can be made from information given.

82) The K_a of carbonic acid is 4.3×10^{-7}.

$$H_2CO_3 \rightleftharpoons H^+ + HCO_3^-$$

This means that H_2CO_3 is a _____.

A) good hydrogen–ion acceptor   B) poor hydrogen–ion acceptor

C) good hydrogen–ion donor   D) poor hydrogen–ion donor

83) A substance with a K_a of 1×10^{-5} would be classified as a _____.

A) strong acid   B) weak acid   C) strong base   D) weak base

Problems

1) Calculate the hydrogen–ion concentration $[H^+]$ for an aqueous solution in which $[OH^-]$ is 1×10^{-11} mol/L. Is this solution acidic, basic, or neutral?

2) If the hydroxide–ion concentration is 10^{-7}M, what is the pH of the solution?

3) If the hydroxide–ion concentration is 10^{-9}M, what is the pH of the solution?

4) If the hydrogen–ion concentration is 10^{-11}M, what is the pOH of the solution?

5) If the pH is 10, what is the concentration of hydroxide ion?

6) What is the pH if the hydrogen–ion concentration is 2×10^{-1}M?

7) What is the hydrogen–ion concentration if the pH is 3.7?

8) What is the pOH if the hydrogen–ion concentration is 5.0×10^{-7}M?

9) Find the pH of a solution whose $[OH^-]$ is 2.8×10^{-5}M.

10) A 0.500M solution of a weak acid, HX, is only partially ionized. The $[H^+]$ was found to be 2.63×10^{-3}M. Find the dissociation constant for this acid.

11) Calculate the acid dissociation constant of a weak monoprotic acid if a 0.5M solution of this acid gives a hydrogen–ion concentration of 0.000 1M?

Essay Questions

1) Compare and contrast the properties of acids and bases.

2) Explain how to measure pH using a pH meter.

3) What are acids and bases according to Arrhenius? Give examples.

4) What are acids and bases according to the Bronsted–Lowry theory?

5) What are acids and bases according to Lewis theory? Give examples.

6) What makes a substance a strong acid or a strong base?

7) How is strength different from concentration for acids and bases? Give examples.

Chapter 20 Acids and Bases

Matching Questions

1) Answer: B
2) Answer: E
3) Answer: C
4) Answer: A
5) Answer: D
6) Answer: F
7) Answer: E
8) Answer: C
9) Answer: A
10) Answer: B
11) Answer: D
12) Answer: D
13) Answer: B
14) Answer: C
15) Answer: A
16) Answer: E
17) Answer: F

Multiple Choice and Bimodal Questions

1) Answer: D
2) Answer: D
3) Answer: B
4) Answer: A
5) Answer: A
6) Answer: D
7) Answer: B
8) Answer: C
9) Answer: C
10) Answer: B
11) Answer: B
12) Answer: B
13) Answer: B
14) Answer: D
15) Answer: A
16) Answer: B
17) Answer: C
18) Answer: D
19) Answer: C
20) Answer: B
21) Answer: A
22) Answer: C
23) Answer: D

24) Answer: C

25) Answer: D

26) Answer: A

27) Answer: B

28) Answer: C

29) Answer: B

30) Answer: D

31) Answer: B

32) Answer: B

33) Answer: A

34) Answer: B

35) Answer: A

36) Answer: B

37) Answer: A

38) Answer: A

39) Answer: D

40) Answer: B

41) Answer: A

42) Answer: A

43) Answer: B

44) Answer: C

45) Answer: A

46) Answer: A

47) Answer: B

48) Answer: B

49) Answer: A

50) Answer: D

51) Answer: C

52) Answer: A

53) Answer: C

54) Answer: D

55) Answer: A

56) Answer: B

57) Answer: C

58) Answer: D

59) Answer: E

60) Answer: B

61) Answer: B

62) Answer: C

63) Answer: D

64) Answer: B

65) Answer: B

66) Answer: B

67) Answer: A

68) Answer: C

69) Answer: A

70) Answer: A

71) Answer: D

72) Answer: A

73) Answer: A

74) Answer: A

75) Answer: B

76) Answer: C

77) Answer: C

78) Answer: D

79) Answer: B

80) Answer: D

81) Answer: D

82) Answer: D

83) Answer: B

Problems

1) Answer: $K_W = [H^+] \times [OH^-]$

$$[H^+] = \frac{K_W}{[OH^-]}$$

$$= \frac{1 \times 10^{-14} \; mol^2/L^2}{1 \times 10^{-11} \; mol/L}$$

$= 1 \times 10^{-3} \; mol/L$
The solution is acidic.

2) Answer: 7.0

3) Answer: 5.0

4) Answer: 3.0

5) Answer: $10^{-4}M$

6) Answer: $pH = -\log [H^+] = -\log (2 \times 10^{-1})$
$= -(\log 2 + \log 10^{-1})$
$= -(.301) - (-1) = 0.7$

7) Answer: $-\log [H^+] = pH = 3.7$
$\log [H^+] = -3.7$
$[H^+] = antilog(-3.7)$
$[H^+] = 0.000\,20\,M$

8) Answer: $pOH = 14 - pH$
$pH = -\log[H^+] = -\log(5.0 \times 10^{-7})$
$pH = 6.3$
$pOH = 14 - 6.3 = 7.7$

9) Answer: $K_W = [OH^-] \times [H^+]$

$$[H^+] = \frac{K_W}{[OH^-]}$$

$$[H^+] = \frac{1 \times 10^{-14} \, mol^2/L^2}{2.8 \times 10^{-5} \, mol/L} = 3.6 \times 10^{-10}M$$

$$pH = -log[H^+]$$
$$= -log(3.6 \times 10^{-10})$$
$$= 9.4$$

10) Answer:

	HX	H+	X-
Initial	0.500M	0M	$2.63 \times 10^{-3}M$
Change	$-2.63 \times 10^{-3}M$	$+2.63 \times 10^{-3}M$	$+2.63 \times 10^{-3}M$
Equlib	0.497M	$2.63 \times 10^{-3}M$	$2.63 \times 10^{-3}M$

$$K_a = \frac{[H^+] \times [X^-]}{[HX]}$$

$$= \frac{(2.63 \times 10^{-3}M) \times (2.63 \times 10^{-3}M)}{0.497M}$$

$$= 13.9 \times 10^{-6}M = 1.39 \times 10^{-5}M$$

11) Answer: $K_a = \dfrac{[H^+] \times [X^-]}{[HX]}$

$$= \frac{(0.000 \, 1M) \times (0.000 \, 1M)}{0.5M - 0.0001M}$$

$$= \frac{0.000 \, 000 \, 01M}{0.499 \, 9M}$$

$$= 0.000 \, 000 \, 02 = 2 \times 10^{-8}$$

Essay Questions

1) Answer: Both acids and bases are electrolytes, they cause indicators to change colors, and they react with each other to form water and a salt. Acids taste sour, while bases taste bitter. Bases feel slippery. Acids react with some metals to produce hydrogen gas.

2) Answer: Wash the electrodes in distilled water. Dip the electrodes in a buffer at pH 7, and calibrate the meter. Wash the electrodes again. Then measure the pH of the solution. Store the electrodes in a distilled water solution.

3) Answer: According to Arrhenius, acids give up a proton to water and bases give up a hydroxide in water. Hydrochloric acid is an Arrhenius acid because it gives up its proton as it dissolves in water. Sodium hydroxide is an Arrhenius base because it gives up its hydroxide as it dissolves in water.

4) Answer: According to the Bronsted–Lowry theory, acids donate protons to other substances and bases accept protons from other substances. Ammonia accepts a proton from water and therefore acts as a Bronsted–Lowry base. The water donates the proton to ammonia and therefore acts as a Bronsted–Lowry acid.

5) Answer: According to the Lewis theory, acids accept a pair of electrons to form a covalent bond and bases donate an electron pair to form a covalent bond. The hydrogen ion accepts electrons from the hydroxide ion to make water. The hydrogen ion is the Lewis acid and the hydroxide ion is the Lewis base.

6) Answer: Its acid or base dissociation constant must be large, so it ionizes completely in water. Hydrochloric acid and sodium hydroxide ionize completely and are a strong acid and a strong base, respectively.

7) Answer: A strong acid ionizes well and a concentrated acid dissolves well. The same is true for strong and concentrated bases. Ammonia is a weak base because it ionizes incompletely, but it is concentrated because it dissolves well.

Chapter 21 Neutralization

Matching Questions

Chapter 21: Matching I

1) buffer

2) common ion

3) common ion effect

4) end point

5) equivalence point

6) equivalent

A) solution in which pH is kept relatively constant

B) amount of acid that gives 1 mole of hydrogen ions

C) point at which numbers of acid and base equivalents are equal

D) lowering of solubility by addition of shared ion

E) ion of both salts in a solution

F) point at which neutralization is achieved in a titration

Chapter 21: Matching II

7) gram equivalent mass

8) neutralization

9) normality

10) salt hydrolysis

11) solubility product constant

12) titration

A) number of equivalents of solute in 1 L of solution

B) reaction in which an acid and a base produce a salt and water

C) process in which dissociated salt accepts or donates hydrogen ions to water

D) mass of 1 equivalent

E) product of concentrations raised to the powers of their coefficients

F) procedure used to determine the concentration of an acid or base

Multiple Choice and Bimodal Questions

1) What products result from a neutralization reaction?

    A) acids and bases

    B) water only

    C) a salt only

    D) a salt and water

    E) polar covalent compounds

2) What is obtained when phosphoric acid and magnesium hydroxide are mixed?

    A) magnesium phosphate plus water

    B) magnesium hydride

    C) hydrogen–magnesium alloy

    D) hydrogen gas

    E) water only

3) What are the products of the reaction of one mole of $Mg(OH)_2$ and one mole of H_2SO_4?

    A) $MgSO_4 + H_3O^+ + H_2O$ B) $MgSO_4 + 2H_2O$

    C) $MgH_2 + H_3SO_4$ D) $MgSO_4 + H_3O^+ + OH^-$

4) How many moles of sodium hydroxide are needed to neutralize 3.0 moles of phosphoric acid?

    A) 1.0 mol   B) 3.0 mol   C) 6.0 mol   D) 9.0 mol   E) 12 mol

5) How many moles of magnesium hydroxide are needed to neutralize 2.0 moles of phosphoric acid?

    A) 2.0 mol   B) 3.0 mol   C) 4.0 mol   D) 5.0 mol   E) 6.0 mol

6) What is the concentration of hydrochloric acid if 20.0 mL of acid is neutralized by 30.0 mL of 0.10M sodium hydroxide?

    A) 0.030M   B) 0.070M   C) 0.15M   D) 0.30M

7) What is the concentration of sulfuric acid if 50 mL of acid is neutralized by 10 mL of 0.1M sodium hydroxide?

    A) 0.005M   B) 0.01M   C) 0.25M   D) 0.5M

8) How many equivalents are in 2 L of 2M sulfuric acid?

    A) 2 equiv   B) 4 equiv   C) 6 equiv   D) 8 equiv   E) 10 equiv

9) How many equivalents are in 1.0 L of 0.50M aluminum hydroxide?

    A) 0.50 equiv   B) 1.0 equiv   C) 1.5 equiv   D) 2.0 equiv   E) 3.0 equiv

10) What is the gram equivalent mass of magnesium hydroxide if magnesium hydroxide has a gram molecular mass of 58 g?

   A) 19 g   B) 29 g   C) 58 g   D) 116 g   E) 174 g

11) How many equivalents per mole are there in nitric acid?

   A) 1   B) 2   C) 3   D) 0.5   E) 0.33

12) How many equivalents are there in 29 g of magnesium hydroxide?

   A) 0.5 equiv   B) 1 equiv   C) 2 equiv   D) 3 equiv

13) What is the gram equivalent mass of chromic acid, H_2CrO_4?

   A) 59 g   B) 236 g   C) 2 g   D) 118 g

14) What is the gram equivalent mass of KOH?

   A) 56.1 g   B) 1.0 g   C) 28.1 g   D) 112 g

15) What is the normality of a solution that has 6.0 equivalents in 2.0 liters of solution?

   A) 1.5N   B) 3.0N   C) 6.0N   D) 9.0N   E) 12N

16) What is the normality of a 2M solution of phosphoric acid?

   A) 0.67N   B) 1.5N   C) 2N   D) 4N   E) 6N

17) How many equivalents are there in 60 mL of 0.1N sodium hydroxide?

   A) 0.006 equiv   B) 6 equiv   C) 0.001 6 equiv   D) 1.6 equiv

18) How many liters of 0.10N sulfuric acid contain 0.10 equivalents?

   A) 0.5 L   B) 1.0 L   C) 1.5 L   D) 2.0 L

19) If a stock solution of hydrochloric acid is 3.0N, how many milliliters are needed to make 200.0 mL of 0.10N HCl?

   A) 67 mL   B) 1.5 mL   C) 6.7 mL   D) 15 mL   E) 150 mL

20) What is the concentration of hydrochloric acid if 20.0 mL of acid is neutralized by 30.0 mL of 0.20N sodium hydroxide?

   A) 0.06M   B) 0.14M   C) 0.30M   D) 0.60M

21) What is the concentration of sulfuric acid if 50 mL of acid is neutralized by 10 mL of 0.2N sodium hydroxide?

   A) 0.010M   B) 0.02M   C) 0.5M   D) 1M

22) How many milliliters of 0.20N NaOH are required to neutralize 30.0 mL of 0.50N HCl?

   A) 12 mL   B) 50 mL   C) 75 mL   D) 100 mL

23) A 100.0–mL sample of hydrobromic acid, HBr, is titrated to an end point with 24.0 mL of 1.5N NaOH. What is the concentration of HBr?

   A) 1.4N   B) 0.72N   C) 3.1N   D) 0.36N

24) How many grams of sodium hydroxide are in 500 mL of a 0.1N NaOH solution?

    A) 2 g   B) 4 g   C) 20 g   D) 40 g

25) A solution labeled 1N H_2SO_4 contains how many moles of H_2SO_4 per liter?

    A) 1 mol/L   B) 2 mol/L   C) 0.5 mol/L   D) 0.2 mol/L

26) What type of reaction is an acid–base reaction?

    A) single replacement   B) double replacement

    C) combination   D) decomposition

27) The equation that summarizes the reaction of an acid with a base is _____.

    A) $H_2O \rightarrow H^+ + OH^-$ B) $H_2O + H_3O^+ \rightarrow 2H_2O + H^+$

    C) $H^+ + OH^- \rightarrow H_2O$ D) $H_2O + H^+ \rightarrow H_3O^+$

28) This equation is representative of what type of reaction?
$H_2SO_4 + Mg(OH)_2 \rightarrow MgSO_4 + 2H_2O$

    A) hydrolysis   B) combination   C) neutralization   D) buffering

29) What measuring instrument is used in a titration?

    A) graduated cylinder

    B) buret

    C) volumetric pipet

    D) syringe

    E) Erlenmeyer flask

30) What is the purpose of a titration?

    A) to determine the color of an indicator

    B) to determine the concentration of acid or base

    C) to determine the concentration of acid only

    D) to determine the volume of base

31) A solution that contains 1 mole of the diprotic acid oxalic acid ($H_2C_2O_4$) per liter is _____.

    A) 1N   B) 0.5N

    C) 2.0N   D) none of the above

32) Calculate the concentration of silver ion when the solubility product constant of AgI is 10^{-16}.

    A) $10^{-16}M$ B) $10^{-8}M$ C) $10^{-4}M$ D) $10^{-2}M$

33) What is the concentration of aluminum ions if the solubility product constant of $Al(OH)_3$ is 27×10^{-32}.

    A) $10^{-32}M$ B) $10^{-16}M$ C) $10^{-8}M$ D) $10^{-4}M$

34) Given the reaction at equilibrium:

$$Zn(OH)_2(s) \rightarrow Zn^{2+}(aq) + 2OH^-(aq)$$

What is the expression for the solubility product constant, K_{sp}, for this reaction?

A) $K_{sp} = \dfrac{[Zn^{2+}] \times [OH^-]}{[Zn(OH)_2]}$

B) $K_{sp} = \dfrac{[Zn(OH)_2]}{[Zn^{2+}] \times [2OH^-]}$

C) $K_{sp} = [Zn^{2+}] \times [2OH^-]$

D) $K_{sp} = [Zn^{2+}] \times [OH^-]^2$

35) The solubility product constant of calcium hydroxide is 6.5×10^{-6}. If 0.10 mol of sodium hydroxide is added to 1 L of 0.0010M $Ca(OH)_2$, what is the final concentration of calcium ion?

A) 6.5×10^{-6}M
B) 6.5×10^{-5}M
C) 6.5×10^{-4}M
D) 6.5×10^{-3}M
E) 6.5×10^{-2}M

36) A water solution of which compound will turn blue litmus red?

A) K_2CO_3 B) NH_4Cl C) $NaOH$ D) $NaCl$

37) Which substance when dissolved in water will produce a solution with a pH greater than 7?

A) CH_3COOH B) $NaCl$ C) $NaC_2H_3O_2$ D) HCl

38) Which salt hydrolyzes water to form a solution that is acidic?

A) KCl B) $NaCl$ C) NH_4Cl D) $LiCl$

39) A solution of one of the following compounds is acidic because one of its ions undergoes hydrolysis. The compound is _____.

A) $NaCl$ B) CH_3COONa C) NH_4Cl D) NH_3

40) A basic solution would result from the hydrolysis of one of the ions in this compound. The compound is _____.

A) $NaNO_3$ B) NH_4Cl C) CH_3COONa D) $CaCl_2$

41) The hydrolysis of water by the salt of a weak base and a strong acid should give a solution that is _____.

A) weakly basic   B) neutral   C) strongly basic   D) weakly acidic

42) What does a buffer do?

A) keeps the pH of a solution constant

B) keeps the salt concentration of a solution constant

C) keeps the sodium concentration constant

D) keeps the chloride concentration constant

43) What substances are present in a buffer?

    A) a weak base or acid and its salt   B) a weak base or acid only

    C) a hydrolyzing salt only   D) a salt only

44) What are the primary buffer systems used in the human body?

    A) carbonic acid–bicarbonate; monohydrogen phosphate–dihydrogen phosphate

    B) carbonic acid–bicarbonate; acetic acid–phosphate acetate

    C) carbonic acid–bicarbonate; ammonium ion–phosphate ammonia

    D) monohydrogen phosphate–dihydrogen phosphate; acetic acid phosphate–acetate

    E) monohydrogen phosphate–dihydrogen phosphate; ammonium ion–ammonia

45) Which of the following reactions shows what happens when hydrochloric acid is added to an ammonium ion–ammonia buffer?

    A) $H^+ + NH_3 \rightarrow NH_4^+$ B) $H^+ + NH_4^+ \rightarrow NH_5^{2+}$

    C) $Cl^- + NH_3 \rightarrow NH_3Cl^-$ D) $Cl^- + NH_4^+ \rightarrow NH_4^+Cl^-$

46) Which of the following reactions shows what happens when sodium hydroxide is added to an ammonium ion–ammonia buffer?

    A) $OH^- + NH_3 \rightarrow NH_3OH^-$ B) $OH^- + NH_4^+ \rightarrow NH_3 + H_2O$

    C) $Na^+ + NH_3 \rightarrow Na^+NH_3$ D) $Na^+ + NH_4^+ \rightarrow NH_4Na^{2+}$

47) The reaction that takes place when an acid is added to an acetate buffer (CH_3COOH/CH_3COO^-) is _____.

    A) $CH_3COO^- + H^+ \rightarrow CH_4 + CO_2$ B) $CH_3COOH + H^+ \rightarrow CH_3COO^- + H_2$

    C) $CH_3COO^- + H^+ \rightarrow CH_3COOH$ D) $CH_3COOH + OH^- \rightarrow CH_3COO^- + H_2O$

48) Which of the following would NOT make a good buffering system?

    A) sulfate ion and sulfuric acid   B) bicarbonate ion and carbonic acid

    C) ammonia and ammonium ion   D) acetate ion and acetic acid

49) What is the solubility product constant equal to?

    A) the equilibrium constant

    B) the equilibrium constant times the concentration of water

    C) the equilibrium constant times the concentration of undissolved solid

    D) the equilibrium constant of water

50) At 25°C, which salt is less soluble than AgI?

    A) ZnS   B) AgCl   C) $BaSO_4$ D) AgBr

51) Which compound is LEAST soluble in water?

    A) $BaSO_4$ B) $PbCrO_4$ C) $AgCl$ D) $PbSO_4$

52) Which compound is MOST soluble in water?

    A) $Ca(OH)_2$ B) CuS C) $CaCO_3$ D) Ag_2S E) PbS

53) Which groups of compounds are generally soluble in water?

    A) sulfites   B) carbonates   C) sulfides   D) nitrates

54) What does the addition of a common ion do to the solubility of that ion?

    A) increases it   B) decreases it   C) does not affect it

55) What happens when the ion product concentration of the ions in a mixture is greater than the solubility product constant of the compound?

    A) A precipitate forms.   B) No precipitate forms.

    C) A new reaction occurs.   D) The common ion is removed.

56) The solubility product constant for zinc carbonate is 10^{-10}. If 0.1M sodium carbonate and 0.1M zinc nitrate are mixed, what happens?

    A) A zinc carbonate precipitate forms.

    B) No precipitate forms.

    C) A sodium nitrate precipitate forms.

57) Given the system at equilibrium:

    $AgCl(s) \rightarrow Ag^+(aq) + Cl^-(aq)$

    When 0.1M HCl is added to the system, the point of equilibrium will shift to the _____.

    A) right and the concentration of $Ag^+(aq)$ will decrease

    B) right and the concentration of $Ag^+(aq)$ will increase

    C) left and the concentration of $Ag^+(aq)$ will decrease

    D) left and the concentration of $Ag^+(aq)$ will increase

Problems

1) Write a complete and balanced equation for the following acid–base reaction:
$H_2SO_4 + Al(OH)_3 \rightarrow$

2) Write a complete and balanced equation for the following acid–base reaction:
$HCl + Mg(OH)_2 \rightarrow$

3) Write a complete and balanced equation for the following acid–base reaction:
$H_3PO_4 + Ca(OH)_2 \rightarrow$

4) Write a complete and balanced equation for the following acid–base reaction:
$HNO_3 + NH_4OH \rightarrow$

5) Calculate the concentration of hydrochloric acid if 30.0 mL of this acid is neutralized by 40.0 mL of 0.010M sodium hydroxide.

6) Calculate the concentration of sulfuric acid if 60.0 mL of this acid is neutralized by 10.0 mL of 0.010M sodium hydroxide.

7) Calculate the concentration of potassium hydroxide if 60.0 mL of this base is neutralized by 25.0 mL of 0.010M hydrochloric acid.

8) How many equivalents are in 500 mL of a solution that has a concentration of 1M sodium hydroxide?

9) How many equivalents are in 1.0 L of a 3.4M solution of sulfuric acid?

10) How many equivalents of sulfuric acid does it take to neutralize 4 equivalents of aluminum hydroxide?

11) What is the gram equivalent mass of nitric acid, if it has a gram molecular mass of 63 g?

12) How many equivalents per mole are there in phosphoric acid?

13) How many equivalents are in 61 g of strontium hydroxide (gram molecular mass = 122 g)?

14) How many equivalents are in 61.5 g of sulfurous acid, H_2SO_3?

15) What is the normality of a solution that has 8.0 equivalents in 4.0 L of solution?

16) What is the normality of a 4.0M solution of phosphoric acid?

17) What is the normality of a 0.050M solution of aluminum hydroxide?

18) What is the normality of a solution in which 49 g of phosphoric acid (gram molecular mass = 98 g) is dissolved in 6.0 L?

19) How many equivalents are in 20 mL of 0.2N sodium hydroxide?

20) How many liters of 0.1N sulfuric acid contain 0.3 equivalents?

21) If a stock solution of hydrochloric acid is 6.0N, how many milliliters are needed to make 300.0 mL of 0.10N hydrochloric acid?

22) How much of a 5.0N H_2SO_4 stock solution would you need to make 600.0 mL of 0.40N H_2SO_4?

23) How many milliliters of 0.6N H_2SO_4 are required to neutralize 90 mL of 0.4N NaOH?

24) A 50.0–mL sample of hydrobromic acid, HBr, is titrated to an end point with 24.0 mL of 1.40N NaOH. What is the concentration of HBr?

25) Write the equation for the reaction that occurs when hydrochloric acid is added to an ammonium ion–ammonia buffer?

26) Write the equation for the reaction that takes place when sodium hydroxide is added to an ammonium ion–ammonia buffer?

27) Give the reactions for the addition of an acid and a base to an ammonium ion–ammonia buffer.

28) Calculate the concentration of silver ion if the solubility product constant of AgBr is 10^{-10}.

29) Calculate the concentration of chloride ion if the solubility product constant of $AlCl_3$ is 27×10^{-64}.

30) The solubility of $CaSO_4$ in water is 0.67 gram per liter of solution. Calculate the K_{sp}.

31) The solubility product constant of calcium hydroxide is 6.5×10^{-6}. If 0.01 mol of sodium hydroxide is added to 1 L of 0.01M $Ca(OH)_2$, what will the final concentration of calcium ion be?

32) Will a precipitate form when 0.96 g $(NH_4)_2CO_3$ is mixed with 0.20 g $CaBr_2$ in 10 L of solution? $(K_{sp} = 4.5 \times 10^{-9})$

Essay Questions

1) What happens in a neutralization reaction? Use an example.

2) Explain how the process of titration can be used to determine the concentration of a base.

3) Explain the differences between an equivalent, a gram equivalent mass, and equivalents per mole.

4) How does a buffer work when acids and bases are added to it? Use an example.

5) Explain the common ion effect.

Chapter 21 Neutralization

Matching Questions

1) Answer: A
2) Answer: E
3) Answer: D
4) Answer: F
5) Answer: C
6) Answer: B
7) Answer: D
8) Answer: B
9) Answer: A
10) Answer: C
11) Answer: E
12) Answer: F

Multiple Choice and Bimodal Questions

1) Answer: D
2) Answer: A
3) Answer: B
4) Answer: D
5) Answer: B
6) Answer: C
7) Answer: B
8) Answer: D
9) Answer: C
10) Answer: B
11) Answer: A
12) Answer: B
13) Answer: A
14) Answer: A
15) Answer: B
16) Answer: E
17) Answer: A
18) Answer: B
19) Answer: C
20) Answer: C
21) Answer: B
22) Answer: C
23) Answer: D
24) Answer: A
25) Answer: C
26) Answer: B
27) Answer: C
28) Answer: C

29) Answer: B

30) Answer: B

31) Answer: C

32) Answer: B

33) Answer: C

34) Answer: D

35) Answer: C

36) Answer: B

37) Answer: C

38) Answer: C

39) Answer: C

40) Answer: C

41) Answer: D

42) Answer: A

43) Answer: A

44) Answer: A

45) Answer: A

46) Answer: B

47) Answer: C

48) Answer: A

49) Answer: C

50) Answer: A

51) Answer: B

52) Answer: A

53) Answer: D

54) Answer: C

55) Answer: A

56) Answer: A

57) Answer: C

Problems

1) Answer: $3H_2SO_4 + 2Al(OH)_3 \rightarrow 2Al_2(SO_4)_3 + 6H_2O$

2) Answer: $2HCl + Mg(OH)_2 \rightarrow MgCl_2 + 2H_2O$

3) Answer: $2H_3PO_4 + 3Ca(OH)_2 \rightarrow Ca_3(PO_4)_2 + 6H_2O$

4) Answer: $HNO_3 + NH_4OH \rightarrow NH_4NO_3 + H_2O$

5) Answer: $0.010M \times \dfrac{40.0 \text{ mL}}{30.0 \text{ mL}} = 0.013\,M$

6) Answer: $0.010M \times \dfrac{10.0 \text{ mL}}{60.0 \text{ mL}} \times \dfrac{1 \text{ equivalent}}{2 \text{ equivalent}}$

   $= 0.000\,83\,M$

7) Answer: $0.010M \times \dfrac{25.0 \text{ mL}}{60.0 \text{ mL}} = 0.004\,2\,M$

8) Answer: $500 \text{ mL} \times \dfrac{1 \text{ equivalent}}{1 \text{ mol}} \times \dfrac{1 \text{ mol}}{L} \times \dfrac{1 \text{ L}}{1000 \text{ mL}}$

   $= 0.5 \text{ equivalent}$

9) Answer: $1.0 \text{ L} \times \dfrac{2 \text{ equivalent}}{1 \text{ mol}} \times \dfrac{3.4 \text{ mol}}{\text{L}}$

$= 6.8 \text{ equivalent}$

10) Answer: 4

11) Answer: Each mole of nitric acid contains one equivalent.

gem = 63 g

12) Answer: 3

13) Answer: $Sr(OH)_2$ contains 2 equivalents per mole.

$$\dfrac{61 \text{ g} \times \dfrac{2 \text{ equiv}}{\text{mole}}}{122 \dfrac{\text{g}}{\text{mole}}}$$

$= 1 \text{ equiv}$

14) Answer: gfm H_2SO_3 = 82 g

$61.5 \text{ g } H_2SO_3 \times \dfrac{1 \text{ mol } H_2SO_3}{82 \text{ g } H_2SO_3} \times \dfrac{2 \text{ equiv}}{1.0 \text{ mol } H_2SO_3}$

$= 1.50 \text{ equiv}$

15) Answer: normality $= \dfrac{8.0 \text{ equiv}}{4.0 \text{ L}} = 2.0\text{N}$

16) Answer: H_3PO_4 contains 3 equiv/mole.

normality $= \dfrac{3 \text{ equiv}}{\text{mol}} \times \dfrac{4.0 \text{ mol}}{\text{L}} = 12\text{N}$

17) Answer: $Al(OH)_3$ contains 3.0 equiv per mole.

normality $= \dfrac{3.0 \text{ equiv}}{\text{mol}} \times \dfrac{0.050 \text{ mol}}{\text{L}} = 0.15\text{N}$

18) Answer: H_3PO_4 contains 3 equiv/mole.

$\dfrac{49 \text{ g}}{98 \text{ g/mol}} \times \dfrac{3 \text{ equiv}}{\text{mol}}$

$= 1.5 \text{ equiv}$

normality $= \dfrac{1.5 \text{ equiv}}{6.0 \text{ L}} = 0.25\text{N}$

19) Answer: equiv = normality x vol

$= \dfrac{0.2 \text{ equiv}}{\text{L}} \times 20 \text{ mL} \times \dfrac{1 \text{ L}}{1000 \text{ mL}}$

$= 0.004 \text{ equiv}$

20) Answer: vol $= \dfrac{\text{equiv}}{\text{normality}}$

$= \dfrac{0.3 \text{ equiv}}{0.1 \text{ equiv/L}}$

$= 3 \text{ L}$

21) Answer: $V_1 \times N_1 = V_2 \times N_2$

$V_1 = V_2 \times \dfrac{N_2}{N_1}$

$= 300.0 \text{ mL} \times \dfrac{0.10\text{N}}{6.0\text{N}}$

$= 5.0 \text{ mL}$

22) Answer: $V_1 \times N_1 = V_2 \times N_2$

$$V_1 = V_2 \times \frac{N_2}{N_1}$$

$$= 600.0 \text{ mL} \times \frac{0.4N}{5N}$$

$$= 48 \text{ mL}$$

23) Answer: $V_1 \times N_1 = V_2 \times N_2$

$$V_1 = V_2 \times \frac{N_2}{N_1}$$

$$= 90 \text{ mL} \times \frac{0.4N}{0.6N}$$

$$= 60 \text{ mL}$$

24) Answer: $V_1 \times N_1 = V_2 \times N_2$

$$N_1 = \frac{V_2}{V_1} \times N_2$$

$$= \frac{24.0 \text{ mL}}{50.0 \text{ mL}} \times 1.40N$$

$$= 0.672N$$

25) Answer: $H^+ + NH_3 \rightarrow NH_4^+$

26) Answer: $OH^- + NH_4^+ \rightarrow NH_3 + H_2O$

27) Answer: $H^+ + NH_3 \rightarrow NH_4^+$; $OH^- + NH_4^+ \rightarrow NH_4OH$

28) Answer: $K_{sp} = [Ag][Br] = 10^{-10}$
$[Ag] = [Br]$
$[Ag]^2 = 10^{-10}$
$[Ag] = \sqrt{10^{-10}} = 10^{-5}$

29) Answer: $K_{sp} = [Al^{3+}][Cl^-]^3 = 27 \times 10^{-64}$
let $[Al^{3+}] = x$; then $[Cl^-]^3 = 3x$
$(x)(3x)^3 = 27 \times 10^{-64}$
$27x^4 = 27 \times 10^{-64}$
$x^4 = 1 \times 10^{-64}$
$x = 1 \times 10^{-16}$
$[Cl^-]^3 = 3x = 3 \times 10^{-16}$

30) Answer: $CaSO_4(s) \rightarrow Ca^{2+}(aq) + SO_4^{2-}(aq)$

gfm $CaSO_4 = 136.1 \text{ g/mol}$

$$\frac{0.67 \text{ g}}{1 \text{ L}} \times \frac{1 \text{ mol}}{136.1 \text{ g}} = 4.9 \times 10^{-3}$$

$$K_{sp} = [Ca^{2+}][SO_4^{2-}]$$

$$= [4.9 \times 10^{-3}M][4.9 \times 10^{-3}M]$$
$$= 2.4 \times 10^{-5}M^2$$

31) Answer: $K_{sp} = [Ca^{2+}][OH^-]^2 = 6.5 \times 10^{-6}M^3$

$[Ca^{2+}][0.1M]^2 = 6.5 \times 10^{-6}M^3$

$[Ca^{2+}][0.000\ 1M^2] = 6.5 \times 10^{-6}M^3$

$[Ca^{2+}] = \dfrac{6.5 \times 10^{-6}M^3}{0.000\ 1M^2}$

$= 6.5 \times 10^{-3}M$

32) Answer: $0.96\ g\ (NH_4)_2CO_3 \times \dfrac{1\ mol}{96\ g\ (NH_4)_2CO_3} = 0.01M$

$\dfrac{0.01M}{10\ L} = 1 \times 10^{-3}M$

$0.2\ g\ CaBr_2 \times \dfrac{1\ mol}{200\ g\ CaBr_2} = 0.001\ mol$

$\dfrac{0.001M}{10L} = 1 \times 10^{-4}M$

$[Ca^{2+}][CO_3^{2-}] = (1 \times 10^{-4}M) \times (1 \times 10^{-3}M)$

$= 1 \times 10^{-7}M^2$

Yes, a precipitate will form because the ion product is larger than the K_{sp}.

Essay Questions

1) Answer: An acid reacts with a base to produce a salt and water. When hydrochloric acid reacts with sodium hydroxide, the hydrogen and hydroxide ions form water and the sodium and chloride ions form sodium chloride.

2) Answer: A measured amount of the base is placed in a beaker. An acid–base indicator is added. A buret is used to add acid of a known concentration (the standard solution). Additional acid is added until the indicator shows that neutralization has occurred. This is the end point of the titration. The amount of acid added is then recorded. Based on the concentration and amount of acid added, the number of moles of acid added may be calculated. The equation for the neutralization reaction is used to determine the number of moles of base needed to neutralize that amount of acid. The concentration of the base can be calculated from the number of moles of base and its volume.

3) Answer: An equivalent is the number of moles of acid or base needed to give one mole of hydrogen or hydroxide ions. A gram equivalent mass is the mass needed to give one mole of hydrogen or hydroxide ions. The number of equivalents per mole is the number of moles of hydrogen or hydroxide ions in one mole of a substance.

4) Answer: If small amounts of strong acid are added to a buffer, the weak base of the buffer neutralizes the acid. If small amounts of strong base are added to a buffer, the weak acid of the buffer neutralizes the base.

5) Answer: A common ion is an ion that is added to a solution which already contains a large amount of the ion from the original solute. Addition of a common ion causes the solubility product constant to be exceeded and thus lowers the solubility. For example, the solubility of AgCl is less in a solution of $AgNO_3$ than in pure water because of the presence of the common ion, Ag^+, in the solution.

Chapter 22 Oxidation–Reduction Reactions

Matching Questions
Chapter 22: Matching I

1) oxidation number

2) half–reaction

3) oxidizing agent

4) reducing agent

5) spectator ion

A) substance that accepts electrons

B) reaction showing either the reduction or the oxidation reaction

C) integer related to the number of electrons under an atom's control

D) substance that donates electrons

E) ion that is present, but does not participate in an oxidation–reduction reaction

Multiple Choice and Bimodal Questions

1) If an atom is reduced in a redox reaction, what must occur to another atom in the system?
   A) It must be oxidized.
   B) It must be reduced.
   C) It must be neutralized.
   D) Nothing need happen to another atom in the system.

2) In the reaction of sodium with oxygen, which atom is reduced?
   A) sodium   B) oxygen   C) both   D) neither

3) In the reaction of sodium with oxygen, which atom is the reducing agent?
   A) sodium   B) oxygen   C) both   D) neither

4) In the reaction of calcium with chlorine, which atom is the oxidizing agent?
   A) calcium   B) chlorine   C) both   D) neither

5) In the reaction of calcium with chlorine, which atom is oxidized?
   A) calcium   B) chlorine   C) both   D) neither

6) In the reaction of hydrogen with iodine, which atom is oxidized?
   A) hydrogen   B) iodine   C) both   D) neither

7) In the reaction of hydrogen with iodine, which atom is the reducing agent?

   A) hydrogen   B) iodine   C) both   D) neither

8) Identify the reducing agent in the following reaction.
   $2Na + S \rightarrow Na_2S$

   A) Na   B) S   C) Na_2S D) Na^+

9) Identify the reducing agent in the following reaction.
   $2Na + 2H_2O \rightarrow 2NaOH + H_2$

   A) Na   B) H_2O C) NaOH   D) H_2

10) Identify the oxidizing agent in the following reaction.
    $CH_4 + 2O_2 \rightarrow CO_2 + H_2O$

    A) CH_4 B) O_2 C) CO_2 D) H_2O

11) What is reduced in the following reaction?
    $S + Cl_2 \rightarrow SCl_2$
    (Hint: Chlorine is the more electronegative element.)

    A) Sulfur is reduced to SCl_2.   B) Chlorine is reduced to SCl_2.

    C) Chlorine is oxidized to SCl_2.   D) Sulfur is the oxidizing agent.

12) Identify the oxidizing agent in this reaction.

    $I^- + MnO_4^- \rightarrow I_2 + MnO_2$

    A) I^- B) MnO_4^- C) I_2 D) MnO_2

13) What are transferred in an oxidation–reduction reaction?

    A) protons   B) ions   C) electrons   D) atoms

14) Which type of reaction provides the main source of energy on earth?

    A) reduction   B) oxidation   C) neutralization   D) decomposition

15) What is another name for an oxidation–reduction reaction?

    A) O–reaction   B) R–reaction   C) redox reaction   D) oxred reaction

16) When iron oxide becomes iron, what type of reaction occurs?

    A) oxidation   B) reduction   C) neutralization   D) combination

17) Why is the term reduction used when ores are processed to produce metals?

    A) Volume is reduced.   B) Atomic number is reduced.

    C) The number of metal atoms is reduced.   D) Temperature is reduced.

18) In which of the following types of reaction are electrons lost?

A) reduction   B) oxidation   C) neutralization

19) Why is oxygen reduced in the reaction of hydrogen with oxygen to make water?

A) It pulls electrons toward itself.

B) It pushes electrons toward the hydrogens.

C) It absorbs a proton.

D) It releases a proton.

20) When hydrogen is added to carbon, what happens to the carbon atom?

A) It is oxidized.   B) It is reduced.

C) It is neutralized.   D) It decomposes.

21) Oxidation is _____.

A) a gain of electrons   B) a gain of hydrogen

C) a loss of electrons   D) a loss of oxygen

22) What is the oxidation number of magnesium in magnesium chloride?

A) –1   B) 0   C) +1   D) +2   E) +3

23) What is the oxidation number of sulfur in hydrogen sulfide?

A) –2   B) –1   C) 0   D) +1   E) +2

24) What is the oxidation number of hydrogen when it is not in a hydride?

A) –2   B) –1   C) 0   D) +1   E) +2

25) What is the oxidation number of oxygen when it is not in a peroxide?

A) –2   B) –1   C) 0   D) +1   E) +2

26) What is the oxidation number of chlorine in chlorine gas?

A) –2   B) –1   C) 0   D) +1   E) +2

27) What is the sum of the oxidation numbers in calcium carbonate?

A) –2   B) –1   C) 0   D) +1   E) +2

28) What is the sum of the oxidation numbers in the phosphate ion?

A) 0   B) –1   C) –2   D) –3   E) –4

29) Give the oxidation number for each atom in NH_4Cl.

A) N = +3, H = –4, Cl = +1   B) N = –3, H = +1, Cl = –1

C) N = +3, H = +1, Cl = –1   D) N = –3, H = –1, Cl = +1

30) Identify the atom that increases in oxidation number in the following redox reaction.
$2MnO_2 + 2K_2CO_3 + O_2 \rightarrow 2KMnO_4 + 2CO_2$

A) Mn   B) O   C) K   D) C

31) Which atom has a change in oxidation number of –3 in the following redox reaction?
$K_2Cr_2O_7 + H_2O + S \rightarrow KOH + Cr_2O_3 + SO_2$

A) K   B) Cr   C) O   D) S

32) Which element increases its oxidation number in the following reaction?
$2Na + 2H_2O \rightarrow 2NaOH + H_2$

A) sodium   B) hydrogen   C) oxygen   D) none

33) What is defined as the charge an atom would have in a compound if its bonding electrons were assigned to the more electronegative atom?

A) reduction number

B) oxidation number

C) valence

D) electropositivity

E) electron affinity

34) The oxidation number of sulfur in each of the following is +6 EXCEPT for _____.

A) SO_3 B) Na_2SO_4 C) SO_4^{2-} D) $S_2O_4^{2-}$

35) In which of the following compounds is the oxidation number of nitrogen different from the other three?

A) NO_3^- B) N_2O_5 C) NH_4Cl D) $Ca(NO_3)_2$

36) $Zn^{2+} \rightarrow Zn$ represents _____.

A) oxidation   B) reduction

C) hydrolysis   D) none of the above

37) $Sn^{2+} \rightarrow Sn^{4+}$ represents _____.

A) oxidation   B) reduction

C) hydrolysis   D) none of the above

38) What is the TOTAL increase in oxidation number for the atom that is oxidized in the following balanced redox equation?

$Cr_2O_7^{2-} + 8H^+ + 3SO_3^{2-} \rightarrow 2Cr^{3+} + 3SO_4^{2-} + 4H_2O$

A) +2   B) +6   C) –3   D) –6

39) What is the change in oxidation number of oxygen in the reaction of aluminum with oxygen gas to make aluminum oxide?

A) –2   B) –1   C) 0   D) +1   E) +2

40) What is the change in the oxidation number of chromium when $K_2Cr_2O_7$ becomes $CrCl_3$?

A) 0   B) –1   C) –2   D) –3   E) +4

41) What is the change in oxidation number of manganese when MnO_2 becomes Mn_2O_3?

    A) 0   B) –1   C) –2   D) –3   E) –4

42) In the following unbalanced reaction, which atom is reduced?
$H_2O + Cl_2 + SO_2 \rightarrow HCl + H_2SO_4$

    A) hydrogen   B) oxygen   C) chlorine   D) sulfur

43) In the following unbalanced reaction, which atom is oxidized?
$HNO_3 + HBr \rightarrow NO + Br_2 + H_2O$

    A) hydrogen   B) nitrogen   C) oxygen   D) bromine

44) Which element decreases its oxidation number in the following reaction?
$BiCl_2 + Na_2SO_4 \rightarrow 2NaCl + BiSO_4$

    A) bismuth   B) chlorine   C) sodium   D) oxygen   E) none

45) Which element increases its oxidation number in the following reaction?
$3KOH + H_3PO_4 \rightarrow K_3PO_4 + 3H_2O$

    A) potassium
    B) oxygen
    C) hydrogen
    D) phosphorus
    E) none

46) Which element decreases its oxidation number in the following reaction?
$I_2 + 2KCl \rightarrow 2KI + Cl_2$

    A) iodine   B) potassium   C) chlorine   D) none

47) What coefficient of H^+ balances the atoms in the following half–reaction?
$H^+ + MnO_2 \rightarrow Mn^{2+} + H_2O$

    A) 1   B) 2   C) 3   D) 4   E) 5

48) What number of electrons balances the charges in the following half–reaction?

$SO_2 + 2H_2O \rightarrow SO_4^{2-} + 4H^+$

    A) 1   B) 2   C) 3   D) 4   E) 5

49) What is the reduction half-reaction for the following unbalanced redox equation?

$Cr_2O_7^{2-} + NH_4^+ \rightarrow Cr_2O_3 + N_2$

    A) $Cr_2O_3 \rightarrow Cr_2O_7^{2-}$ B) $Cr_2O_7^{2-} \rightarrow Cr_2O_3$

    C) $NH_4^+ \rightarrow N_2$ D) $N_2 \rightarrow NH_4^+$

50) What will the coefficient of HNO_3 be when the following equation is completely balanced using the smallest whole–number coefficients?
$HNO_3 + MnCl_2 + HCl \rightarrow NO + MnCl_4 + H_2O$

 A) 5   B) 2   C) 3   D) 6

51) What is the oxidation half–reaction for the following unbalanced redox equation?

$Cr_2O_7^{2-} + Fe^{2+} \rightarrow Cr^{3+} + Fe^{3+}$

 A) $Cr^{3+} \rightarrow Cr_2O_7^{2-}$ B) $Fe^{2+} \rightarrow Fe^{3+}$

 C) $Fe^{3+} \rightarrow Fe^{2+}$ D) $Cr_2O_7^{2-} \rightarrow Cr^{3+}$

52) What is the first step in balancing a redox reaction by the oxidation number change method?
 A) Connect the oxidized and reduced forms of the atoms.
 B) Identify the reduced and oxidized atoms.
 C) Assign oxidation numbers to all the atoms.
 D) Choose coefficients to make the change in oxidation number equal to 0.
 E) Check the balance of charges and atoms.

53) What is the next–to–the–last step in balancing a redox reaction by the oxidation number change method?
 A) Assign oxidation numbers to all the atoms.
 B) Choose coefficients to make the change in oxidation number equal to 0.
 C) Connect the oxidized and reduced forms of the atoms.
 D) Identify the reduced and oxidized atoms.
 E) Check the balance of charges and atoms.

54) In the following unbalanced reaction, what is the total increase in oxidation number for the oxidized atoms?
$H_2O + Cl_2 + SO_2 \rightarrow HCl + H_2SO_4$

 A) 0   B) +1   C) +2   D) +3   E) +4

55) In the following unbalanced reaction, what is the total decrease in oxidation number for the reduced atoms?
$HNO_3 + HBr \rightarrow NO + Br_2 + H_2O$

 A) 0   B) –1   C) –2   D) –4   E) –3

56) Which of the following reactions is a redox reaction?
 A) acid–base   B) double–replacement   C) combustion

57) What is shown by a half-reaction?
  A) oxidation or reduction of an ion or molecule
  B) neutralization of an ion or molecule
  C) decomposition of an ion or molecule

58) Which oxidation reduction reactions are best balanced by the half-reaction method?
  A) covalent reactions   B) acid-base reactions
  C) ionic reactions   D) intermolecular reactions

59) What is the first step in balancing a redox reaction by the half-reaction method?
  A) Balance the atoms in each half-reaction.
  B) Write the two half-reactions.
  C) Write the equation showing ions separately.
  D) Balance the charges in each half-reaction.
  E) Make the charges of both half-reactions equal.

60) What is the next-to-the-last step in balancing a redox reaction by the half-reaction method?
  A) Balance the atoms in each half-reaction.
  B) Write the two half-reactions.
  C) Write the equation showing ions separately.
  D) Balance the charges in each half-reaction.
  E) Make the electron changes of both half-reactions equal.

61) What is the ionic form of the following unbalanced equation?
   $MnO_2 + HNO_2 \rightarrow Mn(NO_3)_2 + H_2O$

  A) $MnO_2 + HNO_2 \rightarrow Mn^{2+} + NO_3^- + H_2O$

  B) $MnO_2 + H^+ + NO_2^- \rightarrow MnNO_3 + H_2O$

  C) $Mn^{4+} + O^{2-} + H^+ + NO_2^- \rightarrow Mn^{2+} + NO_3^- + H_2O$

  D) $Mn^{2+} + O^{2-} + H^+ + NO_2^- \rightarrow Mn^{2+} + NO_3^- + H_2O$

62) What is the reduction half-reaction in the following unbalanced equation?
   $I_2 \rightarrow I_3^- + I^-$

  A) $I_2 + 2e^- \rightarrow 2I^-$ B) $I_2 + 6H_2O \rightarrow 2I_3^- + 12H^+ + 10e^-$

  C) $2I^- \rightarrow I_2 + 2e^-$ D) $2I_3^- + 12H^+ + 10e^- \rightarrow I_2 + 6H_2O$

63) Identify the oxidation half–reaction among the following.

    A) $Sn^{2+} \rightarrow Sn^{4+} + 2e^-$ B) $Cl_2 + 2e^- \rightarrow 2Cl^-$

    C) $O_2 + 4H^+ + 4e^- \rightarrow 2H_2O$ D) $Fe^{3+} + e^- \rightarrow Fe^{2+}$

64) When the half–reactions $Br_2 + 2e^- \rightarrow 2Br^-$ and $Na \rightarrow Na^+ + e^-$ are combined, the balanced redox equation is:

    A) $Na + Br_2 + e^- \rightarrow Na^+ + 2Br^-$ B) $Na + Br_2 \rightarrow Na^+ + 2Br^-$

    C) $2Na + Br_2 \rightarrow 2Na^+ + 2Br^-$ D) $Na + Br_2 + 2e^- \rightarrow Na^+ + 2Br^- + e^-$

65) Which of the following is a reduction half–reaction?

    A) $Zn \rightarrow Zn^{2+} + 2e^-$ B) $NO + 2H_2O \rightarrow N^-_3 + 4H^+ + 3e^-$

    C) $Na \rightarrow Na^+ + e^-$ D) $2H^+ + 2e^- \rightarrow H_2$

66) To balance the oxygen and hydrogen for a redox reaction that takes place in basic solution, it is necessary to use _____.

    A) H_2O and H^+ B) H_2O, only   C) H_2O and OH^- D) OH^-, only

Problems

1) In the reaction of magnesium with oxygen, which atom is the reducing agent?

2) In the reaction of iron with chlorine, which atom is the oxidizing agent?

3) What is the oxidation number of magnesium in magnesium iodide?

4) What is the sum of the oxidation numbers in lithium carbonate?

5) What is the change in oxidation number of chromium when $Na_2Cr_2O_7$ becomes CrI_3?

6) In the following unbalanced reaction, which atom is reduced?
   $H_2O + Br_2 + SO_2 \rightarrow HBr + H_2SO_4$

7) In the following unbalanced reaction, which atom is oxidized?
   $HNO_3 + HI \rightarrow NO + I_2 + O_2$

8) In the following unbalanced reaction, what is the total decrease in oxidation number for the reduced atoms?
   $HNO_3 + HI \rightarrow NO + I_2 + H_2O$

9) What element decreases its oxidation number in the following reaction?
   $CuCl_2 + Na_2SO_4 \rightarrow 2NaCl + CuSO_4$

10) What is the ionic form of the following unbalanced equation?
   $MoO_2 + HNO_2 \rightarrow MoNO_3 + H_2O$

11) What is the oxidation half-reaction in the following unbalanced equation?

$$I_2 \rightarrow IO_3^- + I^-$$

12) What coefficient of H^+ balances the atoms in the following half-reaction?

$$H^+ + PbO_2 \rightarrow Pb^{2+} + 2H_2O$$

13) Combine these two half-reactions to form a balanced redox equation.

$$Cl_2 + 2e^- \rightarrow 2Cl^- \text{ and } Cr \rightarrow Cr^{3+} + 3e^-$$

14) Balance the following redox equation, using the oxidation number change method. Show all your work.

$$Fe_2O_3 + CO \rightarrow Fe + CO_2$$

Essay Questions

1) What are the steps of the oxidation number change method of balancing redox reactions?

2) What are the steps of the half-reaction method of balancing redox reactions?

Chapter 22 Oxidation–Reduction Reactions

Matching Questions

1) Answer: C

2) Answer: B

3) Answer: A

4) Answer: D

5) Answer: E

Multiple Choice and Bimodal Questions

1) Answer: A

2) Answer: B

3) Answer: A

4) Answer: B

5) Answer: A

6) Answer: A

7) Answer: A

8) Answer: A

9) Answer: A

10) Answer: B

11) Answer: B

12) Answer: B

13) Answer: C

14) Answer: B

15) Answer: C

16) Answer: B

17) Answer: A

18) Answer: B

19) Answer: A

20) Answer: B

21) Answer: C

22) Answer: D

23) Answer: A

24) Answer: D

25) Answer: A

26) Answer: C

27) Answer: C

28) Answer: D

29) Answer: B

30) Answer: A

31) Answer: B

32) Answer: A

33) Answer: B

34) Answer: D

35) Answer: C

36) Answer: B

37) Answer: A

38) Answer: B

39) Answer: A

40) Answer: D

41) Answer: B

42) Answer: C

43) Answer: D

44) Answer: E

45) Answer: E

46) Answer: A

47) Answer: D

48) Answer: B

49) Answer: B

50) Answer: B

51) Answer: B

52) Answer: C

53) Answer: B

54) Answer: C

55) Answer: E

56) Answer: C

57) Answer: A

58) Answer: C

59) Answer: C

60) Answer: E

61) Answer: C

62) Answer: A

63) Answer: A

64) Answer: C

65) Answer: D

66) Answer: C

Problems

1) Answer: magnesium

2) Answer: chlorine

3) Answer: +2

4) Answer: 0

5) Answer: –3

6) Answer: bromine

7) Answer: iodine

8) Answer: –3

9) Answer: none

10) Answer: $Mo_2 + H^+ + NO_2^- \rightarrow Mo^{2+} + NO_3^- + H_2O$

11) Answer: $I_2 \rightarrow IO_3^-$

12) Answer: 4

13) Answer: $2Cr + 3Cl_2 \rightarrow 2Cr^{3+} + 6Cl^-$

14) Answer:

$$\overbrace{}^{2 \times (-3) = -6}$$

$$\begin{array}{cccc} +3 - 2 & +2 - 2 & 0 & +4 - 2 \\ Fe_2O_3 & + \; CO & \longrightarrow \; Fe & + \; CO_2 \end{array}$$

$$\underbrace{}_{3 \times (+2) = +6}$$

$$Fe_2O_3 + 3CO \rightarrow 2Fe + 3CO_2$$

Essay Questions

1) Answer: Assign oxidation numbers to all the atoms. Identify the oxidized and reduced atoms. Connect the oxidized and reduced forms of the atoms with a line. Use coefficients to make the total change in oxidation number equal for both the oxidation and die reduction. Check the balance of atoms and charges.

2) Answer: Write out the equation in ionic form. Write the two half-reactions. Balance the atoms in each half-reaction. Balance the charges in each half-reaction. Multiply each half-reaction by a factor that will make the charges equal in both. Add the half-reactions, leaving out terms that appear on both sides.

Chapter 23 Electrochemistry
Matching Questions
Chapter 23: Matching I

1) anode

2) battery

3) fuel cell

4) half–cell

5) cathode

A) one part of a voltaic cell in which either oxidation or reduction occurs

B) a group of cells that are connected together

C) a voltaic cell in which a fuel substance undergoes oxidation and from which electrical energy is obtained continuously

D) the electrode at which reduction occurs

E) the electrode at which oxidation occurs

Chapter 23: Matching II

6) electrode

7) electrolysis

8) salt bridge

9) voltaic cell

10) dry cell

A) a voltaic cell in which the electrolyte is a paste

B) a process in which electrical energy is used to bring about a chemical change

C) a conductor in a circuit that carries electrons to or from a substance other than a metal

D) an electrochemical cell that is used to convert chemical energy to electrical energy

E) a tube containing a conducting solution

Multiple Choice and Bimodal Questions

1) A zinc–copper cell is constructed:

   $Zn \mid Zn^{2+}(1M) \mid\mid Cu^{2+}(1M) \mid Cu$.

   What occurs to the mass of the copper electrode as the reaction proceeds? (Zinc is above copper in the activity series of metals.)

   A) It decreases.   B) It increases.   C) It remains the same.

2) Who invented the first electrochemical cell?

   A) Michael Faraday

   B) Alessandro Volta

   C) James Maxwell

   D) Benjamin Franklin

   E) Ernest Rutherford

3) In a zinc–copper cell, $Zn \mid Zn^{2+}(1M) \mid\mid Cu^{2+}(1M) \mid Cu$, which electrode is negative?

   A) $Zn(s)$ B) $Cu^{2+}(aq)$ C) $Zn^{2+}(aq)$ D) $Cu(s)$

4) What happens in an electrochemical process?

   A) Chemical and electrical energy are interconverted.

   B) Mechanical and light energy are interconverted.

   C) Helium gas is produced.

5) Which metal is the most easily oxidized?

   A) highly active metal

   B) moderately active metal

   C) slightly active metal

6) How can a redox reaction be used as a source of electrical energy?

   A) Two half–reactions must be physically separated.

   B) One half–reaction must involve two metals.

   C) Two half–reactions must involve more than one electron.

   D) One half–reaction must use a metal wire electrode.

7) Ions of which of the following metals are the most easily reduced?

   A) potassium   B) calcium   C) iron   D) lead   E) mercury

8) Which of the following metals is oxidized by calcium ions?

   A) potassium   B) zinc   C) iron   D) lead   E) mercury

9) Which metal ion is reduced by lead?

   A) potassium   B) calcium   C) nickel   D) cadmium   E) mercury

10) A clean strip of copper is dipped into a solution of magnesium sulfate. Magnesium is above copper in the activity series of metals. Predict what you will observe.

    A) The copper strip becomes magnesium-plated.

    B) Copper dissolves and the solution turns blue.

    C) No reaction occurs.

    D) Bubbles of hydrogen gas appear on the copper.

11) A clean iron nail is dipped into a solution of silver nitrate. Iron is above silver in the activity series of metals. Predict what you will observe.

    A) No reaction occurs.

    B) The iron nail will become silver-plated.

    C) Bubbles of oxygen gas will form on the iron nail.

    D) The iron will be reduced.

12) What happens in a voltaic cell?

    A) Chemical energy is changed to electrical energy.

    B) Electrical energy is changed to chemical energy.

    C) Electrical energy is changed to magnetic energy.

    D) Magnetic energy is changed to electric energy.

13) What occurs in a half-cell?

    A) oxidation only   B) reduction only

    C) oxidation or reduction, but not both   D) both oxidation and reduction

14) What is the relation of the two half-cells in a voltaic cell?

    A) They are separated by an impenetrable barrier.

    B) They are separated by a porous partition or salt bridge.

    C) They are in direct contact with no separation.

15) At which electrode does oxidation occur in a voltaic cell?

    A) anode only

    B) cathode only

    C) both anode and cathode

16) Which electrode in a voltaic cell has excess positive charge on it?

    A) anode only   B) cathode only

    C) both anode and cathode   D) neither anode nor cathode

17) Which electrode is labeled as positive in a voltaic cell?

    A) anode only   B) cathode only

    C) both anode and cathode   D) neither anode nor cathode

18) From which electrode do the free electrons originate before they go around the circuit in a voltaic cell?

   A) anode only   B) cathode only

   C) both anode and cathode   D) neither anode nor cathode

19) At which electrode do ions in solution become reduced to metal in a voltaic cell?

   A) anode only   B) cathode only

   C) both anode and cathode   D) neither anode nor cathode

20) How is the circuit completed in a voltaic cell?
   A) Electrons go through the wire and positive ions go through the solution from anode to cathode.
   B) Electrons go through the solution and positive ions go through the wire from anode to cathode.
   C) Positive ions go through the solution and electrons go through the wire from cathode to anode.
   D) Positive ions go through the wire and electrons go through the solution from anode to cathode.

21) Which ions of the solution contribute to the current in the solution?

   A) positive only   B) negative only   C) positive and negative

22) Which of the following factors does NOT affect the voltage produced in a voltaic cell?

   A) metal of the electrodes   B) concentrations of ions

   C) temperature   D) pressure

23) What is the nature of the electrolyte in a dry cell?

   A) solid   B) paste   C) liquid

24) What is the electrode in the center of the most common dry cell made of?
   A) copper
   B) zinc
   C) iron
   D) graphite
   E) magnesium

25) What metal is oxidized in the most common dry cell?
   A) copper
   B) zinc
   C) iron
   D) carbon
   E) magnesium

26) What is reduced in the most common dry cell?

    A) copper

    B) zinc

    C) manganese dioxide

    D) carbon

    E) magnesium

27) Which of the following describes a dry cell?

    A) It contains boric acid, which is a solid acid.

    B) The graphite rod does not undergo reduction, even though it is the cathode.

    C) It can be recharged many times.

    D) all of the above

28) Of what does a battery consist?

    A) a dry cell   B) a series of cells

    C) a fuel cell   D) a series of half–cells

29) What oxide is used in the lead storage battery?

    A) PbO   B) PbO_2 C) SO_2 D) SO_3

30) What is the voltage of a single cell in a lead storage battery?

    A) 1 V   B) 1.5 V   C) 2 V   D) 2.5 V   E) 3 V

31) What electrolyte is used in a lead storage battery?

    A) hydrochloric acid

    B) sulfuric acid

    C) lead acetate

    D) lead nitrate

    E) potassium hydroxide

32) What happens to the concentration of the acid when a lead storage battery is discharging?

    A) It increases.   B) It decreases.   C) It stays the same.

33) How is a lead storage battery recharged?

    A) A direct current is applied to it.

    B) A magnet is held close to it.

    C) Alternating current is forced through it.

34) In a fully charged lead storage battery, the cathode grid is packed with _____.

    A) spongy lead   B) lead sulfate   C) lead(IV) oxide   D) sulfuric acid

35) When a lead storage battery discharges _____.
   A) the concentration of sulfuric acid increases
   B) the concentration of sulfuric acid decreases
   C) the concentration of lead sulfate in the battery decreases

36) What happens in a hydrogen–oxygen fuel cell?
   A) Oxygen diffuses through the cathode.
   B) Oxygen diffuses through the anode.
   C) Hydrogen diffuses through the cathode.
   D) Hydrogen and oxygen are mixed before entering the anode.

37) What is the waste product of a hydrogen–oxygen fuel cell?
   A) hydroxide   B) water
   C) hydrogen chloride   D) potassium oxide

38) What is the electrolyte in the hydrogen–oxygen fuel cell?
   A) sulfuric acid
   B) hydrochloric acid
   C) potassium hydroxide
   D) sodium hydroxide
   E) water with sodium chloride

39) Which of the following is true about fuel cells?
   A) They only produce energy in short bursts.
   B) They are inexpensive.
   C) They have never been built or used.
   D) They can be designed so that they emit no pollutants.

40) What is the standard cell potential of a cell made of Ni/Ni^{2+} and Zn/Zn^{2+}, if the reduction potentials are –0.25 V and –0.76 V respectively?
   A) –1.01 V   B) –0.51 V   C) +0.51 V   D) +1.01 V

41) What is the standard cell potential of a hypothetical cell made of Na/Na^+ and Zn/Zn^{2+} if the reduction potentials are –2.71 V and –0.76 V respectively?
   A) –3.47 V   B) –1.95 V   C) +1.95 V   D) +3.47 V

42) What is the standard cell potential of a hypothetical cell made of Na/Na^+ and F_2/F^- if the reduction potentials are –2.71 V and +2.87 V respectively?
   A) –5.58 V   B) –0.16 V   C) +0.16 V   D) +5.58 V

43) Which reaction occurs when bromine is added to an aqueous solution of iodide ions?
   A) $2I^- + Br_2 \rightarrow I_2 + 2Br^-$ B) $I_2 + 2Br^- \rightarrow Br_2 + 2I^-$
   C) $2I^- + 2Br^- \rightarrow I_2 + Br_2$ D) $I_2 + Br_2 \rightarrow 2I^- + 2Br^-$

44) Which metal will react spontaneously with Cu^{2+}(aq) at 25°C?

    A) Ag   B) Au   C) Mg   D) Hg

45) Which ion can be most easily reduced?

    A) Cu^{2+} B) Zn^{2+} C) Ni^{2+} D) Ca^{2+}

46) What is the cell potential?

    A) the difference in reduction potentials of the half–cells

    B) the difference in oxidation potentials of the half–cells

    C) the sum of reduction potentials of the half–cells

    D) the sum of oxidation potentials of the half–cells

47) At what concentration of ion is the standard cell potential measured?

    A) 0.01M   B) 0.1M   C) 1.0M   D) 1%   E) 10%

48) At what pressure must the gases participating in the reaction be for the standard cell potential to be measured?

    A) 1 atm   B) $1 \, N/m^2$ C) 1 mm Hg   D) $1 \, lb/in^2$

49) At what temperature is the standard cell potential measured?

    A) 0°C   B) 4°C   C) 20°C   D) 25°C   E) 100°C

50) What standard reduction electrode has a half–cell potential of 0.00 V?

    A) oxygen   B) hydrogen   C) lithium   D) fluorine   E) water

51) What symbol is used to show the standard reduction potential of an oxidation reaction in a half–cell?

    A) E_0^{oxid} B) E_{oxid}^0 C) E_0^{red} D) E_{red}^0

52) What is the normal sign of the standard reduction potential for a metal and its ion?

    A) negative   B) positive   C) zero

53) If the standard reduction potential of a half–cell is positive, which redox reaction is spontaneous when paired with a hydrogen electrode?

    A) oxidation   B) reduction   C) both   D) neither

54) How are the standard reduction potentials of half–cells determined?

    A) by direct measurement

    B) by comparison with a hydrogen electrode

    C) by variation of experimental conditions

55) What is the relative standard reduction potential of the half-cell reaction that will be a reduction reaction?

    A) positive   B) negative

    C) more negative than the other half-cell   D) more positive than the other half-cell

56) In which direction will the following reaction go, if the standard reduction potentials are 0.80 V for Ag/Ag^+ and -0.44 V for Fe/Fe^{2+}?

    $Ag^+ + Fe \rightarrow Ag + Fe^{2+}$

    A) forward

    B) reverse

    C) No such reaction can occur.

57) What occurs in anodizing?

    A) Metal ions are reduced.   B) Nonmetal ions are reduced.

    C) Metals are dissolved.   D) Metals are oxidized.

58) At which electrode (anode or cathode) does oxidation occur in an electrolytic cell?

    A) anode   B) cathode   C) both   D) neither

59) Which electrode (anode or cathode) is designated as positive in an electrolytic cell?

    A) anode   B) cathode   C) both   D) neither

60) Which of the following is the name of a process in which electrical energy causes a chemical reaction?

    A) hydrolysis   B) electrolysis   C) oxidation   D) electronation

61) What type of redox reaction is commonly subjected to electrolysis?

    A) spontaneous

    B) nonspontaneous

    C) either, depending on the conditions

62) What is the direction of electron flow in an electrolytic cell?

    A) from cathode to anode   B) from anode to cathode   C) in either direction

63) What electrolyte can be used to electrolyze water?

    A) hydrochloric acid only

    B) sodium chloride only

    C) sodium hydroxide only

    D) any electrolyte that is not easily reduced or oxidized

64) What is the pH near the anode in the electrolysis of water?

    A) less than 7   B) 7   C) more than 7

65) What is produced in the electrolysis of brine?
   A) chlorine gas and sodium only
   B) chlorine gas and hydrogen gas only
   C) chlorine gas and oxygen gas only
   D) chlorine gas, sodium hydroxide, and hydrogen gas

66) What is produced at the anode in the electrolysis of brine?
   A) chlorine gas
   B) hydrogen
   C) oxygen
   D) sodium hydroxide
   E) sodium

67) What is produced at the cathode in the electrolysis of molten sodium chloride?
   A) sodium   B) chlorine gas
   C) sodium hypochlorite   D) sodium hydroxide

68) Which of the following is accomplished in a Down's cell?
   A) The products are kept apart.
   B) Sodium chloride is electrolyzed.
   C) Fresh sodium chloride is delivered on request.
   D) all of the above

69) In the electrolysis of brine, the substance produced at the cathode is _____.
   A) chlorine   B) oxygen   C) sodium   D) hydrogen

70) Which of the following is true for an electrolytic cell?
   A) It changes electrical energy into chemical energy.
   B) It is the type of cell used in electroplating.
   C) It uses an electric current to make a nonspontaneous reaction go.
   D) all of the above

71) Which half-reaction occurs at the negative electrode in an electrolytic cell in which an object is being plated with silver?
   A) $Ag^0 + 1e^- \rightarrow Ag^+$ B) $Ag^0 \rightarrow Ag^+ + 1e^-$
   C) $Ag^+ + 1e^- \rightarrow Ag^0$ D) $Ag^+ \rightarrow Ag^0 + 1e^-$

72) Oxygen and copper are produced during the electrolysis of a $CuSO_4$ solution. Which reaction occurs at the negative electrode?
   A) The copper atom is oxidized.   B) The copper ion is reduced.
   C) The oxygen atom is oxidized.   D) The oxygen ion is reduced.

73) What occurs in electroplating?
   A) deposition of a salt layer on a metal
   B) deposition of a metal layer on a material
   C) decomposition of a metal layer
   D) decomposition of a salt layer

74) In electroplating, the object to be electroplated is placed at _____.
   A) the anode
   B) the cathode
   C) either the anode or cathode

Problems

1) What is the standard cell potential of a voltaic cell made of Cu/Cu^{2+} and Fe/Fe^{2+}, if the reduction potentials are +0.34 V and –0.44 V respectively?

2) What is the standard cell potential of a hypothetical voltaic cell made of K/K^+ and Zn/Zn^{2+} if the reduction potentials are –2.93 V and –0.76 V respectively? Why must this cell be only "hypothetical"?

3) What is the standard cell potential of a hypothetical cell made of Na/Na^+ and Cl^-/Cl_2 if the reduction potentials are –2.71 V and +1.36 V respectively?

4) In which direction will the following reaction proceed if the standard reduction potential for Ag/Ag^+ is +0.80 V and that for Ni/Ni^{2+} is –0.25 V?
   $Ag^+ + Fe \rightarrow Ag + Fe^{2+}$

Essay Questions

1) Explain what occurs in an electrochemical cell.

2) What are the components of a voltaic cell?

3) Describe a common dry cell.

4) Describe the lead storage battery.

5) Describe a fuel cell.

6) What is the standard cell potential?

7) What occurs in an electrolytic cell? Give an example.

8) Give the sign of the electrodes and the reaction that occurs at each for both voltaic and electrolytic cells.

9) What occurs in electroplating?

Chapter 23 Electrochemistry
Matching Questions
1) Answer: E
2) Answer: B
3) Answer: C
4) Answer: A
5) Answer: D
6) Answer: C
7) Answer: B
8) Answer: E
9) Answer: D
10) Answer: A

Multiple Choice and Bimodal Questions
1) Answer: B
2) Answer: B
3) Answer: A
4) Answer: A
5) Answer: A
6) Answer: A
7) Answer: E
8) Answer: A
9) Answer: E
10) Answer: C
11) Answer: B
12) Answer: A
13) Answer: C
14) Answer: B
15) Answer: A
16) Answer: D
17) Answer: B
18) Answer: A
19) Answer: B
20) Answer: A
21) Answer: C
22) Answer: D
23) Answer: B
24) Answer: D
25) Answer: B
26) Answer: C
27) Answer: B
28) Answer: B
29) Answer: B

30) Answer: C

31) Answer: B

32) Answer: B

33) Answer: A

34) Answer: C

35) Answer: B

36) Answer: A

37) Answer: B

38) Answer: C

39) Answer: D

40) Answer: C

41) Answer: C

42) Answer: C

43) Answer: A

44) Answer: C

45) Answer: A

46) Answer: A

47) Answer: C

48) Answer: A

49) Answer: D

50) Answer: B

51) Answer: B

52) Answer: A

53) Answer: B

54) Answer: B

55) Answer: D

56) Answer: A

57) Answer: D

58) Answer: A

59) Answer: A

60) Answer: B

61) Answer: B

62) Answer: B

63) Answer: D

64) Answer: A

65) Answer: D

66) Answer: A

67) Answer: A

68) Answer: A

69) Answer: D

70) Answer: D

71) Answer: C

72) Answer: B

73) Answer: B

74) Answer: B

Problems

1) Answer: 0.34V –(–0.44V) = 0.78V

2) Answer: –0.76 V – (–2.93) V = +2.17 V

   The cell is "hypothetical" because, in reality, the potassium metal of the K/K^+ half–cell will react violently with the aqueous solution of potassium ions.

3) Answer: 1.36 V – (–2.71) V = +4.07 V

4) Answer: 0.80 V – (–0.25) V = +0.065 V

   Direction is forward because sign of standard potential is positive.

Essay Questions

1) Answer: Electrical energy is converted into chemical energy or vice versa. Electrons are transferred from one atom to another, for instance from zinc to copper. One substance changes from oxidized to reduced form, and the other substance does the opposite. The substance losing electrons more easily is the one that is oxidized.

2) Answer: A voltaic cell consists of two half–cells separated by a salt bridge or porous partition. One half–cell, the anode, is made of two substances in which oxidation occurs; this half–cell is called the anode. In the other half–cell, the cathode, reduction occurs. The connection of two half–cells causes a redox reaction to take place.

3) Answer: The common dry cell consists of a zinc container with a paste made of manganese(IV) oxide, zinc chloride, ammonium chloride, and water. Its cathode is a carbon rod, embedded in the paste. Reduction of the manganese dioxide occurs at this rod. The cell's anode is the zinc container.

4) Answer: A lead storage battery usually has six cells. Each cell has lead and lead oxide electrodes. At the anode, lead is oxidized. At the cathode, lead oxide is reduced. The electrolyte is sulfuric acid.

5) Answer: A fuel cell may use hydrogen, methane, or ammonia for fuel. The oxidizer is oxygen, chlorine, or ozone. The gases diffuse through porous carbon electrodes. The fuel is oxidized in the anode compartment. A hot solution of potassium hydroxide acts as the electrolyte. If the fuel is hydrogen and the oxidizer is oxygen, water is produced.

6) Answer: It is the measured cell potential at 25°C, 101.3 kPa pressure, and concentrations of 1M, for both half–cells. The hydrogen electrode has been established as the half–cell with a half–cell potential of 0.0 V.

7) Answer: In an electrolytic cell oxidation occurs at the anode and reduction at the cathode. The reaction is not spontaneous and must be driven by an external electrical voltage. The current transfers electrons from one atom to another. In the electrolysis of water, the water is reduced to hydrogen at the cathode and oxidized to oxygen at the anode.

8) Answer: In both the voltaic and the electrolytic cell, oxidation occurs at the anode and reduction occurs at the cathode. In the voltaic cell, the cathode is positive and the anode is negative. In the electrolytic cell, the anode is positive and the cathode is negative.

9) Answer: The object to be plated is the cathode. Metal ions are reduced and deposited onto the object to form a coat. The anode is the plating metal, and the electrolytic solution contains ions of the plating metal. The pH, concentration, and conductivity of the plating solution must be controlled.

Chapter 24 The Chemistry of Metals and Nonmetals
Matching Questions
Chapter 24: Matching I

1) ozone

2) peroxide

3) protium

4) deuterium

5) nitrogen

6) sulfur

7) tritium

8) oxygen

A) isotope of hydrogen having atomic mass number 3

B) a diatomic element containing a triple covalent bond

C) unstable molecule of three oxygen atoms

D) a diatomic element containing unpaired electrons

E) isotope of hydrogen having atomic mass number 2

F) isotope of hydrogen having atomic mass number 1

G) ion in which two oxygen atoms are combined

H) occurs in rhombic and monoclinic forms

Chapter 24: Matching II

9) allotrope

10) hydrogenation

11) neon

12) plastic sulfur

13) CFCs

14) legumes

15) sand

A) allotrope that is noncrystalline

B) mixed with oxygen to create artificial atmospheres.

C) plants that contain nitrogen–fixing bacteria

D) compounds that destroy ozone molecules

E) one of two or more different forms of an element that can exist in the same physical state

F) process used to convert liquid vegetable oils to solid fats

G) silicon oxide

Chapter 24: Matching III

16) slaked lime

17) aluminum

18) borax

19) Monel metal

20) ore

21) bronze

A) an alloy of copper and tin

B) a mineral used for the commercial production of a metal

C) used in pottery glaze, glass–making, and water softening.

D) the most abundant metal in the earth's crust

E) calcium hydroxide

F) an alloy of nickel and cobalt

Multiple Choice and Bimodal Questions

1) What is the missing product in the following reaction?
$2Li + 2H_2O \rightarrow 2LiOH + \underline{\hspace{1cm}}$

   A) H_2 B) $2H_2$ C) H_2O D) $2H_2O$ E) LiH

2) Alkali metals are _____ .

   A) slightly reactive   B) moderately reactive   C) highly reactive

3) Alkali metals are obtained _____.
   A) readily in their pure elemental form
   B) only from salts dissolved in the oceans
   C) only from solid salt deposits
   D) from dissolved salts and from solid salt deposits

4) Which alkali metals are the most reactive?
   A) lithium and sodium
   B) sodium and potassium
   C) potassium and rubidium
   D) rubidium and cesium

5) Which property would be associated with a very active metal?
   A) a tendency to form unstable compounds
   B) reduction to the atomic state by carbon
   C) only found in nature in the combined form
   D) high ionization energy

6) Alkali metals are _____.
   A) highly reactive
   B) found free in nature
   C) very strong
   D) all of the above

7) Alkaline earth metals are _____.
   A) slightly reactive
   B) moderately reactive
   C) highly reactive

8) Alkaline earth metals are commonly found _____.
   A) as pure metals
   B) in ocean salts only
   C) in salt deposits only
   D) in ocean salts and salt deposits

9) What process is used to extract calcium from its chloride salts?
   A) Frasch process
   B) reaction with oxygen
   C) electrolysis
   D) zone melting
   E) centrifugation

10) Which alkaline earth metal is the most reactive?
   A) beryllium
   B) magnesium
   C) calcium
   D) strontium
   E) barium

11) What is the term used to describe the reaction of alkaline earth oxides and water?
   A) electrolysis
   B) slaking
   C) combustion
   D) distillation
   E) hydrolysis

12) Calcium and magnesium are _____.
   A) found free in nature
   B) alkaline earth elements
   C) more reactive than sodium and potassium
   D) all of the above

13) Calcium oxide is commonly called _____.
   A) slaked lime   B) lime   C) limestone   D) chalk

14) How does the density of aluminum compare with the density of most other metals?
   A) It is lower.   B) It is about the same.   C) It is higher.

15) What is the most abundant metal in the earth's crust?
   A) aluminum   B) calcium   C) iron   D) potassium   E) sodium

16) Why does aluminum NOT corrode in air?
   A) It is unreactive.
   B) It does not react with oxygen.
   C) It requires water to react.
   D) A protective layer of aluminum oxide forms on the aluminum surface preventing further reaction.

17) In nature, aluminum is most commonly found _____.
   A) in its elemental state   B) in ocean salts
   C) in ore deposits   D) in sodium compounds

18) Aluminum _____.
   A) corrodes easily
   B) is very rare
   C) is the most abundant metal in the earth's crust
   D) is found free in nature

19) In what form is lead normally found in nature?
   A) lead chloride
   B) lead nitride
   C) lead oxide
   D) lead sulfide
   E) lead phosphate

20) Tin and lead are each _____.
   A) slightly reactive   B) moderately reactive   C) highly reactive

21) What are the components of bronze?
   A) copper and lead
   B) copper and tin
   C) copper, tin, and lead
   D) copper, tin, and zinc
   E) copper, lead, and zinc

22) What are the components of solder?
   A) lead and bismuth
   B) lead and mercury
   C) lead and tin
   D) tin and bismuth
   E) tin and mercury

23) Tin _____.
   A) is a metal of Group 3A   B) in SnF_2 is an ingredient in toothpaste
   C) has an ore called galena   D) is none of the above

24) Which of the following is NOT characteristic of nonmetals?
   A) poor electrical conductivity   B) covalent bonding
   C) high electronegativity   D) malleability

25) What is the formula for the gaseous compound of nitrogen and hydrogen?
   A) NH_2 B) NH_3 C) NH_4

26) What is the most abundant element in the earth's crust?
   A) hydrogen   B) iron   C) carbon   D) oxygen   E) sulfur

27) Which material is NOT a common oxygen–containing rock?
   A) quartz   B) sand   C) limestone   D) gypsum   E) galena

28) Which of the following materials is the most common source of oxygen for industrial purposes?
   A) sand   B) limestone   C) air   D) sea water   E) ozone

29) What type of magnetism does oxygen display?
   A) diamagnetism
   B) paramagnetism
   C) ferromagnetism
   D) electromagnetism

30) What is the major use of oxygen gas?
   A) welding
   B) the production of ozone
   C) steelmaking
   D) ore refining

31) When two forms of an element are in the same physical state, what are they called?
   A) isotopes
   B) allotropes
   C) tropes
   D) homotropes
   E) homeotropes

32) What is the relative strength of ozone as an oxidizing agent?
   A) low
   B) average
   C) high

33) Paramagnetism occurs in _____.
   A) liquid oxygen
   B) all forms of oxygen
   C) sulfur
   D) nitrogen

34) Ozone is _____.
   A) an allotrope of oxygen
   B) a pale blue gas
   C) a strong oxidizing agent
   D) all of the above

35) Many metallic oxides react with water to form _____.
   A) acids
   B) bases
   C) salts

36) How are oxides of most elements prepared?
   A) by heating with ozone
   B) by heating with air
   C) by heating with oxygen
   D) by electrical discharge in oxygen
   E) by ultraviolet discharge in oxygen

37) In the Frasch process, what is used to liquefy sulfur?
   A) molten sulfur
   B) steam
   C) superheated water
   D) ammonium hydroxide
   E) sulfuric acid

38) To make the Frasch process work, how many concentric tubes are needed?

A) 1   B) 2   C) 3   D) 4

39) What is NOT a property of sulfur?

A) absence of taste

B) absence of odor

C) brittleness

D) yellow color

E) high solubility in water

40) Which allotropic form of sulfur is not crystalline?

A) monoclinic   B) rhombic   C) amorphous   D) flowers

41) How many sulfur atoms are present in the ring that is characteristic of the crystal forms of sulfur?

A) 6   B) 8   C) 10   D) 12

42) At approximately what temperature does sulfur melt?

A) 100°C   B) 400°C   C) 1000°C   D) 2000°C   E) 4000°C

43) What compound forms when hydrogen reacts with sulfur?

A) hydrogen sulfide

B) hydrogen sulfite

C) hydrogen sulfate

D) dihydrogen sulfite

E) dihydrogen sulfate

44) The allotropic forms of sulfur are _____.

A) monoclinic, rhombic, and amorphous   B) plastic, glassy, and diclinic

C) rhombic, square, and triangular   D) monoclinic, diclinic, and triclinic

45) Sulfur _____.

A) has a strong odor   B) is a green liquid

C) is a reactive element   D) all of the above

46) What is the main use of sulfur?

A) to produce vulcanized rubber

B) to make sulfuric acid

C) to make bleaches

D) to make pesticides

E) to make explosives

47) Selenium is _____.

    A) a semiconductor   B) a good conductor in the light

    C) is used in xerography   D) all of the above.

48) Sulfuric acid is most frequently used for what industrial purpose?

    A) fertilizer production   B) steel production

    C) drug production   D) pesticide production

49) What happens when sulfur is heated with most metals?

    A) The sulfur atoms are destroyed.

    B) Compounds called sulfides are produced.

    C) Compounds called sulfides are broken down.

    D) The metal atoms are destroyed.

50) Which of the following statements is NOT true of nitrogen gas?

    A) It is colorless.

    B) It is odorless.

    C) It is tasteless.

    D) It is very soluble in water.

    E) It is unreactive.

51) What process is used to make ammonia commercially?

    A) Solvay process

    B) Ostwald process

    C) Haber–Bosch process

    D) Frasch process

    E) Bessemer process

52) Which of the following statements is NOT true of ammonia gas?

    A) It is colorless.

    B) It is odorless.

    C) It is highly soluble in water.

    D) It is made of polar molecules.

    E) It has a high heat of vaporization.

53) What nitrogen compound is made into nitric acid commercially?

    A) pure nitrogen gas

    B) pure ammonia

    C) ammonium nitrate

    D) ammonium sulfate

    E) sodium nitrate

54) Which of the following nitrogen compounds is a weak base?
   A) nitric acid   B) nitrogen dioxide
   C) aqueous ammonia   D) ammonium sulfate

55) Which of the following is NOT a use of nitric acid?
   A) etching
   B) fertilizer production
   C) dye–making
   D) explosive production
   E) refrigeration

56) In the Ostwald process, what is made commercially from ammonia gas?
   A) nitrogen
   B) carbon
   C) carbon dioxide
   D) nitric acid
   E) chlorine

57) The Ostwald process is used to prepare _____.
   A) ammonia   B) nitric acid
   C) elemental nitrogen   D) nitroglycerine

58) Ammonia is _____.
   A) a liquid at room temperature   B) insoluble in water
   C) extremely soluble in water   D) both A. and B.

59) Where are halide ions obtained commercially?
   A) from volcanic rock   B) from ocean water
   C) from sedimentary rock   D) from deposits of the pure elements

60) Which halogen is the most electronegative?
   A) iodine   B) bromine   C) chlorine   D) astatine   E) fluorine

61) How is fluorine gas made?
   A) by electrolysis
   B) by heating
   C) by distillation
   D) by centrifugation
   E) by zone refining

62) How is chlorine gas made?

    A) by electrolysis

    B) by heating

    C) by distillation

    D) by centrifugation

    E) by zone refining

63) How is hydrogen chloride obtained?

    A) by heating chlorine in air   B) by electrolysis of chlorine compounds

    C) by distillation from sea water   D) by burning hydrogen and chlorine

64) How is bromine isolated from concentrated seawater that is in a state free of chloride ions?

    A) by treatment with chlorine gas   B) by treatment with iodine

    C) by electrolysis   D) by heating with hydrogen

65) What is the raw material of commercial iodine production today?

    A) seaweed

    B) sodium iodate

    C) sodium iodide

    D) halide deposits

    E) sodium nitrate

66) Chlorine is prepared commercially by _____.

    A) electrolysis of a sodium chloride solution

    B) reaction of iodine with HCl

    C) fractional distillation of liquid air

    D) decomposition of sylvite

67) Which halogen occurs in nature in the pure state?

    A) fluorine

    B) chlorine

    C) iodine

    D) bromine

    E) none of the above

68) Which halogen is the least reactive?

    A) fluorine   B) chlorine   C) iodine   D) bromine

69) With which elements do halogens form covalent compounds?

    A) most of the alkali metals   B) most of the alkaline earth metals

    C) most of the oxygen group   D) most of the aluminum group

70) Fluorine is _____.

    A) electropositive   B) electronegative

    C) very reactive   D) a strong reducing agent

71) What is the chief use of hydrogen fluoride?

    A) in fertilizer production

    B) in dye–making

    C) in drug manufacture

    D) in etching

    E) in rubber production

72) Which halogen is used to make non–stick coatings?

    A) fluorine   B) chlorine   C) iodine   D) bromine

73) Which of the following is NOT a use of fluorine?

    A) uranium enrichment

    B) refrigerant production

    C) polymer building

    D) bleaching

    E) etching

74) Which of the following is NOT a use of chlorine?

    A) bleaching   B) water purification

    C) polymer building   D) etching

75) Bromine is used in _____.

    A) photographic film

    B) etching

    C) fertilizers

    D) dyes

    E) polymers

76) The common halogens are ___ _.

    A) sulfur, oxygen, and nitrogen   B) fluorine, chlorine, and bromine

    C) all gases at room temperature   D) metals of Group 3A

77) Of iron, nickel, and cobalt, which are NOT resistant to corrosion?

    A) iron and nickel only   B) iron and cobalt only

    C) iron, nickel, and cobalt   D) iron only

78) Which of the following properties is exhibited by the transition metals?

    A) ductility   B) malleability   C) conduction   D) all of the above

79) What are the components of Monel metal?

A) nickel and cobalt

B) nickel and iron

C) nickel and copper

D) cobalt and copper

E) cobalt and iron

80) Copper is used commonly in _____.

A) pipes and wires

B) structural metal

C) paint

D) thermometers

E) lamps

81) Silver halides are used commonly in _____.

A) photographic film   B) paint

C) structural metals   D) mirror coatings

82) Today, most silver is obtained _____.

A) from its sulfide ore

B) from its oxide ore

C) from quartz rock

D) as a by-product of the refining of copper, lead, and zinc ores

E) as a by-product of gold ore-refining

83) Which of the following metals is the most malleable and most ductile?

A) copper   B) silver   C) gold   D) lead   E) tin

84) Gold is commonly used _____.

A) to produce mechanically strong alloys

B) as the structural material in satellite components

C) as the heat-sensitive material in thermometers to be used in measuring temperatures above 1000°C

D) to plate contacts in microcircuits

85) Gold is particularly valuable to the high-tech industries because of its properties of _____.

A) corrosion resistance, high electrical conductivity, and high thermal conductivity

B) mechanical strength, ductility, and malleability

C) low melting point, mechanical strength, and corrosion resistance

D) ductility, high vapor pressure, and high thermal conductivity

86) Which organ or organ system is most affected by mercury poisoning?
   A) central nervous system
   B) kidney
   C) red blood cells
   D) liver
   E) reproductive system

87) Which of the following equations summarizes the reactions that occur in a blast furnace?
   A) $3Fe_2O_3(s) + CO(g) \rightarrow 2Fe_3O_4(s) + CO_2(g)$
   B) $Fe_3O_4(s) + CO(g) \rightarrow 3FeO(s) + CO_2(g)$
   C) $FeO(s) + CO(g) \rightarrow Fe(s) + CO_2(g)$
   D) $Fe_2O_3(s) + 3CO(g) \rightarrow 2Fe(s) + 3CO_2(g)$

88) Where are most hydrogen atoms located on earth?
   A) water
   B) organic molecules
   C) fossil fuels
   D) atmosphere
   E) rocks

89) What is the isotope of hydrogen having atomic mass number 3?
   A) deuterium   B) protium   C) tritium   D) helium   E) lithium

90) What is the major industrial use of hydrogen gas?
   A) the production of ammonia
   B) the production of sulfuric acid
   C) the production of synthetic rubber
   D) the production of solid fats from vegetable oils
   E) the production of synthetic oil

91) What is the term for the process of hardening oils by adding hydrogen in the presence of a catalyst?
   A) hydrolysis
   B) hydrogenation
   C) hydration
   D) hydrazining
   E) saponification

92) Tritium is an isotope of _____.
   A) nitrogen   B) oxygen   C) hydrogen   D) sulfur

93) Hydrogen shares some characteristics with _____.
   A) halogens
   B) noble gases
   C) earth metals
   D) A. and B.
   E) B. and C.

94) Hydrogen is no longer used in lighter–than–air balloons because _____.
   A) it is explosive   B) helium is lighter than hydrogen
   C) helium is less expensive than hydrogen   D) both B. and C.

95) In the Bosch process, what hot material is steamed?
   A) iron filings
   B) natural gas
   C) coke
   D) zinc
   E) sulfuric acid

Problems

1) Write the balanced equation for the reaction of cesium with water.

2) Write the balanced equation for the reaction of magnesium with water.

3) Calculate the percent (by mass) of aluminum in Al_2O_3.

4) Calculate the mass percent of oxygen in SiO_2.

5) Determine the oxidation state of nitrogen in $NaNO_3$.

Essay Questions

1) Describe the properties of the alkali metals.

2) Describe some of the common uses of alkali metals and their compounds.

3) Describe the properties of the alkaline earth metals.

4) Describe some of the common uses of the alkaline earth metals and their salts.

5) Describe the important properties of tin and lead. Indicate several significant uses for each of these metals and their compounds.

6) Explain how oxides are formed. Indicate how metallic oxides and nonmetallic oxides differ in their reactions with water. Explain what a peroxide is and give an example.

7) Describe the properties of sulfur and indicate what its primary uses are.

8) Describe the properties of sulfuric acid and indicate what its primary uses are.

9) Name several important nitrogen compounds and describe their uses.

10) How is ammonia made?

11) Describe the properties of the halogens. Also describe the primary uses of the halogens and their compounds.

12) Describe the properties of the transition metals and indicate some important uses of these elements and their compounds.

13) Describe the properties of iron, cobalt, and nickel. Indicate some common uses of these elements and their compounds.

14) Describe the properties of copper, silver, and gold. Indicate some important uses of these elements.

15) Select one of the common transition metals described in this chapter. List the most important physical and chemical properties of this metal. Then describe several uses of the metal that depend on these properties.

16) How is hydrogen prepared?

17) Explain why the halogens do not exist in the free state in nature.

Chapter 24 The Chemistry of Metals and Nonmetals

Matching Questions

1) Answer: C
2) Answer: G
3) Answer: F
4) Answer: E
5) Answer: B
6) Answer: H
7) Answer: A
8) Answer: D
9) Answer: E
10) Answer: F
11) Answer: B
12) Answer: A
13) Answer: D
14) Answer: C
15) Answer: G
16) Answer: E
17) Answer: D
18) Answer: C
19) Answer: F
20) Answer: B
21) Answer: A

Multiple Choice and Bimodal Questions

1) Answer: A
2) Answer: C
3) Answer: D
4) Answer: D
5) Answer: C
6) Answer: A
7) Answer: C
8) Answer: D
9) Answer: C
10) Answer: E
11) Answer: B
12) Answer: B
13) Answer: B
14) Answer: A
15) Answer: A
16) Answer: D
17) Answer: C
18) Answer: C

19) Answer: D

20) Answer: A

21) Answer: B

22) Answer: C

23) Answer: B

24) Answer: D

25) Answer: B

26) Answer: D

27) Answer: E

28) Answer: C

29) Answer: B

30) Answer: C

31) Answer: B

32) Answer: C

33) Answer: A

34) Answer: D

35) Answer: B

36) Answer: C

37) Answer: C

38) Answer: C

39) Answer: E

40) Answer: C

41) Answer: B

42) Answer: A

43) Answer: A

44) Answer: A

45) Answer: C

46) Answer: B

47) Answer: D

48) Answer: A

49) Answer: B

50) Answer: D

51) Answer: C

52) Answer: B

53) Answer: B

54) Answer: C

55) Answer: E

56) Answer: D

57) Answer: B

58) Answer: C

59) Answer: B

60) Answer: E

61) Answer: A

62) Answer: A

63) Answer: D

64) Answer: A

65) Answer: B

66) Answer: A

67) Answer: E

68) Answer: C

69) Answer: C

70) Answer: B

71) Answer: D

72) Answer: A

73) Answer: D

74) Answer: D

75) Answer: A

76) Answer: B

77) Answer: D

78) Answer: D

79) Answer: C

80) Answer: A

81) Answer: A

82) Answer: D

83) Answer: C

84) Answer: D

85) Answer: A

86) Answer: A

87) Answer: D

88) Answer: A

89) Answer: C

90) Answer: A

91) Answer: B

92) Answer: C

93) Answer: D

94) Answer: A

95) Answer: A

Problems

1) Answer: $2Cs + 2H_2O \rightarrow 2CsOH + H_2$

2) Answer: $Mg + 2H_2O \rightarrow Mg(OH)_2 + H_2$

3) Answer: Al: $2 \times 27\ g = 54\ g$
O: $3 \times 16\ g = 48\ g$
Total mass = 102 g

$\dfrac{54\ g}{102\ g} \times 100\% = 53\%$ aluminum

4) Answer: Si: $1 \times 28.0 \text{ g} = 28.0 \text{ g}$

O: $2 \times 16.0 \text{ g} = 32.0 \text{ g}$

Total mass = 60.0 g

$\dfrac{32.0 \text{ g}}{60.0 \text{ g}} \times 100\% = 53.3\%$ oxygen

5) Answer: +5

Essay Questions

1) Answer: Alkali metals are soft, lustrous, and reactive. They have a large atomic size and low density. They also have low ionization energies. Alkali metals are good conductors of heat and electricity. Salts of alkali metals are very soluble in water.

2) Answer: The metals are used as reducing agents. Sodium is used as a heat conductor, and also as a light source in sodium–vapor lamps. Alkali peroxides are used as oxidizing agents in bleaches and disinfectants. Sodium metal is used in the production of lye (NaOH). Liquid sodium is used in nuclear reactors to remove heat from the reactor core. Sodium hydroxide is a very strong base and it is used in the production of a variety of materials, including soap, petroleum, synthetic textiles, and paper pulp.

3) Answer: They are soft, lustrous, conductive, and reactive (but less so than the alkali metals in each of these categories). They have low densities and low ionization energies (not as low as the alkali metals in these two categories). Salts of alkaline earth metals are very soluble, but not as soluble as salts of alkali metals.

4) Answer: Magnesium is used in alloys. Magnesium oxide is used in firebrick and insulation. The hydroxides of alkaline earth metals are strong bases; calcium hydroxides are used in the manufacture of building mortar and bleaching powder, and in water softening. A suspension of magnesium hydroxide (milk of magnesia) is used as a laxative and antacid. Marble (metamorphic rock formed from limestone) is used as a structural material.

5) Answer: Tin and lead are heavy metals that are lustrous, conductive, and relatively unreactive. Tin is a component of bronze and solder and is used as a coating to protect iron or steel from corrosion. Stannous (tin) fluoride is used in toothpaste. Lead is used in solder and in pipes. Tetraethyl lead was used as an antiknocking agent in gasoline.

6) Answer: Oxides of most elements can be formed by heating the element in the presence of oxygen. Metal oxides react with water to form bases. Nonmetallic oxides react with water to form acids. Peroxides are compounds that can release the peroxide ion, O_2^{2-}. An example is hydrogen peroxide which is colorless, viscous, and reactive.

7) Answer: Sulfur is a yellow, tasteless, odorless, and brittle solid. It is insoluble in water. It has allotropes that may be monoclinic or rhombic crystals. When heated it becomes plastic sulfur. It has an eight–member ring structure. Sulfur is used in the production of vulcanized rubber, paper, fungicides, fertilizers, matches, fireworks, insecticides, explosives, drugs, paints, plastics, and dyes.

8) Answer: Sulfuric acid is a dense, oily, and colorless liquid that dissolves well in water. It is a strong oxidizing acid. Concentrated sulfuric acid dissolves readily in water, liberating large amounts of heat. This affinity for water makes sulfuric acid a strong dehydrating agent. Sulfuric acid has a variety of uses. It can be used to make hydrochloric acid from sodium chloride. It can also be used in dehydrating materials, in making fertilizer, in pickling iron and steel, and in refining petroleum.

9) Answer: Ammonia is a base that is used in fertilizers and refrigerants, and in the making of nitric acid. Nitric acid is used to etch, to make fertilizers, to make dyes, and to make explosives. Nitrates and nitrites are used for fertilizer. Nitrogen is also a component of proteins and nucleic acids.

10) Answer: Ammonia is produced primarily by the Haber-Bosch process. In this process, nitrogen and hydrogen gases are reacted under conditions of high heat and pressure, and in the presence of an iron catalyst.

11) Answer: Nitric acid is produced primarily by the Ostwald process. In this process, ammonia is first oxidized in air to form nitric oxide. The nitric oxide is then oxidized to form nitrogen dioxide. The nitrogen dioxide is then reacted with water to form nitric acid.

12) Answer: In general, transition metals are conductive, ductile, malleable, lustrous, and have many different oxidation states. Transition metals are often used as structural materials, because of their strength and corrosion resistance. Titanium alloys are used in high-performance aircraft engines and missiles. White titanium dioxide, TiO_2, is commonly used as a pigment in paint. Chromium is a hard, brittle metal with a white luster. It is extremely resistant to corrosion and is an ideal coating for iron or steel objects. Chromium is an important ingredient of stainless steel.

13) Answer: These elements are dense, conductive, and magnetic. They have high melting points. Nickel and cobalt, unlike iron, are resistant to atmospheric corrosion. Monel metal is a strong, corrosion-resistant alloy of copper and nickel that is used in propeller shafts of seagoing vessels. Stellite, an alloy of cobalt, chromium, and tungsten, is used in high-speed cutting tools and drill bits. Iron is used in the manufacture of steel. Nickel and cobalt are also used in the manufacture of steel.

14) Answer: These metals are lustrous, very conductive, and unreactive. Copper is used in electrical wiring and in plumbing for pipes that carry hot or cold water. Silver has a high luster and is used as a coating on the backs of mirrors. Silver halides are light-sensitive and are used in photographic processes. Gold is the most malleable and ductile of all metals. The corrosion-resistance of gold, coupled with its good thermal conductivity, make gold valuable to high-tech industries, where it is used to plate contacts in microcircuits and to cover the external surfaces of satellite components.

15) Answer: Answers should include: ductility, luster, hardness, strength, corrosion-resistance, lower density than iron, can be alloyed with other metals, can be electroplated onto other metals, and has low chemical activity, is magnetic, catalyzes chemical reactions, and has several oxidation states.

16) Answer: Hydrogen can be prepared in a variety of ways. It can be made from water by electrolysis or by passing steam over red hot iron filings (Bosch process), or by reacting zinc and sulfuric acid. It can also be prepared by reacting steam with natural gas in the presence of a nickel catalyst (steam reforming), or by passing steam over white hot ore. Small quantities can be prepared.

17) Answer: The halogens do not exist in the free state in nature because the halogens are among the most reactive of the nonmetals. The reactivity of the halogens is a result of their valence electron structure. An atom of any halogen has seven valence electrons. It needs to gain one electron to acquire a stable electron configuration (that of the noble gases). To gain this electron, the halogen atom must bond, ionically or covalently, with another atom. The tendency to bond is strong because the halogen atom has a strong attraction for the additional electron.

Chapter 25 Hydrocarbon Compounds

Matching Questions

Chapter 25: Matching I

1) alkanes

2) alkenes

3) alkynes

4) arenes

A) special group of unsaturated cyclic hydrocarbons

B) organic compounds containing one or more carbon–carbon triple bonds

C) organic compounds containing one or more carbon–carbon double bonds

D) hydrocarbons that contain only single covalent bonds

Chapter 25: Matching II

5) substituent

6) structural isomers

7) geometric isomers

8) stereoisomers

9) asymmetric carbon

10) trans configuration

11) cis configuration

A) arrangement in which substituted groups are on the same side of the double bond

B) arrangement in which substituted groups are on opposite sides of the double bond

C) compounds that have the same molecular formula, but different molecular structures

D) molecules of the same molecular structure that differ only in the arrangements of their atoms in space

E) carbon atom to which four different groups are attached

F) compounds that differ only in the geometries of their substituted groups

G) atom or group of atoms that takes the place of a hydrogen in a parent hydrocarbon molecule

Chapter 25: Matching III

12) hydrocarbon

13) homologous series

14) unsaturated compound

15) saturated compound

16) complete structural formula

17) condensed structural formula

A) organic compound that contains only carbon and hydrogen atoms

B) group of compounds in which there is a constant increment of change in molecular structure from one compound in the series to the next

C) formula showing all the atoms and bonds in a molecule

D) formula from which some of the bonds and/or atoms of a molecule are left out

E) organic compound that contains fewer than the maximum number of hydrogens

F) organic compound that contains the maximum number of hydrogens

Chapter 25: Matching IV

18) aromatic hydrocarbon

19) aliphatic hydrocarbon

20) peat

21) lignite

22) bituminous coal

23) anthracite coal

A) brown coal; has carbon content of approximately 50%

B) soft coal; has carbon content of 70–80%

C) any hydrocarbon compound in which the bonding is like that of benzene

D) any hydrocarbon compound that does not contain rings

E) soft, brown, spongy, fibrous material having very high water content

F) hard coal; has carbon content of over 80%

Multiple Choice and Bimodal Questions

1) How many double covalent bonds are in an alkane?

  A) none

  B) one

  C) two

  D) three

  E) The number varies.

2) How many valence electrons surround a carbon atom?

  A) 1 B) 2 C) 3 D) 4

3) With how many covalent bonds does each carbon atom participate in an organic compound?

  A) 1 B) 2 C) 3 D) 4 E) 5

4) How many carbons are in a molecule of hexane?

  A) 3 B) 4 C) 5 D) 6 E) 7

5) What is the name of the alkane having five carbons?

  A) hexane B) methane C) octane D) pentane E) propane

6) What is the name of the compound having the following formula?

$$H-\underset{\underset{H}{|}}{\overset{\overset{H}{|}}{C}}-\underset{\underset{H}{|}}{\overset{\overset{H}{|}}{C}}-\underset{\underset{H}{|}}{\overset{\overset{H}{|}}{C}}-\underset{\underset{H}{|}}{\overset{\overset{H}{|}}{C}}-\underset{\underset{H}{|}}{\overset{\overset{H}{|}}{C}}-\underset{\underset{H}{|}}{\overset{\overset{H}{|}}{C}}-\underset{\underset{H}{|}}{\overset{\overset{H}{|}}{C}}-H$$

A) butane   B) decane   C) ethane   D) heptane   E) octane

7) What is the substituent on the following compound?
$CH_3CH_2CH_2CH_2Cl$

A) Cl

B) CH_2Cl

C) CH_2CH_2Cl

D) CH_3

E) CH_2

8) What prefix is used to represent the substituent $CH_3-CH_2-CH_2-$?

A) propen-   B) propyne-   C) propyl-   D) propoyl-   E) propal-

9) If a substituent appears four times in a compound, what prefix is used?

A) di-   B) mono-   C) penta-   D) tetra-   E) tri-

10) What is the name of the following compound?

$$CH_3-CH-\underset{\underset{CH_3}{|}}{CH}-\overset{\overset{CH_3}{|}}{CH}-\overset{\overset{CH_3}{|}}{CH}-CH_3$$

A) trimethylpentane   B) 2-methyl-3-methyl-4-methylpentane

C) 2,2-dimethyl-3-methylpentane   D) 2,3,4-trimethylpentane

11) What is the IUPAC name for the following compound?

$$CH_2-\underset{\underset{CH_3}{|}}{CH}-CH_2-\underset{\underset{CH_2}{|}}{\overset{\overset{CH_3}{|}}{C}}-CH_3$$
$$\;\;\;\;|\;\;\;\;\;\;\;\;\;\;\;\;\;\;\;\;\;\;|$$
$$\;CH_3\;\;\;\;CH_3\;\;\;\;\;\;\;\;\;CH_3$$

A) 2-ethyl-2,4,5-trimethylpentane   B) 2-ethyl-2,4-dimethylhexane

C) 3,5,5-trimethylheptane   D) 3,3,5-trimethylheptane

12) What is the name of the compound $CH_3CH(CH_3)C(CH_3)_3$?

    A) 2,2,3–trimethylbutane   B) tetramethylpropane

    C) 1,1,1,2–tetramethylpropane   D) isoheptane

13) What is the physical state of the smallest alkanes at room temperature?

    A) gas

    B) liquid

    C) solid

    D) gas or liquid

    E) gas, liquid, or solid

14) What is the simplest hydrocarbon containing a carbon–carbon bond?

    A) urea   B) ammonia   C) methane   D) ethane   E) graphite

15) The carbon–carbon bonds in alkanes are _____.

    A) double bonds   B) quite polar

    C) free to rotate   D) none of the above

16) What is the general formula for a continuous–chain alkane?

    A) C_nH_n B) C_nH_{n+2} C) C_nH_{2n} D) C_nH_{2n+2} E) C_nH_{2n-2}

17) What is the simplest alkane?

    A) butane   B) ethane   C) methane   D) pentane   E) propane

18) What increment of change occurs between propane and butane in the alkane series?

    A) —CH—

    B) —CH$_2$—

    C) —CH$_3$—

    D) —CH$_2$=

    E) —CH$_3$=

19) Which of the following is a condensed structural formula for propane?

    A) C_3H_8 B)

$$
\begin{array}{ccccccc}
 & H & & H & & H & \\
 & | & & | & & | & \\
H-\!\!\!& C &\!\!\!-\!\!\!& C &\!\!\!-\!\!\!& C &\!\!\!-H \\
 & | & & | & & | & \\
 & H & & H & & H &
\end{array}
$$

    C) $CH_3CH_2CH_3$ D) C—C—C

20) Which carbon skeleton is different from the other three?

A)

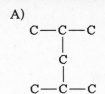

B)

C—C—C
|
C—C
|
C—C

C)

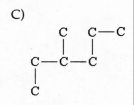

D)

C—C
|
C
|
C
|
C—C
|
C

21) A saturated continuous–chain hydrocarbon with seven carbons is _____.
   A) hexane   B) octane   C) heptane   D) heptene

22) The condensed structural formula for 2,2,3–trimethylbutane is _____.
   A) $CH_3CH_2(CH_3)CH(CH_3)_2$ B) $CH_3C(CH_3)_2C(CH_3)_3$
   C) $CH_3C(CH_3)_2CH(CH_3)_2$ D) $CH_3CH_2CH(CH_3)C(CH_3)_3$

23) The name of an alkyl group that contains two carbon atoms is _____.
   A) diphenyl   B) ethyl   C) dimethyl   D) propyl

24) Which of the following compounds is a structural isomer of butane?
   A) 2–methylbutane   B) 2,2–dimethylbutane
   C) 2–methylpropane   D) 2,2–diethylpropane

25) Which of the following carbon skeletons represents a compound that is a structural isomer

of C—C—C—C—C—C?

A)

```
C — C — C — C
|
C — C — C
```

B)

```
C — C — C
|
C — C — C — C
```

C)

```
        C
        |
C — C — C — C
        |
        C
```

D)

```
C — C — C — C -- C
            |
            C — C
```

E)

```
C
|
C — C — C — C
|       |
C       C
```

26) In which of the following compounds is hexane most likely to dissolve?
   A) water
   B) ammonium hydroxide
   C) acetic acid
   D) ethyl alcohol
   E) nonane

27) Which of the following compounds has the lowest boiling point?
   A) heptane   B) 2–methylhexane
   C) 2,3–dimethylpentane   D) 2,2,3–trimethylbutane

28) Why is a carbon–hydrogen bond essentially nonpolar?
   A) Neither atom is ionic.
   B) Free electrons cancel any polarity.
   C) The electron pair is shared equally.
   D) Van der Waals forces overcome polarity.

29) Structural isomers have _____.
   A) the same molecular formula
   B) different physical and chemical properties
   C) the same elemental composition
   D) all of the above

30) Hydrocarbons in general are _____.
   A) soluble in water   B) chemically reactive
   C) less dense than water   D) all of the above

31) A structural isomer of hexane is _____.
   A) 2,2–dimethylbutane   B) cyclohexane
   C) benzene   D) 2–methylpentene

32) What is the name of the hydrocarbons with double covalent bonds?
   A) alkanes   B) alkenes   C) alkynes   D) alkyls   E) alkones

33) Which of the following compounds is an unsaturated hydrocarbon?
   A) methane   B) propyne   C) nonane   D) ammonia   E) ethyl

34) What is the name of the smallest alkyne?
   A) butyne   B) ethyne   C) methyne   D) propyne

35) Which compound is an alkene?
   A) methane   B) nonene   C) butyne   D) propanone

36) In which of the following compounds does rotation occur around a covalent bond between carbons?
   A) ethane   B) ethene   C) ethyne

37) An organic compound that contains only carbon and hydrogen and a triple bond (all the other bonds are single bonds) is classified as an _____.
   A) alkane   B) alkene   C) alkyne   D) arene

38) Which lettered carbon is the asymmetric carbon in the following compound?

$$\begin{array}{c} \overset{a}{CH_2} - \overset{b}{CH_3} \\ | \\ \overset{c}{H-C-CH_3} \\ | \\ \overset{}{CH_2} - CH_2 - CH_3 \\ d \end{array}$$

A) a

B) b

C) c

D) d

E) No asymmetric carbon is present.

39) Which lettered carbon is the asymmetric carbon in the following compound?

$$\begin{array}{c} \overset{a}{CH_3}\ \overset{b}{CH_2} - CH_3 \\ | \qquad | \\ \overset{c}{H-C} - \overset{d}{C} - OH \\ | \qquad | \\ OH\ \ OH \end{array}$$

A) a

B) b

C) c

D) d

E) No asymmetric carbon is present.

40) What is the configuration of the following compound?

$$\begin{array}{c} Cl \qquad Cl \\ \backslash \qquad / \\ C=C \\ / \qquad \backslash \\ H \qquad H \end{array}$$

A) cis   B) trans   C) both   D) neither

41) Which of the following compounds has its substituents in the trans position?

A)
$$\begin{array}{c} H \qquad H \\ \backslash \qquad / \\ C=C \\ / \qquad \backslash \\ Cl \qquad Cl \end{array}$$

B)
$$\begin{array}{c} H \qquad Cl \\ \backslash \qquad / \\ C=C \\ / \qquad \backslash \\ Cl \qquad H \end{array}$$

C)
$$\begin{array}{c} H \qquad Cl \\ \backslash \qquad / \\ C=C \\ / \qquad \backslash \\ H \qquad Cl \end{array}$$

D)
$$\begin{array}{c} Cl \qquad Cl \\ \backslash \qquad / \\ C=C \\ / \qquad \backslash \\ Cl \qquad Cl \end{array}$$

42) What is the name of the following compound?

HC—CH
HC   C—CH$_2$—CH$_2$—CH$_2$—CH$_2$—CH$_3$
HC=CH

A) pentylcyclohexane	B) cyclopentylhexane
C) phenylpentane	D) phenylhexane

43) What is the name of the following compound?

HC—C—CH$_2$—CH$_3$
HC   C—CH$_2$—CH$_3$
HC=CH

A) diethylbenzene	B) m–diethylbenzene
C) o–diethylbenzene	D) p–diethylbenzene

44) What is the name of the following compound?

CH$_3$—C—CH
HC   C—CH$_2$—CH$_3$
HC=CH

A) 1-methyl-3-ethylbenzene	B) 1-ethyl-3-methylbenzene
C) 1-methyl-4-ethylbenzene	D) 1-ethyl-4-methylbenzene

45) Hydrocarbons containing a saturated carbon ring are called _____.
   A) cyclic hydrocarbons
   B) aromatic hydrocarbons
   C) aliphatic hydrocarbons
   D) alkylated hydrocarbons
   E) oxygenated hydrocarbons

46) What type of hydrocarbon is the following compound?
   CH$_3$—CH$_2$—CH$_2$—CH$_2$—CH$_2$—CH$_3$

A) aliphatic	B) aromatic	C) cyclic	D) unsaturated

47) What compound is the simplest of the arenes?
   A) methane
   B) ethene
   C) ethyne
   D) cyclohexane
   E) benzene

48) Which of the following molecules does NOT display resonance?

A) benzene

B) phenylethane

C) cyclohexylbenzene

D) cyclohexane

49) Which type of coal has the highest carbon content?

A) anthracite

B) bituminous

C) lignite

D) peat

50) What is the main hydrocarbon component of natural gas?

A) benzene

B) ethane

C) ethene

D) methane

E) propane

Problems

1) Draw the complete structural formulas for methane and ethane.

2) Draw the molecular formula, the complete structural formula, the carbon skeleton, and the three different condensed structural formulas, for pentane.

3) What is the name of the following compound?

$$CH_3-CH(CH_3)-CH_2-CH(CH_3)-CH_2-CH_3$$

4) What is the name of the following compound?

$$CH_3-C(CH_3)(CH_3)-CH_2-CH(CH_2CH_3)-CH_2-CH_2-CH_2-CH_3$$

5) What is the name of the following compound?

$$CH_3-CH_2-CH(CH_2CH_3)-CH_2-CH(CH_3)-CH_3$$

6) What is the condensed structural formula for 2,2–dimethylbutane?

7) Draw the carbon skeletons for the structural isomers of C_5H_{12}.

8) Draw the two structural isomers of butane.

9) Give the complete structural formula for 3–methyl–1–pentene.

10) What is the name of the following structure?

$$CH_3 - CH = \overset{\overset{\displaystyle CH_3}{|}}{C} - CH_2 - \overset{\overset{\displaystyle CH_3}{|}}{\underset{\displaystyle CH_2}{CH}} - CH_2 - CH_3$$

11) Name this compound:

12) Draw the correct structural formula for 4–ethyl–2,6–dimethyl–2–heptene.

13) Draw the complete structural formulas for the cis and trans configurations of 2–pentene.

14) Draw the geometric isomers of 3–methyl–2–pentene.

15) Draw a hydrocarbon molecule that has one asymmetric carbon.

16) Draw a hydrocarbon molecule that has two asymmetric carbons.

17) Identify the asymmetric carbon in this compound.

18) Draw the carbon skeletons of the resonant structures of a hydrocarbon that exhibits resonance.

19) Name the following compound:

HC—CH
//   \\
HC   C—CH$_2$—CH$_2$—CH$_2$—CH$_3$
\\   /
HC=CH

20) Draw the carbon skeleton of 2–phenylpentane.

21) Draw the carbon skeleton of 1,4–diethylbenzene.

22) Draw the structural formula for 2,4–diphenylpentane.

23) Write a chemical equation for the complete combustion of ethane.

24) Write a balanced equation for the complete combustion of heptane.

Essay Questions

1) Explain why carbon is able to form such a wide variety of compounds.

2) Silicon is in the same chemical family as carbon, but it does not form nearly as many different compounds. Why is this?

3) Given the name of an alkane, indicate how you can reconstruct its structural formula according to IUPAC rules.

4) Describe the arrangement of hydrogen atoms in ethene. What is the significance of this arrangement?

5) Describe the arrangement of atoms in ethyne. What is the significance of this arrangement?

6) Why does the presence of a double or triple bond have little effect on the physical properties of a hydrocarbon?

7) Explain how geometric isomers differ from each other. Describe the difference between the trans and cis configurations of geometric isomers. Provide an example of each configuration for molecules that exhibit geometric isomerism.

8) What are stereoisomers? Provide examples.

9) What is the principle for identifying an asymmetric carbon? Give an example of a carbon compound with an asymmetric carbon and an example of a similar carbon compound without an asymmetric carbon.

10) Explain the concept of resonance. Give an example of a compound that displays resonance.

11) Describe the process of "cracking" and give an example.

12) What are the stages in the formation of coal from organic material?

13) Describe the various products that can be obtained by the distillation of coal.

14) Why is burning coal a major source of pollution?

Chapter 25 Hydrocarbon Compounds

Matching Questions

1) Answer: D
2) Answer: C
3) Answer: B
4) Answer: A
5) Answer: G
6) Answer: C
7) Answer: F
8) Answer: D
9) Answer: E
10) Answer: B
11) Answer: A
12) Answer: A
13) Answer: B
14) Answer: E
15) Answer: F
16) Answer: C
17) Answer: D
18) Answer: C
19) Answer: D
20) Answer: E
21) Answer: A
22) Answer: B
23) Answer: F

Multiple Choice and Bimodal Questions

1) Answer: A
2) Answer: D
3) Answer: D
4) Answer: D
5) Answer: D
6) Answer: D
7) Answer: A
8) Answer: C
9) Answer: D
10) Answer: D
11) Answer: D
12) Answer: A
13) Answer: A
14) Answer: D
15) Answer: C

16) Answer: D

17) Answer: C

18) Answer: B

19) Answer: C

20) Answer: C

21) Answer: C

22) Answer: C

23) Answer: B

24) Answer: C

25) Answer: C

26) Answer: E

27) Answer: D

28) Answer: C

29) Answer: D

30) Answer: C

31) Answer: A

32) Answer: B

33) Answer: B

34) Answer: B

35) Answer: B

36) Answer: A

37) Answer: C

38) Answer: C

39) Answer: C

40) Answer: A

41) Answer: B

42) Answer: C

43) Answer: B

44) Answer: B

45) Answer: A

46) Answer: A

47) Answer: E

48) Answer: D

49) Answer: A

50) Answer: D

Problems

1) Answer:

$$
\begin{array}{ccc}
 & \text{H} & \\
 & | & \\
\text{H}-&\text{C}&-\text{H} \\
 & | & \\
 & \text{H} &
\end{array}
\qquad
\begin{array}{ccccc}
 & \text{H} & & \text{H} & \\
 & | & & | & \\
\text{H}-&\text{C}&-&\text{C}&-\text{H} \\
 & | & & | & \\
 & \text{H} & & \text{H} &
\end{array}
$$

2) Answer: molecular formula: C_5H_{12}

complete structural formula:

$$H-\overset{\overset{\displaystyle H}{|}}{\underset{\underset{\displaystyle H}{|}}{C}}-\overset{\overset{\displaystyle H}{|}}{\underset{\underset{\displaystyle H}{|}}{C}}-\overset{\overset{\displaystyle H}{|}}{\underset{\underset{\displaystyle H}{|}}{C}}-\overset{\overset{\displaystyle H}{|}}{\underset{\underset{\displaystyle H}{|}}{C}}-\overset{\overset{\displaystyle H}{|}}{\underset{\underset{\displaystyle H}{|}}{C}}-H$$

carbon skeleton: C—C—C—C—C

condensed structural formula (C—H and C—C bonds understood):
   $CH_3CH_2CH_2CH_2CH_3$

condensed structural formula (C—H bonds understood):

   $CH_3-CH_2-CH_2-CH_2-CH_3$

condensed structural formula (all bonds understood):
   $CH_3(CH_2)_3CH_3$

3) Answer: 2,4–dimethylhexane

4) Answer: 4–ethyl–2,2–dimethyloctane

5) Answer: 4–ethyl–2–methylhexane

6) Answer: $(CH_3)_3CCH_2CH_3$

7) Answer:

$$\text{C}-\text{C}-\text{C}-\text{C}-\text{C} \qquad \text{C}-\overset{\overset{\displaystyle \text{C}}{|}}{\text{C}}-\text{C}-\text{C} \qquad \text{C}-\overset{\overset{\displaystyle \text{C}}{|}}{\underset{\underset{\displaystyle \text{C}}{|}}{\text{C}}}-\text{C}$$

8) Answer:

$$H-\overset{\overset{\displaystyle H}{|}}{\underset{\underset{\displaystyle H}{|}}{C}}-\overset{\overset{\displaystyle H}{|}}{\underset{\underset{\displaystyle H}{|}}{C}}-\overset{\overset{\displaystyle H}{|}}{\underset{\underset{\displaystyle H}{|}}{C}}-\overset{\overset{\displaystyle H}{|}}{\underset{\underset{\displaystyle H}{|}}{C}}-H \quad \text{and} \quad$$

9) Answer:

$$CH_2{=}CH-\overset{\overset{\displaystyle CH_3}{|}}{CH}-CH_2-CH_3$$

10) Answer: 5–ethyl–3–methyl–2–hexene

11) Answer: 6–ethyl–3,8–dimethyl–4–nonene

12) Answer:

```
                                 H
                                 |
                     H       H—C—H    H
                     |       |        |
                     |    H—C—H       |
                 H—C—H       |     H—C—H
                     |       |        |
                     H       |        H
                     |       |        |
         H—C—C = C—C—C—C—C—H
             |           |  |  |  |  |
             H           H  H  H  H  H
             |
             H
```

13) Answer:

```
    H       CH₂CH₃          CH₃      CH₂CH₃
     \      /                 \      /
      C = C                    C = C
     /      \                 /      \
   CH₃       H               H        H
```

14) Answer:

```
   CH₃      CH₂CH₃          CH₃       CH₃
     \      /                 \       /
      C = C                    C = C
     /      \                 /       \
    H       CH₃              H       CH₂CH₃
```

15) Answer:

```
           CH₂CH₃
            |
    H —— *C —— CH₃
            |
           CH₂ —— CH₂ —— CH₃
```
The asymmetric carbon is starred.

16) Answer:

```
           CH₃ CH₃
            |   |
    H —— *C – *C —— H
            |   |
           CH₂ CH₂
            |   |
           CH₃ CH₃
```

17) Answer:

```
          H   H    H   H
          |   |    |   |
    H —— C —— C —— *C —— C —— H
          |   |    |   |
          H   H    H   H
```
Carbon #2 (*)

18) Answer:

```
      C—C            C=C
     /    \         /    \
    C      C  ⇌    C      C
     \    /         \    /
      C=C            C—C
```

19) Answer: butylbenzene or 1–phenylbutane

20) Answer:

```
      C—C         C
     /    \       |
    C      C —— C—C—C—C—C
     \    /
      C=C
```

21) Answer:

22) Answer:

23) Answer: $2C_2H_6 + 7O_2 \rightarrow 4CO_2 + 6H_2O$

24) Answer: $C_7H_{16}(l) + 11O_2(g) \rightarrow 7CO_2(g) + 8H_2O(l)$

Essay Questions

1) Answer: Carbon has four valence electrons and can therefore form four covalent bonds. Carbon can bind other atoms and it can also bind to itself. Carbon–carbon bonds are quite stable, and this fact, coupled with its capacity to form four covalent bonds, enables carbon to form long chains that may be either straight or branched; carbon atoms can also be joined to each other in ring structures. Carbon can also form double and triple bonds with itself This allows for even greater variety in the types of carbon compounds that can be formed.

2) Answer: Silicon forms short chains, but they are unstable in an oxygen environment.

3) Answer: (1) Find the root word (ending in –ane) in the hydrocarbon name. Then write the longest carbon chain to create the parent structure.
(2) Number the carbons of this parent carbon chain.
(3) Identify the substituent groups. Attach the substituents to the numbered parent chain at the proper positions.
(4) Add hydrogens as needed.

4) Answer: The hydrogen atoms all lie in the same plane and are separated by angles of 120. This arrangement provides the maximum possible separation of hydrogen atoms (and, therefore, the maximum possible separation of shared electron pairs). Further separation would result in the breaking of bonds.

5) Answer: The two carbons and two hydrogens are all on the same line. The hydrogen atoms are separated from each other by an angle of 180. The reason for this arrangement is that it permits the maximum possible separation of the hydrogen atoms (and, therefore, the maximum possible separation of shared electron pairs). Further separation would result in the breaking of bonds.

6) Answer: The major attractions between alkanes, alkenes, or alkynes are weak van der Waals forces. Consequently, the introduction of a double or triple bond into a hydrocarbon does not have a dramatic effect on its physical properties.

7) Answer: Geometric isomers differ only in the geometry of their substituted groups. Geometric isomerism is possible whenever each carbon of a double bond has at least one substituent. In the trans configuration, the substituted groups are on opposite sides of the double bond. In the cis configuration, the substituted groups are on the same side of the double bond. Examples are trans–2–butene and cis–2–butene.

$$\begin{array}{cc}
\underset{CH_3}{\overset{H}{\diagdown}}C=C\underset{H}{\overset{CH_3}{\diagup}} & \underset{H}{\overset{CH_3}{\diagdown}}C=C\underset{H}{\overset{CH_3}{\diagup}} \\
\text{trans–2–butene} & \text{cis–2–butene}
\end{array}$$

8) Answer: Stereoisomers are molecules of the same molecular structure that differ only in the arrangement of their atoms in space. Stereoisomerism is analogous to handedness. Two stereoisomers are different from each other in the way that a right and left hand are different from each other. Stereoisomerism is possible in carbon molecules only when a carbon has four different groups attached. The carbon is then said to be asymmetric. The four groups can be arranged in two, and only two, fundamentally different ways around this asymmetric carbon. The stereoisomers cannot be superimposed; they are mirror images. An example of a compound having stereoisomers is CHFClBr.

9) Answer: An asymmetric carbon is one that has four different substituents.

$$\begin{array}{cc}
F-\overset{\displaystyle H}{\underset{\displaystyle H}{C}}-Cl & F-\overset{\displaystyle H}{\underset{\displaystyle Br}{{}^*C}}-Cl \\
\text{no asymetric carbon} & \text{asymetric carbon}
\end{array}$$

10) Answer: Resonance occurs when two or more equally valid structures can be drawn for a molecule. The benzene molecule exhibits resonance. In benzene, each carbon atom can participate in a double bond. A double bond may be formed on one side of the carbon and a single bond may be formed on the other side. However, the reverse structure can also be formed. Benzene is said to resonate between these equally possible structures.

11) Answer: Cracking is a controlled process by which hydrocarbons are broken down or rearranged into smaller, more useful molecules. Hydrocarbons are cracked with the aid of a catalyst or by The use of heat. High molecular mass fractions obtained in petroleum distillations are "cracked" to produce the more useful short–chain components of gasoline and kerosene.

12) Answer: The first stage is the formation of an intermediate material known as peat. Peat is a soft, brown, spongy, fibrous material. It has a very high water content. If peat is left in the ground, it eventually loses most of its fibrous texture, and becomes lignite (brown coal). Lignite is much harder than peat and has a higher carbon content (50%). The water content of lignite is still high, however. Additional pressure and heat slowly change lignite to bituminous coal (soft coal). Bituminous coal has a lower water content and a higher carbon content (70–80%) than lignite. Additional pressure can convert bituminous coal to anthracite coal (hard coal). Anthracite has a lower water content and higher carbon content (over 80%) than bituminous coal.

13) Answer: Coal may be distilled to provide a variety of products, including coal gas, coal tar, ammonia, and coke. Coal gas consists mainly of hydrogen, methane, and carbon monoxide. Coal tar can be distilled further to yield benzene, toluene, naphthalene, phenol, and pitch. Coke is used as a fuel in many industrial processes. The ammonia from distilled coal is converted to ammonium sulfate for use as a fertilizer.

14) Answer: Coal consists largely of condensed ring compounds of very high molecular mass. Due to the high proportion of these aromatic compounds in coal, the burning of this fuel produces more soot than does the burning of the more aliphatic fuels obtained from petroleum. In addition, the majority of the coal burned in North America contains about 7% sulfur which burns to form SO_2 and SO_3 which are major pollutants.

Chapter 26 Functional Groups and Organic Reactions

Matching Questions

Chapter 26: Matching I

1) functional group

2) hydroxyl group

3) carbonyl group

4) ether

5) carboxyl group

A) a specific arrangement of atoms in an organic compound that is capable of characteristic chemical reactions

B) a carbon atom and an oxygen atom joined by a double bond

C) a carbonyl group attached to a hydroxyl group

D) a compound in which oxygen is bonded to two carbon atoms

E) the OH functional group in alcohols

Multiple Choice and Bimodal Questions

1) What is the name of the functional group in the following compound?

$$CH_3—O—\overset{\overset{\displaystyle O}{\|}}{C}—CH_2—CH_3$$

A) halogen

B) hydroxyl

C) carbonyl

D) carboxylic acid

E) ester

2) What is the common name of the following compound?

$$CH_3 — \underset{\underset{CH_3}{|}}{\overset{\overset{CH_3}{|}}{C}} — Br$$

    A) isopropyl bromide
    B) butyl bromide
    C) isobutyl bromide
    D) sec-butyl bromide
    E) tert-butyl bromide

3) What functional group reacts with an alkane by a substitution reaction?
    A) amino   B) carbonyl   C) carboxyl   D) halogen   E) hydroxyl

4) What type of compound is $CH_3—O—CH_2—CH_2—CH_3$?
    A) alcohol   B) aldehyde   C) ether   D) ketone   E) ester

5) What type of compound is the following?

$$CH_3 — \overset{\overset{O}{\|}}{C} — CH_2 — CH_3$$

    A) alcohol   B) aldehyde   C) ether   D) ketone   E) ester

6) The most important way to classify organic compounds is by _____.
    A) the number of carbon atoms in the longest chain
    B) functional group
    C) the type of carbon-carbon bonds
    D) reactivity

7) Which halocarbon has the highest boiling point?
    A) 1-chloropropane
    B) 2-chloropropane
    C) 1-dichloropropane
    D) 2-dichloropropane
    E) 1,2,3-trichloropropane

8) Which of the following compounds is trichloromethane?

A)

B)

$$Cl - \underset{\underset{CH_3}{|}}{\overset{\overset{Cl}{|}}{C}} - Cl$$

C)

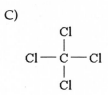

D)

$$Cl - \underset{\underset{CH_3}{|}}{\overset{\overset{Cl}{|}}{C}} - CH_3$$

9) What is the common name of the following alcohol?

$$CH_3 - CH_2 - CH_2 - CH_2 - \underset{\overset{|}{OH}}{\overset{}{C}}H - CH_3$$

A) sec–hexyl alcohol   B) tert–hexyl alcohol

C) isohexyl alcohol   D) hexyl alcohol

10) What substance is added to an organic molecule to test for the degree of saturation?

A) water

B) hydrogen gas

C) bromine

D) hydrogen bromide

E) hydrogen chloride

11) Name the following compound.

$$CH_3 - CH_2 - CH_2 - CH_2 - O - C_6H_5$$

A) cyclohexylbutyl ether

B) butylcyclohexyl ether

C) phenylbutyl ether

D) butylphenyl ether

E) none of the above

12) Name the compound $CH_3CH_2OCH_2CH_2CH_3$.

A) diethyl ether   B) dipropyl ether

C) ethylpropyl ether   D) pentane oxide

13) An example of a secondary alcohol is shown by the structure _____.

A) CH_3CH_2OH

B)
$$CH_3CH_2\underset{\underset{\displaystyle OH}{|}}{C}HCH_3$$

C) $CH_3CH_2CH_2OH$

D)
$$CH_3CH_2\underset{\underset{\displaystyle OH}{|}}{C}(CH_3)_2$$

14) Which of these compounds would you expect to be most soluble in water?

A) CH_3CH_2Cl

B) $CH_3CH_2CH_2F$

C) $CH_3CH_2CH_2CH_3$

D) $CH_3CH_2CH_2OH$

15) Which of the following compounds is a secondary alcohol?

A) $CH_3—CH_2—CH_2—CH_2OH$

B)
$$CH_3—CH_2—\underset{\underset{\displaystyle H}{|}}{\overset{\overset{\displaystyle OH}{|}}{C}}—CH_3$$

C)
$$CH_3—CH_2—\underset{\underset{\displaystyle CH_3}{|}}{C}H—CH_3$$

16) Which of the following compounds is a glycol?

A) $CH_3—CH_2—CH_2—CH_2OH$

B) $CH_3—CH_2—O—CH_2—CH_3$

C) $HOH_2C—CH_2—CH_2—CH_2OH$

D) $CH_3—CH_2—CH_2—CHO$

17) Phenols are characterized by _____.

A) their behavior as gases

B) ether linkages

C) an —OH group on a benzene ring

D) their use as flavoring agents

18) Which pair of formulas represents the same compound?

A) C_2H_5OH; CH_3OCH_3

B) CH_3CH_2CHO; CH_3CH_2COOH

C) $(CH_3)_2CO$; CH_3OCH_3

D) $CH_3COH(CH_3)_2$; $(CH_3)_3COH$

19) Which of the following is true of isopropyl alcohol?

A) It has a relatively high boiling point.

B) It is insoluble in water.

C) It is completely odorless.

D) It is white.

20) Which of the following alcohols is a main component of fats and oils?

    A) ethanol

    B) isopropyl alcohol

    C) ethylene glycol

    D) glycerol

    E) phenol

21) Which of the following alcohols is used in antifreeze?

    A) ethanol

    B) isopropyl alcohol

    C) ethylene glycol

    D) glycerol

    E) phenol

22) Based on your knowledge of intermolecular forces, which of these would you expect to have the highest boiling point?

    A) propanal   B) propane   C) acetone   D) 1–propanol

23) What is the carbon skeleton of the product formed in the following reaction?

    C_3H_6 + HBr → _____

    A) C—C≡C—Br   B) C—C—C—Br

    C) C—C—Br≡C   D) C—C—Br—C

24) In an addition reaction, which bond of the reactant is broken?

    A) carbon–carbon single bond   B) carbon–hydrogen single bond

    C) carbon–carbon double bond   D) carbon–hydrogen double bond

25) Which carbon skeleton represents an ether?

    A) C—C—C—O—C—C—C

    B) C—C—C—C—C—C≡O

    C)

$$
\begin{array}{c}
\quad\quad\quad\quad\quad\quad O \\
\quad\quad\quad\quad\quad\quad \parallel \\
C-C-C-C-C-C
\end{array}
$$

    D)

$$
\begin{array}{c}
\quad\quad\quad\quad\quad\quad\quad O \\
\quad\quad\quad\quad\quad\quad\quad \parallel \\
C-C-C-C-C-C-O
\end{array}
$$

    E) none of the above

26) Which of the following compounds has the lowest boiling point?

    A) diethyl ether   B) 2–butanol   C) diphenyl ether   D) 4–octanol

27) What is the name of the following compound?

$$C_6H_5—\overset{\overset{\displaystyle O}{\|}}{C}—H$$

A) phenylhyde
B) cyclohexylhyde
C) benzaldehyde
D) phenol aldehyde
E) cyclohexyl aldehyde

28) What is the name of the following compound?

$$CH_3—\overset{\overset{\displaystyle O}{\|}}{C}—CH_2—CH_2—CH_3$$

A) 2-butanone   B) 2-pentanone   C) 4-butanone   D) 4-pentanone

29) Name this compound:

$$\overset{\overset{\displaystyle O}{\|}}{CH_3CCH_2CH_3}$$

A) butane   B) butanal   C) butanol   D) butanone

30) Which carbon skeleton represents an aldehyde?

A) C—C—C—C═O

B)

$$C—C—\overset{\overset{\displaystyle O}{\|}}{C}—C$$

C)

$$C—C—C—\overset{\overset{\displaystyle O}{\|}}{C}—O$$

D) C—C—C—C—O

E) none of the above

31) Which carbon skeleton represents a ketone?

A) C—C—C—C=O

B)

$$\begin{array}{c} \text{O} \\ \| \\ \text{C—C—C—C} \end{array}$$

C)

$$\begin{array}{c} \text{O} \\ \| \\ \text{C—C—C—C—O} \end{array}$$

D) C—C—C—C—O

E) none of the above

32) Which of the following compounds has the highest boiling point?

A) 2–pentanone

B) pentane

C) pentene

D) chloropentane

E) chloropentene

33) Aldehydes have the general structure _____.

A)   B)   C)   D)

$$\begin{array}{c} \text{O} \\ \| \\ \text{R—C--OR} \end{array}$$

34) A ketone has the general structure _____.

A) R—O—R   B)

$$\begin{array}{c} \text{R—C—R} \\ \| \\ \text{O} \end{array}$$

C)   D)

$$\begin{array}{c} \text{R—C—OR} \\ \| \\ \text{O} \end{array}$$

35) Which carbon skeleton contains a carboxyl group?

A) C—C—C—O

B) C—C—C=O

C)

$$\begin{array}{c} \text{O} \\ \| \\ \text{C—C—C—O} \end{array}$$

D)

$$\begin{array}{c} \text{O} \\ \| \\ \text{C—C—C} \end{array}$$

E) none of the above

36) Which of the following carbon skeletons represents a carboxylic acid?

A) C—C—C—C—C—O

B) C—C—C—C—C=O

C)

$$CH_3—C—C—C—\overset{\overset{\displaystyle O}{\|}}{C}—OH$$

C—C—C—C—C—OH (with O double bonded to 5th carbon)

D)

C—C—C—C—C (with O double bonded to 2nd carbon)

37) Which of the following compounds is known as acetic acid?

A)

$$CH_3—\overset{\overset{\displaystyle O}{\|}}{C}—H$$

B) CH₃—CH₂OH

C)

$$CH_3—\overset{\overset{\displaystyle OH}{|}}{\underset{\underset{\displaystyle H}{|}}{C}}—OH$$

D)

$$CH_3—\overset{\overset{\displaystyle O}{\|}}{C}—OH$$

38) Carboxylic acids with long hydrocarbon chains are called _____.
A) oils
B) fats
C) fatty acids
D) oily acids
E) none of the above

39) Which of the following compounds is the most soluble in water?
A) propanal
B) 1-bromopropane
C) propane
D) propanoic acid

40) A carboxylic acid with six carbons in a straight chain would be named _____.
A) phenolic acid
B) hexanalic acid
C) dimethylbutanoic acid
D) hexanoic acid

41) If an aldehyde is oxidized, what type of molecule does it become?
A) alkane
B) alkene
C) ketone
D) alcohol
E) carboxylic acid

42) When an oxygen atom is attached to a carbon atom, the carbon atom becomes more _____.

   A) oxidized   B) reduced   C) acidic   D) basic

43) Which of the following compounds is the most reduced?

   A) ethene

   B) carbon dioxide

   C) propanone

   D) ethanoic acid

   E) ethane

44) Which of the following compounds will produce the most energy when completely oxidized?

   A) butane

   B) butene

   C) butanal

   D) butanol

   E) butanoic acid

45) Which of the following is a test for aldehydes?

   A) Fehling's test   B) flame test   C) Butler's test   D) acid test

46) What is the expected product when l–propanol is oxidized?

   A) propanal

   B) propanone

   C) propanoic acid

   D) propene

   E) propane

47) Which carbon skeleton represents an ester?

   A) C—C—C—C—C—O—C—C

   B)

$$C-C-C-C-\overset{\overset{\displaystyle O}{\|}}{C}-C-C$$

   C)

$$C-C-C-C-\overset{\overset{\displaystyle O}{\|}}{C}-O-C-C$$

   D)

$$C-C-C-C-C-C-\overset{\overset{\displaystyle O}{\|}}{C}-O$$

   E) none of the above

48) Which of the following compounds has the highest boiling point?
   A) butane
   B) 1-butanol
   C) butanal
   D) ethyl acetate
   E) butanoic acid

49) Esters contribute which property to fruits?
   A) odor   B) color   C) texture   D) skin thickness

50) Which compound reacts with a carboxylic acid to form an ester?
   A) alkane
   B) alkene
   C) alcohol
   D) aldehyde
   E) carboxylic acid

51) What is the monomer used as the building block in polyethylene?
   A) ethane   B) ethene   C) chlorethane   D) chloroethene

52) What type of chemical bond links the monomers in a polymer?
   A) ionic bond   B) hydrogen bond   C) metallic bond   D) covalent bond

53) What happens in a condensation reaction?
   A) head-to-tail joining of monomers   B) side-by-side joining of monomers
   C) cross-linking of monomers   D) substitution of a halogen on monomers

Problems

1) What is the functional group in $CH_3-O-CH_2-CH_2-CH_2-CH_3$?

2) Write the general structure for halocarbon compounds.

3) Write the general structure for aldehyde compounds.

4) What is the IUPAC name of the following compound?

$$\begin{array}{c} F \\ | \\ CH_3-CH_2-CH-CH_3 \end{array}$$

5) What is the common name of the following compound?

$$CFH=CH_2$$

structure:

```
 F   H
 |   |
 C = C
 |   |
 H   H
```

6) Write an equation using structural formulas for the reaction of benzene and chlorine.

7) Write complete, balanced equations for the reaction of 2–pentene and water. Use structural formulas.

8) What is the name of the following compound?

```
        OH
        |
CH3 — CH — CH2 — CH3
```

9) Complete the following reaction.
   $$C_4H_8 + HBr \rightarrow$$

10) What is the name of the following compound?
    CH3—CH2—CH2—O—CH2—CH2—CH3

11) Write the general structure for carboxylic acid compounds.

12) Write the general structure for ester compounds.

13) What is the name of the following compound?
    CH3—CH2—CH2—CHO

14) Draw the structure of benzaldehyde.

15) What is the expected product when the following compound is oxidized?
    CH3—CH2—CH2—CH2OH

16) Complete the condensation polymerization reaction between two amino acids to form a peptide bond:

```
      R   O                    R   O
      |   ||                   |   ||
H — N — C — C — OH   +   H — N — C — C — OH  →
      |   |                    |   |
      H   H                    H   H
```

Essay Questions

1) Give an example of a substitution reaction and describe what happens in the reaction.

2) Compare the properties of the alcohols with the properties of the halocarbons and the alkanes.

3) Give an example of an addition reaction and describe what happens in the reaction.

4) Compare the properties of the aldehydes and ketones with the properties of alcohols, ethers, alkanes, and halocarbons.

5) Compare the properties of the carboxylic acids with the properties of the other compounds with functional groups.

6) Describe oxidation–reduction reactions of organic molecules. Give an example.

7) Describe a polymerization condensation reaction. Give an example.

Chapter 26 Functional Groups and Organic Reactions

Matching Questions

1) Answer: A
2) Answer: E
3) Answer: B
4) Answer: D
5) Answer: C

Multiple Choice and Bimodal Questions

1) Answer: E
2) Answer: E
3) Answer: D
4) Answer: C
5) Answer: D
6) Answer: B
7) Answer: E
8) Answer: A
9) Answer: A
10) Answer: C
11) Answer: D
12) Answer: C
13) Answer: B
14) Answer: D
15) Answer: B
16) Answer: C
17) Answer: C
18) Answer: D
19) Answer: A
20) Answer: D
21) Answer: C
22) Answer: D
23) Answer: B
24) Answer: C
25) Answer: A
26) Answer: A
27) Answer: C
28) Answer: B
29) Answer: D
30) Answer: A
31) Answer: B
32) Answer: A
33) Answer: B
34) Answer: B

35) Answer: C

36) Answer: C

37) Answer: D

38) Answer: C

39) Answer: D

40) Answer: D

41) Answer: E

42) Answer: A

43) Answer: E

44) Answer: A

45) Answer: A

46) Answer: C

47) Answer: C

48) Answer: E

49) Answer: A

50) Answer: C

51) Answer: B

52) Answer: D

53) Answer: A

Problems

1) Answer: ether

2) Answer: R—X

3) Answer:

$$\begin{array}{c} O \\ \parallel \\ R-C-H \end{array}$$

4) Answer: 2–fluorobutane

5) Answer: vinyl fluoride

6) Answer:

7) Answer:

$$CH_3-O-\overset{\overset{\displaystyle O}{\parallel}}{C}-CH_2-CH_3$$

8) Answer: 2–butanol

9) Answer: C_4H_9Br

10) Answer: dipropyl ether

11) Answer:

$$\begin{array}{c} O \\ \parallel \\ R-C-OH \end{array}$$

12) Answer:

$$R \!-\! \overset{\overset{\displaystyle O}{\|}}{C} \!-\! O \!-\! R$$

13) Answer: butanal

14) Answer:

15) Answer: $CH_3 \!-\! CH_2 \!-\! CH_2 \!-\! COOH$

16) Answer:

Essay Questions

1) Answer: $CH_4 + Br_2 \rightarrow CH_3Br + HBr$

   The halogen replaces the hydrogen because it is more reactive.

2) Answer: Alcohols are capable of intermolecular hydrogen-bonding. Consequently, they boil at higher temperatures than alkanes and halocarbons containing comparable numbers of atoms. In addition, because of their polar hydroxyl end, alcohols are generally more soluble in water than are alkanes or halocarbons. The solubility of alcohols varies with the length of the nonpolar hydrocarbon chain. Alcohols of up to three carbons are soluble in water in all proportions. Alcohols of four carbons or more are generally much less soluble in water. Because of their nonpolar end, alcohols tend to be soluble in nonpolar solvents.

3) Answer: $CH_2\!=\!CH_2 + HCl \rightarrow CH_3CH_2Cl$

   One of the bonds in a carbon–carbon double bond is somewhat weaker than a carbon–carbon single bond. In an addition reaction this weaker bond is broken and replaced by two single bonds. In the above reaction, the weaker carbon–carbon bond of the alkene is broken and replaced by two single bonds, one between carbon and hydrogen and one between carbon and chlorine.

4) Answer: Aldehydes and ketones are normally liquids or solids at room temperature. They cannot form intermolecular hydrogen bonds and therefore have lower boiling points than the corresponding alcohols. They have polarities that are between those of alcohols and the other compounds. They therefore tend to have solubilities and boiling points between those of alcohols and the other compounds.

5) Answer: Carboxylic acids are the most polar of these compounds. Therefore, carboxylic acids have the highest boiling points and are the most soluble in water. Carboxylic acids are volatile liquids or waxy solids.

6) Answer: $CH_3 \!-\! CH_3 \rightarrow CH_2\!=\!CH_2 + H_2$

   In a dehydrogenation reaction, two hydrogens are removed from a hydrocarbon chain and a carbon–carbon double bond is formed. Removal of the hydrogens is oxidation and therefore involves the removal of electrons. The removed hydrogen carries the electrons away and is itself reduced. The hydrocarbon that remains is oxidized.

7) Answer: $HOOCCOOH + HOCH_2 \!-\!\! CH_2OH \rightarrow$

$$HOOCCOOCH_2 \!-\!\! CH_2OH + H_2O$$

A dicarboxylic acid combines with a dihydroxy alcohol to link one carboxy end to one hydroxy end, leaving one carboxy and one hydroxy at the ends of the new molecule. At these new ends, additional units can be attached. Water is removed in each step, and so this is a dehydration. The polymer formed is a polyester.

Chapter 27 The Chemistry of Life

Matching Questions
Chapter 27: Matching I

1) peptide

2) monosaccharide

3) protein

4) zwitterion

5) nucleotides

A) a peptide with more than 100 amino acids

B) a simple carbohydrate molecule

C) monomers that make up DNA and RNA

D) an internal salt of an amino acid

E) any combination of amino acids in which the amino group of one acid is united with the carboxyl group of another through an amide bond

Multiple Choice and Bimodal Questions

1) What is the fundamental unit of life?
   A) the element   B) the nucleus   C) energy   D) the cell

2) What are the two major byproducts of photosynthesis?
   A) heat and light   B) glucose and oxygen
   C) carbon dioxide and water   D) heat and oxygen

3) What is the name of the process in which cells directly use solar energy to make food?
   A) polymerization   B) cellular oxidation
   C) photosynthesis   D) cellular reduction

4) Which of the following is not contained in a prokaryotic cell?
   A) cell wall   B) nucleus   C) chromosomes   D) cell membrane

5) What functional group is present in all carbohydrates?
   A) amino   B) halogen   C) carboxyl   D) carbonyl   E) ester

6) The simple sugars are also called _____.

  A) alcohols   B) carboxylic acids
  C) cycloalkanes   D) monosaccharides

7) What type of reaction produces a disaccharide from two monosaccharides?

  A) addition   B) condensation
  C) acid–base   D) dehydrogenation

8) Which form of polysaccharide is found in animals?

  A) starch   B) glycogen   C) sucrose   D) glucose   E) fructose

9) What is the repeating unit of cellulose?

  A) fructose   B) sucrose   C) glucose   D) starch   E) glycogen

10) Differences between amino acids are normally due to differences in which part of the molecule?

  A) amino group
  B) carboxyl group
  C) central carbon
  D) side chain
  E) isolated hydrogen

11) A zwitterion is what type of chemical substance?

  A) acid   B) base   C) alcohol   D) nonmetal   E) salt

12) A peptide bond is a bond between which functional groups?

  A) amino and alcohol
  B) amino and carboxyl
  C) carboxyl and alcohol
  D) carbonyl and carbonyl
  E) carboxyl and carboxyl

13) Amino acids form _____.

  A) weak bases   B) molecular compounds
  C) internal salts   D) polysaccharides

14) Proteins are poly-_____.

  A) esters   B) acetals   C) peptides   D) amines

15) What is the role of an enzyme?

  A) speeds up biochemical reactions
  B) causes biochemical reactions
  C) is a product in biochemical reactions
  D) provides extra heat for biochemical reactions

16) In which of the following substances can a lipid NOT dissolve?
   A) water
   B) alcohol
   C) ketone
   D) carboxylic acid
   E) halocarbon

17) A triglyceride is a compound of glycerol and _____.
   A) alcohol   B) ether   C) alkene   D) alkyne   E) fatty acid

18) Saponification is what type of reaction?
   A) hydrolysis   B) dehydrogenation
   C) hydrogenation   D) acid–base

19) An ester of a long–chain fatty acid and a long–chain alcohol is _____.
   A) a fat   B) an oil   C) a triglyceride   D) a wax

20) How many bases are available to make the twenty common amino acids?
   A) an infinite number   B) twenty
   C) four   D) three

21) How many bases are needed to specify one amino acid?
   A) one   B) three   C) four   D) twenty

22) How many termination code words are there?
   A) three   B) four   C) twenty   D) thousands

23) Substitutions, additions, or deletions of one or more nucleotides in a DNA molecule is called _____.
   A) a gene mutation   B) transcription
   C) coding   D) anemia

24) The technique of identifying a person from a sample of hair, skin cells, or body fluid is called _____
   A) recombinant DNA technology   B) genetic coding
   C) DNA fingerprinting   D) genetic sequencing

25) Approximately what percentage of a human's DNA is used for coding information for the synthesis of proteins?
   A) 5%   B) 25%   C) 95%   D) 99%

26) DNA has which of the following functions in the body?

    A) It transfers cell products.

    B) It confers structure on the cell.

    C) It makes enzymes work more efficiently.

    D) It stores the information needed to make protein.

27) A nucleotide contains which of the following functional groups?

    A) phosphate   B) halogen   C) sulfur   D) carboxyl

28) Base–pairing in DNA involves _____.

    A) covalent bonds   B) ionic bonds

    C) hydrogen bonds   D) acid–base reaction

29) A typical nucleotide is composed of _____.

    A) base + sugar   B) sugar + phosphate

    C) base + phosphate   D) base + phosphate + sugar

30) Why do A and T (and G and C) pair in a DNA double helix?

    A) Hydrogen bonds form between them.

    B) Covalent bonds form between them.

    C) Van der Waals forces are thus maximized.

    D) Ionic interactions are thus maximized.

    E) The nitrogenous bases overlap in this arrangement.

31) Which reactions are responsible for producing the heat that maintains your body's temperature?

    A) metabolism   B) catabolism   C) anabolism   D) photosynthesis

32) Which of the following molecules is responsible for transmitting the energy needed by cells.

    A) ATP   B) APP   C) adenine   D) RNA

33) Which of the following terms represents the entire set of chemical reactions carried out by an organism?

    A) anabolism   B) catabolism   C) metabolism   D) omnibolism

Essay Questions

1) Describe the similarities of prokaryotic and eukaryotic cells.

2) Describe in words the reaction that takes place during photosynthesis.

3) Describe the process of making sucrose. Give an example.

4) Describe the process of making soap.

5) What are nucleic acids, and why are they important?

6) Explain the basic steps of recombinant DNA technology.

7) Explain the differences between an offspring of two parents and the clone of a parent

8) Compare and contrast catabolism and anabolism.

Chapter 27 The Chemistry of Life
Matching Questions
1) Answer: E
2) Answer: B
3) Answer: A
4) Answer: D
5) Answer: C

Multiple Choice and Bimodal Questions
1) Answer: D
2) Answer: B
3) Answer: C
4) Answer: B
5) Answer: D
6) Answer: D
7) Answer: B
8) Answer: B
9) Answer: C
10) Answer: D
11) Answer: E
12) Answer: B
13) Answer: C
14) Answer: C
15) Answer: A
16) Answer: A
17) Answer: E
18) Answer: A
19) Answer: D
20) Answer: C
21) Answer: B
22) Answer: A
23) Answer: A
24) Answer: C
25) Answer: A
26) Answer: D
27) Answer: A
28) Answer: C
29) Answer: D
30) Answer: A
31) Answer: B
32) Answer: A
33) Answer: C

Essay Questions

1) **Answer:** Both types of cells contain chromosomes and the chemicals necessary for life encased in a cell membrane.

2) **Answer:** Energy from the sun reduces carbon dioxide in the presence of water and produces glucose and oxygen.

3) **Answer:**

$$\begin{array}{ccccccc} & H & & CH_2OH & & H & CH_2OH \\ & | & & | & & | & | \\ -C & -OH & + & -C-OH & \rightarrow & -C-O-C- & + H_2O \\ & | & & | & & | & | \\ & & & & & H & \end{array}$$

One glucose molecule and one fructose molecule are joined through an ether linkage. A water molecule is removed.

4) **Answer:** Vegetable and/or animal fat or oil is heated with an excess of sodium hydroxide. Then sodium chloride is added to form sodium salts of the fatty acids produced. These salts separate as a thick layer of crude soap. Glycerol is an important by-product of the reaction and is recovered by evaporating the water layer. The crude soap is then purified.

5) **Answer:** Nucleic acids are polymers found primarily in cell nuclei. There are two types of nucleic acid, DNA and RNA. DNA stores the information needed to make proteins. It also governs the reproduction of cells and new organisms. RNA has a key role in the transmission of the information stored in DNA.

6) **Answer:** A portion of a DNA chain is cleared (cut out), a new DNA chain is inserted into the gap created by the cleavage, and then the chain is rejoined.

7) **Answer:** An offspring has a genetic code that is a mixture of the parents genetic code, while a clone has the identical genetic code of its parent.

8) **Answer:** Catabolism and anabolism are both part of an organism's metabolism. In catabolism, food and unneeded cellular components are degraded into simpler compounds, producing energy. In anabolism, simple compounds are synthesized into more-complex biological molecules through reactions requiring energy.

Chapter 28 Nuclear Chemistry
Matching Questions
Chapter 28: Matching I

1) positron

2) alpha particle

3) beta particle

4) transuranium element

5) gamma radiation

6) transmutation

A) element with atomic number greater than 92

B) high–energy electromagnetic radiation

C) energetic electron from decomposed neutron

D) particle of charge +1 and mass equal to that of an electron

E) emitted helium nucleus

F) conversion of an atom of one element to an atom of another element

Chapter 28: Matching II

7) fission

8) fusion

9) Geiger counter

10) radioisotope

11) scintillation counter

12) neutron absorption

13) neutron moderation

A) radiation detector that makes use of a phosphor–coated surface

B) slowing down of neutrons to speed up nuclear reaction

C) radiation detector that makes use of a gas–filled metal tube

D) element with unstable nucleus

E) combination of two nuclei to form a large nucleus

F) splitting of nucleus into two similar–sized pieces

G) absorption of neutrons to slow down nuclear reaction

Multiple Choice and Bimodal Questions

1) Who discovered radioactivity?
    A) Marie Curie
    B) Ernest Rutherford
    C) George Geiger
    D) Antoine Becquerel
    E) Albert Einstein

2) How many neutrons are in the nucleus of iodine–131 (atomic number 53)?
    A) 53   B) 78   C) 127   D) 131

3) Uranium–235 atoms have how many protons? (atomic number = 92)
    A) 92   B) 143   C) 235   D) 327

4) What is the charge on an alpha particle?
    A) –2   B) –1   C) 0   D) +1   E) +2

5) How many neutrons are there in an alpha particle?
    A) 0   B) 1   C) 2   D) 3   E) 4

6) What is the change in the atomic number when an atom emits an alpha particle?
    A) decreases by 2
    B) decreases by 1
    C) remains the same
    D) increases by 1
    E) increases by 2

7) What is the change in atomic mass when an atom emits an alpha particle?
    A) decreases by 2
    B) decreases by 1
    C) remains the same
    D) increases by 1
    E) increases by 2

8) What is the change in atomic number when an atom emits a beta particle?

   A) decrease by 2

   B) decrease by 1

   C) 0

   D) +1

   E) +2

9) What is the change in atomic number when an atom emits gamma radiation?

   A) decreases by 2

   B) decreases by 1

   C) remains the same

   D) increases by 1

   E) increases by 2

10) Why do radioactive isotopes emit radiation?

   A) They have too low a ratio of protons to neutrons in the nucleus

   B) They have too high a ratio of protons to neutrons in the nucleus

   C) They have too low or too high a ratio of protons to neutrons in the nucleus

   D) They have too low a ratio of protons to electrons in the atom

   E) They have too high a ratio of protons to electrons in the atom

11) What does an unstable nucleus NOT do to become more stable?

   A) rearrange its protons and neutrons

   B) emit radiation

   C) change its number of protons and/or neutrons

   D) change its number of electrons

12) An unstable nucleus _____.

   A) may have too many neutrons   B) may have too few neutrons

   C) loses energy by emitting radiation   D) all of the above

13) What particle is emitted in alpha radiation?

   A) electron   B) photon

   C) helium nucleus   D) hydrogen nucleus

14) Which symbol is used for an alpha particle?

   A) $^{2}_{2}He$ B) $^{2}_{4}He$ C) $^{4}_{2}He$ D) $^{4}_{4}He$

15) What thickness of what material is necessary to stop an alpha particle?

   A) three feet of concrete   B) three inches of lead

   C) sheet of aluminum foil   D) sheet of paper

16) What is a beta particle?

   A) a photon
   B) an electron
   C) a helium nucleus
   D) a hydrogen nucleus

17) What particle decomposes to produce the electron of beta radiation?

   A) proton   B) neutron   C) electron   D) muon   E) pion

18) What symbol is used for beta radiation?

   A) $_{0}^{0}e$ B) $_{-1}^{0}e$ C) $_{0}^{-1}e$ D) $_{-1}^{-1}e$

19) What is the change in atomic mass when an atom emits a beta particle?

   A) decreases by 2
   B) decreases by 1
   C) remains the same
   D) increases by 1
   E) increases by 2

20) What thickness of what material is necessary to stop a beta particle?

   A) three feet of concrete
   B) three inches of lead
   C) sheet of aluminum foil
   D) sheet of paper

21) What does gamma radiation consist of?

   A) photons
   B) electrons
   C) helium nuclei
   D) hydrogen nuclei

22) What is the change in atomic mass when an atom emits gamma radiation?

   A) decreases by 2
   B) decreases by 1
   C) remains the same
   D) increases by 1
   E) increases by 2

23) What thickness of what material will stop gamma radiation?

   A) three inches of lead
   B) one inch of water
   C) sheet of aluminum foil
   D) sheet of paper

24) The most penetrating form of radiation is _____.

   A) alpha radiation
   B) beta radiation
   C) gamma radiation
   D) visible radiation

25) Ionizing radiation that consists of helium nuclei is _____.

   A) X–radiation
   B) gamma radiation
   C) beta radiation
   D) alpha radiation

26) Which of these could stop the penetration of an alpha particle?
   A) the top layer of your skin   B) aluminum foil
   C) a piece of paper   D) all of these

27) A neutron breaks down forming _____.
   A) an alpha particle   B) a proton, only
   C) a proton and an electron   D) a helium nucleus

28) Electromagnetic radiation includes _____.
   A) alpha particles and X–rays   B) gamma rays and X–rays
   C) beta particles and gamma rays   D) gamma rays and alpha particles

29) Which of the following is NOT true concerning an alpha particle?
   A) It has a mass of 4 amu.   B) It has a 1+ charge.
   C) It is a helium nucleus.   D) It contains 2 neutrons.

30) Which type of ionizing radiation can be blocked by clothing?
   A) beta particle   B) X–radiation
   C) gamma radiation   D) alpha particle

31) If an isotope undergoes beta emission _____.
   A) the mass number changes
   B) the atomic number changes
   C) protons are given off
   D) the number of neutrons remains the same

32) Which radiation has a positive charge?
   A) alpha   B) beta   C) gamma

33) If the half–life of a radioactive material is 8 years, how many years will it take for one half of
   the original amount of material to decay?
   A) 2 years   B) 4 years   C) 8 years   D) 16 years   E) 32 years

34) The half–life of radon–222 is four days. After how many days is the amount of radon–222
   one–sixteenth of its original amount?
   A) 16   B) 12   C) 20   D) 24   E) 36

35) A piece of wood found in an ancient burial mound contains only half as much carbon–14 as
   a piece of wood cut from a living tree growing nearby. If the half–life ($t_{1/2}$) for carbon–14 is
   5730 years, what is the approximate age of the ancient wood?
   A) 1432.5 years   B) 2856 years   C) 5730 years   D) 1460 years

36) After 42 days, 2 g of phosphorus–32 has decayed to 0.25 g. What is the half–life of
   phosphorus–32?
   A) 5.4 days   B) 6 days   C) 8 days   D) 14 days

37) If the half–life of sodium–24 is 15 hours, how much remains from a 10.0 g sample after 60 hours?

   A) 0.63 g   B) 1.3 g   C) 2.5 g   D) 5.0 g

38) What is the half–life of iodine–131 if, after 24 days, 0.125 g remains from a 1.00–g starting sample?

   A) 3 days   B) 6 days   C) 8 days   D) 12 days

39) What particle is needed to complete this nuclear reaction?

$$^{222}_{86}Rn \rightarrow\ ^{218}_{84}Po + \underline{\qquad}$$

   A) $^{4}_{2}He$ B) $^{0}_{-1}e$ C) $^{1}_{1}H$ D) $^{1}_{0}n$

40) Which of the following particles is needed to complete this nuclear equation?

$$^{55}_{25}Mn +\ ^{2}_{1}H \rightarrow \underline{\qquad} + 2\,^{1}_{0}N$$

   A) $^{56}_{27}Co$ B) $^{27}_{25}Mn$ C) $^{55}_{26}Fe$ D) $^{58}_{24}Cr$

41) What particle is needed to complete this equation?

$$^{14}_{7}N + \underline{\qquad} \rightarrow\ ^{14}_{6}C +\ ^{1}_{1}H$$

   A) $^{1}_{0}n$ B) $^{0}_{-1}e$ C) $^{4}_{2}He$ D) $^{0}_{+1}e$

42) To what element does polonium–214 (atomic number = 84) decay when it loses an alpha particle?

   A) $^{210}_{82}Pb$ B) $^{210}_{82}Po$ C) $^{214}_{82}Pb$ D) $^{214}_{86}Rn$

43) To what does plutonium–239 (atomic number 94) decay when it loses an alpha particle?

   A) $^{235}_{92}Pu$ B) $^{235}_{92}U$ C) $^{237}_{90}Th$ D) $^{239}_{95}Am$

44) What is the approximate ratio of neutrons to protons for atoms below atomic number 20?

   A) 1   B) 1.5   C) 2

45) What is the approximate number of neutrons in an atom with 90 protons?

   A) 90   B) 120   C) 135   D) 180   E) 225

46) How does a relatively small atom, with too few neutrons, undergo radioactive decay?
   A) by emitting alpha radiation
   B) by emitting beta radiation
   C) by emitting gamma radiation

47) How does a very large atom undergo radioactive decay?

A) by emitting alpha radiation

B) by emitting beta radiation

C) by emitting gamma radiation

48) Above what atomic number are all atoms radioactive?

A) 20   B) 51   C) 82   D) 103

49) What type of radioactive decay will occur in an atom of atomic number 87 and atomic mass 224?

A) emission of an electron

B) emission of a positron

C) emission of an alpha particle

50) Which half–life indicates the most stable element?

A) 2 days   B) 2 weeks   C) 2 years

51) What is the approximate half–life of uranium–238?

A) weeks

B) years

C) thousands of years

D) millions of years

E) billions of years

52) Which of these naturally occurring radioisotopes would be most useful in dating objects thought to be millions of years old?

A) carbon–14, $t_{1/2} = 5.73 \times 10^3$ years   B) potassium–40, $t_{1/2} = 1.28 \times 10^9$ years

C) thorium–234, $t_{1/2} = 25$ days   D) radon–222, $t_{1/2} = 3.8$ days

53) Radioisotopes taken internally for medical reasons _____.

A) must be eliminated from the body slowly

B) should be fissionable isotopes

C) are usually deposited in fat tissue

D) should have a short half–life

54) Who performed the first artificial transmutation of the elements?

A) Willard Libby

B) Antoine Becquerel

C) Marie Curie

D) Ernest Rutherford

E) Enrico Fermi

55) Above what atomic number are the transuranium elements?

A) 82   B) 92   C) 102   D) 110

56) A transmutation reaction must always involve _____.

  A) a change in the number of electrons in the atom

  B) a decrease in the number of neutrons in the nucleus of an atom

  C) an increase in the number of neutrons in the nucleus of an atom

  D) a change in the number of protons in a nucleus of an atom

57) The production of carbon–14 _____.

  A) takes place in the upper atmosphere

  B) is mostly due to fallout from nuclear explosions

  C) occurs to a large extent in nuclear reactors

  D) occurs during photosynthesis in plants

58) What particle does argon–39 (atomic number 18) lose when it decays to potassium–39 (atomic number 19)?

  A) neutron   B) electron   C) proton   D) alpha particle

59) In what physical state is the material at the center of the sun?

  A) solid   B) liquid   C) gas   D) plasma

60) What happens to an atomic nucleus in nuclear fission?

  A) It absorbs another nucleus.

  B) It absorbs an electron, proton, or alpha particle.

  C) It splits into one large, and one small, piece.

  D) It splits into many small pieces.

  E) It splits into two pieces of similar size.

61) What happens in a chain reaction?

  A) Products that start a new reaction are released.

  B) Reactants that have two parts split.

  C) Products that are radioactive are made.

  D) Reactants that are radioactive are used.

62) How is the heat removed from a nuclear reactor?

  A) by water only

  B) by liquid sodium only

  C) by liquid sodium or water

63) What does a moderator do in a nuclear reactor?

  A) It slows down the neutrons.

  B) It slows down the reaction.

  C) It slows down the flow of the coolant.

64) What does neutron absorption accomplish in a nuclear reactor?

    A) It slows down the reaction.   B) It speeds up the reaction.

    C) It increases the rate of heat absorption.   D) It recycles the fuel.

65) What substances are used as moderators in a nuclear reactor?

    A) carbon and water   B) liquid sodium and water

    C) plutonium and neptunium   D) cadmium or other metals

66) What substances are used as neutron absorbers in a nuclear reactor?

    A) carbon and water   B) liquid sodium and water

    C) plutonium and neptunium   D) cadmium or other metal

67) Which of these processes results in a "splitting" of atoms?

    A) a chemical reaction   B) a fusion reaction

    C) a fission reaction   D) an ionizing reaction

68) Controlled nuclear chain reactions _____.

    A) take place in nuclear reactors   B) are always fusion reactions

    C) never produce radioactive by-products   D) are characteristic of atomic bombs

69) In nuclear fission _____.

    A) certain atoms break into fragments when struck by neutrons

    B) a chain reaction occurs

    C) energy is released as heat

    D) all of the above

70) Which of the following statements is correct?

    A) Water is used to moderate (slow down) neutrons in a nuclear reactor.

    B) Carbon control rods are used to absorb neutrons in a nuclear fission reaction.

    C) A very high temperature is required to initiate a nuclear fission reaction.

    D) The energy released from the sun is the result of a nuclear fission reaction.

71) What two nuclei are fused in the main fusion reaction of the sun?

    A) hydrogen and hydrogen

    B) hydrogen and helium

    C) helium and helium

72) What structure is used to confine a plasma?

    A) centrifuge   B) "magnetic bottle"

    C) scintillation counter   D) laser beams

73) A reaction in which two light nuclei combine to form a heavier nucleus is termed _____.

    A) fission   B) a chemical reaction

    C) background radiation   D) fusion

74) Nuclear fusion _____.
A) takes place in the sun
B) occurs when large nuclei fuse together
C) produces hydrogen nuclei
D) all of the above

75) What is the main detector of a Geiger counter?
A) ionizable gas in a metal tube
B) phosphor–covered surface
C) plates of ionizable plastic
D) potassium metal surface

76) What type of radiation is best detected by a Geiger counter?
A) alpha radiation only
B) beta radiation only
C) gamma radiation only
D) alpha and beta radiation only
E) all types of radiation

77) What is the main detector of a scintillation counter?
A) ionizable gas in a metal tube
B) phosphor–covered surface
C) plates of ionizable plastic
D) potassium metal surface

78) What type of radiation is best detected by a scintillation counter?
A) alpha radiation only
B) beta radiation only
C) gamma radiation only
D) alpha and beta radiation only
E) all types of radiation

79) What instrument is used routinely to check a person's exposure to radiation?
A) Geiger counter
B) scintillation counter
C) film badge

80) Ionizing radiation not emitted by the decay of a radioisotope is _____.
A) alpha radiation
B) beta radiation
C) gamma radiation
D) X–radiation

81) A device that is used primarily for the detection of beta radiation is _____.
A) the film badge
B) the scintillation counter
C) the Geiger counter
D) all of the above

82) What are tracers used for?
A) to study reaction mechanisms
B) to detect elements
C) to treat cancer

83) Which cells are the most sensitive to ionizing radiation?

    A) cells that do not divide

    B) cells that divide slowly

    C) cells that divide rapidly

Problems

1) Complete the following nuclear reaction:

$$_{\overline{}92}U \rightarrow \, _2^4He + \, _{\overline{}}^{231}Th$$

2) The radioisotope radon–222 has a half–life of 3.8 days. How much of a 10.0–g sample of radon–222 would be left after approximately 15 days?

3) Iodine–131, a radioisotope, has a half–life of 8 days. If the amount of iodine–131 in a sample is 32 g, how much iodine–131 will remain after 32 days?

4) After 252 days, a 12.0–g starting sample of scandium–42 contains only 1.5 g of the isotope. What is the half–life of scandium?

Essay Questions

1) Distinguish between alpha particles, beta particles, and gamma rays. Indicate how the atomic number and atomic mass number change when each type of radiation is emitted.

2) What happens in the artificial transmutation of an element? Give an example.

3) Explain how the sun produces its energy.

4) Describe the ways in which ionizing radiation can be detected. Distinguish between film badges, Geiger counters, and scintillation counters.

Chapter 28 Nuclear Chemistry

Matching Questions

1) Answer: D
2) Answer: E
3) Answer: C
4) Answer: A
5) Answer: B
6) Answer: F
7) Answer: F
8) Answer: E
9) Answer: C
10) Answer: D
11) Answer: A
12) Answer: B
13) Answer: G

Multiple Choice and Bimodal Questions

1) Answer: D
2) Answer: B
3) Answer: A
4) Answer: E
5) Answer: C
6) Answer: A
7) Answer: A
8) Answer: D
9) Answer: C
10) Answer: C
11) Answer: D
12) Answer: D
13) Answer: C
14) Answer: C
15) Answer: D
16) Answer: B
17) Answer: B
18) Answer: B
19) Answer: C
20) Answer: C
21) Answer: A
22) Answer: C
23) Answer: A
24) Answer: C
25) Answer: D
26) Answer: D
27) Answer: C

28) Answer: B

29) Answer: B

30) Answer: D

31) Answer: B

32) Answer: A

33) Answer: C

34) Answer: A

35) Answer: C

36) Answer: D

37) Answer: A

38) Answer: C

39) Answer: A

40) Answer: C

41) Answer: A

42) Answer: A

43) Answer: B

44) Answer: A

45) Answer: C

46) Answer: B

47) Answer: A

48) Answer: C

49) Answer: C

50) Answer: C

51) Answer: E

52) Answer: B

53) Answer: D

54) Answer: D

55) Answer: B

56) Answer: D

57) Answer: A

58) Answer: B

59) Answer: D

60) Answer: E

61) Answer: A

62) Answer: C

63) Answer: A

64) Answer: A

65) Answer: A

66) Answer: D

67) Answer: C

68) Answer: A

69) Answer: D

70) Answer: A

71) Answer: A

72) Answer: B

73) Answer: D

74) Answer: A

75) Answer: A

76) Answer: B

77) Answer: B

78) Answer: E

79) Answer: C

80) Answer: D

81) Answer: C

82) Answer: A

83) Answer: C

Problems

1) Answer: $^{231}_{92}U \rightarrow {}^{4}_{2}He + {}^{231}_{94}Th$

2) Answer: 15 days/3.8 days = approximately 4 half–life periods have passed
After 4 half–life periods, 1/16 of the sample will remain.
10.0 g x 1/16 = 0.625 g remaining

3) Answer: 32 days = 4 half–life periods. 1/16 of the original sample remains.
32 g x 1/16 = 2.0 grams remaining.

4) Answer: If one–eighth of the sample remains, the isotope must have decayed through 3 half–life periods. Three half–life periods is 252 days, so one half–life period is 84 days. The half–life of scandium–42 is 84 days.

Essay Questions

1) Answer: Alpha particles are helium nuclei; they have 2 protons and 2 neutrons. Alpha particles have low energy. Beta particles are electrons or positrons. They have medium energy. Gamma rays are electromagnetic radiation. They have high energy. Alpha particle emission reduces atomic number by 2 and atomic mass number by 4. Beta particle emission increases atomic number by 1 and does not affect atomic mass number. Gamma ray emission does not affect atomic mass number or atomic number.

2) Answer: In artificial transmutation, atoms of one element are bombarded with high energy particles to convert them into other elements. For example, nitrogen–14 can be converted to fluorine–18 by being bombarded with alpha particles.

3) Answer: The energy released from the sun is the result of nuclear fusion, or thermonuclear, reactions. Fusion occurs when two light nuclei combine to produce a nucleus of heavier mass. In solar fusion, hydrogen nuclei (protons) are fused to make helium nuclei. The reaction requires two beta particles.

$$4\,{}^{1}_{1}H + 2\,{}^{0}_{-1}e \rightarrow {}^{4}_{2}He + energy$$

4) Answer: Film badges use unexposed film to detect radiation. When developed, dark patches indicate radiation exposure. Geiger counters measure the ionization of gas in a tube with a voltage across it; the gas is ionized by contact with a charged particle, such as a beta particle. Geiger counters are used primarily for the detection of beta radiation. Scintillation counters emit light when struck by ionizing radiation; the number of light flashes and their respective energies are recorded electronically. Scintillation counters have been designed to detect all types of ionizing radiation.